What Every Fidelity Investor Needs *to* Know

What Every Fidelity Investor Needs to Know

JAMES LOWELL

BICENTENNIAL
1807
WILEY
2007
BICENTENNIAL

John Wiley & Sons, Inc.

Lowell, James.
    What every Fidelity investor needs to know / James Lowell.
        p.   cm.
    Includes index.
    ISBN-13: 978–0-470–03627–3 (cloth)
    ISBN-10: 0–470–03627–3 (cloth)
    1. Mutual funds—United States.   2. Fidelity Funds (Firm)   3. Investments—United States.   I. Title.
    HG4930.L688 2007
    332.63'27—dc22   2006021654

Printed in the United States of America

10 9 8 7 6 5 4 3 2 1

CONTENTS

PREFACE

I have been called a "Fidelity fanatic" so often that I no longer pause and try and decipher what the intention behind that characterization is; for a significant portion of my professional life, I have clearly and distinctly focused on Fidelity as a brilliant single resource for any investor's range of investment needs and objectives. This book's aim is to enable you to take advantage of all that Fidelity has to offer, and to benefit from my years of personal and professional experience with regard to thinking, writing, and talking about Fidelity as well as successfully investing in it.

My personal relationship with Fidelity began before I even knew it was beginning: spending summer months across the street from a family that, as far as I was concerned, had three great playmates, a sound knowledge of sailing and square dancing, and had been rumored to have had lunch with the Queen of England. It wasn't until I had turned the corner from youth to adulthood that I began to know more about these neighbors; as it turns out, not only did the Johnson's own Fidelity, but their wealth was significantly greater than that of the queen's—in fact, several queens put together.

Perhaps because of my upbringing (I was born with a silver spoon in my mouth, but ever since that day I've had to earn the rest of the place setting on my own), I was not taken with their wealth so much as by its genius. To this day, the Johnsons can travel wherever they like without an entourage of paparazzi and protection. They can do good works anonymously (and they do!). They can enjoy the fruits of their prosperity by focusing on their own family. They can talk about subjects of interest and matters of importance that have little or nothing to do with the stock market; but they can also talk stocks like no other family I've met, save my own.

The Johnsons' focus on doing good work is in the original DNA of Fidelity. Yes, it's a business seeking to profit, and yes this means that you need to be mindful of your own purse strings when receiving anything even remotely approaching advice from the self-interested employees of the firm. But the fact that Fidelity really grew under the auspices of a more democratic model for practicing the investment business—the discount brokerage (as opposed to full-service brokerage model, which I discuss in the first chapter of this book)—set Fidelity on the right course from nearly the get-go, a course that sought to deliver investment products that outperformed their market benchmarks for a reasonable (i.e., low) fee, all the while delivering some of the best active management minds to Main Street investors (as opposed to ivory tower institutions or ultra-high-net-worth trust funds).

But it's important that you know right from the start of this book that, while I may be a Fidelity fanatic, as my years of unbiased and purely independent prose reveal, I'm not a simple-minded fan. There are more than enough loose bolts on the good ship Fidelity; and spotting them, bringing them to light, and suggesting the best steps to take to tighten them up is part and parcel of what I do for my subscribers at my multiple-award-winning www.fidelityinvestor.com. As you'll learn in this book, some ways are better than others to navigate the numerous decks of Fidelity; many hands on the deck are well worth following, and some ought to be encouraged to jump ship.

On that latter note, I always make it a point to call attention to the fact that I am not a clever purveyor of a claim to independence, selling an elixir of performance prediction whose biggest purchasers, in the form of licensing fees for promotional purposes, are the fund firms themselves. I'll leave that misguided path to the leading rating services, which derive a significant portion of their revenue diet from the very firms they claim to be independently rating. I've never had much of an interest in quid pro quo.

I have always had a significant interest in the markets and their machinations. I didn't grow up talking baseball. Table talk at my family dinner table was stocks, bonds, and roast beef. My grandfather was an accomplished businessman and philanthropist in a long lineage of them.

My father was just moving from a traditional role as a rising star in a staid investment bank to establish his own investment company. My uncles were all in the business in one way or another; one was a star manager at Fidelity (a shooting star, as it turned out). Wherever we traveled, and whenever we broke bread with nonfamily members, there was little else but talk of the markets (except the random conversations about a rogue poet, astronomer, or politician).

Looking back, that upbringing led through direct and indirect ways to where I stand today: independent-minded and focused on the investment world through an excellent lens—Fidelity. Looking ahead, there are significant transitions in store for Fidelity as we know it today, not the least of which is the succession issue and the status of being privately held. I have no doubt that the Johnsons will orchestrate a successful transition for themselves and their shareholders in due course. For now, as I write this, Ned Johnson stands at the helm, navigating the increasingly competitive waters with a steady hand and keen eye. Where am I? Look for me in the crow's nest; the best place to spot trouble and bounty dead ahead. In fact, consider this book your invitation to join me for the rewarding view.

ACKNOWLEDGMENTS

This book presents you with the experience, insights, and input of many knowlegeable people. While it's true that my own personal and professional experience as the leading independent authority on investing in Fidelity funds is deeply relevant here, one of the reasons I have focused on Fidelity as the best one-stop shop for every investor is that its business model is so closely aligned with that of our highest-minded universities, where knowledge and collegiality matter more than office politics and braggarts.

Frederick P. Gabriel, Jr., executive editor of *InvestmentNews*, was instrumental in bringing this book to fruition. From the beginning, Gabriel helped me to interpret the vision of this book. His contributions and diligence enabled this book to leave no Fidelity stone unturned.

I'm fortunate to have many colleagues and friends who are in the business of thinking about and acting on the markets at home and abroad. My right and left hands at FundWorks, Inc., David Cohne and Karen Frost, are two oars in the water without whom I'd be rowing in circles or sitting becalmed.

My partners in two significant businesses outside of FundWorks, Inc., are constant sources of new angles and ideas. Dan Wiener, the leading independent authority on Vanguard funds and the editor of the multiple-award-wining *Independent Adviser* for Vanguard Investors (www.adviseronline.com), is the Lance Armstrong of business cycles and risk-adjusted returns; David Thorne, a quixotic Gandalph trespassing lightly in circles of power and knowing is a mover of molehills and mountains; Dan Silver's mastery of cross-border mergers has created an emerging market over which he carefully presides; John Mileszko's ability to pitch any batter puts Kurt Schilling to shame and makes him an easy candidate for any managing director's hall of fame.

Bud Sheppard is the most mindfully dogged and determined revolutionary this side of 1776; may his regard for doing what is right meet with the rewards he justly deserves.

All these people have lent various degrees of energy and support for this book in particular and my life's work in general, and I remain deeply thankful to each.

At John Wiley & Sons, Bill Falloon's distant beckoning, Emilie Herman's disciplined determination, and Stacey Farkas' savvy scrutinizing made my ether world of ideas a living, breathing manuscript.

Many other professionals, friends, mentors, and family members have had a hand in lifting this work from the recesses of thought, through scribe, to pen. To name a few would be to do the rest an unspoken injustice; suffice it to say that my investment in them is long term.

Finally, this book's ending sets the stage for another beginning, one in which I'm bound in the happiness and love of fidelity to my family, who know the toll of hard work and the merrymaking it provides.

What Every Fidelity Investor Needs to Know

PART ONE

Fidelity: Past, Present, and Future

ONE

Fidelity

Past, Present, and Future

Fidelity is the world's largest mutual fund company, bar none.

With more than $1.1 trillion in mutual fund assets and more than 19 million shareholders, Fidelity Investments has long ruled the mutual fund industry.

In fact, you could say that Fidelity was and still is in no small measure responsible for the growth of the mutual fund industry itself.

It is a Goliath, even in the land of Goliaths.

From its headquarters on Devonshire Street in Boston's financial district, 60-year-old Fidelity employs nearly 40,000 people; offers over 300 actively managed, index-focused, and ETF-based funds; and casts its investment shadow across the globe.

The sun never sets on Fidelity.

While Fidelity is known as a leading provider of financial services, its empire is vastly greater than its mutual fund company and offerings. Its services extend far beyond mutual funds to include discount brokerage services, retirement services, estate planning, securities execution and clearance, life insurance, real estate, publishing, venture capital, outsourcing, and even a national executive limousine service (aptly named *Boston Coach* which, by the way, I recommend highly).

Although it has occasionally stumbled, Fidelity has a long and illustrious history of success as a business—as a business that has been able to reinvent itself to not only compete with changing times and changing leadership in the financial services landscape, but to lead and dominate that landscape time and again.

That success can be traced to traits not typically associated with Boston's Puritan roots: guts and gusto. But ingenuity, hard work, and an eye for global trade has always been part of the Hub's heritage ("the Hub" being the nickname given to Boston precisely because of its intense historical focus on global commerce). In Fidelity's founder, one Boston trust lawyer named Edward C. Johnson II, the twain met.

Johnson hailed from a distinguished and wealthy Brahman family. Smart and ambitious, he earned a degree in business from Harvard College and went on to graduate from Harvard Law School.

But Johnson didn't rest on his social standing—or even on his intellect. Graced with an independent spirit and a voracious appetite for adventure, Johnson soon found himself seduced by Wall Street, a place he once described as one "in which it was every man for himself, no favors asked or given."

In 1943, at the age of 45, Johnson assumed the reigns of the 13-year-old Fidelity fund. Even by the standards of the financial markets six decades ago, the fund's $3 million in assets represented a modest sum. Three years later, Johnson established Fidelity Management and Research Company to act as an investment adviser to Fidelity Fund, which by then had grown to $13 million. That 400 percent gain in three years would be a harbinger of growth to come.

Johnson was an imperious leader, one who likened playing the market to being England's Sir Francis Drake in the midst of a sea battle. By setting high standards, and by rewarding individuals who met those standards, Johnson cultivated a highly competitive money management culture that continues to distinguish Fidelity from most of its peers today. Under Johnson, Fidelity became known as a place where employees were almost fanatical—if not downright, cutthroat—in their quest to meet exacting standards set by Johnson himself.

In fact, Johnson's steadfast pursuit of individual excellence led him to reject the popular notion that mutual funds were best managed by investment committee. To his way of thinking, funds were best run by individuals—individuals who were smart, decisive, and empowered to make investment decisions. The focus on the manager, not the fund, has been imprinted on each and every Fidelity manager, past and present.

In 1947, Johnson launched a second fund, the Fidelity Puritan Fund. The income-oriented balanced fund was positioned as a less-aggressive offering than the Fidelity Fund. The principle of diversification both in terms of investment choices and as the basis for investment decisions remains a core component of Fidelity's money management business and investment discipline to this day.

Although money flowed into Fidelity at a healthy clip—by 1956, the firm had $256 million in assets under management—Johnson was in no rush to grow his young money management firm. In fact, it wasn't until 1958, long after Americans had begun to develop an appetite for risk in the financial markets, that he launched two funds aimed at what we now consider to be aggressive growth investors.

One of the new funds, Fidelity Capital, was created at the behest of Fidelity stock analyst Gerald Tsai Jr., whose no-holds-barred style of investing would transform into a Wall Street star in the go-go days of the 1960s.

Two years later, the other new growth fund, Fidelity Trend, would become the first management assignment held by Johnson's son Edward C. "Ned" Johnson III, who joined Fidelity as a research analyst in 1957. The younger Mr. Johnson shared his father's passion for investing and quickly distinguished himself as a stock picker par excellence.

Eventually, Ned would replace his father at Fidelity's helm—a move that would mark a dramatic turning point in Fidelity's history.

The 1960s were heady years for Fidelity—and for all of Wall Street, for that matter. Tsai, a native of Shanghai, became the first "star" manager to rise from Fidelity's ranks. But Tsai's bold and adventurous investing style, which involved taking big positions in a stock and then bailing out just before its short-term run-up was about to end, soon became the poster child of Wall Street's appetite for risk in those days.

Fidelity, it seemed, had become Wall Street's "it" money management firm. Assets, for example, reached $4.3 billion in 1969, up dramatically from $500 million at the beginning of the decade.

But, neither the run of economic prosperity nor the breakneck growth that Fidelity experienced because of it would go unchallenged. Thanks to inflation and a deteriorating U.S. economy, the Dow Jones Industrial Average, which had reached a peak in 1968, began a tortuous series of drops that culminated with a 40 percent decline in one year—1973–1974—preceded by tough years. (Fortunately for Fidelity, Tsai had struck out on his own in 1965, before the market turned so decisively against his hyperaggressive investing style.) Still, as a result of the broader market's decline, mutual fund shareholders across America began to yank money from their investment accounts, killing off dozens of fund companies and brokerage houses in the process.

Fidelity, of course, survived. But it did more than merely survive; it learned a lesson about its own need to diversify its business, which it took to heart and put into practice. And, even though the best example of learning from such past experience to better maneuver through difficult times took 28 years to materialize, when the market crash of 2000–2002 took place, erasing nearly 47 percent of the value of the S&P 500, and competitors like Charles Schwab were forced to lay off more than half their workforce, Fidelity not only hired more workers, but gained share in the brokerage marketplace.

But let's get back to earlier times. Fidelity's assets under management dropped to $2.4 billion by the end of 1974; nearly a 50 percent drop.

A Family Affair

In the midst of that tumult, Edward C. Johnson II turned to one person for help: his son.

Even though he was only 42 years old when he was appointed president of Fidelity in 1972, Edward C. "Ned" Johnson III, had earned the respect and admiration of Fidelity's stock-picking team. In fact, the returns he posted while managing Fidelity's famed Magellan in the 1960s would prove even better than when the much larger fund was in the hands of über-investor Peter Lynch (see Figure 1.1).

Ned Johnson was more than a good stock picker, however. He was a visionary—a visionary with a knack for product development as well as an early appreciation for the essential business and philosophical role technology would play in Fidelity's continued success.

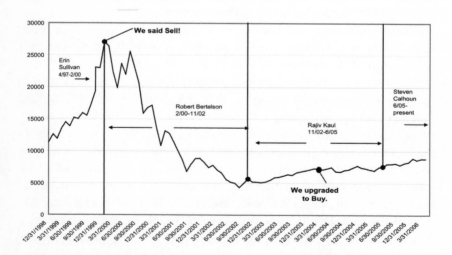

FIGURE 1.1 Manager changes at Fidelity Aggressive Growth

Source: www.fidelityinvestor.com

With the sky-high-oil-priced economy still in the tank, stocks, and mutual funds that invested in them, had become persona non grata in the portfolios of many American investors. Recognizing this, the younger Johnson set out to recast Fidelity as a company that would appeal to the more skittish investors of that era.

Innovation: Back to Basics

How did he go about doing that? By using the simplest, most efficient, and what proved to be most profitable instrument available (and one that most money managers treated with disdain): a money market fund that also doubled as a checking account. Faced with high inflation and interests rates, many yield-hungry yet conservative investors were flocking to money market funds. Fidelity did not open the first money market fund, but adding the check-writing feature was Johnson's idea.

Launched on May 31, 1974, Fidelity Daily Income Trust (FDIT) was not only successful in attracting some $500 million from low-yield (or zero-yield) savings or checking accounts during the first seven months of its existence, it also established the secretive Fidelity mascot. Even to this day, when you walk through the inner sanctums leading to Ned Johnson's office you'll find glass cases lined with all manners of frog sculptures, the ticker symbol for Fidelity's first money market fund, FDIT. Two years later, Fidelity unveiled another major investment innovation, tailor-made for the shell-shocked conservative investors of the 1970s: It was the nation's first open-end municipal bond fund.

In 1977, the same year Ned Johnson's succession was completed by his ascension to chairman and chief executive, Fidelity expanded its menu of bond offerings to include its first junk-bond vehicle, the Devon Bond Fund (now Capital & Income).

But Ned Johnson was focused on things other than money market and bond funds. Internally, he had also turned his attention to building Fidelity's technological prowess. Thanks to Johnson's commitment to computerization and the skill of operations manager Bob Gould, Fidelity would finish the decade by also distinguishing itself through the automation of its back-office operations as well as through the creation of a sophisticated telephone customer service system.

Initially, the calls pouring in to Fidelity's toll-free lines were all handled by live operators. By 1979, however, the Fidelity Automated Service Telephone (FAST)—forerunner of the account service systems now standard throughout the industry—was up and running.

The economy finally bottomed out with the 1980–1982 recession. In response to President Ronald Reagan's massive tax cuts and a lowering of interest rates, the Dow Jones Industrial Average in August 1982 broke free of the malaise that had plagued it since 1968 and took off on an upward trajectory.

By that time, Fidelity had amassed some $10 billion in assets. But two-thirds of those assets were held in money market accounts, which generated far less fee revenue than stock funds. On the bright side, the money pooled in those accounts was already sitting in Fidelity's coffers.

Now it was up to Fidelity to convince its money market investors to dip their toes back into the stock market—and to do it through Fidelity.

The 1982 to 1987 bull market was unlike any other. The trials and tribulations of the 1970s had raised the awareness of many ordinary investors to the concept of yield. As stocks began to improve and interest rates declined, money fund investors naturally looked to stock funds for higher returns. Fidelity, which had billions in money fund assets and an impressive stock team that included a promising young manager named Peter Lynch, was ideally suited to reap the benefits of the Reagan boom. But stellar fund performance alone doesn't build a business; human capital is equally essential. And it was here, long before the notion of complementary CEOs became the buzz of the business world, that Ned had another remarkable success: He hired a man who would be instrumental in shaping Fidelity's future. His name: Jim Curvey.

James C. "Jim" Curvey joined Fidelity in 1982 as vice president of human resources, and a short time later became senior vice president of administration. Together, Ned and Jim would build Fidelity into the powerhouse it is today; Ned focusing on innovative product and service ideas, and Jim translating those ideas into the key hires that could implement them.

In 1987, Curvey started Fidelity Capital—the company's new business development arm—and served as its president until 1997, when he was named president and chief operating officer of Fidelity. During his tenure at Capital, the organization grew from a fledgling group of venture businesses with $10 million in revenues to a company that both operated and invested in businesses and had revenues of $270 million.

Curvey was named president and chief operating officer in 1997, a position he held until July 2000, when he became head of Fidelity Strategic Investments, the umbrella organization for Fidelity's capital, venture investing and real estate operations. He narrowed his focus to Fidelity's telecommunications interests in January 2002. "When Ned asked me to oversee day-to-day operations of the whole company in 1997, we were going through a difficult period in which performance of our funds and other parts of Fidelity weren't up to our standards," Curvey said. "Working with a terrific team of Fidelity people, we got back on the right track, where we remain today."

During Curvey's tenure as president and COO, Fidelity had some of its best years ever. The company grew from 24,000 to 31,000 employees from 1997 to 2000, while its assets under management increased 82 percent to $973.4 billion (at July 1, 2000). Net sales, revenue and operating income also increased dramatically during 1997, 1998, and 1999, with operating income in 1999 totaling more than twice its what it was in 1997.

When, at the age of 67 Jim announced his retirement from Fidelity on November 13, 2003, he had this to say: "The past 20 years have filled me with the great satisfaction of helping Ned (Chairman Edward C. III) Johnson to build one of the finest financial services firms in the world. It's been an exciting time. From starting and growing Fidelity Capital, to serving as president of the company, to focusing on our telecommunications interests, I've been challenged, rewarded, and blessed. But it's time now for a new generation of Fidelity people to take on the challenges we face today."

Ned returned the compliment: "Everything I asked Jim Curvey to do over the past 20 years was done eagerly and well," said Johnson. "Jim brought intelligence, experience and dedication to each task he undertook, and he was always willing to tell it like it was. I will miss the guidance he provided to Fidelity and the counsel he provided to me. The work of Jim Curvey over the past 20 years is one of the major factors behind the success that Fidelity has enjoyed. He set an example for all of us and he will be missed."

Today, Curvey remains a member of the board of directors of FMR Corp., Fidelity's parent company, and of COLT, the pan-European telecommunications company in which Fidelity is a major investor. Curvey also is a director of Geerlings & Wade, Inc., and Reading is Fundamental, and a member of the Corporation of Northeastern University, the Boston College Carroll School of Management Board of Advisors, and the Villanova University Board of Trustees.

Without Jim Curvey, Fidelity could have easily been just another spoke in the Hub's money management wheel. And without star managers, Fidelity's asset gathering wheel could have stood still.

Long before Morningstar thought up its popular star rating system, Fidelity cottoned on to the star power of its managers. In fact, if you were to name one mutual fund manager, chances are it would be this Fidelity one: Peter Lynch.

To describe Peter Lynch's stock-picking skill as "legendary" is not an overstatement. During his 13-year tenure at Magellan's helm, Lynch led the fund to a 2,703 percent return, far exceeding the 574 percent gain by the S&P 500 during the same period.

Even in the early days of his reign, Lynch's performance did not go unnoticed by investors. As assets began pouring into the fund, Magellan—and Lynch—soon began to receive a level of attention from the media not seen at Fidelity since the days of Gerry Tsai.

Lynch also received an intense level of attention from within Fidelity—particularly from Fidelity's cadre of eager young security analysts who were hell-bent on duplicating his eclectic investing style. Lynch's habit of grilling analysts about every facet of a company's balance sheet, coupled with the analysts' desire to meet his standards exacting standards, turned Fidelity into a veritable boot camp for hotshot stock pickers.

Under Lynch, Magellan's assets ballooned from $22 million in 1977 to $13.1 billion—a sum larger than Fidelity's entire asset base a decade earlier—when he retired in 1990.

Needless to say, Johnson's mutual fund empire was back in full swing.

By 1986, the Fidelity organization offered 70 retail mutual fund offerings, which the company promoted with print advertising, direct mail solicitations, and television spots, as well as through a growing number of walk-in investor centers.

Then came October 19, 1987, the day the Dow Jones Industrial Average fell 508 points and the bull market came to a crashing end. Almost overnight, the greed and gluttony that had come to define Wall Street during the first half of the 1980s was swept away. In its wake remained a nation of shell-shocked investors and thousands of investment industry workers without jobs.

Ultimately, the crash of 1987 would prove more of a hiccup than a heart attack. Fidelity ended 1987 with $75 billion in assets, down moderately from its record high of $80 billion.

But two years later Fidelity's assets would pass the $100 billion mark.

Fidelity sailed into the 1990s with its characteristic surefootedness. The combination of low inflation and high employment—not to mention reduced government deficits and high productivity growth—had turned Fidelity into a moneymaking machine. In fact, Fidelity's assets under management would skyrocket to $955 billion at the end of 1999, from $109 billion at the beginning of 1990.

But the 1990s were also an era of uncertainty for Fidelity. Lynch, who had attained superstar status at the helm of the nation's largest and most successful stock fund, announced plans to retire in 1990s at age 46. Though Fidelity was well stocked with smart, aggressive stock pickers, Lynch's departure proved more than a glancing blow to Fidelity's celebrity status on Wall Street.

Fidelity also faced intense and often brutal competition in the 1990s. Much of that competition came from one firm: Vanguard Group Inc.

Vanguard had found a way to distinguish itself from Fidelity by becoming a leader in low-cost money market funds and index funds. The popularity of both products in the late 1980s and early 1990s called into question one of Fidelity's main reasons for being—that is, to provide small investors access to professional money management they would never be able to afford otherwise.

But Johnson was not about to let Vanguard blunt his edge with investors. Early in 1989, Fidelity launched the Spartan Money Market Fund. By shouldering the fund's expenses—and offering above-average yield—Fidelity was successful in attracting assets, not to mention more media attention. In the first six months, Spartan Money Market picked up about $2.5 billion in assets. A year later the fund would grow to a whopping $8.3 billion.

Buoyed by the success of the money market fund, Johnson, in the spring of 1990, unveiled the Spartan Market Index Fund. The fund, which was later renamed the Fidelity Market Index Fund, was designed to track the performance of the Standard & Poor's 500 Index. Once again, Johnson fought Vanguard by absorbing some of the fund's expense, and once again he was successful in bringing boatloads of new assets into the company.

But the 1990s also posed considerable challenges to Fidelity on the investment front. In 1994, its fund managers were hurt by investing too aggressively. Then, in 1995 and 1996, many managers took a hit for investing too conservatively.

Most notably, Jeff Vinik, then the manager of Magellan, injected a big dose of government bonds into the "stock" fund, causing it to stumble. Vinik "left" the fund, and Fidelity, in 1996.

Another big challenge facing Johnson in the 1990s had to do with turnover of portfolio managers. Since Fidelity's managers tend to be the cream of the crop, Johnson has long had to contend with them being heavily recruited by rivals. For a while, being part of the Fidelity machine provided enough cachet to keep talented managers.

But with the growing popularity of hedge funds in the mid- to late 1990s, Fidelity—as well as other fund companies—began to lose some of its stars. While Fidelity managers are well compensated, successful hedge fund managers earn two or three times what they would at the helm of a mutual fund.

So, in 1995, Johnson did the unthinkable: He gave Fidelity's top executives and fund managers a 51 percent stake in FMR Corporation, the firm's parent company. The move, which marked one of the largest transfers of voting control to employees in corporate history, reduced Johnson's stake in Fidelity to 12 percent (from almost 25 percent).

It also made Abigail Johnson, at that time manager of Fidelity OTC and the only one of Johnson's children active in the business, Fidelity's biggest shareholder, with a 24.5 percent stake.

Fidelity's performance improved over the next several years, thanks in large part to Johnson's efforts to impose more discipline on portfolio managers and to hold them more accountable for their performance results.

Then came the new millennium.

The bear market of 2000–2002 was difficult for the entire mutual fund industry. Fidelity was no exception. Besides having to cope with the collapse of the technology stocks and the fact that growth-oriented companies were being spurned by investors, Fidelity had to adapt to something else: Regulation Fair Disclosure (Reg FD).

Enacted in 2000, Reg FD bars public companies from selectively disclosing information to certain shareholders or investors. The rule change was intended to level the playing field between institutional and individual investors.

Once again, Fidelity's edge—which was based in part on the ability of its managers to use the Fidelity name to gain exclusive access to the CEOs of big companies—was under attack. On an asset-weighted basis, Fidelity's U.S. stock funds beat just 50 percent of their peers in 2004, down from 53 percent in 2003. In 2002, the funds beat 61 percent of their peers.

Something else would soon come under attack: Johnson's seat at the head of the board that oversees every one of Fidelity's mutual funds.

Since 1946, a member of the Johnson family has served as chairman of the board overseeing Fidelity's funds. But in 2004, the Securities and Exchange Commission issued a landmark ruling requiring that 75 percent of fund directors—including its chairman—be independent of the company managing the funds' assets.

For Johnson, who had clearly taken a lead in trying to block the proposal from being passed, it was a devastating blow to his ego.

In the months leading up to the ruling, Johnson spoke personally to William H. Donaldson, who was chairman of the SEC at the time. He also traveled to Washington—and made thousands of dollars in political contributions—to curry favor with key legislators.

The rule change, originally set to take effect in early 2006, has been put on hold pending the outcome of a legal challenge by the U.S. Chamber of Commerce.

Meanwhile, Magellan went from being famous to being infamous. Robert Stansky, who became manager of Magellan in June 1996, faced a barrage of criticism for his inability to significantly beat the Standard & Poor's 500 Index, against which Fidelity compares the fund. Fidelity itself was criticized for allowing Magellan to grow too big to deliver impressive returns.

After more than a decade of tepid performance, Johnson, in October 2005, finally replaced Robert Stansky as the fund's manager. It's easy to see why. Under Stansky, the fund returned an average of 6.9 percent a year, compared with 8.1 percent for the S&P 500.

The fund, which is now in the hands of Harry Lange, currently has $50.2 billion in assets, down from an all-time high of $106 billion in early 2000.

In the annals of Fidelity's history, 2005 will go down as the year of the "dwarf toss."

In July, Fidelity got word that the SEC may file civil charges stemming from allegations that Fidelity traders accepted excessive gifts and entertainment from brokers who did business with the company.

Among gifts allegedly accepted by one Fidelity trader was a bacchanalian bachelor party, complete with scantily clad women and a round or two of "dwarf tossing," which reportedly involves throwing a dwarf in a Velcro suit at a Velcro-covered wall.

Moreover, the Office of the U.S. Attorney launched an investigation into whether brokers from other firms plied Fidelity traders with drugs and prostitutes in order to win their business.

Fidelity immediately launched its own investigation into the matter. As a result, a total of 16 employees were disciplined (14 late last year and 2 more earlier this year) for violations of company policy regarding gifts and gratuities. Meanwhile, Scott DeSano, who had headed Fidelity's stock trading desk, was transferred to another business unit.

In September of that year, Fidelity revealed that the SEC is eyeing a second area of potential charges against it in connection with gifts and entertainment its traders accepted from other brokerage firms.

For Fidelity, the allegations were unprecedented and humiliating. This is, after all, a firm that sailed unscathed through the 2003–2004 improper trading scandal—a scandal that led to more than $2 billion in fines and mandatory fee cuts and involved dozens of fund companies. Should it be charged, Fidelity vows to "vigorously defend itself" against any allegations unsupported by facts and data.

For Johnson, however, the charges were no doubt personal. That's because the very suggestion that Fidelity's traders would take part in such base pursuits goes against the refined, dignified culture that he and his father dedicated their lives to cultivating at Fidelity.

Johnson, who at 75 years of age shows no sign of relinquishing the scepter at Fidelity, has recently taken steps to restore the firm's reputation. For example, he's hired more analysts to allow Fidelity's research team to focus more heavily on specific segments of the market. Along the same lines, he has also implemented a plan to develop so-called career analysts to allow analysts to deepen their knowledge in their area of expertise.

In May 2005, Fidelity disclosed sweeping changes in the ranks of its most senior managers. As part of those changes, Abigail P. Johnson, Johnson's daughter and long considered his successor, relinquished her role as president of Fidelity's investment unit to assume the same title at Fidelity Employer Services Company, the subsidiary responsible for providing retirement and other benefits programs to employers for their employees.

She was replaced at the helm of Fidelity Research & Management Company by Stephen Jonas, a 19-year veteran of the company and its chief financial officer.

As part of the shake-up Johnson assembled a brand-new management team to run the investment group. On that team is Boyce I. Greer, who is head of equity research/asset allocation, a newly created position at Fidelity. Mr. Greer's appointment marks the first time the executive who oversees research is reporting directly to the executive in charge of the entire investment unit—once again signaling Johnson's single-minded focus on restoring Fidelity's research edge.

Today, Fidelity continues to evolve and innovate. In 2003, Fidelity met a brand-new competitor head on when it launched its first and only exchange traded fund, the Fidelity Nasdaq Composite Index Tracking Stock, known as OneQ. Despite being late to the game in terms of its foray into the exchange traded fund (ETF) market, OneQ was the first ETF to track the Nasdaq Composite Index.

The recent management changes at Fidelity have also raised new questions about who is being groomed to replace Johnson.

In recent years, Abigail Johnson has been widely expected to succeed her father. But that long-assumed succession plan was called into question by some last year when Abigail stepped down as head of the company's investment operations. It was further questioned in October 2005 when Abigail reduced her personal ownership in Fidelity and again two months later when she stepped down from her role as a member of the Fidelity mutual fund board of trustees.

Regardless of who is at the helm, Fidelity is sure to be a dominant force—if not the dominant force—in the mutual fund industry for a long time.

"I am generally satisfied with our accomplishments over the years," wrote Johnson in the company's 2005 annual report, which is distributed to employees to provide an update on the company's far-flung businesses. "However, we must not allow our success in the past to lead to complacency in the future, because there is much that needs to be done."

TWO

Navigating Fidelity in the Real World

Your Guide to Opening and Understanding Your Fidelity Accounts

I t's *your* move.

While Fidelity, through its mighty marketing machine, has no doubt been courting you for years, it's generally up to you to take the first step toward establishing a relationship with Fidelity. This may sound like twisted road, but in fact it lies at the heart of Fidelity's single biggest contribution to the financial services industry: its discount brokerage business model.

At the time Fidelity stepped onto the world stage, there was no competition among major brokerages. They were only too happy to charge an arm and a leg for their lackluster services and were also intent on never letting you have an uninterrupted dinner—ever.

Brokers need to eat, too. Therein lies the rub.

There's a saying you've no doubt heard, trite and not always true: Brokers leave you broker. And without tarring a whole group of salespeople with one brush (oops, guess I just did), the fact is that brokers make a living from the commissions they earn for selling you the products they bought with your money. With commission-based compensation, a salesperson's own self-interest lies in selling you wares regardless of whether you truly need them, which means the core rule of investing, "caveat emptor" (buyer beware) doubly applies.

Oh sure, good brokers, like any persuasive salespeople, can convince you that you need more new clothes if you want to become the new emperor, but if you want to build your own financial empire, Fidelity's innovative discount brokerage means dialing into or, more likely, clicking onto, its services.

Trouble is, they won't call you—you'll have to make the first move.

Unlike a traditional brokerage model like Merrill Lynch, Fidelity doesn't have 14,000 brokers doing its bidding. Instead, its discount brokerage model relies on us doing some of the legwork.

The first step of such legwork usually involves opening a brokerage account.

Fidelity, like any self-respecting financial services company, makes it easy to open a brokerage account from the privacy of your own home—or at least to get the ball rolling. Gone are the days when would-be investors felt obligated to don their best "power suits," trudge down to their nearest Fidelity Investor Center, and pray the branch representative didn't fall off his or her chair in a fit of laughter when they plunked down their $2,500 initial deposit (in the form of crumpled bills, quarter rolls, and ha'pennies).

Despite the ease of opening an account online and all the online advantages that Fidelity lets you plug into (see Chapter 4 to learn how to navigate Fidelity's online world), I would encourage you to open your Fidelity account at one of the firm's 110 Investor Centers—especially if you are new to investing. Even if you're a seasoned Fidelity investor but have never been to a Fidelity branch, I'd encourage you to do so. For starters, it will give you the chance to ask questions, get immediate answers, and establish a rapport with the people behind Fidelity. (Note: Fidelity, like most discount brokers, has a reputation for high turnover in its branches, so don't get too attached to your Fidelity branch rep. Do, however, get familiar with the branch office.) Being there can actually be a bonding experience; you'll be surrounded by other investors like yourself.

How do you find the Fidelity branch nearest you? Easy. You can find the most up-to-date list of Fidelity Investor Centers at the end of this chapter, or try going to Fidelity's web site (www.fidelity.com). There, under the "Customer Service" tab in the upper right-hand corner, you will find the familiar "Contact Us" option. After selecting that option, you will be redirected to a screen that, among other things, enables you to locate Fidelity Investor Centers by city and state.

Fidelity also gives you the option of using your zip code to find the nearest Fidelity Investment Center.

If that doesn't work, simply scroll back to the "Contact Us" page and select the option that allows you to send an e-mail to Fidelity. If you are in need of instant gratification, select the new and nifty option that allows you to instant-message a Fidelity representative.

For those of you who don't know an IM from an M&M, there's always that thing attached to the wall with a curlicue cord (I think they still call it a telephone). Dial 800-FIDELITY (800–343–3548) and a Fidelity representative should be able to point you in the right direction.

Opening a Brokerage Account

When it comes to buying mutual funds, exchange traded funds (ETFs), stocks, bonds, and options, you'll not only need to open a brokerage account, you'll be best served by choosing the right one.

A brokerage account, which requires a minimum of $2,500 to open, also gives you access to more than 4,500 Fidelity and non-Fidelity mutual funds, index funds, and exchange traded funds. Opening a brokerage account is much like opening a checking account at your local bank, and there are some important things to keep in mind, chief among them, fees.

Make no mistake, like all financial services companies, Fidelity is out to make a dime off your buck. To do that, it charges different customers different fees based on their level of trading activity as well as the amount of money they keep in their Fidelity account.

So-called Gold-level customers (those who keep at least $1 million in their accounts or who keep at least $25,000 and make at least 120 trades a year) pay the lowest fees.

The cost of trading a stock through a Fidelity representative, for example, is $35 for the first 1,000 shares and 35 cents for each additional share.

For the same transaction, Fidelity's two other levels of customers, Silver and Bronze, would pay $45 for up to the first 500 shares and 45 cents for each share thereafter and $55 for up to 100 shares plus 14 cents for each additional share, respectively.

To put the distinction into perspective, suppose you are fortunate enough to be one of Fidelity's Gold-level customers and you want to buy 2,500 shares of Dogs Gone Styled Inc., a company that operates a chain of dog-washing salons across the country. Shares of the company are trading at $37 each under the ticker symbol DGS.

As a Gold-level customer, you could expect to pay a commission of $87.50 to invest in Dogs Gone Styled. A Silver-level customer, however, would pay $135 for the same transaction and a Bronze-level customer would pay $391.

Here's a quick summary of the distinctions between the three levels of accounts when it comes to trading stocks:

1. **Bronze:** Available to all customers.
   - *Online*—$19.95 for up to the first 1,000 shares, plus 15 cents for each additional share.
   - *Automated telephone*—$45 for up to the first 500 shares, plus 45 cents for each additional share.
   - *Fidelity representative*—$55 for up the first 100 shares, plus 14 cents for each additional share.

2. **Silver:** Available to households with $50,000 in assets at Fidelity or those with $25,000 in assets that carry out 36 trades a year. Also available to any household that makes 72 trades a year.
   - *Online*—$10.95 for up to the first 1,000 shares, plus 15 cents for each additional share.
   - *Automated telephone*—$25 for up to the first 1,000 shares, plus 25 cents for each additional share.
   - *Fidelity representative*—$45 for up to the first 500 shares, plus 45 cents for each additional share.

3. **Gold:** Open to households with $1 million in assets at Fidelity or those with $25,000 in assets that make at least 120 trades a year.
   - *Online*—$8 for all trades
   - *Automated telephone*—$20 for up to the first 1,000 shares, plus two cents for each additional share.
   - *Fidelity representative*—$35 for up to the first 1,000 shares, plus 35 cents for each additional share.

HINT➤ Fidelity reevaluates the level of pricing it charges each of its customers every November. If your level changes in between that reevaluation (e.g., Uncle Windsor dies and you come into a huge inheritance), it's up to you to bring it to Fidelity's attention in order to get the discount.

HINT➤ If you are not the only person in your home with a Fidelity account, make sure you request a "Household Relationship Form" from a Fidelity representative, or download one from Fidelity's web site. By filling out the form, you may qualify for lower commissions—even if your account alone does not meet the required minimum. You don't have to be married, or even friends, to consolidate more than one account into a "household relationship."

Navigating the World's Largest Fund Company

Of course, there's much more to opening an account than simply opening it. Fidelity is the largest fund company in the world, in terms of both assets managed and funds offered. All those choices can get confusing, as can all the rules, forms, and fees necessary to the buying and holding of your investments. This section is designed to help you navigate Fidelity's service options, rules, and fees. To help keep them in check the following topics will be covered:

- Best Fidelity Service
- Using the Internet for More Efficient Service
- Handling Service Mistakes
- Sidestepping Fidelity Minimums
- Understanding and Minimizing Fidelity Fees
- Fidelity's Other Fees
- Mistakes to Avoid
- Fidelity's New Funds
- Buying Closed Funds
- Switching Rules at Fidelity
- Services for Big Investors
- Minimize Capital Gains Taxes
- Maybe You Shouldn't Reinvest
- USA, All the Way!

Best Fidelity Service

Feeling overwhelmed when you open an account at Fidelity is natural. You have to call, click, or visit the company, then wait for the mail, e-mail, or person to deliver the needed forms, fill them out, and send them back. And if you make a mistake or omit something, you may have to go through another slow round-trip mail, e-mail, or branch visit! The best way around this (at least if you're not on the Internet) is to go to one of Fidelity's 110 Investor Centers if you live near one (addresses for many of which are at the back of this book). The forms are all right there at the centers, and so is a fair amount of investment research. Moreover, Investor Center employees are generally more knowledgeable than Fidelity phone reps and can usually give you more time and assistance. One caveat, however: Although they may have the time and expertise to give you advice on picking your investments, I've heard that they are encouraged to steer investors into certain types of funds, especially variable annuity plans. (For more on these plans, check Chapter 14; it's all about VIP funds.)

Using the Internet for More Efficient Service

I know what most of you are thinking: You have Internet access, or you have a friend with a cable modem service at home or work, or your local library may have terminals and people to help you use them. With access to a computer and the help of someone who's been on the Web before, you can view or print out useful information in just five minutes, saving several days of waiting for the mail or making a trip to a Fidelity Investor Center. For some of us, this is as natural as picking up a phone. But if the Internet is still a brave new world to you, don't be intimidated; instead, get educated. You can start by heading to a Fidelity branch near you or by picking up the phone and asking someone at a branch office to help you navigate www.fidelity.com. Don't be embarrassed to ask questions until you understand. It's in Fidelity's best interest, and yours, for you to be plugged in.

Fidelity's Web site at www.fidelity.com has more material than you could fit inside most college libraries: account forms and downloadable fund prospectuses, daily share prices (NAVs), fund sectors, and top holdings; a wide array of independent research material; calculating tools that may prove useful, such as one (IRA Evaluator) to help you pick the right type of IRA (Roth, deductible or nondeductible traditional IRA) and another (Growth Calculator) to help you evaluate your growth projections.

It's a remarkable resource, which I discuss more in depth in Chapter 3.

Handling Service Mistakes

Mistakes happen. Fidelity isn't immune to them. No one is. Has Fidelity ever made a mistake with your account? Bought Small Cap Retirement instead of Small Cap Stock, or, heaven forbid, lost track of $50,000 of your money? When Fidelity makes service mistakes, it's important that you take the right steps to resolve the issue in your favor. The most important thing you can do to protect yourself, at Fidelity or any financial services firm, is to keep a file with all your records. (Such a file can also come in handy at tax time.)

The most important records are those confirming your transactions and your purchases and sales of mutual funds, stocks, and other investments. How you record these depends on which method you use to make your trade. Basically, you can make trades in the following ways: (1) with a real person, (2) using the FAST touch-tone phone system, (3) on the Web at www.fidelity.com, or (4) through your broker.

With a real person, Fidelity has audiotapes it can check if there's a transaction problem; with the Web site, you can print out trade confirmations; but with an automated phone service like Fidelity's FAST, it can be impossible to prove Fidelity made a mistake. (If you write down your transaction number, you can prove that something was done, but if Fidelity's computers insist that you bought when you wanted to sell, then there's little you can do to prove otherwise.)

While computers may be more reliable than people when it comes to making transactions, the computer transactions aren't backed up by audiotapes. For safety's sake, use humans or Fidelity's Web site, not FAST, for Fidelity fund trades. (For brokerage trades you may want to use automated systems to keep commissions low or Fidelity's web site to get an even deeper discount, but for Fidelity mutual fund transactions, it costs you nothing to stick with real people.)

Whichever way you trade, *always write down that long transaction number!* (If you use the Web site, you can easily print it out.) Since it's a long collection of numbers and letters, you might make an error, so also write down the name of the service rep and the date and time of your call. (If you have the transaction number and/or the name of the service representative you talked to and the time and date of the call, Fidelity account managers can find the audiotape of your conversation and fix any mistakes they may have made; if not, you may be out of luck.) As soon as you receive confirmation of your trade by mail, check it to make sure it's the transaction you requested, then save it in your Fidelity file. If there's any problem, it's your responsibility to catch it quickly and bring it to Fidelity's attention.

Again, this is important: When you get your confirmation in the mail, check it immediately. If you find the problem a few days after the transaction, chances are it will be more easily correctable than if you call Fidelity a year later to complain. For example, a stock you thought you bought (but didn't) probably would not have gotten out of your price range within a few days, and it's also more likely Fidelity will make a change.

If there is a problem, call Fidelity customer service (1–800–544–6666) to report it, and see if it can be corrected while you wait on the phone, or at least within a few days. If you have the relevant records, it should be. If you're not satisfied, call customer service and ask for a supervisor or a product manager. These service reps have more seniority and experience in solving problems.

Finally, if customer service can't help you, write to Ned Johnson, Fidelity's president. Remember to include any reference numbers, what you've tried so far to correct the problem, and photocopies (not the originals!) of any relevant mailed correspondence. Many investors have achieved satisfaction by these means. Write to:

Edward C. Johnson III
Office of the President
Fidelity Investments
82 Devonshire Street
Boston MA 02109

Sidestepping Fidelity Minimums

Many Fidelity investors think they must have $2,500 to invest in a Fidelity fund. The minimum for IRA and Keogh accounts *used to be* $500, but no longer. Now it's $2,500 with an additional investment minimum of $250. (Regardless of your other retirement plans, if you have earned income, you can fund an IRA; at worst it just might be a nondeductible IRA.)

Is there a way around the $2,500 minimum? With a regular investment plan (called the *automatic account builder* at Fidelity), you can start with at little as $100 and add as little as $100 at a time. You can have these $100 purchases automatically deducted from your bank account every month (or every third month), from your Fidelity money market account every month (or every second, third, or even every twelfth month), or from your paycheck (every pay period).

For children, you can also open a Uniform Gift to Minors Act (UGMA) account with only $1,000. You're limited to Blue Chip, Growth & Income, Puritan, Asset Manager, and Cash Reserves. On the upside, Blue Chip's 3 percent load is waived for this program, and there are some tax advantages to these accounts, especially for children over 14, who are taxed at their own rate. On the downside, your children can take the money and run once they reach 18; and if they are looking for any college aid, this UGMA will count against them much more than savings in the parents' name.

Small investors can technically open an account with $2,500 and then move some or most of that money into another fund. But this method has its drawbacks: Once a year, on the second Friday in November, Fidelity can levy a charge of $12 on fund accounts holding less than $2,000. It's waived if the account was opened after September 30 for the current calendar year or if the account was opened after January 1 of the current calendar year and uses the automatic account builder. On accounts under $2,000, Fidelity also reserves the right to close out your account (returning your money to you, of course), but first gives you 30 days' warning to meet the minimum, cash out on your own timing, or exchange to another of your funds.

Fidelity's Spartan funds have higher minimums: $25,000 minimum initial investment for retirement and nonretirement accounts, with the same small balance fee caveat ($12.00 if the balance is less than $2,000, waived if the account was opened after September 30 for the current calendar year or if the account was opened after January 1 of the current calendar year and uses the automatic account builder). In return, they generally have slightly lower annual expense ratios than non-Spartan funds.

Understanding and Minimizing Fidelity Fees

Fidelity's retail funds charge several kinds of fees—but by 2005, one fee you won't find on any Fidelity fund, including its Select funds, is a front-end load. (Long-standing Fidelity investors know that about a third of Fidelity's growth funds, all of its region-specific international funds, and all its Select funds used to levy a 3 percent front-end sales charge, which meant that for every dollar you invested, 3 cents was paid to Fidelity to market the fund and 97 cents was invested on your behalf in shares of the fund.) The fact that Fidelity is a pure no-load fund shop is good news. (Note that Advisor funds, which are sold by brokers, come with potentially higher front-end loads as well as annual 12b-1 fees. Also, Variable Insurance Products (VIP) funds have added 0.8 percent annual "mortality" expenses. For these reasons, we do not generally recommend Advisor funds and caution investors to discuss the purchase of any VIP plan with a qualified accountant manager, financial planner, or tax adviser.)

Keeping track of the fees you've paid and ordering transactions properly no longer means paying less. But something that has never been made clear to me is where the "load credit" went. The thing about having ever paid a sales load on a Fidelity's retail fund is that you never had to pay it twice on the same money. Once you paid a 3 percent load on a sum of money, you could transfer it around Fidelity without having to pay another load to buy another load fund. For this reason, it made sense for you to bite the bullet and buy an appropriate 3 percent load fund if that was the most appropriate for your objectives.

Under the load system, when moving money among Fidelity funds, it paid to know what shares you already paid a load on—and how Fidelity moved those shares. For example, when you exchanged money from one fund to another, the shares moved out in descending order of credited load, first 3 percent, then 2 percent, finally 0 percent. (Fidelity used to charge 2 percent loads on some growth and income funds.) If you owned 1,000 shares of a fund, with 500 credited at 3 percent and 500 credited at 0 percent, the 3 percent shares used to be used first to purchase shares of a new fund. If you exchanged 500 shares into a no-load fund and the rest into a load fund, you ended up paying a load on the second transaction. You could have avoided that by switching the order: Exchange into the load fund now using the 3 percent shares, then exchange into the no-load fund later using the 0 percent money.

More simply, you could have made both of the transactions at the same time. Purchases of new funds worked in the same order: with load funds purchased first and no-loads following. In the preceding example, if you had bought the two funds at the same time, the 3 percent load money would go to buy the 3 percent load fund, and the 0 percent money would go to buy the no-load fund—automatically.

If you were shifting money among several funds, it paid to keep in mind the principle that, whenever possible, load money should be used for load funds and no-load money for no-load funds. To match loads, you had to know which loads have been credited to what money. If in doubt, you could call Fidelity Customer Service at 1–800–544–6666. A Fidelity rep could give you that information and could even offer you a strategy for minimizing loads while obtaining the funds you want.

Finally, if you had $10,000 in money that paid a load, and it grew within that load fund to $20,000, the whole $20,000 was credited with paying the load. That was true whether the gains resulted from an increase in share price or from distributions. Once that money left Fidelity, you lost credit for any loads that were paid on it.

But what happened to that load credit when Fidelity went pure no-load?

Fidelity's Other Fees

Following are some additional fees you should be aware of.

Short-Term Trading Fee

Many funds charge a fee for selling a fund within a certain period of its purchase. This fee, which varies from 0.75 percent in the first month on Selects ($7.50 thereafter), to 3 percent on sales made within three years on Small Cap Stock, is also paid into the fund to offset trading expenses. (Small Cap Stock has the strictest rules because small-cap stocks are relatively illiquid, i.e., difficult to trade without moving the market price and/or incurring significant transaction costs.) The only way to avoid these fees is to avoid rapidly trading affected funds—probably a good idea anyway, both for tax reasons and because few people can consistently do well by making a lot of very short term trades. These fees are listed on the online fund snapshots at fidelity.com and in each month of my *Fidelity Investor*'s Performance Review.

Exchange Fee

In addition to the variable redemption fee on Selects, there is a $7.50 fixed fee on Select exchanges. In addition, many Spartan funds charge $2 per check redemption and $5 for other exchanges (these fees are waived on accounts holding over $50,000).

Low Account Fees

As detailed earlier in "Sidestepping Fidelity Minimums," every November Fidelity can levy a charge of $12 on fund accounts holding less than $2,000.

Expense Ratios

In addition to the more visible fees that are charged to you, all mutual funds have expenses, which are deducted incrementally and expressed on an annual basis. These expenses pay the costs of managing and servicing the fund (at Fidelity, typically about 0.6 percent annually for a bond fund, 1.0 percent for a growth fund, and 1.5 percent for an international fund). While expense ratios can be important, especially with income funds, they are already taken into account when fund returns are shown. Bottom line: If a stock fund has a good record, that's much more important than whether its expense ratio is high (at least at Fidelity; occasionally a non-Fidelity fund will do well in a given year despite an outrageous expense ratio of, say, 5 percent or more; such a fund should be avoided). For bond funds, long-run studies have shown that, except for junk bonds, active management adds very little to fund returns and that expense ratios account for more than half the variability in returns among funds with similar objectives. (For money markets, expenses account for almost 100 percent of return variability.) That's why my *Fidelity Investor* lists expense ratios for bond and money market funds every month in its Performance Review.

12b-1 Fees

You've probably heard of something called a 12b-1 fee, which is also included in the expense ratio and is used to pay for selling the fund, as an alternative to a sales load. While Fidelity has 12b-1 plans in place at many funds in case the SEC decides to call some of its service expenses sales-related (e.g., mailing a prospectus), it doesn't currently charge any 12b-1 fees on its retail funds (they are on its broker-sold Advisor funds).

Trading Costs

A fund's expense ratio does not include its underlying trading costs, which are largely hidden. A fund's commission charges can be found—in dollar terms—in the fund's Statement of Additional Information, also known as the Prospectus Part B. (You can get it by calling Fidelity customer service.) But this commission figure cannot, of course, take into account the fact that share prices can be affected by a fund's buying or selling, or even by bid/ask spreads. A fund with a large turnover ratio (e.g., more than 100 percent per year) will have more significant trading costs, but remember that new managers are likely to have a high turnover in their first year as they replace old holdings with their own favorites. Also, an aggressive growth fund such as Aggressive Growth will naturally have a higher turnover (218 percent) than a conservative growth and income fund (e.g., Puritan, 80 percent), and an index fund will have the lowest turnover of all (Spartan Market Index's turnover is 3 percent). Also, if a fund manager can achieve good returns with high turnovers, that's fine with us. (Conversely, a sudden increase in turnover after a period of poor performance may indicate fund flailing more than fund thinking.)

Mistakes to Avoid

The Fidelity investor's most common and costly mistake is picking funds on an ad hoc basis, buying a fund here and a fund there based on what looks hot or what is being advertised by Fidelity rather than systematically constructing a portfolio which meets one's objectives. The fact is, almost any fund can be a good pick for some person, some of the time, and any fund can be a bad pick for someone else, or at another time. And while Fidelity's managers may choose to advertise a fund when they feel it's likely to perform well looking ahead, it's at least as likely that their marketing choices are based on what has been performing well and has a good past record that's easy to sell. Further, a fund advertisement cannot, of course, take your particular situation into account.

Likewise, it's a mistake to seek fund-picking advice from Fidelity service representatives. Fidelity employees can't give you objective fund advice for several reasons. First, there are legal restrictions preventing them from doing so (except in the most oblique way). Second, they're expected to answer scores of phone calls a day; they don't really have the time either to understand your situation or to explain their thinking. Third, unless they're taking night courses on their own, they aren't really qualified to give investment advice beyond telling you what Fidelity will allow you to do—and Fidelity will just as easily allow you to buy the wrong fund as the right one. Finally, they're Fidelity employees. Do you think that a Fidelity employee will ever actually tell you to *sell* a Fidelity fund? Think again!

Fidelity's New Funds

If you haven't heard that Fidelity's new funds do better than its old ones, let me be the first to break the good news to you: They tend to. While I wish it were true that all of Fidelity's new funds delivered market-beating gains, since that way we wouldn't have to think twice about how to invest (we'd simply lump our money into the "can't lose" new fund machine), the truth is that this machine on the whole works inconsistently well. During the past decade, several new growth funds and most new international funds did, as a whole, show an outperformance pattern that is statistically significant.

But among these, growth funds invested in small- to mid-cap areas were the rule of those that *trended* to outperform their peers, by about 4 percent in the first year and 7 percent in the first two years. I think this streak is more than just luck. On the international fund front, the news is statistically and significantly much better: All of Fidelity's new international funds have trended to outperform by as much as two times their index's return in the first and second year of their launch.

Why might a new fund do better than the competition? There are at least five possible reasons: (1) The manager has a very small (manageable) amount of money to manage. (2) There are no asset outflows, only inflows. (3) The fund's purchases should tend to drive up the stocks held in the fund. (4) Fidelity may be smart about timing new fund launches so they come out when they'll do well. (5) Fidelity may give the new fund an outsized share of the best purchases, especially initial public offerings (IPOs), since Fidelity wants the new fund to succeed. Note that all of these factors should logically work better for small-cap funds. Note also that reason 5 would imply legally questionable behavior on Fidelity's part, and Fidelity has denied any such conscious attempts to help new funds at the expense of other funds.

Buying Closed Funds

After much speculation, Fidelity finally (on September 30, 1997, when the fund had reached over $60 billion in assets) closed Magellan fund because it had just gotten *too big*. The company had previously closed the much smaller (then just over $1 billion) New Millennium in 1996 because its manager (Neal Miller) was having trouble picking his favorite small- and mid-cap stocks while having to put a lot of money to work. Other closed funds: Contrafund, Growth Company, Mid Cap Stock, Small Cap Stock, International Discover . . . the list goes on and on and is likely to get longer as assets swell and managers want to ensure that they can invest all the incoming cash rather than let it build to performance-impacting results.

Existing shareholders can typically add to their accounts in any of these closed funds. (And if your company offers one of them in its 401(k) plan, you can start buying it through that plan.) This has led to the idea that you can get an existing shareholder to transfer a few dollars of his or her holding to you, and then you can add more money to this new account. Unfortunately, while this technique works at many closed non-Fidelity funds, Fidelity now only allows existing shareholders to transfer their *entire* account; there can be no net gain in owners of any of these closed funds.

To avoid being locked out of a fund, if you're closing out a big position in one of these closed funds but think you might want to own it in the future, leave $2,500 in the account to keep it active.

Switching Rules at Fidelity

Except for money markets and Select funds, Fidelity generally allows you to exchange out of any given Fidelity fund only four times per year. If you exceed this number, Fidelity reserves the right to terminate your exchange privilege. (It will never prevent you from withdrawing your money out of Fidelity.) Some people may tell you that you can get around this limit by opening multiple fund accounts—but not only will that give you more paperwork headaches, having multiple accounts "under common ownership or control" will further limit your ability to make meaningful switches. (Fidelity combines all trades made by you or made under the same tax ID number.)

There is one way you can increase the possible number of partial (under 50 percent of an effective position) withdrawals. That's by owning multiple funds with similar objectives. In each fund category chapter in this book, I provide correlation tables to help you spot funds that behave alike and those that don't. For example, if you own only one growth fund, you can exchange out four times per year, but if you own two growth funds, you can exchange out eight times per year (four from each fund). But owning two different growth funds won't help you if you're making market-timing trades (or selling mostly or entirely out of the market, for whatever reason), since you'd still only be able to clear out of growth funds as a whole on four occasions per year.

What if you want to take money out of Fidelity on a monthly basis, without substantially altering the makeup of your portfolio? You might think you should make monthly exchanges from each of your funds into a money market and then write a monthly money market check, but then you'd be way over your limit on fund exchanges (12 exchanges instead of 4). If you make the exchanges into money market four times a year, then you might run into trouble if market conditions or changes in your strategy require a fifth or sixth exchange; you'd also have less of your assets working for you in your non-money-market funds. What should you do? Set up a Systematic Withdrawal Plan so money is taken out of each fund on a monthly basis and a check sent to you. Just remember that you may not want to do this on a load fund, especially if you are at the same time adding money to a Fidelity nonretirement account, which will be subject to loads; once money leaves Fidelity, you lose credit for any loads that were paid on it. Also remember that all withdrawals are taxable events (i.e., except for IRAs and other retirement accounts, they generate capital gains or losses).

Services for Big Investors

Fidelity offers Portfolio Advisory Services (PAS) to help you allocate and manage your portfolio of $200,000 or more. However, it charges 1 percent per year for this service (lower for larger accounts) and doesn't claim to be giving much consideration to minimizing your taxes. On that score, the company offers PAS Special Option for investors with $500,000 or more at Fidelity. With this option, Fidelity employees help track and minimize taxes (maximize after-tax returns) on your account of funds and individual stocks and other securities, at the cost of 1.1 percent per year (again, less for larger accounts).

However, while you will get better service (including access to Fidelity's most experienced and competent service reps) and pay no sales loads on any Fidelity funds, fees of around 1 percent per year are likely to prove more significant than one-time sales loads. And from what I've seen so far, the advice given to PAS clients isn't as individualized as you might expect, and here, too, you can't expect Fidelity employees to tell you to dump a fund just because it's in *your* interest to do so. If you have $200,000 to invest, you can get clear, comprehensive, and objective advice for $2,000 a year from a good independent planner. Of course, it may be easier to just go with Fidelity than to find your own independent planner; if you are interested in PAS, call 1–800–544–3455.

Minimize Capital Gains Taxes

You probably know that it's a bad idea to buy funds right before their big annual distributions in December, except for IRAs and other retirement accounts (where it doesn't matter). That's because distributions don't mean more money for you—they just mean paying taxes on a portion of what's already yours (fair enough if you held the fund for a while and shared in the gains, not so fair if you've just bought the fund or are hold-ing it for a loss). Here is a lesser-known way to reduce your tax payments.

Figuring Your Capital Gains

If you've sold part of a long-term fund position, don't let Fidelity calcu-late your taxes. If you do, you'll be staring at more taxes than you may otherwise owe. Fidelity gives you gains only as calculated by the average cost method, and with a partial sale that will *virtually never* be the cheap-est method! You can often save a bundle on your taxes by using the spe-cific shares method. Here's how.

First, you need good records that show what you paid for your fund shares. This is also known as their *cost basis*. If you made several purchases or had the fund's dividends reinvested, then different shares will have dif-ferent costs. (If you bought the fund in only one purchase and did not have any distributions, then the average cost method and every other method will result in the same gains and taxes, so use Fidelity's numbers. The same applies if you have sold out of the fund in one fell swoop.) With specific shares, you'll need to specify which specific shares to sell in order to gain the best tax advantages for yourself. You will generally want to minimize taxes by selling the most expensive shares. If the fund has tended to go up since you first purchased it, these will tend to be the most recently purchased shares.

Unfortunately, if you've already sold shares in the account of the same fund (including writing a check on your non-money-market fund), you're stuck using whatever calculation method you've used in the past, most likely either the average cost method calculated by Fidelity or the first in, first out (FIFO) method, which often generates the highest taxable gain. If you haven't, you're free to use specific shares. Once you've specifically identified the shares you want to sell (usually the most expensive), call Fi-delity Customer Service, specify that you're using specific shares, and place a sell order for whatever amount of the fund you wish (e.g., the 318 shares purchased on 12/4/95, the 372 shares purchased on 12/4/98, and the 410 shares purchased on 12/4/99). Then send Fidelity a follow-up let-ter explaining exactly the same trade, and keep a copy for your tax records. Although this is a legal fiction and means nothing real to Fidelity, having done it, you can (and in fact now *must*) use the specific shares method when you file your taxes.

Maybe You Shouldn't Reinvest

December's a big month for fund distributions. Many funds pay out 5 per-cent or more of their assets in capital gains and/or income distributions.

And all that money can be easily and automatically reinvested in its source fund without paying any loads or fees. But many investors should *not* take advantage of this Fidelity feature. Don't reinvest your distributions in taxable accounts if there's any real chance you'll need the money, whether it's to pay taxes, to spend, or to rebalance your fund portfolio. Instead you should take the Directed Dividends option, with dividends and capital gains paid into a money market.

If you do reinvest a distribution and then need to take it out of the fund, you're probably going to have to pay some more taxes. (You're certainly going to have more tax-time paperwork.) That is, you'll realize a gain (or perhaps a loss) on the shares, on top of paying a tax on the reinvestment amount itself. There'll likely be long-term gains because Fidelity uses the average cost method of figuring gains. (As detailed earlier, you won't be credited with selling the most recent purchases, but will in effect mostly be selling many longer-term shares which have a lot of gains. But as also noted, you can sell specific shares, albeit with more paperwork on your part.)

USA, All the Way!

Most Fidelity investors should not have a regular Fidelity Fund Account. Instead, if they have at least $10,000 at Fidelity, they should look into an Ultra Service Account (USA). This is a brokerage account with a money market with free checking (and no $2,500 minimum on the money market). It allows you to buy Fidelity mutual funds with no more costs or restrictions than regular Fidelity Fund investors, but it also offers many more options.

Income investors can own individual Treasury bonds, notes, and bills. These have no credit risk—like the safest of government bond funds—but because you buy them once and don't pay fund expenses, they often offer a higher yield. Their maturities can also be tailored to exactly meet your objectives and need for principal, and unlike bond funds, you'll know exactly how much you'll get back when the bonds mature.

Many growth investors will like the ability to buy mutual funds from other fund companies, often (with "no transaction fee" funds) with no sales load and with no higher expense ratio than if they had a separate account at that fund company. Stock investors may also choose to own individual stocks. This doesn't have to be a high-risk strategy, and for "buy and hold" investors it can mean deferring capital gains indefinitely without the need for using a variable annuity, IRA, or other tax-deferred account. (Unlike stock funds, stocks generally have no capital gains distributions, only the generally much smaller dividend income distribution.)

THREE

You've Got Mail!

Understanding Your Fidelity Statement

Fidelity spends millions, yes millions of dollars a year on something that doesn't make one thin dime for the company: your statements— both hard copy and, of course, increasingly, online. Yet, while Fidelity's statements are the cleanest and clearest examples of account holdings and performance that I've seen (and I've seen hundreds of different attempts at doing this one thing), most of Fidelity's hard work is not only not appreciated, it's never even seen. That's kind of funny, given that it's a report that's all about *your* money.

Your monthly and quarterly statements are the most valuable documents you'll receive from Fidelity. Therefore, it's important—no, make that critical—that you take time to understand the information contained in it.

Believe it or not, you'll be ahead of the game if you even bother to glance at your account statements. Indeed, the vast majority of investors toss their statements in the trash without so much as opening the envelopes they arrive in. Besides being a total waste of a small rain forest in Brazil, ignoring your account statement is, well, how to put this delicately . . . *stupid*. It's almost like walking into a gym, plunking down $1,000 for a one-year membership, and then never going back to work out. (Okay, I've done that. But I have never *not* opened my monthly statements since, after all, it's all about my money.)

If nothing else, your account statement lets you know whether you are richer or poorer than the previous month or quarter. It also lets you know whether your stocks, bonds, or mutual funds are performing as you had expected; and it alerts you to when it may be time to pull the plug on a particular investment, double up on another, or look for gains to harvest for an upcoming cash need.

Math Anxiety 101

Of course, there's an explanation for why most account statements go from the mailbox to the trash can in a nanosecond: Most people suffer from a mild form of math anxiety that makes opening the envelope an emotionally daunting task. Couple that latent math anxiety with fear of not being able to secure one's own financial future, and you have a monthly reminder of one of your nightmares. There's also an assumption about statements born of past experiences, not the least of which stems from balancing your checkbook; statements consisting of financial information are often difficult—if not impossible—to read, much less understand. Most financial services companies put out statements that make William Faulkner's *The Sound and the Fury* look like a "Dick and Jane" book. Still, compared to other mutual fund companies, Fidelity's statements are a good resource.

They could be better. For the most part, brokerage statements don't give you the information you need to follow your portfolio's performance easily, to track it's long- and intermediate-term performance against appropriate market benchmarks. And in this regard, Fidelity's statements are no exception.

For example, your Fidelity statement does not tell you how your investments have done in terms of percentage gains or losses over an extended period of time. Nor does Fidelity provide any assistance in helping you compare your investments to appropriate benchmark indexes.

Why is this information crucial to understanding your investment results? Because, like many things in life, investment returns are *relative*. While you may have been happy as a clam to earn 33.4 percent on your investment in Fidelity Aggressive Growth in 2003, your enthusiasm would probably have been tempered had you known that the average fund in the same category gained more than 36 percent that same year.

Another useful piece of information that is missing from Fidelity's statement involves fees. Like most fund companies, Fidelity does not tell you what you are paying in charges related to your funds' underlying expenses. It's easy enough to do. If you have $10,000 in a mutual fund that has an expense ratio of 1.6 percent, you are paying Fidelity $160 a year for the privilege of investing in that fund, or $13.33 a month.

Fidelity also leaves out figures that reflect the total monthly, quarterly, or year-to-date commissions that it earned on your account. While you may receive commission information for a specific transaction in a confirmation statement for that transaction, having that information spelled out in an account statement would provide a more complete picture of your dealings with the firm.

Of course, you don't have to be Sherlock Holmes to figure out why Fidelity doesn't provide those details on its account statements: It doesn't want to draw undue attention to how much you are *paying* it to help manage your investments.

That said, ignoring your Fidelity statement is not an option—or not an option you're going to find me supporting.

Your Portfolio Summary

The envelope please.

This is where you go to get the big picture of how your accounts are doing at Fidelity. Since most investors just want to know whether they've made or lost money, the first thing Fidelity shows is the total market value of your accounts on the first day covered by the statement. This is listed next to the line that begins with "Beginning market value as of . . ."

Next Fidelity, gives you an overview of what happened during the month or quarter. The "change in investment value" line reveals whether you made or lost money on your investments. In addition to reflecting any appreciation or deprecation of your holdings due to price changes, the change in investment value reflects any income earned during the statement period, less any transaction costs, sales charges, or fees.

After that, in the line that begins "Ending market value as of . . . ," Fidelity lets you know the market value of your accounts on the last day of trading.

Comparing the market value of your investments at the beginning and end of the reporting period allows you to quickly determine whether you have made money or lost money. But to figure out the percentage loss or gain, you will have to do the math yourself.

Lucky for you, that math is fairly simple. All you need to do is subtract the beginning market value of your investments from the ending market value, then divide that result by the ending market value, and finally, multiply your answer by 100; that is the percentage change in your investment.

The formula looks like this:

$$[(\text{Ending market value} - \text{beginning market value}) \div (\text{ending market value})] \times 100$$

Unfortunately, Fidelity gives you the market value of your investments only at the beginning and ending of the month or quarter. To track your investments over a longer period of time, you'll need to dig up your old statements and calculate the performance yourself.

The line marked "Ending Net Value" results from multiplying the price per share of every stock or mutual fund you own by the total number of shares and then subtracting from that anything you may owe on the account, such as margin debt. In other words, it's a close approximation of what you would have pocketed had you decided to liquidate all your Fidelity accounts on the last day covered by the statement (not including commission costs).

Finally, if there is any doubt about where you fall on Fidelity's fee schedule, here is where you will get your answer. The line marked "Your portfolio commission schedule" is where you will find out whether Fidelity considers you a Gold, Silver, or Bronze customer.

Remember, this part of the portfolio is the view from 30,000 feet. It does not tell you how any particular investment performed during the period covered by the statement. And it doesn't tell you how much dividend income a particular security may have brought in. If you want that kind of information, you will have to dig a little deeper into your statement.

Value by Account

If the "Your Portfolio Summary" represents a look at your account from 30,000 feet, this section is a look at your account from 15,000 feet. In this part of your statement, you find a list of all your accounts at Fidelity and the assets held in each of those accounts. Unlike many mutual fund companies and brokerages, Fidelity makes it easier for you to put the numbers in context by giving you the value of the assets at both the beginning and end of the statement period.

Income Summary

In the "income summary" section, you find breakdown of income earned on your investments by tax status. For example, if you have a traditional brokerage account and a Roth IRA at Fidelity, the income earned during the statement period is labeled "taxable" and "tax-free," respectively. Fidelity also provides a "Year to Date" summary of income generated by your account.

It is important to review this section, because an increase in account value may be the result of the income reflected in this section as opposed to an increase in the value of your holdings. It is also important to review this section to make sure your investment income is correctly being classified as either "taxable" or "tax-free."

The income summary includes dividends, capital gains, and interest.

Dividends: Simply put, dividends are cash distributions that companies make to their shareholders. When a dividend distribution is made, you have the option of pocketing the cash or buying more shares. Many people choose to have their dividends automatically reinvested.

Capital gains: This represents any gains you, or to a mutual fund you are invested in, realized on the sale of a stock or bond. In other words, it is the difference between a security's sale price and its purchase price. Typically, capital gains distributions made by mutual funds are done once a year, and you can opt to receive the distribution as cash or use it to buy more shares. For nonretirement accounts, all capital gains distributions are taxable.

Interest: As with a bank, Fidelity pays you interest on money that is in your cash reserve account. You may also earn interest on your bond investments.

Your Portfolio Details

If the devil is in the details, you'll want to wear oven mitts when reviewing this part of your account statement.

Here is where you will find a complete chronological record of all the activity in each of your accounts during the statement period. On the first page of your statement, Fidelity provides you with a portfolio summary of all your accounts. Here you get the same sort of summary—only on an account-by-account basis.

The first thing you'll notice here is that the account number is displayed prominently near the top of the page. Below that are the "Account Summary" and the "Income Summary." As it did in the "Portfolio Summary" part of your statement, Fidelity provides you with the value of each particular account at the beginning and the end of the statement period.

In addition, you will find detailed information about your holdings in each account. For each position in the account, Fidelity lists the name of the security, the ticker symbol of that security (if applicable), the number of shares, the price per share at the end of the statement date, the total cost basis of those shares (what you paid for them), the value of those shares at the beginning of the statement period, and the total market value of the shares at the end of the statement period.

In the "transaction details" section, you will find a thorough list of transactions that were posted to your account since the last statement period. The most common entries appearing in this section include purchases of securities, sales of securities, margin interest charges, receipt of dividends, and dividend reinvestments.

The dates of the transactions are reflected as the settlement dates and may not reflect the actual dates the trades were executed.

Additional Information about Your Investment Report

Here is where you will find important messages and notices regarding your account. These messages may include up-to-date information on new developments in the mutual fund industry and regulatory announcements.

Finding Errors

While Fidelity processes billions of transactions a year without a problem, it does occasionally blunder. Checking for errors is another reason why it's important to thoroughly review your account statements. If you have more than one account at Fidelity, you'll want to make sure that any money you send to the firm lands in the right account. With retirement accounts, you'll want to make sure your contributions are credited for the correct tax year.

If you do find a mistake, call Fidelity immediately (800–544–6666).

Record Keeping

Okay, so you have reviewed your account statement and feel fully informed about the status of your relationship with Fidelity. Now, can you toss your statement in the garbage can?

No!

Since most of the information contained in your account statement goes back only to the previous month or quarter, it's important that you keep your past statements. Without those statements, you have no way of analyzing your investment results over an extended period of time.

If you don't already have a good record-keeping system in place, you better start thinking about one. There are many different ways to create a record-keeping system that can work for you. A good system will contain a category labeled "Investing," and that category will have two components—an active file and an inactive file.

Your Active Files

Account statements, trade documentation, and written memos of any conversations you have had with a Fidelity representative are just some of the items to keep in your active investment file.

Your Inactive Files

An inactive file is a repository where you can research your spending, saving, and investing history. The main advantage of maintaining an inactive file is the ability to research your own questions. Instead of spending valuable time on the telephone with a Fidelity representative, you will be able to come up with your own answers about a transaction that took place more than a year ago.

FOUR

Fidelity.com

Online Investing at Fidelity

I n its infancy, *online investing* meant checking your account balance, gathering a few delayed stock quotes, and, maybe, trying your mouse at a trade or two.

Then came the Internet revolution.

Never mind Asimov's I-robot. Today's investor, like it or not, has been transformed into a new type of being; I-Internet.

Nowhere was this revolution more anticipated, better facilitated, and consistently upgraded and activated than at Fidelity.

At its core, Fidelity is and has always been a technology company wrapped in a mutual fund disguise.

This meant that while other companies were (and still are) playing a game of tech catch-up, Fidelity was able to plug its clients into the revolution, catching the first tech wave rather than watching it roll on by in the early 1960s. Fidelity caught the next big wave in the 1990s while most of its competitors (except Schwab) missed it completely and found themselves waiting for the next set. Today, one could easily argue that Vanguard is still dead in the water when it comes to providing technology, technological know-how and real-time solutions for its clients. Sometimes being cheap is, well, just being cheap.

In the years rolling up to Y2K (2000), suddenly, nearly every big financial services company—firm in its conviction that the Internet would have a profound impact on the way it ran its business—began plowing billions of dollars into their online offerings. Stock quotes went real time. The cost of online trading plummeted as companies such as Fidelity, Charles Schwab, and T.D. Waterhouse went head-to-head for on-line accounts. Ameritrade and E*Trade were born. And ordinary investors, armed with millisecond market access, gained the ability to track portfolios, research their own investments, and trade 'em.

Fidelity, which in 1995 became the first major mutual fund company to create a home page on the World Wide Web, emerged at the forefront of that revolution. Indeed, thanks to Chairman Edward C. "Ned" Johnson III's fascination with technology (not to mention his willingness and ability to spend big bucks on that technology), Fidelity has been running a top-notch, no-holds-barred discount brokerage operation online for more years than many online brokerages have been in existence.

Sure, some of the content on Fidelity's Web site is biased, self-serving, and promotional in nature. Not surprisingly, there are subtle and not-so-subtle ways of calling attention to the wares on your own store's shelf. But with such features as access to a wide range of truly independent re-search (sorry, Morningstar, in my book you don't qualify) tools that allow you to analyze your level of diversification and give you the ability to im-mediately chat live with a flesh-and-blood representative from your per-sonal computer, ever-enhanced versions of its site and site's features born of the feedback from the top down and the bottom up, Fidelity's online capabilities are well worth getting to know—and use.

In fact, in a recent survey by J.D. Powers and Associates of online in-vestor satisfaction, Fidelity ranked number 3 in overall satisfaction, be-hind Vanguard Group at number 2 and Scottrade at number 1. The fact that Vanguard ranked second had to have heads shaking at Fidelity; there's no comparison between the two sites—save for the fact that Van-guard's retail clientele may be so accustomed to seeing and getting less that they don't know how to benchmark what they've got versus what other firms offer. Even www.janus.com is a far more useful and user-friendly site than www.vanguard.com.

At the beginning of 2006, Fidelity had more than 6.6 million online ac-counts, which accounted for more than 60 percent of its total number of retail accounts. Assets in those online accounts totaled more than $500 billion, or 75 percent the company's total retail assets.

Of course, Fidelity didn't get to be an online heavyweight overnight. In fact, the company's extensive menu of online services has evolved and continues to evolve.

Fidelity's Online Evolution

Let's take a closer look at Fidelity's efforts to harness the power of technology.

THE TECHNOLOGY TIME LINE

1965 Edward C. "Ned" Johnson III purchases Fidelity's first mainframe computer.

1974 Fidelity offers the financial industry's first toll-free number to field calls from prospective investors.

1979 Fidelity launches a voice-activated computer response system aimed at the general public.

1983 Fidelity introduces Fidelity Automated Service Telephone (FAST) and becomes the first major financial services company to use a voice-activated computer answering system.

1984 Fidelity develops software application to offer trading via the personal computer.

1991 Fidelity introduces a check processing imaging system.

1992 Fidelity unveils Fidelity On-Line Xpress (FOX), a software program that allows customers direct assess to their accounts through their personal computers.

1993 Fidelity introduces a forms processing imaging system.

1995 Fidelity becomes the first mutual fund company to create a home page on the World Wide Web.

Fidelity launches a Spanish language toll-free telephone service.

Fidelity becomes the first major retirement services provider to distribute employee education and interactive planning tools on the World Wide Web.

1996 Fidelity begins offering 401(k) access and transactions over the Internet.

1998 Fidelity offers its customers wireless access for monitoring and managing investments from just about anywhere in the United States.

Fidelity launches PortfolioPlanner, an interactive, Internet-based planning service for 401(k) plan participants.

1999   Fidelity hosts its first Webcast featuring portfolio managers and financial analysts.

Fidelity launches Powerstreet, a package of Internet-based financial planning and trading tools.

Fidelity unveils My Fidelity, which allows customers to create a personal start page on its Web site.

Fidelity expands its wireless offerings and becomes the first financial services firm to offer wireless trading.

2000   Fidelity launches its Full View aggregation service. This gives investors the ability to aggregate all their financial information, including accounts at other firms, into one place.

2001   Fidelity enables real-time customer support online on its Web site through Instant Messaging.

Fidelity launches Web pages with online tools and resources specifically designed for interactive television users.

Fidelity expands Fidelity PortfolioPlanner, making it one of the first online planning tools that integrates data from multiple accounts.

Fidelity becomes the first financial services company to offer in-vehicle investment services via OnStar's hands-free, voice-enabled, Virtual Advisor.

2005   Fidelity gives the public free access to Portfolio Review, which allows investors to evaluate their investments and determine whether their holdings are properly diversified.

Fidelity unveils several enhancements to its Web site, including one that allows customers to access interactive account statements.

Navigating Fidelity.com

So you want in on the action? And who can blame you? People have been talking about this online investing thing for years.

First, is the hype worth the type? Be sure you know both the advantages and the limitations of the sites you're considering. The following checklist will help you do this at a glance, but be sure you get answers to your questions *before* you make your final move.

✔ Do you have the ability to trade stocks, options, mutual funds, and bonds?

✔ What is the cost per trade? For example, what is the cost per trade for up to 5,000 shares in regard to market or limit orders conducted over the Internet? Is there a discount for using the Internet as opposed to your touch-tone phone?

✔ Are there hidden charges? Are additional charges imposed, such as in-activity fees and postage and handling fees?

✔ Are the accounts protected? For example, one site offers up to $50 million per customer ($500,000 under SIPC, including $100,000 for cash claims) and an additional $49.5 million in protection provided by Aetna Casualty and Surety Company—which means that if you strike it rich and the company goes belly up, you're covered. (Note: This coverage isn't for market losses, but is more like FDIC Insurance at your bank.)

✔ When do you get confirmation? Will you receive confirmation of orders within seconds of execution (with portfolio updated automatically), within hours, or within in days?

✔ Do you have access to free real-time quotes, and how many (some sites offer up to 100 per day)?

✔ Is there free, unlimited portfolio access and the ability to create charts as well as to monitor investments in real time?

✔ Do you get free company news, market news, and other information on stocks, bonds and mutual funds?

✔ Do you have free access to fundamental analysis, technical and earnings estimates, and charting services oriented to technical investors.

Putting your money where your mouse is is no easy task—it tests your nerves as well as your wires. But the time saved, the research gleaned, and the advice pooled and sifted make the advent of online investing much more than a cool trend. In fact, with the mere flick of your wrist, you can take control of your financial life.

Fidelity can help.

The question is, where do you go from here? Well, if you have a personal computer and access to a high-speed Internet connection, I'll show you.

But first, you must ask yourself a basic question: What's in it for me?

Well, here's a short list of what's in store for you at www.fidelity.com:

1. Access up-to-date account balances.
2. Review recent transactions that affect your account.
3. Trade stocks, bonds, and mutual funds.

4.   Access thousands of independent research reports from many of Wall Street's top analysts, including Lehman Brothers Holding Inc. and Standard & Poor's Corp.

5.   Screen stocks, bonds, and mutual funds based on more than 100 criteria.

6.   Chat live with Fidelity representatives through the firm's instant messaging services.

7.   Set alerts to notify you of news and events that could affect your portfolio.

8.   Transfer funds from one account to the other.

9.   View your account statement online.

You Online

Computer on. Browser humming. Click into www.fidelity.com. What you see: Fidelity's home page. What you get: a portal into all things Fidelity.

While the home page is always being updated, you are most likely looking at various promotions of the company's products and services. Fidelity also uses this page to post messages it deems important to shareholders. As of this writing, for example, there is a message aimed at shareholders of its mighty Magellan Fund, informing them that the fund's net asset value recently dropped 18.33 percent due to a dividend distribution.

From here, you should look to the upper left side of the screen, where you will see a box labeled "Customer Login." Put your arrow on the box and click on it. Your screen changes and a new one appears. You are probably looking at a screen that asks you to enter your Social Security number (or a customer ID) and a personal identification number.

Having an account at Fidelity does not automatically give you online access to that account. If you have not already registered with Fidelity to access your account online, you must do so by clicking on the words "New User Registration" at the right side of the page. There you will be asked to provide your Social Security number as well as your date of birth and zip code so that Fidelity can verify your identity before beginning the process that will allow you to access your account online.

If you are a registered user, enter your Social Security number (or your customer ID) as well as your personal identification number.

The first thing will appear on your screen is a list of your accounts at Fidelity. At the top of the screen, you will see "Portfolio Total," which gives you the total market value of all your accounts. It's important to look at the small print at the bottom of the screen to find the date and time the market value of your holdings was last updated.

As with the first page of your paper account statement, this is where you get the big-picture view of all your accounts at Fidelity. At the top of the screen, you will see five tabs that allow you to look more closely at different aspects of your total portfolio.

1. *Summary* gives you a snapshot of the total market value of each account. Next to each account you will also see a box that says "Select Action." Clicking on that box allows you to drill down for more information specific to that account, such as positions, balances, orders, and history.

2. *Portfolio Positions* brings up each position in each account. For each position, it also gives the amount of shares you own, the price of each share, the market value of the position, and the change in market value since the position was added to the portfolio. Next to each position, you will also see a box that says "Action." Clicking on the box gives you the option of adding to your position, reducing your position, compiling research on the security, or viewing various "lots" that went into building your position.

3. *Portfolio Research* brings up each position in your accounts as well as a chart that depicts the one-year performance of that position's stock price. While the chart automatically defaults to a one-year view of the share price, you have the option of recalibrating the chart to look at various time periods, ranging from one day to 10 years. On this view, you will also find a list of recent news stories pertaining to each position.

4. *Portfolio Analysis* is where things start to get interesting. This tool allows you to categorize your investments to give you a better understanding of your portfolio's diversification. This tool takes into account any individual securities you own, as well as the underlying securities in each of your mutual funds, to present you with a more transparent view of your exposure to such major asset classes as domestic stocks, foreign stocks, bonds, and money market funds.

Scroll a little farther down the page and you will see the Equity Style Profile. This chart shows you where your domestic stock holdings fall on the size and valuation continuum. Does your portfolio fall squarely into the large-cap growth box? While that's great when that investment style is in favor, it's a catastrophe when large-cap growth stocks fall out of favor. You might want to think about diversifying your portfolio a bit.

Next comes the Equity Industry Sector graph. This chart classifies your domestic stock holdings into 13 major industry sectors: Software, Hardware, Media, Telecom, Healthcare, Consumer Services, Business Services, Financial Services, Consumer Goods, Industrial Materials, Energy, Utilities, and Unknown. Even better, you get to see how your domestic stock investments in different industries compare against the Wilshire 5000 Equity Index, a proxy representation of the broad domestic market.

In this section, you will also find a Bond Style Profile chart. Basically, this chart shows you the overall style of the assets classified as domestic bond investments using two common measures: credit quality and duration. *Credit quality* is divided into investment-grade—that is, those with a credit rating of BBB or higher—and non-investment-grade, which consists of bonds rated below BBB. Since government bonds are not rated by any rating agencies, Fidelity includes them in the investment grade camp. *Duration*, which is a measure of the average time it will take you to fully recover the principal and interest payments, allows you to compare bonds of different maturities and coupon rates.

This chart does more than show you the style of the bonds in your portfolio. It also compares your portfolio's style to the Lehman Brothers Universal Bond Index, which is a measure of the broad domestic bond market.

It's important to note that the category marked "unknown" includes any bonds held individually or through a mutual fund.

The Bond Credit Ratings charts shows your bond portfolio broken down by the individual credit ratings of the bonds in your portfolio. By giving you a percentage breakdown of the bonds in your portfolio that are rated AAA, AA, BBB, BB, B, or Below B, you get a good idea of how much risk is embedded within your portfolio.

The Taxable Bond Sector chart classifies your taxable bonds into five categories: Government and Agency, Mortgage and Asset-Backed, Investment Grade Credit, Non-Investment Grade Credit, and Others. You can also see how your taxable bond investments compare to the Lehman Brothers Universal Bond Index, which includes more than 10,000 taxable bonds.

The Municipal Bond Sector chart classifies your municipal bond investments into general obligation munis, revenue munis, and other munis. It also shows you how your muni investments compare to the Lehman Brothers Municipal Bond Index, which generally includes more than 40,000 individual municipal bonds and is a widely used proxy for municipal bonds.

Under the Portfolio Analysis tab, you will also find a link titled Hypothetical Trade Tool, which allows you to see the potential effects of a trade on your asset allocation, concentration, stock, and bond styles. If you are selling securities, this tool also evaluates any potential gains or losses you will incur with the sale.

5. *Statements/Records* allows you to immediately view your quarterly statements going back more than two years. In this section, you also have access to trade confirmations, tax forms pertinent to your portfolio, and prospectuses and annual reports of your Fidelity funds.

Some Ink about Online Statements

So you're getting pretty comfortable with this whole online thing? Why not consider viewing your account statements online? While I firmly believe that paper account statements are crucial to a good record-keeping system (call me old-fashioned), Fidelity's online statements offer several advantages that you can't get with paper.

1. *Convenience:* You can't beat the immediacy of online statements—and you never have to let another vacation go by without checking on your portfolio. (What? Oh, I thought that was a good thing!)

2. *Customization:* You can customize your online statement to see only the accounts you are most interested in.

3. *Links:* With links to such tools as Portfolio Analysis and Portfolio Review, Fidelity's online statements make it easier to perform a quick analysis of your portfolio. Links to up-to-date stock quotes and research also make it easier for you to research individual holdings in your portfolio.

Trading Stocks, Bonds, and Funds Online at Fidelity

On your mark, ready, set . . . go.

You did the hard work. You scoured though the annual and quarterly reports, you read what the analysts are saying, and you're confident Dogs Gone Styled Inc. (DGS), our hypothetical dog-washing empire, is going to make Google Inc. look like a penny stock.

It's time to go online and invest in that puppy.

Let's assume you want to buy 100 shares of DGS at the market value.

After you go through the login process, you will be taken to a page that contains a listing of all your accounts at Fidelity. Next to each account you will see the "Select Action" box, which you should be pretty familiar with by now.

A. *Click on "Select Action" and select "Trade Stocks."* This will take you to a box titled "Trade Stocks-Standard Session." At the top of the box you should see your account number, your account's net worth as well as the amount of cash available to you to make a purchase.

B. *Click on the "Action Box."* You have four options:
1. *Buy:* Buy a security.
2. *Buy to Cover:* An order placed to close out a short position in a particular stock.
3. *Sell:* Sell a security.
4. *Sell Short:* Selling a security you do not own. The shares are loaned from a broker or another margin account and the proceeds of the sale secure the loan.

C. *Click on "Buy."*

D. *In the box next to "Symbol," enter "DGS."* If you don't know the symbol, you may look it up by clicking on "symbol lookup."

E. *In the box next to "Quantity" enter "100."* If you are selling shares, you may select the option that allows you to sell all the shares.

F. *Click on box next to "Order Type."* You have eight options:
1. *Market Order:* A buy or sell order that is executed immediately at the best price available.
2. *Limit Order:* An order in which the buyer or seller specifies the price at which they're willing to buy or sell. For limit orders to buy, the stock is eligible to be purchased at or below your limit price, but never above it. When you place a limit order to sell, the stock is eligible to be sold at or above your limit price, but never below it.
3. *Stop Loss:* An order that becomes a market order if and when a security sells at or below the specified stop price. It is used to protect yourself against a potential downward slide of a security.
4. *Stop Limit:* A stop order that becomes a limit order if and when a specified price level has been reached.
5. *Trailing Stop Loss ($):* A stop-loss order in which the stop-loss price is set at some fixed dollar value below the market price. If the market price rises, the stop-loss price rises proportionately, but if the stock price falls, the stop-loss price doesn't change. This technique allows an investor to set a limit on the maximum possible gain.
6. *Trailing Stop Loss (%):* A stop-loss order in which the stop-loss price is set at some fixed percentage below the market price. If the market price rises, the stop-loss price rises proportionately, but if the stock price falls, the stop-loss price doesn't change. This

technique allows an investor to set a limit on the maximum possible gain.

7. *Trailing Stop Limit ($):* The dollar you set as part of a trailing stop limit, which works just like a trailing stop-loss order except that the order becomes a limit order (instead of a market order) when the order is triggered. When the market is moving in your favor, your trailing stop order's stop price trails the market by the trail amount. When the market is moving against you, the stop price does not change.

8. *Trailing Stop Limit (%):* The percentage value you set as part of a trailing stop limit, which works just like a trailing stop-loss order except that the order becomes a limit order (instead of a market order) when the order is triggered. When the market is moving in your favor, your trailing stop order's stop price trails the market by the trail amount. When the market is moving against you, the stop price does not change.

G. **Select "Market Order."** Note: Be extremely careful when placing market orders when the market is closed. If placed, your order will be eligible for trading on the following business day, and the value of your security may open significantly higher or lower than where it closed the day the previous day.

H. **Click on "Time in Force" box.** You have six options:

1. *Day:* Order is canceled if it cannot be executed before the current day's market close (4 p.m. ET)

2. *Good 'til Cancelled:* Order is generally good for 120 days. If the order is not executed after 120 days, the order is automatically canceled.

3. *Fill or Kill:* This restriction requires that the order is immediately completed in its entirety or it is canceled.

4. *Immediate or Cancel:* This restriction requires that a broker immediately enter a bid or offer at a limit price you specify. All or only a portion of the order can be executed. Any portion of the order not immediately completed is canceled.

5. *On the Open:* This restriction requires that the order be executed as close as possible to the opening price for a security. All or part of the order can be executed. Any part of the order that cannot be executed at the opening price is canceled.

6. *On the Close:* This restriction requires that the order be executed as close as possible to the closing price for a security. All or any part of the order that cannot be executed at the closing price is canceled.

I. *Select "Day."*

J. *Click on the "Conditions" box.* You have four choices:

   1. *None:* No restrictions are placed on the execution of the order.

   2. *All or None:* Indicates the order can be used only as a Good 'til Cancelled limit order.

   3. *Do Not Reduce:* A condition on a Good 'til Cancelled limit order to buy or stop an order to sell a security. This condition prevents the order limit or stop price from being reduced by the amount of the dividend when a stock goes ex-dividend or the stock's price is reduced due to a split.

   4. *All or None/Do Not Reduce:* A condition on an order indicating that the order can only be used as a Good 'til Cancelled limit order.

K. *Select "None."* Next, you have to decide the "Trade Type." You have two options:

   1. *Cash:* Uses available cash in your cash account at Fidelity.

   2. *Margin:* Allows you to borrow against securities you own to purchase other securities.

L. *Select "Cash."*

M. *Click on "Preview Order."* Fidelity provides you with a breakdown of how much the trade is costing you, with and without the commission.

N. *If you are satisfied, click on "Place Order."* Piece of cake. Now for your next order.

Beyond Fidelity.com

Let's face it, smart investors (yourself among them) will know how to rule the information that is most relevant to them—whereas foolish investors will let the information rule them. In these turbocharged fund investing times, survival of the swiftest (in terms of both getting the right information at the right time and knowing how to apply it) determines who will thrive in the market—and who will merely survive. One key: Get plugged in.

Gotta get plugged in. Otherwise, you'll be left to the mercy of someone else's research, recommendations, and timing of your trades. (It's only money.) On the other hand, plugging into online investing can give you total control over your own investments. It's easy once you know how.

It's no secret that Fidelity.com provides a way to keep fully current with your Fidelity accounts' investments as well as the range of themes that affect them. But beyond the account info glut, the net also provides the most efficient way to research and invest in mutual funds, stocks, and bonds. It's also a place where glib opinion can look as authoritative as proven research, and charlatans can appear to be authentic. Just as caveat emptor applies to any investor and potential investment, so, too, does it apply to information about them.

Access to information doesn't guarantee successful use of it. But, despite the disconnects, online investing is here to stay.

Major Players and Niche Sources

Nothing new under the sun? Check out "sun" using your Web browser and you will see there's plenty that's new. But don't stare at the sun too long. You've come this far; the next level is up to you. And that's learning where some of the most significant investment sources on the World Wide Web are located. You can always start a search by using Google or Yahoo (www.yahoo.com) and typing in the name of the subject matter (i.e., "economy," "stocks," "mutual funds") or a specific name (e.g., name of a company, security, or mutual fund) in which you are interested. Or you can check out the following hot sites that shouldn't be missed.

Stocks, Bonds, and Mutual Funds

Use your browser to help locate any sites that are exchange specific. As of this writing, not one of the three major U.S. stock exchanges (NYSE, AMEX, Nasdaq) had official Web sites. However, by the time you read this, chances are all the major exchanges will be out there—in cyberspace awaiting your cursory glance. Fortunately, the Web isn't all that constrained by what it lacks—since it offers so much. Take a look at one or more of the following sites.

Ipodata.com is a unique web site that offers investors the ability to track initial public offerings—plus a searchable database of those IPOs. Although bonds shouldn't be a large part of your portfolio (see Chapter 12), if you want information about them you can click into bondsonline.com; and also be sure to visit the Federal Reserve Bank of New York site for quotes on U.S. Treasuries and bonds (ustreas.gov).

Some leading full-service brokerages offer free sites worth visiting, but you might have to yield your name to enter, which could translate into never having an uninterrupted dinner again in your lifetime—since brokers love to call when you're home. Still, the information available on the following is first-rate:

Merrill Lynch   www.ml.com

Morgan Stanley   www.morganstanley.com

Company Research

If you're thinking about buying stock in a company, and you want to know more than just its name, check out EDGAR, the SEC's web site. Electronic Data Gathering and Retrieval (EDGAR) is the SEC's database of electronic corporate filings. Here you'll find filings from most publicly traded companies—from large-caps to small-caps. EDGAR provides customized company reports as well as bulk data. To get there, go to edgar-online.com.

Online Investment Research

Bloomberg.com. A more conventional and more comprehensive means for finding financial facts and overall market views is Bloomberg .com. You get much more than mere coverage—you get in-depth analysis, market quotes, and access to a range of market experts and money managers that frequent Bloomberg's site on a daily basis. You can also zip into a number of market and industry comparison charts that can give you a snapshot of how your overall portfolio may be doing.

CNNfn.com. A comprehensive one-stop shop for the daily planet. Here you'll find all the news headlines, as well as a comprehensive market watch. Keeping in tune with the daily pulse of regional and international markets may leave you crying in your beer. But staying fully informed is one way to stay ahead of the herd—and it's not hard to do. Of course, if you're interested only in regular checkups, you can turn to the weekly overviews.

EIU.com. EIU is an acronym for Economist Intelligence Unit. If you invest in foreign stocks or international stock funds, you can't afford to overlook this site, which covers 190 countries, including emerging and newly emerging markets. EIU's core value is its consistent, objective analysis of trends in 190 countries. Its uniquely informed commentators and commentary, including more than 500 analysts, consultants, and researchers, provide reliable and accurate intelligence to a client base that consists of the world's leading businesses, financial institutions, and government agencies. It would be hard to find another site that offers more expertise, greater coverage, or a stronger reputation for accuracy and insight.

Fidelityinvestor.com. This is the home page of my multiple-award-wining, independent investment advisory newsletter. It's a member-only service.

Fundalarm.com. This site provides unique "sell" recommendations on funds.

Morningstar.com. An informed and efficient way to gather a lot of fund information, but be wary of the star rating system; it's been shown more than once that 1-Star funds trounce 5-Star funds.

Marketwatch.com. If you want to hot-list only one site for all your investment resource needs, you could choose Dow Jones's Marketwatch.com and rest assured that your investment-related bases will be well covered. If you're looking for the top- and bottom-performing mutual funds, the best and worst fund managers, the largest funds, fund ownership of stocks, and sector and fund-by-sector performance numbers, you got 'em. If you want to look beyond a single rating system for funds, and for more commentary on individual funds in relation to their peers, it's all here.

Together, all the preceding sites provide the most efficient, comprehensive sources for fund information on the Web. But there's much more you need to learn about the Web before you can consider yourself its master.

Your Personalized Fidelity Fund Tracking System

If you want get really *technical* and be in greater control of the broader number of Fidelity funds (and the markets, industries, and stocks they invest in) you'll need to move beyond the obvious fund sites and create your own spreadsheet.

Gasp.

Deep breath.

You can do this.

Yes. You can.

Now I know that the very word *spreadsheet* probably has every math anxiety hair on the back of your neck standing on end. But it can be done; I'll walk you through it.

The carrot: Doing so will enable you to gain a broader and more meaningful picture of your funds' performance as well as the performance of other similar and dissimilar funds, stocks, bonds, indexes, and so forth. And, after taking 10 minutes to read this and 10 minutes to set it up, it will take you only 10 minutes a day to view and update your very own marketwatch.

Although many portfolio management programs are available, I have long preferred the flexibility and control that comes from working with raw data and a simple Excel spreadsheet program. All I use to keep track of the daily performance of 800 or so stocks, funds, ETFs, and indexes is a Web browser to cull the data (I use Yahoo!), and Microsoft Excel to manage the data.

True, CNBC's right here in my office. But I like to see the daily, weekly, monthly, and year-to-date performance of each and every fund in my possible universe—not just in my actual portfolio—and I like to be able to view each part and the sum of the whole for my real and model portfolios.

There are many sources of free pricing data. I use Yahoo!, which allows me to track multiple portfolios (of up to 200 securities each) and whose data are easy to copy into my Excel spreadsheet. With a stock symbol (or five-letter fund code) I can get prices on just about any security. Ten minutes a day and I have a broad view of how every pick I've made is faring relative to an array of appropriate broad market, narrow industry, and regional measures. (A few of the newest and smallest funds are not listed, but they're within a click or two once you know where to find 'em—more on that in a moment.) Yahoo! also lists news articles that mention any of the funds and stocks I track—fresh news that I can and do use every day in a way that keeps me ahead of the herd and up-to-the-minute about each piece of my portfolio pie.

To show returns, I use a spreadsheet that keeps track of a month's worth of daily prices. The spreadsheet includes the investment's year-to-date return through the end of the previous month and its share price (or net asset value, NAV) on the last day of the previous month.

Total returns for the day, week, and month-to-date are simply derived from the last share price divided by the end-of-month share price multiplied by a factor for any dividends within the month. For example, if a fund's share price has gone from $10.00 to $10.45 during the month, without any distributions, then its return is 4.5 percent, or $100 \times [(10.45 \div 10.00) - 1] \times$ the distribution multiplier; in this simple case the distribution multiplier is just 1. Year-to-date (YTD) returns are shown by compounding the previous end-of-month YTD return by the present month-to-date return.

Distributions can be hard to keep track of and, as a result, are a potential glitch in my system, but I've learned to look for them and integrate them when they occur. Fortunately, most are on a fairly regular schedule, available from the fund companies. Barron's also shows distributions after the fact, and sizable distributions can usually be spotted by an unexpectedly negative one-day return for a fund, and then the size can be confirmed with a call to the fund company or a check of its Web site.

In the spreadsheet, the aforementioned distribution multiplier is simply 1 + (dividend ÷ reinvestment price). My Daily Report spreadsheet has separate distribution multiplier columns for the month-to-date, week, and day returns. The dividends of the month-to-date multipliers are of course cleared out at the beginning of each month, the others more often as the affected time periods elapse.

For bond funds, which have gradually accrued interest instead of occasional share-price-lowering distributions, there is a further multiplier that estimates income accrued for the month to date, using the funds' yield and the date of the month. I do not bother showing week-to-date or one-day income accrual, as these small numbers will rarely affect returns much.

Return errors are almost always the result of a missed distribution or stock split. To make sure I'm not carrying forward errors from one month to the next, I do check my end-of-month YTD returns against another published source such as the newspaper listings and/or the relevant fund company.

Stock splits, like dividends, lead to unexpectedly negative returns. Splits are generally easier to catch, because most are 2 to 1 or greater, leading to one-day returns on the order of –50 percent. Usually, a check of company news by ticker will quickly confirm the split (or will mention the stock's devastating decline!). There are many such sources for recent company news. I tend to use those found at smartmoney.com and cbsmarketwatch.com. There are also Web sites featuring stock split news (e.g., www.2-for-1.com), or search "stock splits" on Yahoo to find other sites.

Yahoo! has many indices in its database, (e.g., the S&P 500, Dow 30, Nasdaq Composite), but these are raw index values, not total return numbers. You'll have to either forget about index income or, like me, estimate accruing income intramonth and correct for exact figures on a monthly basis. Barra.com shows exact monthly total returns for the S&P 500, 400, and 600 indexes, including Growth and Value indexes, usually on the second business day of the month.

On the Morgan Stanley site (msci.com), go to MSCI (Morgan Stanley Capital International). There you'll find daily index values for its famous EAFE index, as well as all the country and regional indexes you could possibly desire. Postings are generally available each weekday by 9:00 a.m. Eastern time, but they are sometimes several hours late, especially with crucial end-of-month data. Be patient. Be persistent.

If you have one or more portfolios, it's a relatively simple matter to track their values, and thus returns, using a row of your spreadsheet. For each day, the value of the portfolio is simply given by a formula summing up the number of shares in each relevant fund or stock. These formulas will, of course, have to be updated to account for any distributions and trading.

The Mouse that Roars

In just 10 minutes a day you can create your own relevant marketwatch and see strong or troubling signs in every investment you own and track. If one stock or fund takes a significant nosedive, I first look for a distribution or split. If that hasn't been the culprit, I review Yahoo!'s daily news and also click into bloomberg.com for the thin read. If the fund or stock is losing ground relative to the industry benchmark over 30 trading days, even if there's no punishing news, I know my manager isn't making the grade. And I need to review my more focused sources (www.fidelityinvestor.com and www.fundalarm.com) to try to ferret out the possible reasons for this. One other advantage of this Fidelity Daily: It is a constant in the ever-changing Web universe—a reliable constant by which I still measure most others.

PART TWO

Fidelity's 401(k) Focus: Retirement Planning and Platforms

FIVE

Your Golden Years Begin with Copper

Planning Your Retirement through Fidelity

It's back.

That nagging voice inside you're head.

So what if Harrison Ford says that 60 is the new 50. He's got more money set aside than most developing countries.

You, on the other hand, are . . . how to put this delicately . . . getting older.

Yes. You are.

And unless you know something I don't, you're retirement dollars aren't going to come from pennies from heaven.

No.

You'll have to secure your own financial future with hard-won, wisely saved, and smartly invested pennies on every dollar you earned.

Even if you're the new 30, which means you're at least 40, with every passing year that the sand runs through the hourglass of your biological time, it's running about twice as fast through the hourglass of your financial planning time.

And that nagging voice inside your head is right: *Time is running out.*

Maybe, you're not quite at the point where the aches and pains in your joints dictate when you wear your raincoat. Maybe you haven't started using TiVo to record the 6 p.m. news. Maybe you still think a Rave review has something to do with your last lost weekend. No matter.

Little by little, it is happening: You're getting older, and the days for securing your financial future are getting fewer.

Your Future Retirement *Is* Fidelity's Future

In the Herculean effort to secure your own financial future you're not alone. In fact, when it comes to providing the information, resources, investment vehicles, and planning you need for your retirement, nobody does it better than Fidelity.

Chances are, if you have any money in a 401(k) plan, you already know this, albeit subliminally. Fidelity wasn't the first fund firm on the retirement planning block; I'll give that distinction to T. Rowe Price who, nearly 20 years ago, was at the cutting edge of helping investors mature into retirees through smart retirement planning. But that was 20 years ago. Ever since, Fidelity has been way, way out in front of its closest competitor in terms of securing the largest share of the defined distribution, a.k.a. 401(k), market, providing retirement planning services and platforms, establishing the broadest array of retirement-related investment vehicles, and creating the most comprehensive campaign for retirement awareness.

That's a lot to crow about. Of course, Fidelity's interest is, at its core, self-interest. Fidelity understands that it has arguably helped more Americans to be able to afford to retire than any other firm; and once they do retire, it doesn't want to give up a dime, let alone a large slice of its revenue source: fees.

But Fidelity has a discount brokerage instinct up its sleeve; it already knows that it will have to compete not just on performance and asset growth, but on cost and income distribution. To be able to do all those things at once, Fidelity is in the midst of transitioning itself into its next trillion dollar business: processing.

Processing may sound fairly bland. On the one hand, it is. It entails everything about controlling any and all financial transactions right down to the postage paid on the monthly statements sent. But if you think that's small potatoes, consider that automatic data processing (ADP) makes a multi-billion-dollar living doing just that. (In fact, one out of every five 401(k) statements is processed by ADP.) But part and parcel of Fidelity's future is to capitalize more fully and wholly on the myriad applications that comprise processing your financial life. Fidelity wants to be (by virtue of its processing ability, which is born of its long-standing technological savvy and innovativeness) your private bank for pennies on trillions of dollars rather than dimes on billions of dollars. In this, I think they're taking the Wal-Mart business model and applying it to the rarified world of private banking (wherein your portfolio is constantly massaged to respond to your growth and income distribution needs), while at the same time products relating to everything from insurance issues to home buying to charitable giving are offered up to you on tax-efficient platforms.

That's why, when all is said and done, your future retirement is Fidelity's future—and consequently, Fidelity investors have an ally for the life of their assets.

There Is No Time Like the Past

One of the biggest hurdles to really saving for your retirement, rather than passively participating in one form of automatic savings or another—such as not having the maximum amount of your pay slotted into a 401(k)—is the belief that you have to start bigger, bolder, better.

You don't.

Believe it or not, now is the time to begin preparing for retirement—before you begin looking like your driver's license picture. Actually, if you are like most Americans, it's probably *past* the time to begin planning for retirement. According to a study released by Fidelity Investments in May 2006, about 83 percent of U.S. workers believe they are not socking away enough cash for retirement, up from 78 percent a year earlier.

The 2006 Retirement Confidence survey, which is widely considered one of the most comprehensive reports on the state of retirement preparedness, equates many Americans' retirement plans to a piece of Swiss cheese—full of holes. Many Americans have accumulated only modest retirement savings, have underestimated the percentage of their preretirement income they are likely to need in retirement, and have no idea of how much money they will need to live comfortably once they retire.

Just for the record: The general rule of thumb is that you will need 80 percent of what you currently spend. For example, if your current annual pretax income is $80,000, and you are able to save $10,000, you would need to replace 80 percent of $70,000, or $56,000, to maintain your current standard of living. Of course, the big unknown in all of this is what you will be earning in 10, 20, 30, or 40 years when you retire.

The annual survey, which is sponsored by the Employee Benefit Research Institute in Washington, D.C., found that 68 percent of workers say they and their spouses have accumulated less than $50,000 in retirement savings. Predictably, this modest level of saving is more prevalent among younger workers; 88 percent of workers ages 25 to 35 have less than $50,000 saved for retirement compared with 52 percent of workers ages 55 and older.

Despite their rather modest savings, 24 percent of workers say they are *very confident* they will have enough money to live comfortably in retirement and another 44 percent say they are *somewhat confident*.

Welcome to la-la land.

You Need to Create Your Own Safety Net

In the old days, most Americans could count on retiring with a gold watch and a lifetime pension. Today, they might still get the gold watch, but the pension has probably fallen by the wayside. Taking the place of that are 401(k) accounts, individual retirement accounts, savings accounts, and Social Security (assuming it is still around). Most likely you will spend your Bingo years living off of some combination of all four.

For employers, the decline of pension plans is good business; it frees them from the responsibility of having to fund such plans. It also releases them from the responsibility of investing wisely for your retirement. But what's good for the goose ain't exactly grand for the gander. (And don't forget, *you're the gander*.) The burden of investing wisely today for a secure financial future falls squarely on your shoulders. As I said at the outset, the good news is that Fidelity offers many attractive investment alternatives to help steer you through your golden years. The bad news is that it's up to you to understand, select, and monitor the ones that are most appropriate for you based on your risk tolerance and time line. (Chapter 18 provides 10 model portfolios that can help give you a sense of how you're current portfolio ought to look based on 10 distinct time lines.) Moreover, while Fidelity, and other firms, do an excellent job of providing you with educational material, they can't provide you with the one thing you need most: *independent advice*.

Fidelity's Retirement Plan and Planning Clout

Without a doubt, Fidelity knows the retirement game inside and out. It dominates the retirement field. In fact, retirement accounts, such as IRAs and 401(k) plans constitute 56 percent of Fidelity's assets under management. In all, about 17 million investors depend on Fidelity to help them with their retirement goals.

More than any other fund company in the world, Fidelity has positioned itself to attract a good chunk of the trillions of dollars that are about to go into play as the nation's 76 million baby boomers retire over the next decade. While other fund companies grew fat and lazy chasing after the low-hanging fruit in the late 1980s and early 1990s, Fidelity looked ahead and saw that, in addition to investment services, baby boomers would need help spending and managing their money after retirement.

After all, the average retired household will have nine—yes, nine—sources of income, ranging from Social Security to 401(k) plans to three or four IRA accounts. Fidelity wants a hand in every till, and if they succeed, I think that, for the most part, you'll be glad they did.*

Fidelity Retirement Income Advantage

In mid-2004, the world got its first glimpse of Fidelity's vision when the company unveiled Fidelity Retirement Income Advantage, a groundbreaking program aimed at helping boomers plan for, monitor, and manage their finances as they make the transition from saving for retirement to living in retirement. So serious is Fidelity about helping boomers through retirement assets that it spent more than $70 million getting Fidelity Retirement Income Advantage off the ground.

To be sure, other fund companies heard Fidelity's wake-up call. In the months that followed the launch of Fidelity Retirement Income Advantage, dozens of financial services firms rolled out similar products aimed at retiring boomers. Many of the same firms, Fidelity included, also significantly beefed up their staffs of in-house retirement experts.

Here's what the program has to offer:

- *Retirement plan:* A powerful interactive tool allows you to plan for your retirement by factoring in a wide variety of risks, ranging from inflation to rising health care costs.

- *Income management account:* Once your plan is created, it can be tracked online—not only to see whether your investments are performing as expected, but also whether you are withdrawing the appropriate amount of money.

- *Guidance:* You get the chance to meet with one of Fidelity's so-called retirement experts for help in creating an investment asset mix appropriate for your age, goals, and risk tolerance. Fidelity's adviser can also help you determine how much you can afford to withdraw from your

---

* See my comments on Fidelity's contribution to the financial services industry in Chapter 1. Most investors forget that Vanguard, for example, started off as a load fund shop and, to this day, remains one of the biggest defenders of the hedge fund industry, since its actively managed funds are sub-advised by firms that make the lion's share of their revenue through their hedge fund fees. The irony, let alone shareholder jeopardy, that having open-end funds invested long run, often by the same managers who are running hedge funds and can short the same issues for the benefit of their bigger-ticket clients, is a scandal that the SEC almost addressed in 2005, but in no small part due to intensive lobbying by Vanguard, reverted to being content to ignore. I mention this here since unregulated hedge funds could come to play a devastating role in the financial markets, and so wreak havoc on your financial future. Become alarmed!

retirement accounts and which accounts you should draw from first. While the meeting is designed to take place over the telephone, you can arrange to meet with a flesh-and-blood adviser through one of Fidelity's investment centers.

So far, Fidelity Retirement Income Advantage is free. But Fidelity has suggested it may soon begin charging a nominal fee for accounts with less than $100,000 in assets. So, if you are within 10 years of retirement, it's definitely worth checking out at Fidelity's online "Retirement Resource Center" (http://personal.fidelity.com/retirement/).

Freedom from Funds in One Freedom Fund

Prior to the launch of Fidelity Income Retirement Advantage, Fidelity developed another product line specifically aimed at capturing retirement assets: Fidelity Freedom Funds (for my review of these funds in detail, see Chapter 9).

Fidelity Freedom Funds are age-based life-cycle funds that offer the power of a diversified set of mutual funds wrapped up in a single fund, with the added benefit of professional asset allocation. Fidelity introduced the series in 1996 and has been tinkering with and refining the lineup ever since. Today, Fidelity offers 12 Freedom Funds, including one fund that invests mainly in bonds, for those who have already reached retirement.

First, let's step back and talk about life-cycle investing.

The basic premise of life-cycle investing is easy: Using decades of past performance of stocks, bonds, and cash, it is possible to come up with an asset allocation that is appropriate for any goal and for any point on the life cycle. Think of it as investing on autopilot. When you put your money into a life-cycle fund, you are putting it into a fund that automatically gravitates toward a more conservative mix of stocks, bonds, and cash as your retirement date draws closer.

For example, Fidelity's 2050 Fund, which is aimed at investors who expect to retire sometime between 2048 and 2052, holds 70 percent of its assets in U.S. stocks, 10 percent of its assets in international stocks, and 20 percent of its assets in junk bonds. Meanwhile, the 2015 Fund, which is aimed at those who expect to retire between 2013 and 2017, invests 47 percent in domestic stocks, 12 percent in international stocks, 6 percent in junk bonds, 31 percent in investment-grade fixed income, and 5 percent in money market accounts.

Life-cycle funds are often lumped together with "lifestyle" funds, which adhere to an asset allocation model based on an investor's risk profile, such as "conservative," "moderate," or "aggressive." Unlike life-cycle funds, lifestyle funds don't shift their asset allocations to become more gradual over time.

As more and more employers foist the responsibility of managing the retirement assets onto their workers, both types of asset allocation funds have become wildly popular—especially in the defined contribution market. Indeed, assets in such funds climbed 19.5 percent, to $132 billion, by the end of 2005 from a year earlier, according to Pensions & Investment's annual survey of the largest managers of U.S. institutional tax-exempt assets.

By Fidelity's own account, 83 percent of plans for which it is a service provider now hold at least one of its Freedom Funds, up from 37 percent five years ago. Also, more than 1,000 of Fidelity's plan clients offer Freedom Funds as a default investment option.

Over the past three years, total assets in all of Fidelity's Freedom product line have climbed more 248 percent, to $45.9 billion as of January 31, 2006. And some of the Freedom Funds now consistently rank among the top-selling funds at Fidelity.

Management Shake-Up

Fidelity's laserlike focus on the retirement market extends far beyond new product development. In one of the surest signs of where Fidelity expects to earn its next trillion (make that $10 trillion!) in assets, the company in 2005 announced that Abigail P. Johnson, daughter of Fidelity's chairman and chief executive Edward "Ned" C. Johnson (and possibly her dad's successor), was named president of Fidelity Employer Services Company, which oversees the administration of 401(k) plans for more than 19 million people employed at more than 14,000 corporations. While many looked at Abigail Johnson's reassignment as something of a demotion from her previous post as the head of Fidelity's (admittedly ailing) mutual fund unit, I am convinced the job change underscores Ned Johnson's belief that Fidelity's future hinges on its ability to rake in trillions in postretirement assets.

Given its focus on retirement, it should come as no surprise that Fidelity offers the full panoply of traditional retirement-related products, such as IRAs, SIMPLE IRAs, SEPs, and more.

Let's take a close look at Fidelity's more traditional retirement offerings.

Individual Retirement Account (IRA)

An Individual Retirement Account (IRA) is a brokerage account that allows earnings to compound over time on either a federally tax-free or tax-deferred basis. A Roth or traditional IRA is widely considered the most advantageous retirement savings vehicle available after an employer-sponsored retirement plan such as a 401(k).

In recent years, Fidelity has become even more aggressive than most fund companies in marketing its IRAs, and that effort appears to be paying off. In April 2006, the company reported that the number of new IRA accounts was up 22 percent compared to the previous year and that savings levels in the accounts increased 25 percent.

The main advantage of an IRA is that it allows your earnings to compound over time on a tax-free or tax-deferred basis. Remember, the power of compound earnings grows stronger the longer the time horizon, so the sooner you start to invest in an IRA the better.

Let's say, for example, at age 40 you decide to put $4,000 a year into an IRA earning an annual rate of return of 8 percent. By the time you are 70 years old, your IRA will have grown to about $532,854. Now let's say you begin making the same annual contributions at the age of 25, just 15 years earlier. Assuming the same annual rate of return, your IRA would have more than $1.8 million in it by the time you reach 70.

You can play *a lot* of bingo with $1.8 million. Please see Figure 5.1.

Fidelity, of course, makes it easy to open an IRA—either over the telephone, online, or in person.

But first you must decide what type of IRA is best for you.

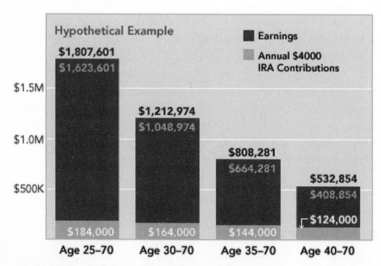

FIGURE 5.1   The power of compound earnings

Source: Fidelity Investments.

If you are under age 70½ and earn less than $110,000 a year (make that $160,000 if you file taxes jointly with your spouse), you have the option of opening either a traditional or Roth IRA.

With a Roth, there is no up-front tax write-off—nor are there taxes to be paid upon retiring, a huge new benefit. Also, because the money is taxed before it is invested, you are not forced to begin withdrawing money from the account at age 70½.

With a traditional IRA, it's crucial to start withdrawing money from your account by the first April 1 that falls after you turn 70½. If you don't, believe it or not, the IRS will zap you with a whopping 50 percent tax.

Essentially, the distinction between a Roth IRA and a traditional IRA comes down to whether you want to pay your taxes now or later. All IRAs offer the benefit of tax-deferral—that is, the tax consequence for trading securities is eliminated. You are, however, taxed once on the money, either when you take it out after retirement (traditional IRAs) or when you earn the money before you put it in (Roth IRAs). For a nondeductible tradi-

Table 5.1   Traditional IRA vs. Roth IRA

	Traditional IRA	Roth IRA
Tax Implications	Money has the potential to grow tax deferred	Money has the potential to grow federally tax-free
	Contributions may be tax-deductible (based on income limits and participation in workplace retirement plans)	Contributions are generally not tax deductible
	Earnings and deductible contributions are subject to tax when withdrawn	Earnings can be withdrawn free of federal tax
Penalties for Accessing Your Money Before Age 59½	10% penalty for withdrawals, subject to certain exceptions	Penalty-free access to your contributions at any time. 10% penalty for withdrawals, subject to certain exceptions
Requirements for Withdrawing Money at age 70½	Minimum required distributions must start at age 70½ Contributions cannot be made after age 70½	You do not have to begin withdrawing money at any age Contributions can be made at any age
Investment Choices	Wide range of investment options	Wide range of investment options

Source: Fidelity Investments.

tional IRA, a portion of the withdrawals are considered "return of contributions" and are therefore exempt from tax, but most of the withdrawals are taxable as income. With Roth IRAs, whose contributions are nondeductible and therefore are taxed like any other income, withdrawals are generally not taxed.

The main distinctions between a Roth and traditional IRA are summarized in the Table 5.1.

SimpleStart IRA

In late 2004, Fidelity rolled out an easy-to-start IRA targeted at investors between the ages of 21 and 40. The IRA, known as the SimpleStart IRA, eliminates some of the usual problems associated with opening IRAs for people in that age group, such as not having a lot of money to invest and not knowing which funds to invest in. SimpleStart IRAs are centered on Fidelity life-cycle funds, which, as I explained earlier, grow more conservative as an investor ages. Instead of requiring the usual $2,500 minimum to open a Fidelity account, SimpleStart incorporates an account-building feature that allows investors to direct a set amount to be transferred automatically from a bank account each month. That amount can be as low as $200 a month.

SimpleStart IRAs are available as both Roth and traditional IRAs. Also, if you are not interested in using a life-cycle fund in your SimpleStart IRA, you have the option of using one of the more than 4,500 mutual funds available through Fidelity.

Inherited IRAs

In dealing with issues involving an inheritance, it is almost always best to consult a professional adviser for help navigating what is likely an emotional and financial minefield. So complicated are inheritances that Fidelity offers trained "inheritor services specialists" to help heirs handle inherited accounts.

Still, I offer here a brief overview of the options available to you when you inherit an IRA. First, an IRA account owner can designate two types of beneficiaries: spouse and nonspouse. Each type has its own requirements and deadlines.

1. *Spouse:* If you inherit an IRA directly from your spouse, you may roll over the inherited IRA assets into your own IRA account, transfer your inherited IRA assets to an Inherited IRA Beneficiary Distribution Account, or disclaim all or part of your inherited IRA assets.

- Rolling over inherited IRA assets into your own IRA is the only option exclusive to surviving spouses. This allows you to roll over your inherited IRA proceeds into your own new or existing IRA and treat the assets as if they were your own. The benefit of this option is that the amount and the timing of the minimum required distributions are based on your age.
- Transferring inherited assets to an inherited IRA makes sense if you are older than your spouse, and your spouse died before age 70½, since it allows you to delay taking the required distributions until your spouse would have turned 70½. If you are younger than age 59½ and need access to the assets right away, it's also good, since it allows you to sidestep the 10 percent early withdrawal penalty.
- Disclaiming all or part of the IRA assets enables you to pass those assets on directly to the next eligible beneficiaries. Any required distributions are then based on the beneficiary's age. If the other beneficiaries are significantly younger, the required distributions would be lower, thereby leaving more assets in the account to grow, tax-deferred. Tax rules require you to disclaim assets within nine months of the IRA owner's death.

2. *Nonspouse:* If you inherit an IRA from a parent or someone other than your spouse, you may transfer the inherited assets to an IRA beneficiary distribution account or disclaim all or part of your inherited IRA assets.

- Transferring inherited assets to an inherited IRA allows you to control both how your inherited assets are invested and who gets those assets after you are gone. Your required distributions will also generally be based on your own life expectancy.
- Disclaiming all or part of your inheritance means the inheritance then gets passed on to the next eligible beneficiaries, and any required distributions are then based on the other beneficiary's age. Tax rules require you to disclaim assets within nine months of the IRA owner's death.

Rollover IRAs

If you are changing jobs or are recently retired, you may want to open what is known as a rollover IRA, which essentially allows you to move any money you may have stashed away in your previous employer's retirement plan into a Fidelity IRA without incurring any tax consequences.

Because you are simply transferring money from one plan into another, your money will continue to remain invested tax-deferred.

401(k)s

Of the 17 million people who keep retirement assets at Fidelity, about 12.9 million do so through 401(k) or 403(b) plans; 403(b) plans work a lot like 401(k) plans but are sponsored by government and nonprofit organizations.

Indeed, 401(k) plans are being offered by more employers as an alternative to traditional pension plans. Essentially, they work like a deductible IRA, but with higher contribution limits: $15,000 for workers under age 50 and $20,000 for workers age 50 and older in 2006.

To participate in a 401(k) plan, you designate a fixed portion of your pretax salary to be deducted from your paycheck to be invested in your company-sponsored investment plan. The main advantage of a 401(k) plan is that it saves you federal (and most likely state) income taxes in several ways. First, the money that goes into your plan is classified as *deferred compensation*, meaning it doesn't show up on your W-2 Form. As a result, it escapes both federal income tax and Social Security taxes, unless your gross income after the 401(k) contribution exceeds the maximum income for which Social Security is withheld.

Depending on where you live, your contribution may also avoid state and local taxes. Second, since your contributions are allowed to grow tax-deferred, your long-term returns are likely to be much higher. Finally, since the money is taken directly out of your paycheck, you won't be tempted to spend it.

To encourage employees to join 401(k) plans, Fidelity is leading a charge to encourage employers to add automatic investment features to their 401(k) plans.

If you have the option of participating in a 401(k) plan, there is almost no excuse for not doing so—especially if your employer matches all or part of your contribution.

Fidelity offers a wide variety of 401(k) options aimed at the self-employed and small to mid-sized businesses. Some, like the Self-Employed 401(k), may be opened online. Others, like standard or tailored 401(k) plans, require face-to-face meetings with Fidelity representatives.

For the Self-Employed

For folks in business for themselves, Fidelity offers a few retirement account options.

Simplified Employee Pension Plan

The simplified employee pension plan (SEP) is basically a quick and easy way to set up a corporate retirement plan. A SEP is especially useful if you are not planning to contribute more than 25 percent of your paycheck.

Essentially, contributions to a SEP are tax-free income paid by an employer to an employee. Employers can contribute to each employee's account the lesser of $44,000 for 2006 or 25 percent of pay (or a lesser percentage, but it must be the same percentage for each employee). Each employee is always 100 percent *vested* (i.e., has total ownership of the money in his or her SEP-IRA). Employees can't put their own money into a SEP, but they can still contribute to an IRA.

As with a traditional IRA, withdrawals are taxed as income, and premature withdrawals (those before age 59½) are generally subject to a 10 percent penalty.

Fidelity allows you to open a SEP online. All you need is about 10 to 15 minutes and some basic information about yourself, such as your Social Security number, your driver's license number (which helps Fidelity verify your identity), and your bank account number and your bank's routing number, both of which can be found on your checks.

Self-Employed 401(k)

The Self-Employed 401(k) is a profit-sharing plan that includes employee salary deferrals. Fidelity sets up Self-Employed 401(k) customer accounts as Keogh profit-sharing accounts. Eligible customers include self-employed individuals and owner-only businesses with no employees other than a spouse. This includes business owners who are incorporated, unincorporated, partnerships, and sole proprietors. Small business owners with multiple employees are not eligible to adopt the Self-Employed 401(k).

The main benefit of a Self-Employed 401(k) is that it allows you to contribute up to 100 percent of the first $15,000 of your self-employment income (make that $20,000 if you are 50 or older). On top of that you can contribute and deduct an additional amount of up to 25 percent of your income, up to $44,000 ($49,000 if age 50 or older) in 2006.

The main disadvantage is that it requires a bit more administration. Specifically, if your plan assets exceed $100,000, you are required to file a Form 5500 with the IRS each year.

SIMPLE IRA

A Savings Incentive Match Plan for Employees (SIMPLE) IRA plan offers small businesses with 100 or fewer employees who earned at least $5,000 in the preceding year an affordable and, yes, simple plan for funding retirements through employee salary reductions and matching employer contributions. Employees can generally contribute up to 100 percent of their pay, up to a maximum of $10,000 in 2006. Employers may match employee contributions dollar for dollar, up to 3 percent of employee wages to a maximum $10,000 (or $12,500 for employees 50 or older) in 2006. Or employers may make a contribution equal to 2 percent of each eligible employee's compensation, up to $4,400.

A SIMPLE plan can be sponsored by most types of organizations, including C and S corporations, partnerships, sole proprietorships, tax-exempt employers, and governmental entities, as long as they don't already sponsor another retirement plan. The employer may allow each employee to choose a financial institution, or the employer may choose the financial institution that will receive all contributions under the plan. In the latter case only, employees have a right to transfer contributions to a SIMPLE IRA at another financial institution without penalty.

It's NeverToo Late

If you find later in life that your savings plan is off track, don't panic. A special provision of the Economic Growth and Tax Relief Reconciliation Act of 2001 allows investors age 50 and over to make catch-up contributions, if allowed by their employer, to IRAs (Roth and traditional), to workplace savings plans such as 401(k)s, 403(b)s, and 457 plans, and to SIMPLE IRAs.

If you are 50 years old, you can take advantage of higher contribution limits in a 401(k) plan or an IRA. This means a 50-year-old can invest an additional $5,000 in a 401(k), bringing the maximum annual amount up to $20,000. For an IRA, you can contribute an additional $500 and an additional $1,000 in 2006 and thereafter.

Saving for College

If you're like most parents and even many grandparents, you probably want to pay for your kids' or grandkid's college education, or at least help with tuition.

The cost of getting a college degree is skyrocketing. But so is the importance of having a degree. Not only is the degree a key to landing the most interesting jobs, with chances for advancement, it offers a big leg up in earnings potential. Studies show that college graduates earn twice as much as high school graduates. On average, college grads earn a stunning $750,000 more in their lifetime than people who finish only high school.

The cost of private colleges is climbing 6 percent a year, faster than inflation or wage growth. In the 2005–2006 year, the average bill for private college was $21,235 a year. That's $84,940 over four years.

In 18 years, that cost is likely to jump to $60,611 a year, or $242,444 over four years, assuming a 6 percent annualized increase in the cost of tuition.

Even if tuition at private schools climbs at a modest 5 percent a year, the cost will reach $51,104 a year in 2024, or $204,416 over four years.

So, if possible, it's wise to start saving.

Fidelity essentially offers two investment vehicles aimed at saving money for Junior's education: a 529 College Savings Plan and a Uniform Gifts to Minors/Uniform Transfers to Minors Account (UGMA/UTMA).

529 College Savings Plan

A 529 college savings plan is an education savings plan operated by a state for the express purpose of helping families save for college. The plans were named after section 529 of the IRS Code, and residents of any state can invest in any plan.

The appeal of these plans is relatively straightforward: Money that is withdrawn from a 529 plan and used to pay for qualified educational expenses is exempt from federal taxes. In many states, qualified distributions are also free from state income taxes.

It's worth noting that the Economic Growth and Tax Relief Reconciliation Act of 2001, which exempts distributions from federal tax laws, is set to expire on December 31, 2010. In the unlikely event the law is not extended, 529 plans will lose their tax-free status.

In a 529 college savings plan, an individual may contribute up to $55,000 a year for each beneficiary on the account ($110,000 a year per married couple), without incurring any gift tax. Most plans, including the ones offered by Fidelity, allow you to invest in a variety of mutual funds.

Fidelity manages four state-sponsored plans: New Hampshire, Arizona, Delaware, and Massachusetts.

Regardless of which state plan to choose, you have two options. One is an age-based strategy that essentially starts out with a high allocation of stocks and gradually shifts more toward bonds and money market funds as your child gets older.

The other is a choice of three static portfolios, each with investments in varying levels of stocks, bonds, or money market funds. With this option, you may invest in one, two, or all three static portfolios.

Fidelity allows you to open a 529 account with a minimum initial investment ranging from $500 to $1,000. That minimum, however, is lowered to $50 provided you agree to contribute $50 a month, or $150 a quarter. The combined balance of accounts for a beneficiary is also capped at between $250,000 and $289,000, depending on which state operates the program.

Fidelity charges a $20 to $30 annual maintenance fee, which it will waive if you make automatic contributions, set up direct deposit, or if the combined value of accounts with the same beneficiary is $25,000 or more.

There are other annual costs to be aware of when investing in one of Fidelity's 529 plans (or any 529 plan, for that matter). In addition to paying your share of the underlying expenses of funds, you can also expect to pay your share of a "program manager fee" charged to the funds by Fidelity. In addition, most states charge a fee to each fund participating in their program.

As a result, you can expect to pay a total annual fee that ranges anywhere between 0.76 and 1.14 percent of the assets in your account, depending on which investment options you choose. For an account with $50,000 in assets, that translates into anywhere from $380 to $570 a year.

Uniform Gifts to Minors/Uniform Transfers to Minors Account (UGMA/UTMA)

Despite its obscenely clunky name, a UGMA/UTMA is easy to understand and even easier to set up. Basically, it is a brokerage account in your child's name. While any assets placed in such an account are considered irrevocable gifts and become the property of the child, you get to control those assets until the child is 18 or 21, depending on your state.

Because the money is owned by Junior, earnings are generally taxed at Junior's—presumably lower—tax rate. Of course, all bets are off if Junior is raking in the dough as a child movie star.

The chief advantage of a UGMA/UTMA account, otherwise known as a *custodial account*, is flexibility. Since it is basically a brokerage account, you have full access to Fidelity's panoply of stock, bond, and mutual fund offerings.

There is also no limit to the amount of money you may contribute over the lifetime of the fund.

The main disadvantage is that the child eventually gains complete control of the assets. Consequently, a UGMA/UTMA account may hurt your child's chances of receiving financial aid.

As with a traditional brokerage account, a UGMA/UTMA account requires a minimum initial deposit of $2,500 to activate. Fidelity charges the same for UGMA/UTMA accounts as it does for all other brokerage accounts.

Fidelity's Mutual Funds: Mutual Funds 101

When most people think of mutual funds, they think of Fidelity. That's because Fidelity isn't simply the largest mutual fund company on earth, it has also spent a lot of years building up the association of itself as *the* fund industry. (See Chapter 1.) And make no mistake, when it comes to investing in mutual funds, no investor ever has to own anything other than a Fidelity fund. Fidelity has more funds in more areas of the market than any other fund company—in fact, more than the combined lineups of many other fund companies.

But this very attribute—being a stellar one-stop shop for fund investors—is also problematic for Fidelity. With more than 300 options to choose from (glance at the fund page in your local business section), including 30 growth funds, 20 international funds, and 40 sector funds (there are many more), how do you begin to make rational investment decisions and specific fund selections? Well, you do so by reading this book and, in particular, this section!

In fact, at the end of this section you should be as much of a Fidelity fund expert as anyone employed by Fidelity—probably more so (unless they, too, are reading this book). Moreover, in Part 4, I'll lay out 10 model portfolios, from *Aggressive Trader* to more standard *Growth* to conservative *Growth & Income* and *Income* investors. These model portfolios will help serve as a compass for navigating what can be an overwhelming array of choices to reach your destined investment objective. But before we get there, we need to begin at the beginning: What are mutual funds, and why is Fidelity the best place, bar none, to invest in them?

Overview

What are mutual funds?

Mutual funds are the great equalizer.

Of course, Bill Gates and Oprah Winfrey can afford to hire top-notch money managers to do their investment bidding. But so can you— through the power of mutual funds.

First, what is a mutual fund? A mutual fund is nothing more than a large pool of professionally managed stocks, bonds, money market instruments, and/or other securities. When you invest in a fund, you buy shares in the fund—not individual shares of all the securities owned by the fund. This allows you to spread your risks across a broad spectrum of companies in a way that is both efficient and affordable.

Believe it or not, the mutual fund is *not* a Fidelity creation—it's not even an American one. While no one is completely sure about the exact origin of mutual funds, some say the first mutual fund took the form of a closed-end investment company launched in the early 1820s in the Netherlands. Others say the first mutual fund goes all the way back to 1774 when a Dutch merchant named Adriaan van Ketwich launched an investment trust aimed at small investors. Interestingly, the name of van Ketwich's fund, Eendragt Maakt Magt, means "unity creates strength."

Regardless of their origin, mutual funds certainly attained their superstar status in the United States.

The first open-end mutual fund, Massachusetts Investors Trust, was launched in the United States on March 21, 1924. (Historical note: My grandfather was on the board that oversaw this newfangled investment idea.) By 1951, the number of funds surpassed 100 and the number of shareholders exceeded 1 million. Today, mutual funds are by far the most popular form of investing in the United States.

Indeed, U.S. investors have more than $9 trillion entrusted to about 8,000 mutual funds, according to the Investment Company Institute, the industry's main trade organization. The number of U.S. households owning mutual funds totaled 53.7 million in 2005, down slightly from 53.9 million in 2004, the ICI said. With the slight drop, some 47.5 percent of U.S. households now own mutual funds, down from 48.1 percent in 2004.

It's easy to see why mutual funds are so popular:

- *From these acorns grow mighty oaks:* The nice thing about mutual funds is that they haven't lost their focus on average investors. Fidelity, for example, sets its investment minimum at $2,500. But retirement account investors can start investing for as little as $200 a month.

- *Diversification:* Most mutual funds invest in dozens of securities. That means every dollar you put into a mutual fund gets divvied up among all those securities. It also means you're getting the highest possible return for the lowest possible risk, given the overall objectives of the fund.

- *Ease of use:* These days, buying or selling a mutual fund is as easy as picking up the telephone or going online.

- *Transparency:* Unlike hedge funds and separately managed accounts, mutual funds are fairly easy to keep an eye on. The Securities and Exchange Commission requires fund managers to disclose their holdings regularly. And tracking the daily, monthly, or yearly performance of a particular mutual fund is as easy as going to the fund company's Web site.

- *Professional money management:* Mutual funds tend to hire the best that money can buy when it comes to investment talent (or at least they try to). Fidelity, for example, is known for aggressively recruiting potential managers from only the best business and finance schools in the country. Then it puts them through a rigorous "boot camp" where they spend years learning the ropes as analysts.

- *Flexibility:* With more than 8,000 mutual funds to choose from, there are funds designed to suit almost every investment strategy and every consumer's preferences. Were you so traumatized by your Aunt Esther's two-pack-a-day cigarette habit that you don't want to give a single penny to the tobacco industry? You can buy a socially conscious fund. Conversely, are you a two-pack-a-day smoker who believes the tobacco industry is doing God's work? There are plenty of funds out there for you.

- *Safety:* Unlike an Internet start-up, a big financial services giant, or a giant energy company, the chances of seeing your mutual fund go belly-up is practically nil. While your chances of losing money are not nil, you are unlikely to wake up one morning to learn that your entire life savings are gone because a few executives in the corner office decided to play fast and loose with the company's books.

Of course, there are also reasons to think twice before placing your hard-earned cash in a mutual fund.

- *Risk:* One of the major misconceptions about mutual funds is that they are inherently less risky than stocks. True, having all your money invested in one stock is much riskier than having it all invested in a mutual fund that is invested in just two companies. But being invested in a mutual fund that is not well diversified is almost as risky.

- *Fees:* All mutual funds charge fees. Since a fund's performance is directly tied to the amount it charges in fees and expenses, paying attention to a fund's expenses is critical. Here are some of the expenses charged by mutual funds:

  - *Loads.* A load is an up-front sales commission charged to and deducted from your initial investment amount. Some funds charge a back-end load, otherwise known as a *deferred sales charge,* which means that a fee is deducted when you cash in on your shares. Load charges range as high as 0.5 percent, but are more commonly in the 3 to 4.5 percent range.

- *12b-1 fees.* Some funds deduct the cost associated with advertising and marketing from the fund's overall assets. The National Association of Securities Dealers limits funds sold by its members to a 12b(1) fee of 0.75 percent, plus a servicing fee of 0.25 percent, for a total of 1 percent.
- *Early-redemption fees.* These fees are designed to discourage investors, particularly market timers, from moving money out of a fund too soon after putting it in (usually 1 to 12 months). They differ from deferred sales charges in that they are paid to the fund, as opposed to the management company.
- *Operating expenses.* All mutual funds charge fees as long as you keep money invested in the fund. The fees pay the portfolio manager as well as administrative costs associated with keeping the fund up and running, such as printing and mailing prospectuses.

Basic Types of Mutual Funds

With more than 8,000 mutual funds in existence, there are funds suitable for just about any investor's portfolio. There are funds that invest in large companies and funds that invest in small ones. There are funds that invest in real estate, bonds, and precious metals. There are funds that invest according to religious values and funds that invest in such vices as alcohol, cigarettes, gambling, and pornography.

If you can't find a mutual fund that suits your needs, you ain't looking hard enough.

Still, most mutual funds fall into a one of several categories. I will explain those categories here.

MONEY MARKET FUNDS

When most people think of mutual funds, they don't think of money market funds. Basically, a money market fund is a type of mutual fund that is required by law to invest in extremely low-risk securities, such as certificates of deposit, government securities, and commercial paper. Whether you are saving money to buy a house or just looking for a place to park your hard-earned cash while you scope out your next big investment, money market funds are ideal because accessing your cash is as easy as writing a check or using an ATM card. And because issuers go to great lengths to keep the NAV at $1, your principal is relatively safe.

Here's how a money market fund works.

As I said, brokerages and fund companies strive to keep the value of a share of a money market fund at exactly $1. How do managers keep the share price at $1? It's not easy. First, fund managers are not allowed to let their average maturity creep past 90 days. Second, they can't really buy anything yielding much more than a three-month Treasury bill. The only way they are able to gain more yield is by investing in corporates (corporate bonds) and, even then, 95 percent of their corporate holdings must have the equivalent of an AAA rating.

While the share price remains fixed, the interest rate paid to the shareholder goes up and down depending on what is happening to the various yields of the instruments in the funds' portfolios.

I have long been an advocate of money market funds for serious investors.

For starters, money market funds offer all the convenience of a checking account, and yet you earn dividends, which are usually higher than the interest paid on a bank savings account.

Of course, many funds offer the convenience of checking. But it is ludicrous to use anything but a money market fund to write checks. That's because each time you write a check on a fund, you are essentially selling shares in the fund to cover the value of the check. As a result, every time a check is cashed, it creates a taxable event that may cost you—depending on the value of those shares.

Because shares in a money market fund are always priced at $1, you don't have to worry about the Internal Revenue Service putting its hand out every time you write a check.

Still, there are risks associated with money market funds. The biggest, of course, involves the mercurial nature of interest rates. The interest rates on many of the vehicles in a money market fund are tied to the whims of the Federal Reserve, which is a group of economists and bankers who are responsible for setting short-term interest rates and manipulating other factors that affect the supply of money. When the Fed wants to add fuel to the fires of economic growth, it lowers some of its key lending rates. Typically, the yields on the vehicles that go into money market funds follow suit. When the Fed wants to keep the economy from gathering too much speed, it simply raises interest rates and, again, yields on short-term interest-bearing securities follow suit.

A sudden and severe rise in interest rates, coupled with heavy shareholder redemptions, could have a negative effect on your money market fund.

Then there's credit risk. If a debt issuer goes into default, then the brokerage and fund companies that bought its IOUs may be left holding the bag. If that happens, the brokerage or mutual fund company may be forced to dip into its reserves and "break the buck." In other words, they would be forced to let the price of a share sink below $1.

Unlike a bank account, a money market fund does not come with FDIC insurance. While that sound's scary at first, it's worth remembering that mutual fund companies and brokerages are required by law to have $1 invested in securities for every $1 that you put in their money market funds. Banks, on the other hand, are required to keep only a fraction of the customers' cash deposits in their coffers, increasing their need for FDIC insurance.

Today, investors have more than $1.85 trillion parked in money market funds. Not surprisingly, Fidelity sponsors not simply one of the biggest money market funds around, but one of the largest mutual funds in any town, Fidelity Cash Reserves, which has more than $80 billion in assets.

STOCK FUNDS

To my way of thinking, a stock fund, also known as an *equity fund,* is the financial steroid that will help grow your portfolio. Consider this: From 1926 to 2005, a diversified portfolio of large-cap stocks produced a rate of return averaging about 10.4 percent a year, which is about seven percentage points higher than the rate of inflation. Over the same period, long-term U.S. Treasury notes returned, on average, 5.08 percent a year.

Of course, there will be years that you earn more than 10.4 percent a year, just as there will be years that you earn less. But, if you are a long-term investor—and I emphasize *long-term*—you should be fairly confident that investing in the stock market will double the purchasing power of your money every 10 years.

Without a doubt, mutual funds are the way to go when investing in the stock market. Basically, a stock fund invests in the individual stocks of public companies. While some funds are encouraged to invest across a broad spectrum of companies, many are confined to stay within strict parameters. A large-cap growth fund, for example, looks for big companies whose earnings are expected to increase substantially, whereas a small-cap value fund looks for small companies that, for various reasons, may be underappreciated by most investors.

The nice thing about investing in a stock mutual fund is that it minimizes your exposure to risk. If a fund holds 100 stocks, and one goes belly-up, you lose only 1 percent of the value of the fund, provided the stock was an average holding.

Stock funds fall into many categories, and within each category there are even more subcategories. One popular way of looking at stock funds is by the valuation of the companies they invest in. A growth fund, for example, invests mainly in stocks that tend to have a high price relative to earnings and provides little if any dividend. In contrast, a value fund seeks to invest in stocks that are considered cheap relative to earnings. Value stocks tend to be the stodgier players in slower-growing defensive or cyclical areas.

Here's a simplified way to corral the herd:

- *Large-cap funds* typically invest at least 75 percent of their equity assets in companies with a market capitalization greater than $14.9 billion.

- *Mid-cap funds* typically invest 75 percent of their assets in companies with a market capitalization greater than $3.8 billion but below $14.9 billion.

- *Small-cap funds* typically invest 75 percent of their assets in companies with a market capitalization below $3.8 billion.

- *Equity-income funds* generally invest at least 65 percent of their net assets in dividend-paying stocks. The rest is invested in convertible securities and bonds. Since the primary purpose of these funds is to generate income, they are usually not suitable for young, more aggressive investors.

- *Growth and income funds* aim to provide growth by investing in well-established companies that pay income, or *dividends*. Some even hold some assets in bonds. They are the kind of funds that should be a cornerstone for your entire portfolio.

- *Balanced funds* favor a blend of stocks and bonds, making them a nice way to shield your portfolio from some of Wall Street's jumpiness without missing out entirely on the action.

SIX

Charitable Giving/ Trust and Estate Planning

At the End of the Day, Giving Is as Good as Receiving

Okay, your last name isn't Trump or Hilton. You don't have tens of billions of dollars in your bank account like Warren Buffett or Bill Gates. So you don't shop with a Chihuahua tucked under your arm and a checkbook in your Prada that knows no bounds nor bounces.

Still, you're as inclined to do good work as any socialite billionaire— maybe even more so. Whether your charitable giving is measured in thousands or thousands and thousands of dollars, if you want to buy some good karma by helping those less fortunate, join the club.

With 76 million baby boomers barreling toward retirement, and many just starting to receive their share of the $10.4 trillion in total inheritances that is expected to pass into their hands by 2040, a growing number of boomers are getting in touch with their inner philanthropists.

Last year, for example, Americans gave $260 billion to charity, up 6 percent from $245 billion collected in the year before that and up from $241 billion two years earlier, according to Giving USA 2005, a study released by Giving USA Foundation.

Of course, the biggest benefactors of this trend will be local churches, homeless shelters, and big charities, such as Habitat for Humanity. But Fidelity, by being one of the first mutual fund companies to spot the lucrative market of helping people give their money away, also stands to benefit by an increase in boomer giving.

Another Fidelity First!

In 1991, Fidelity established the first IRS-approved public charity run by a financial services company, the Fidelity Investments Charitable Gift Fund. Like a community foundation, but on a national scale, the fund allows people to donate money for an immediate tax deduction and then dole out that money over time to a charity, or many charities, of their choice.

The idea has since been copied by such rivals as the Vanguard Group and Schwab.

Today, with more than $3 billion in assets, the Fidelity Investments Charitable Gift Fund is one of the nation's largest independent public charities, and it is the nation's biggest donor-advised fund. In 2005, the fund distributed more than $846 million, making 2005 the biggest grant-making year in its history.

Since its inception, more than 35,000 fund donors have recommended grants totaling more than $5 billion to more than 95,000 public charities.

Fidelity didn't stop there. In its effort to construct a business around assisting do-gooders, as well as those simply trying to keep as much of their money as possible from going to Uncle Sam when they die, Fidelity has also been aggressively building a nationwide personal trust business. In late 2002, Fidelity began managing private charitable foundations for individuals and families with at least $1 million to give away.

Opening a Giving Account

Fidelity Investments Charitable Gift Fund allows you to make a donation and immediately reap the tax benefits that come with that donation. While the fund legally controls the money, Fidelity allows you to "suggest" which causes get that money and when. In other words, the fund—which is basically an assortment of 11 investment pools designed to generate certain levels of returns—acts as an intermediary between donors and charities.

When you put money in Fidelity Investments Charitable Gift Fund, you can deduct the full value (up to 50 percent of your adjusted gross income). For example, if you donate $10,000, your taxable income declines by $10,000. That's a tax saving of $2,800 for someone in the 25 percent bracket.

What's more, the fund also accepts stock, which can lead to even greater tax benefits. If you donate stock that has appreciated since you bought it, you can deduct the full current value of the shares—and you don't have to pay capital gains taxes on your profit.

Let's say you bought 500 shares at $50 each—a total investment of $20,000. The price has since doubled, and the stock is worth $40,000. If you contribute those shares to Fidelity Investments Charitable Gift Fund, you can deduct the full $40,000 value of the shares from your taxable income. Plus, you don't have to pay a cent in capital gains taxes on the $20,000 profit.

In certain circumstances, the fund also accepts residential real estate as well as private stock.

From a donor's perspective, another benefit of the gift fund is that it requires far less paperwork and offers better tax breaks than starting a private family foundation to achieve the same level of flexibility in building a philanthropic portfolio. Since the fund is actually a public charity, reporting donations for tax purposes is also infinitely easier, as it eliminates the need to report a year's worth of charitable donations individually.

Another advantage is that money left in the fund is allowed to grow tax-free, which, over time, could greatly increase the amount of money you have to give away.

The main disadvantage, of course, is loss of control. The fund makes donations only to IRS-approved public charities, which would preclude donations to any foreign charities or private foundations. Because some foreign charities receive funding from U.S. public charities that support international causes, it may be possible to get a donation to those foreign charities through the U.S. public charity.

If you're interested in making charitable donations through a giving account through Fidelity, here's a step-by-step guide to get you going.

Step 1. *Open an account.*

Fidelity allows you to begin the process of opening an account online (www.charitablegift.org), via fax, e-mail, or telephone (800–682–4438).

Step 2. *Make your initial contribution.*

Once your account is officially established, you have 30 days to come up with a minimum contribution of $10,000 in cash, securities, or other eligible assets, such as unencumbered residential real estate, some restricted stock, or the cash value of life insurance policies. Since the fund's trustees must review contributions of anything other than cash or securities, a donation of anything outside the norm would no doubt lengthen the process of getting the account up and running.

Step 3. *Calculate the tax benefits of your contribution.*

The IRS imposes "percentage limitations," which limit the deductions that can be taken as a percentage of your adjusted gross income in the year the deduction is taken. (Contributions in excess of these percentage limitations may be carried forward up to five subsequent years). Deductions for cash are limited to 50 percent of your adjusted gross income. Deductions on appreciated securities held more than a year are limited to 30 percent of adjusted gross income.

Step 4. *Select how the money will be invested.*

Contributions to the Fidelity Charitable Gift Fund are invested in pools managed by Strategic Advisors Inc., a division of Fidelity. When it comes to how your money is invested, you have two options: an *asset allocation pool* or an *individual investment pool.*

Fidelity offers a choice of three asset allocation pools, which are essentially designed to maintain strict allocations to various investment vehicles. Fidelity's Legacy Giving Pool, for example, maintains its exposure to stocks at 70 percent, whereas the Lifetime Giving Pool maintains a 50 percent exposure to stocks.

For the more adventurous philanthropist, and those with more time to more actively manage their contributions, Fidelity offers eight individual investment pools. Through mutual funds, each pool invests specific asset classes, such as international stocks, growth stocks, a mix of stocks and bonds, or money market funds. Fidelity also gives you the option of investing in Fidelity funds only or in a blend of Fidelity and non-Fidelity funds.

Step 5. *Donate to your favorite charities.*

Fidelity imposes a minimum grant recommendation of $250 and increases must be made in $50 increments. If you're just looking to throw an extra $100 bucks to your local church over the holidays, the gift fund isn't right for you.

A Word about Fees

Fidelity, of course, isn't positioning itself as the intermediary between you and your charitable dollars out of the goodness of its heart. Each giving account, with less than $500,000 in assets, is assessed a minimum annual administrative fee of 0.60 percent of assets, or $100, whichever is greater. Accounts with more than $500,000 are charged less.

In addition, Fidelity also charges an annual investment management fee, ranging from 0.79 percent of assets to 0.07 percent, depending on how the assets are invested. You can also expect to pay a commission on any trading activity. Currently, Fidelity charges 1.2 cents a share for a stock trade.

Fidelity Private Foundation Services

Okay, so maybe you *do* have tens of billions of dollars in your bank account—or at least several million—and you want to give some of it away; in that case, setting up a private foundation is an option, especially if you are a bit of a control freak.

Indeed, the biggest advantage of a private foundation is that you maintain almost total control over the charitable donations made by the foundation. Often, private foundations also get to exert enormous influence over how those donations are used by charities.

But that control doesn't come without its own set of headaches. In an effort to ensure they are not used as tax shelters or to funnel money toward less charitable purposes, the government imposes strict rules on private foundations. A private foundation, for example, is required to distribute at least 5 percent of its assets each year. It is also responsible to file annual tax returns, and other documentation, with the IRS.

There's something else to keep in mind when considering a private foundation: Donors to a private foundation are allowed to deduct cash contributions only up to 30 percent of their adjusted gross income, versus 50 percent on contributions to donor-advised funds, such as Fidelity Investments Charitable Gift Fund. Deductions on appreciated securities held more than a year are limited to 20 percent of adjusted gross income.

Fidelity jumped into the business of helping folks set up and manage private foundations in late 1992. Basically, the company provides three services: administration, record keeping, and investment management. Your fees generally depend on the size of the foundation and the number of services you ask Fidelity to provide.

A foundation with $10 million in assets that hires Fidelity to provide administrative and record-keeping services, for example, can expect to pay an annual maintenance fee of $7,500, plus a yearly charge of 0.15 percent on assets, or $15,000.

Trusts

Considering its blue-blood pedigree and the amount of money at stake, it's no surprise that Fidelity is in the trust services business. While it had been quietly peddling trust services to its customers in Massachusetts and California since 1993, Fidelity launched a full-scale national rollout of its trust business in mid-2000.

It's pretty easy to figure out why. In 2004, U.S. personal-trust assets climbed to $1.19 trillion, up from $658.71 billion in 1998, according to VIP

Forum, a Washington-based research group. Also, Fidelity understood that the ability to help its rich and superrich PAS customers spread their wealth was crucial if it expected to keep those customers in its folds.

Through a company called Fidelity Personal Trust Company, Fidelity drives most of its trust business through its 110 Investor Centers. It also sells trust services through tens of thousands of financial advisers across the country.

What exactly is a trust? Good question. While trusts come in dozens of forms, each with varying degrees of complexity, a trust is essentially nothing more than an agreement to hand over assets to someone else, the *trustee*, to manage for beneficiaries. While trusts can have a variety of tax advantages, they can be quite expensive to set up. Trusts also come with annual management and accounting fees that may devour about 1 percent of trust assets each year.

If you are interested in setting up a trust, it's important to hire a lawyer who specializes in estate planning. In addition to being complex (read: a breeding ground for acronyms), trusts are governed by highly complex rules, which vary by state.

Fidelity, through a service called Fidelity Private Portfolio Service, is willing to act as a trustee or as a cotrustee with a family member or other designated individual. If you prefer to keep your current trustee, or simply don't want Fidelity acting in that role, you can also hire Fidelity trust's investment manager.

The minimum investment for trust services at Fidelity is $300,000 for the first accounts and $250,000 for each subsequent account.

You can also hire Fidelity to handle all the paperwork associated with operating the trust and to oversee distributions to the trust's beneficiaries.

PART THREE

Fidelity's Famous Funds & Hidden Gems

SEVEN

Fidelity's Managers

Cultivating the Best Managers and Money Management Culture

According to Abby Johnson, former president of Fidelity Management & Research Company, "This is a business where you get a chance to build a track record. You do your research, you make your recommendations or you buy your stocks, and you live with your moves—and your success or failure against the benchmarks is right out there to be seen."

At Fidelity, investing is a batting average business—*where batting average isn't good enough*. Moreover, it's a business where, despite all the conventional wisdom and services, the batting averages of your individual managers' stock- and/or bond-investing careers matter more than any current rating service or consulting firm can quantify or qualify.

The common use of existing, and subjective, rating services and fund comparison services, and the insistence of consulting firms and investment banks that a "manager" *is* the overall firm and not simply the underlying individual manager is simply and starkly inadequate.

The result? Today's investors are being ill served by the very sources they turn to for advice. The problem? Whether it's Morningstar, Lipper, S&P, or any number of advisory newsletters, all share one fatal flaw: They rate and recommend funds based on the fund's past performance rather than the career performance of the manager who is currently running the fund.

Investing in a fund based on making investment decisions without the objective, quantitative data of each and every manager in any and all investment instruments (open- or closed-end funds, separate accounts, hedge funds), categories and/or capitalization ranges, and/or investment styles is like trying to manage a baseball team without knowing the underlying statistics of all your own players as well as all the known players in the league against whom you compete. That's no way to create a league of one's own—but it is one way in which you can ensure that you'll never beat the average performance of the league.

Fidelity has a long-standing history of offering funds run by individual managers, as opposed to anonymous teams of them, and Fidelity has historically grown its own management talent (culled from the über-competitive environment where junior analysts vie with one another for the best record of successful buy, sell, and hold recommendations in order to advance to analyst, then senior analyst, and ultimately, if they desire, to grab the brass ring of a Select fund, the training ground for managers of diversified funds); this makes Fidelity a perfect microcosm for tracking, ranking, and buying *the manager, not the fund.*

From the inception of www.fidelityinvestor.com, I set out to upset the applecart of the existing fund rating services in two ways. First, I created a purely quantitative manager-ranking system, which has been featured in *Barron's* and the *Wall Street Journal* and on CNBC and MarketWatch.com, to name a few. Second, unlike Morningstar, which is actually revenue- and data-dependent on the fund firms that it claims to "independently" rate, Fidelity Investor, just like this book, is driven by individual subscribers to the service.

Many thousands of members who use our proprietary manager-ranking advice to make investment selections among their 401(k) plans' options or in their own IRAs know the performance advantages and pitfalls of this real-time service. In this book, as in any book, I have had to be very sensitive to the need for, and the value of, both timely and timeless information; since managers change hats frequently at Fidelity and elsewhere, I remind you here that if you are not comparing your manager in each investment category, market benchmark, style, and pool of managers that correlates most closely to him or her (i.e., best fits), then you are not comparing apples to apples and, as a result, are making less-informed investment decisions based on fuzzy math or subjective ratings rather than real, quantifiable, objective numbers.

Why Managers Matter

Among diversified stock, bond, and balanced funds, fund management is the most important determinant of fund performance—and the single most important factor in selecting a manager for the specific allocation role in your overall Fidelity portfolio. Asset allocation plays a fundamental, structural role—but owning the wrong manager in any allocated space renders even the best allocation strategy vulnerable to unseen pitfalls and missed profit potential.

With the narrowly drawn sector or special situation funds, the manager's performance record is relatively less important than the fund's investment objective. Investing in or avoiding a sector or country fund based primarily on its fund manager when management factors are swamped by other fundamental, technical, or even political issues makes little sense. You have to be right about the sector first, and then the manager. However, even among actively managed sector funds, some managers have made a considerable difference versus specific sector benchmarks and more generic vehicles such as exchange traded funds, consistently losing less in downdrafts and gaining more in updrafts.

Similarly, the choice of a single-country fund should generally depend more on the country's and companies' underlying fundamentals than on the manager.

Choices among similar regional funds and among the diversified international and global funds should rest primarily on the fund manager's career record. As with domestic diversified stock, bond, and balanced funds, fund management is the most important determinant of fund performance—and the single most important factor in selecting a manager for the specific regional, international, and global allocation roles in your overall portfolio.

Tracking each fund's performance against a general market index remains the standard for performance measurement and monitoring. It is insufficient, and renders managers of managers vulnerable to significant liabilities as well as missed opportunities.

Calculating the running records of each manager's monthly performances (one can do annual, quarterly, weekly, daily reviews, etc.) relative to highly correlated benchmarks over his or her total career of managing money is the most accurate way to measure and monitor not only past performance, but how that performance was derived during different market cycles and seasons, different objectives, and different risk management challenges and requirements.

Table 7.1 helps put this into perspective: Fidelity's growth, international, and Select fund managers' relative performances over various time periods, through different performance- and risk-related lenses, for their total career, is laid bare.

You can see the extent to which a manager's choices have tended to help (or hurt) fund performance over his or her career.

Table 7.1 Fidelity Funds' Manager Change History

Name As of 4/30/06	Inception	Name As of 4/30/06	Inception	Name As of 4/30/06	Inception
Aggressive Growth	**12/90**	Stephen Peterson	3/96-6/97	Robert Haber	7/98-9/99
Steven Calhoun	6/05-pres	Bob Haber	3/88-3/96	Tom Sweeney	3/96-7/98
Rajiv Kaul	11/02-6/05	Frances Cabour	4/87-2/88	George Domolky	11/87-3/96
Robert Bertelson	2/00-11/02	Bob Haber	11/86-3/87		
Erin Sullivan	4/97/2/00			**Capital Appreciation**	**11/86**
John Hurley	1/97-4/97	**Banking**	**6/86**	Fergus Shiel	10/05-pres
Larry Greenberg	10/93-1/97	Ramona Persaud	2/06-pres	Harry Lange	3/96-10/05
Larry Bowman	4/91-10/93	Heather Lawrence	3/04-1/06	Tom Sweeney	11/86-3/96
Robert Stansky	12/90-3/91	Peter Hirsh	2/02-3/04		
		Samuel Peters	2/00-1/02	**Chemicals**	**7/85**
Aggressive Int'l	**11/94**	Yolanda Taylor	4/99-1/00	Chris Bartel	4/06-pres
Michael Jenkins	1/06-pres			Jill Jortner	2/06-4/06
Rick Mace	9/05-12/05	**Biotechnology**	**12/85**	Matthew Friedman	5/04-1/06
Kevin McCarey	12/99-9/05	Rajiv Kaul	10/05-pres	John Roth	3/02-5/04
Rick Mace	11/94-12/99	Harlan Carere	10/04-10/05	Jonathan Zang	9/99-2/02
		Andraz Razen	3/02-10/04		
Air Transportation	**12/85**	Brian Younger	9/00-2/02	**China Region**	**11/95**
Andrew Hatem	1/05-pres	Yolanda Taylor	2/00-9/00	K.C. Lee	6/05-pres
Harlan Carere	1/04-1/05	Rajiv Kaul	6/98-1/00	Ignatius Lee	1/04-6/05
Heather Lawrence	8/02-1/04			Joseph Tse	11/95-1/04
Matthew Fruhan	1/01-7/02	**Blue Chip Growth**	**12/87**		
Jeffrey Feingold	2/00-1/01	Brian Hanson	4/05-pres	**Computers**	**7/85**
		John McDowell	3/96-pres	Heather Lawrence	4/06-pres
Asset Manager	**12/88**	Michael Gordon	1/93-3/96	James Morrow	8/05-4/06
Dick Haberman	3/96-pres	Steve Kaye	9/90-1/93	Naved Kahn	1/05-8/05
Bob Beckwitt	12/88-3/96	Dick O'Rourke	12/87-8/90	Sonu Kalra	12/02-1/05
				Christian Zann	2/02-12/02
Asset Mgr: Aggressive	**9/99**	**Blue Chip Value**	**6/03**	Telis Bertsekas	6/01-2/02
Dick Haberman	9/99-pres	Brian Hogan	6/03-pres	Lawrence Rakers	1/00-6/01
Asset Mgr: Growth	**12/91**	**Brokerage and Investment**	**7/85**	**Const & Housing**	**9/86**
Dick Haberman	3/96-pres	Charles Hebard	3/06-pres	Nora Creedon	2/06-pres
Bob Beckwitt	12/91-3/96	Brian Kennedy	10/03-3/06	Ramona Persaud	4/04-1/06
		Joshua Spencer	1/02-10/03	Robert Bao	9/02-4/04
Asset Mgr: Income	**10/92**	Jennifer Nettesheim	9/00-1/02	Valerie Friedholm	1/02-8/02
Dick Haberman	3/96-pres			Joshua Spencer	12/00-1/02
Bob Beckwitt	10/92-3/96	**Business Svcs & Outsourcing**	**2/98**	Brian Hogan	4/99-12/00
		Ben Hesse	3/06-pres		
Automotive	**6/86**	James Morrow	3/06-pres	**Consumer Industries**	**6/90**
Anmol Mehra	3/04-pres	Nicola Stafford	10/04-2/06	John Roth	6/04-pres
Robert Bao	1/03-3/04	Dion Hershan	10/03-10/04	Joshua Spencer	1/04-4/04
Kelly Cardwell	7/01-1/03	James Morrow	7/01/-10/03	Christian Zann	12/02-1/04
Douglas Nigen	9/99-7/01	Simon Wolf	1/00-7/01	Brian Hanson	3/02-12/02
				John Porter	9/99-2/02
Balanced	**11/86**	**Canada**	**11/87**		
Lawrence Rakers	2/02-pres	Maxime Lemieux	11/02-pres	**Contrafund**	**5/67**
Robert Ewing	2/00-2/02	Stephen Binder	10/99-11/02	Will Danoff	9/90-pres
Stephen DuFour	7/97-2/00			Jeff Vinik	1/89-9/90

Name	Inception
As of 4/30/06	
Stuart Williams	5/87-12/88
Alan Leifer	5/84-4/87
Ernest Wiggins	7/83-4/84
Leo Dworsky	10/67-6/83
Roland Grim	5/67-9/67
Convertible Securities	**1/87**
Thomas Soviero	6/05-pres
Victor Thay	2/02-6/05
Lawrence Rakers	6/01-2/02
Peter Saperstone	11/00-6/01
Beso Sikharulidze	8/99-11/00
David Felman	7/97-8/99
Stephen DuFour	1/97-6/97
Robert Bertelson	6/96-1/97
Charles Mangum	2/95-6/96
Andrew Offit	3/92-2/95
Harris Leviton	7/90-2/92
Andrew Midler	1/89-6/90
Robert Haber	1/87-12/88
Cyclical Industries	**3/97**
Chris Bartel	12/05-pres
Matthew Friedman	5/04-11/05
Matthew Fruhan	8/02-5/04
Pratima Abichandani	12/00-8/02
Brian Hogan	2/00-12/00
Defense and Aerospace	**5/84**
Andrew Hatem	12/05-pres
Chris Bartel	3/04-11/05
Alexander Sacerdote	10/03-3/04
Matt Fruhan	1/01-10/03
Jeff Feingold	10/98-1/01
Developing Comm	**6/90**
Charlie Chai	5/03-pres
Shep Perkins	6/01-4/03
Rajiv Kaul	2/00-6/01
Disciplined Equity	**12/88**
Steven J. Snider	5/00-pres
Brad Lewis	12/88-4/00
Discovery	**3/98**
Adam Hetnarski	2/00-pres
Jason Weiner	3/98-2/00
Diversified Int'l	**12/91**
William Bower	4/01-pres
Greg Fraser	12/91-4/01

Name	Inception
As of 4/30/06	
Dividend Growth	**4/93**
Charles Mangum	1/97-pres
Steven Wymer	5/95-1/97
Fergus Shiel	4/94-5/95
Abigail Johnson	4/93-4/94
Electronics	**7/85**
James Morrow	2/04-pres
Samuel Peters	2/02-2/04
Brian Hanson	2/00-2/02
Emerging Markets	**11/90**
Bob von Rekowsky	1/04-pres
John Carlson	5/01-12/03
Patricia Satterthwaite	4/00-5/01
David Stewart	11/97-3/00
Richard Hazlewood	7/93-10/97
John Hickling	1/93-7/93
James Lyle	7/92-1/93
John Hickling	11/90-6/92
Energy	**7/81**
Matthew Friedman	6/04-pres
Pratima Abichandani	1/03-6/04
John Porter	3/02-12/02
Scott Offen	9/99-2/02
Energy Service	**12/85**
John Dowd	12/05-pres
Nathan Strik	6/04-12/05
Charles Hebard	2/02-6/04
Nicholas Tiller	2/00-2/02
Environmental	**6/89**
Douglas Simmons	2/04-pres
Jed Weiss	3/03-2/04
Robert Bao	3/02-3/03
Valerie Friedholm	7/01-2/02
Ian Gutterman	11/99-7/01
Equity-Income	**5/66**
Stephen Petersen	7/93-pres
Beth Terrana	9/90-7/93
Bruce Johnstone	10/71-9/90
Equity-Income II	**8/90**
Stephen DuFour	2/00-pres
Bettina Doulton	12/96-2/00
Brian Posner	4/92-12/96
Andrew Midler	8/90-3/92

Name	Inception
As of 4/30/06	
Europe	**10/86**
Trygve Toraasen	1/06-pres
Frederic Gautier	8/05-12/05
David Baverez	1/03-8/05
Thierry Serero	10/98-1/03
Sally Walden	7/92-9/98
John Hickling	2/91-6/92
Penelope Dobkin	10/86-1/91
Europe Cap App	**12/93**
Darren Maupin	1/06-pres
Ian Hart	4/00-12/05
Kevin McCarey	12/93-3/00
Export & Multinational	**10/94**
Victor Thay	10/05-pres
Tim Cohen	2/02-10/05
Douglas Chase	2/00-2/02
Adam Hetnarski	9/98-2/00
Jason Weiner	1/97-9/98
Arieh Coll	10/94-1/97
Fidelity	**4/30**
John Avery	2/02-pres
Nick C. Thakore	6/00-2/02
Beth Terrana	7/93-5/00
Barry Greenfield	3/82-7/93
Malcolm MacNaught	1/75-2/82
Arnold Midwood	10/67-1/75
Fidelity Fifty	**9/93**
Jason Weiner	4/03-pres
Fergus Shiel	6/02-4/03
John Muresianu	1/99-6/02
Scott Stewart	9/93-1/99
Financial Services	**12/81**
Charles Hebard	5/05-pres
Matthew Fruhan	4/04-5/05
Jeffrey Feingold	10/01-4/04
Jim Catudal	2/00-10/01
Focused Stock	**11/96**
Robert Haber	2/04-pres
Bahaa Fam	10/01-2/04
John Chow	4/01-10/01
Tim Krochuk	11/96-4/01
Food and Agriculture	**7/85**
Robert Lee	6/04-pres
Valerie Friedholm	2/03-6/04

Table 7.1 Fidelity Funds' Manager Change History (Continued)

Name As of 4/30/06	Inception	Name As of 4/30/06	Inception	Name As of 4/30/06	Inception
Gal Bronwyn Lese, MD	1/01-2/03	**Home Finance**	**12/85**	Tokuya Sano (co-mgr)	9/02-pres
Matthew Fruhan	11/99-1/01	Valerie Friedholm	5/04-pres	L.C. Kvaal	9/02-1/04
		Jeff Feingold	1/01-5/04		
Four-in-One	**6/99**	Victor Thay	3/99-1/01	**Int'l Small Cap Opp**	**8/05**
Christopher Sharpe	7/05-pres			Andrew Sassine	8/05-pres
Derek Young	7/05-pres	**Independence**	**3/83**		
William Eigen	10/02-7/05	Jason Weiner	4/03-pres	**Japan**	**9/92**
Jennifer Farrelly	6/99-9/02	Fergus Shiel	6/96-4/03	Oko Ishibashi	6/00-pres
Freedom Funds	10/96	Michael Gordon	3/96-6/96	Brenda Reed	12/98-6/00
Jonathan Shelon	3/05-pres	Harris Leviton	3/92-3/96	Shigeki Makino	10/94-12/98
Ren Cheng	10/96-pres	Stuart Williams	9/88-3/92	John Hickling	5/93-9/94
		Michael Kassen	1/85-8/88	Dana Martin	9/92-5/93
Global Balanced	**2/93**	George Vanderheiden	3/83-12/84		
Derek Young	1/06-pres			**Japan Smaller Comp**	**11/95**
Rick Mace	3/96-12/05	**Industrial Equipment**	**9/86**	Kenichi Mizushita	12/96-pres
Bob Haber	2/93-3/96	Chris Bartel	1/03-pres	Simon Fraser	11/95-12/96
Rick Mace	2/93-12/93	Ted Orenstein	3/02-1/03		
		Praveen Abichandani	1/00-2/02	**Large Cap Growth**	**11/01**
Gold	**12/85**			Bahaa Fam	2/04-pres
Daniel Dupont	2/03-pres	**Industrial Materials**	**9/86**	Jeff Kerrigan	11/01-2/04
Niel Marotta	4/00-2/03	Jody Simes	8/03-pres		
		Mark Schmehl	12/00-7/03	**Large Cap Stock**	**6/95**
Growth & Income	**12/85**	Niel Marotta	4/00-12/00	Matthew Fruhan	5/05-pres
Timothy Cohen	10/05-pres			Karen Firestone	4/98-5/05
Steven Kaye	1/93-10/05	**Insurance**	**12/85**	Tom Sprague	3/96-3/98
Andrew Midler	5/92-1/93	Stephen Hermsdorf	3/06-pres	John McDowell	6/95-3/96
Jeff Vinik	9/90-4/92	Charles Hebard	6/04-3/06		
Beth Terrana	12/85-9/90	Ian Gutterman	7/01-6/04	**Large Cap Value**	**11/01**
		Forrest Fontana	9/00-7/01	Bruce Dirks	2/05-pres
Growth & Income II	**12/98**			Ciaran O'Neill	2/04-2/05
James Catudal	10/05-pres	**Int'l Discovery**	**12/86**	Robert Macdonald	11/01-2/04
Victor Thay	6/05-10/05	William Kennedy	10/04-pres		
Louis Salemy	12/98-6/05	Penny Dobkin	4/01-10/04	**Latin America**	**4/93**
		William Bower	5/98-4/01	Brent Bottamini	4/05-pres
Growth Company	**1/83**	John Hickling	3/96-4/98	Adam Kutas	4/05-pres
Steven Wymer	1/97-pres	Rick Mace	1/94-3/96	Claudio Brocado	1/03-4/05
Larry Greenberg	6/96-1/97	John Hickling	4/87-12/93	Margaret Reynolds	6/01-1/03
Bob Stansky	4/87-6/96	Stewart Williams	12/86-3/87	Patti Satterthwaite	4/93-6/01
Rich Fentin	1/83-3/87				
		Int'l Real Estate	**9/04**	**Leisure**	**5/84**
Health Care	**7/81**	Matthew Lentz	1/06-pres	Gopal Reddy	11/05-pres
Harlan Carere	3/05-pres	Steve Butler	9/04-12/05	Aaron Cooper	6/04-10/05
Samel Peters	2/04-3/05			Joshua Spencer	10/03-6/04
Steven Calhoun	3/02-2/04	**Int'l Small Cap**	**9/02**	Alexander Sacerdote	3/02-10/03
Yolanda Taylor	6/00-2/02	Wilson Wong (co-mgr)	7/05-pres	Charles Hebard	1/01-2/02
		Ben Paton (co-mgr)	1/04-pres	Michael Tarlowe	1/00-1/01

Name As of 4/30/06	Inception
Leveraged Co Stock	**12/00**
Thomas Soviero	7/03-pres
David Glancy	12/00-7/03
Low-Priced Stock	**12/89**
Joel Tillinghast	12/89-pres
Magellan	**5/63**
Harry Lange	10/05-pres
Bob Stansky	6/96-10/05
Jeff Vinik	7/92-6/96
Morris Smith	6/90-6/92
Peter Lynch	5/77-5/90
Richard Haberman	1/72-5/77
Edward C. Johnson III	5/63-12/71
Medical Delivery	**6/86**
Matt Sabel	1/05-pres
Jonathan Zang	3/02-1/05
Sanjeev Makan	12/00-2/02
Pratima Abichandani	2/00-12/00
Med Equip & Systems	**4/98**
Aaron Cooper	3/05-pres
Samuel Peters	2/04-3/05
Steven Calhoun	1/02-2/04
Christine Schaulat	9/00-1/02
Mid Cap Growth	**11/01**
Bahaa Fam	2/04-pres
Jeff Kerrigan	11/01-2/04
Mid Cap Value	**11/01**
Bruce Dirks	2/05-pres
Ciaran O'Neill	2/04-2/05
Robert Macdonald	11/01-2/04
Mid Cap Stock	**3/94**
Shep Perkins	1/05-pres
Steven Calhoun	3/05-10/05
Beso Sikharulidze	6/01-1/05
David Felman	8/99-6/01
Katherine Collins	1/97-8/99
Jennifer Uhrig	3/94-1/97
Multimedia	**6/86**
John Roth	5/04-pres
Matthew Friedman	9/03-5/04
Brian Kennedy	3/02-8/03
Victor Thay	1/01-2/02
Michael Tarlowe	1/00-1/01

Name As of 4/30/06	Inception
Natural Gas	**4/93**
James McElligott	11/05-pres
Matthew Friedman	6/05-10/05
Jonathan Zang	1/05-6/05
Naved Khan	10/02-1/05
Douglas Nigen	7/01-9/02
Natural Resources	**3/97**
Matthew Friedman	6/04-pres
Pratima Abichandani	1/03-6/04
John Porter	3/02-12/02
Scott Offen	9/99-2/02
Networking & Infrastructure	**9/00**
Charlie Chai	7/04-pres
Matt Cheyney	2/03-7/04
Chris Bartel	2/02-2/03
Sonu Kalra	1/02-2/02
Jed Weiss	9/00-1/02
New Millennium	**12/92**
Neal Miller	12/92-pres
Nordic	**11/95**
Trygve Toraasen	6/98-pres
Colin Stone	11/95-5/98
OTC Portfolio	**12/84**
Sonu Kalra	1/05-pres
Shep Perkins	4/03-1/05
Jason Weiner	2/00-4/03
Robert Bertelson	1/97-2/00
Charles Mangum	6/96-1/97
Abigail Johnson	4/94-6/96
Alan Radlo	6/90-4/94
Morris Smith	6/86-5/90
Paul Stuka	12/84-5/86
Overseas	**12/84**
Ian Hart	1/06-pres
Rick Mace	3/96-12/05
John Hickling	1/93-3/96
James Lyle	11/91-1/93
Penelope Dobkin	2/91-10/91
George Noble	12/84-1/91
Pacific Basin	**10/86**
Dale Nicholls	10/04-pres
William Kennedy	9/03-10/04
June-Yon Kim	10/02-8/03

Name As of 4/30/06	Inception
William Kennedy	12/98-9/02
Shigeki Makino	5/96-12/98
Simon Fraser	5/93-4/96
Dana Martin	1/92-5/93
John Hickling	5/90-12/91
William Ebsworth	10/86-4/90
Paper & Forest Products	**6/86**
Chris Bartel	3/06-pres
Justin Bennett	3/06-pres
Anmol Mehra	2/04-2/06
Vincent Rivers	10/01-2/04
Adam Segel	3/00-10/01
Pharmaceuticals	6/01
Harlan Carere	1/05-pres
Ian Gutterman	1/05-1/05
Gavin Baker	3/02-1/05
Yolanda Taylor	6/01-2/02
Puritan	**4/47**
Stephen Petersen	2/00-pres
Bettina Doulton	3/96-1/00
Richard Fentin	4/87-3/96
Francis Cabour	11/80-3/87
Patricia Ostrander	11/80-3/87
Frank Parrish	9/77-11/80
Edward Manion	12/76-9/77
Frank Parrish	5/69-12/76
Real Estate Income	**2/03**
Mark Snyderman	2/03-pres
Retailing	**12/85**
Martin Zinny	1/05-pres
Adam Segel	12/02-1/05
Brian Hanson	2/02-12/02
Steven Calhoun	8/99-2/02
Small Cap Growth	**11/04**
Lionel Harris	4/05-pres
Chuck Myers	4/05-3/06
Jamie Harmon	4/05-10/05
Forrest St. Clair	11/04-4/05
Small Cap Ind	**6/93**
Richard Thompson	10/05-pres
Jamie Harmon	4/01-10/05
Tim Krochuck	4/00-4/01
Brad Lewis	6/93-3/00

Table 7.1   Fidelity Funds' Manager Change History *(Continued)*

Name As of 4/30/06	Inception
Small Cap Stock	**3/98**
Paul Antico	3/98-pres
Katherine Collins	4/05-10/05
Richard Thompson	4/05-10/05
Small Cap Value	**11/04**
Thomas Hense	3/06-pres
Katherine Lieberman	11/04-2/06
Software and Computer	**7/85**
Kelly Cardwell	1/03-pres
Christian Zann	12/01/-12/02
Telis Bertsekas	3/00-12/01
Southeast Asia	**4/93**
Allan Liu	4/93-pres
Stock Selector	**9/90**
Jim Catudal	10/01-pres
Bobby Kuo	5/00-10/01
Brad Lewis	9/90-4/00
Strategic Div & Inc	**12/03**
Christopher Sharpe	7/05-pres
Derek Young	7/05-pres
William Eigen	12/03-7/05
Strategic Real Return	**9/05**
Christopher Sharpe	9/05-pres
Derek Young	9/05-pres
Tax Managed Stock	**11/98**
Keith Quinton	2/04-pres
Tim Heffernan	11/98-2/04
Technology	7/81
James Morrow	1/05-pres
Sonu Kalra	2/02-1/05

Name As of 4/30/06	Inception
Telis Bertsekas	1/02-2/02
Christopher Zepf	6/01-1/02
Lawrence Rakers	2/00-6/01
Telecommunications	**7/85**
Brian Younger	3/02-pres
Tim Cohen	9/00-2/02
Transportation	**9/86**
Chris Bartel	4/06-pres
Lindsay Connor	4/06-pres
Jill Jortner	1/05-4/06
Harlan Carere	1/04-1/05
Heather Lawrence	12/01-1/04
Ian Gutterman	9/00-12/01
Trend	**6/58**
Ramin Arani	9/00-pres
Nick Thakore	10/98-6/00
Arieh Coll	1/97-10/98
Abigail Johnson	6/96-1/97
Fergus Shiel	5/95-6/96
Alan Leifer	5/87-5/95
Henry Mehlman	8/82-4/87
Richard Habermann	6/77-8/82
Ross Sherbrooke	11/71-5/77
Edward C. Johnson III	6/58-1/67
Utilities	**11/87**
Douglas Simmons	9/05-pres
Andrew Burzumato	10/03-9/05
Martin Zinny	3/02-10/03
Tim Cohen	9/00-2/02
Peter Saperstone	10/98-9/00
Nick Thakore	8/97-10/98
John Muresianu	12/92-8/97
Jeff Ubben	4/91-12/92

Name As of 4/30/06	Inception
Alan Berro	10/89-3/91
Donald Taylor	1/89-9/89
Sandy Cushman	11/87-12/88
Utilities Growth	**12/81**
Brian Younger	5/03-pres
Shep Perkins	3/02-4/03
John Roth	11/99-2/02
Value	**12/78**
Rich Fentin	3/96-pres
Bettina Doulton	3/95-3/96
Jeffrey Ubben	12/92-3/95
Rich Fentin	4/92-12/92
Brian Posner	9/90-4/92
Ernest Wiggins	6/82-9/90
Henry Mehlman	4/81-6/82
Francis Cabour	3/79-4/81
Dorsey Gardner	1/79-2/79
Paul Haagensen	12/78-12/78
Value Discovery	**12/02**
Scott Offen	12/02-pres
Value Strategies	**12/83**
Richard Fentin	6/05-pres
Harris Leviton	3/96-6/05
Daniel Frank	12/83-3/96
Wireless	**9/00**
Brian Younger	5/03-pres
Shep Perkins	9/00-4/03
Worldwide	**5/90**
Jeffrey Feingold	1/06-pres
Rick Mace	4/01-12/05
Penelope Dobkin	5/90-4/01

You can see whether and to what extent a fund manager is lagging or beating his or her benchmark, and whether he or she is taking on more risk than the investment universe (or, on the other hand, lagging due to holdings in cash, or "diworsifying" by going beyond its single-sector mandate).

You can thus come to know each fund manager's long-term record, whether he or she tends to drift away from the funds' stated asset classes

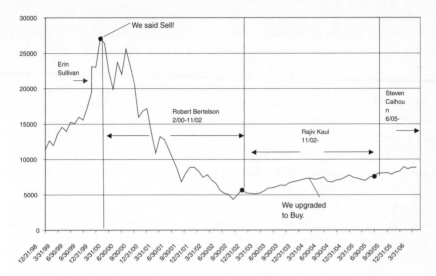

FIGURE 7.1   Manager changes at Fidelity Aggressive Growth

and objectives or stick to them, and whether his or her long-term record is superior after taking risk and all asset-class variables into account.

You can also see that while a big "macro" bet, like loading up on a particular industry, asset class, or country, may explain much of a manager's outperformance over a specific time period, it's not likely to be indicative of future performance.

Having a record in picking large numbers of individual stocks, on the other hand, clearly is. (That's because a small number of big bets can help you—or go against you—almost as a matter of luck, whereas a record of doing well with hundreds of individual stock holdings strongly implies that you're good at picking individual stocks.)

Figure 7.1 shows one fund, Fidelity Aggressive Growth, with many manager changes and illustrates the importance of *who* you own, not just *what* you own.

Managers Scoreboard: By the Numbers

When you calculate and graph each manager's running records in any given investment instrument (open- or closed-end funds, separate accounts, hedge funds), category, and/or investment style (e.g., large-cap growth or micro-cap value), and, for example, you include the results of each manager's long- and shorter-term performances, including a long-term "Risk-Adjusted" relative return number, you can address two critical and fundamental issues at once: Who is in the overall pool of managers, and how does your current manager rank within that pool? Naturally, this leads to two more critical steps: Which managers in the pool are worth considering for selection, and who among them is best suited for your current allocation needs?

Risk-adjusted return is a figure that permits comparisons between the total return of funds (and/or investment models or indices) of varying levels of risk by factoring out differences in volatility. A fund's risk-adjusted return is the return one would obtain with a portfolio holding the fund and enough cash reserves or similar zero-volatility investment (or, for low-risk funds, enough margin) to maintain the risk level of the S&P 500. For a fund with a relative volatility of 1.25, a portfolio would be constructed of 80 percent of that fund and 20 percent of a cash position, giving the hypothetical portfolio a volatility of 1.00. The returns for this hypothetical portfolio would be that fund's risk-adjusted return. For funds compared to an index other than the S&P 500, risk-adjusted return is also calculated for that index. (The risk-adjusted return for the S&P 500 is the same as its actual return, since its relative volatility is by definition exactly 1.00.)

A Fidelity manager's Risk-Adjusted Career Relative Return is his or her return after factoring out both the investment parameters of the fund (e.g., by comparing Select Paper & Forest to a paper and a forest index) and the level of risk the manager has taken relative to that index. Thus, a "neutral" manager, would earn a rating of about 0.0 percent. Any positive number would mean very successful active management, while a negative number would mean relatively unsuccessful active management. That said, industrywide, most managers would earn significantly negative numbers due to fund expenses (often over 1.0 percent), brokerage commissions, and bid/ask spreads.

Fund Manager Ranking Details

Fidelity managers can be listed in order of their "ranking" and "objective" in order to deliver useful investment information to you. Naturally, none of us have all our investments in one or two funds—hopefully, most of us have diversified portfolios that include large-, mid-, small-cap funds as well international funds, bond funds, and so forth.

One "ranking" could be the average of a defined group (by category, objective, style) based on their risk-adjusted "career" relative return (up to 10 years) and their unadjusted "front-weighted average" outperformance (e.g., the average of the career, 5-, 3-, 2-, and 1-year relative performances). In such an example, all performance numbers could be annualized (return per year). The table would then show unadjusted career relative returns and 5-, 3-, 2-, and 1-year relative returns. Gaps in these returns would reflect gaps in lead management positions.

For the more technically minded, one could add career volatilities for the manager's tracking index (or indices) and for the manager, followed by career returns and risk-adjusted returns for the index and the manager, and so see clearly among any group of managers their volatility relative to the correlated market benchmark, group, group average, top quintile, and so on.

Note that the imposition of a benchmark could best be described as an "ideal stock index fund," namely, an index fund proxy that assumes very low expenses (0.2 percent) and no trading costs. This would apply to domestic indices, whereas an "ideal" benchmark for foreign and sector indices would be constructed along the lines of incurring moderately higher expenses (say, 0.4 percent) and no trading costs. Comparison index sources could be Morgan Stanley Capital International, Dow Jones, Goldman Sachs, Standard & Poor's, Barra, Wilshire, Russell. Needless to say, these are very tough benchmarks to beat. Please see Figure 7.2.

Major League Difference

Given how difficult it is for one manager to best the broader market, let alone his or her particular benchmark, style-specific pool of competitor managers, and risk requirements of the investor, investors should be able to find more than peace of mind in the preceding Fidelity Manager Ranking. The numbers yield more than the answer to the most common question, namely, "Who is the best Fidelity manager of any given year?" (The answer is always X), but that doesn't rule out a host of others—it simply highlights who is at the head of the large-cap diversified fund manager class.)

Extra Innings

Analytics: Once you define the investment universe from the standpoint of the managers who comprise it (e.g., Fidelity funds), you can begin to implement a host of existing analytical tools, terms, and systems to better address your own investment discipline and objectives.

Whether it's looking at the total return, relative return, risk-adjusted return, volatility, weighted average, cyclicality, seasonality, style, correlation, and/or risk scattergraphs of the relevant universe of individual managers, you will be fundamentally better informed and, as a result, make fundamentally better investment decisions.

	Name	Current Funds	Start Month	FI Rating	Risk-Adj. Rel. Ret. Career	Front-Weighted Average	Relative Return Career	Relative Return 5 years	Relative Return 3 years	Relative Return 2 years	Relative Return 1 year	Index Volatility	Manager Volatility
1	Thomas Soviero	Lev Company Stock	7/03	8.3	3.5	13.2	14.2				12.1	1.08	1.93
2	Tom Allen	VIP Mid-Cap	2/97	4.3	4.5	4.0	3.7		2.9	4.8	4.8	1.08	0.98
3	Matt Fruhan	Large Cap Stock	11/99	3.8	3.9	3.6	4.6	4.7	4.0	2.5	2.1	1.25	1.11
4	Brian Hogan	Blue Chip Value	4/99	3.5	4.4	2.7	5.5				-0.1	1.27	1.25
5	Joel Tillinghast	Low-Priced	12/89	3.0	4.8	1.3	1.4	3.5	2.3	-1.1	0.5	1.14	0.86
6	Keith Quinton	Tax Managed Stock	2/04	3.0	1.8	4.2	3.8				4.7	1.13	1.53
7	Victor Thay	Conv Securities	12/97	2.8	3.1	2.5	4.3	5.7	-0.2	0.6	2.3	1.39	1.34
8	Will Danoff	Contrafund, VIP Contra	10/86	2.7	3.0	2.5	1.8	3.8	1.3	2.7	2.8	1.02	0.87
9	Steven Wymer	Growth Co	10/90	2.7	1.8	3.5	3.5	2.5	3.8	4.4	3.2	1.24	1.55
10	William Eigen	Start Div & Inc	12/03	2.5	2.4	2.5	1.9				3.1	1.13	1.00
11	Scott Offen	Value Discovery	7/89	1.9	3.0	0.8	2.7	0.2	0.0	0.6	0.7	1.13	1.04
12	Jamie Harmon	SmCapRet, SmCapInd	6/97	1.3	2.6	0.0	1.6	4.3	-3.7	-2.8	0.5	1.25	1.00
13	Tim Cohen	Export & Multi, Destiny	2/99	1.0	0.9	1.1	1.1	1.1	2.4	0.7	0.1	1.41	1.47
14	Steve DuFour	Equity-Inc 2	7/93	0.9	1.2	0.7	1.0	4.4	0.7	-1.8	-0.6	0.87	0.86
15	Sonu Kalra	OTC	2/02	0.8	1.6	0.0	3.1		2.2	0.0	-5.4	1.92	2.01
16	Charles Mangum	Dividend Growth	2/91	0.7	2.1	-0.6	1.8	2.6	-2.0	-4.4	-1.1	1.04	0.99
17	Paul Antico	Small Cap Stock	12/93	0.5	2.3	-1.3	2.8	0.7	-1.5	-1.6	-6.6	1.32	1.27
18	Larry Rakers	Balanced	7/95	0.5	0.1	0.8	-0.5	-0.6	2.5	2.0	0.7	1.55	1.81
19	Robert Haber	Focused Stock	1/86	0.3	-1.8	2.5	-2.2				7.2	1.31	1.35
20	Harry Lange	Capital App, AdvSmCap	5/92	0.3	0.2	0.4	1.2	-1.0	1.8	0.9	-1.2	1.16	1.37
21	Peter Saperstone	Adv Mid-Cap	8/96	0.0	1.4	-1.4	2.1	-1.5	0.4	-3.2	-4.8	1.13	1.22
	Ideal Index Fund			-0.1	-0.1	-0.1	-0.1	-0.1	-0.1	-0.1	-0.1		
22	Robert Chow	Adv Equity-Inc	9/00	-0.3	0.3	-0.8	-0.1	2.9	-1.3	-1.7	-3.8	1.00	0.92
22	Jennifer Uhrig	VIP Growth, Adv Eq Gr	1/88	-0.3	0.6	-1.1	0.6	1.2	-3.0	-1.8	-2.8	1.25	1.21
23	Rajiv Kaul	Aggr Grow	6/98	-0.3	2.4	-3.0	4.8	1.1	-6.0	-5.8	-9.4	1.93	1.95
23	Steven Kaye	Grow & Inc	12/85	-0.4	0.5	-1.3	-0.6	0.9	-2.8	-3.0	-0.8	1.00	0.82
24	Jim Catudal	Stock Sel	8/97	-0.5	0.4	-1.3	0.8	-1.9	-1.2	-2.4	-1.7	1.41	1.59
25	Jason Weiner	Independence, Fifty	12/94	-0.5	1.7	-2.6	2.7	-0.2	-6.0	-5.4	-4.1	1.73	1.68
25	Stephen Petersen	Equity-Inc, VIP E-I, Pur	7/93	-0.5	0.1	-1.1	-0.3	0.8	-1.1	-1.6	-3.3	0.89	0.84
26	Brian Hanson	Bl Chp Gr, Adv Str Gro	2/00	-0.6	0.1	-1.2	-0.5	0.6	-2.4	-2.0	-1.9	2.09	2.17
26	Steven Snider	Disc Eq, VIP AMG	9/97	-1.0	-1.8	-0.3	-1.5	-1.4	0.0	-0.5	2.2	0.82	0.85
27	Bob Stansky	Magellan	5/84	-1.6	-0.5	-2.8	-0.4	-2.9	-3.3	-4.2	-3.3	1.02	1.03
27	Shep Perkins	Mid Cap Stock	8/99	-1.7	-2.0	-1.5	4.6	0.3	-4.1	-3.1	-4.9	2.47	1.77
28	John Avery	Fidelity	7/95	-1.8	-1.8	-1.7	-1.7	-3.0	-1.2	-1.0	-1.8	0.86	0.82
28	Andrew Burzumato	Utilities	10/03	-1.8	-3.4	-0.2	-1.2				0.7	0.85	0.97
29	Ramin Arani	Trend	1/97	-1.8	-1.9	-1.8	-2.7	-1.1	-1.2	-2.3	-1.6	1.21	1.09
29	Louis Salemy	G&I 2, VIP G&I, VIP Bal	8/92	-1.9	-1.0	-2.8	-2.2	0.5	-2.0	-6.0	-4.4	1.05	0.89
30	Rich Fentin	Value	1/83	-2.2	-2.7	-1.8	-1.6	0.0	-1.4	-2.0	-3.8	0.92	1.05
30	Adam Hetnarski	Discovery, Destiny 2	3/96	-2.9	-2.1	-3.6	-2.1	-2.4	-4.0	-6.0	-3.3	1.20	1.30
31	Bettina Doulton	VIP Grow Opps	1/93	-3.3	-3.0	-3.5	-2.8	-4.0	-2.9	-4.1	-3.8	0.92	0.92
31	Bahaa Fam	Structured Growths	5/00	-3.3	-4.5	-2.1	-6.8	-7.3	-3.7	1.5	5.6	0.96	1.27
32	Neal Miller	New Millennium	12/92	-3.3	-1.6	-5.1	2.8	-7.6	-3.7	-7.2	-9.5	1.05	1.86
32	John Porter	Adv/VIP Dyn Cap App	2/96	-4.2	-4.3	-4.1	-4.7	-3.4	-3.0	-6.2	-3.2	1.12	1.12
33	Harris Leviton	Value Strategies	11/87	-5.0	-5.1	-4.9	-2.3	-4.1	-1.0	-4.4	-12.7	0.92	1.42

International Funds

	Name	Current Funds	Start Month	FI Rating	Risk-Adj. Rel. Ret. Career	Front-Weighted Average	Relative Return Career	Relative Return 5 years	Relative Return 3 years	Relative Return 2 years	Relative Return 1 year	Index Volatility	Manager Volatility
1	Wm Kennedy	Int'l Discovery	12/98	10.0	6.7	13.3	9.0	4.7			26.3	1.18	1.41
2	David Bavarez	Europe	1/03	6.0	3.0	9.0	7.3				10.7	1.50	1.75
3	Sano & Patton	Intl Sm Cap	9/02	5.8	6.0	5.6	8.8			4.9	3.0	1.15	1.23
4	Kenichi Mizushita	Japan Small Cos	12/96	4.3	6.7	1.8	12.0	-1.3	-0.5	4.7	-5.7	1.73	1.77
5	William Bower	Divers Int'l	12/94	3.7	4.0	3.5	4.1	5.0	3.1	1.7	3.5	0.99	1.02
6	Allan Liu	SE Asia	6/93	2.8	2.3	3.3	4.0	0.8	1.6	2.9	7.0	1.72	1.67
7	Rob von Rekowsky	Emerging Markets	1/04	1.9	0.6	3.2	2.0				4.3	2.17	2.32
8	Ian Hart	Europe Cap App	4/00	1.7	2.4	1.0	2.7	2.9	-1.8	-0.2	1.3	1.12	1.06
9	Maxime Lemieux	Canada	11/02	1.3	1.0	1.5	0.8			1.8	1.9	1.27	1.24
10	Rick Mace	Overseas, Glo Bal, WW	6/89	0.2	1.2	-0.9	1.4	-0.1	-1.2	-1.1	-3.6	0.84	0.94
11	Kevin McCarey	Aggressive Intl	6/86	0.1	0.2	0.0	0.9	2.2	-0.7	-3.4	0.9	0.96	1.18
12	T Toraasen	Nordic	6/98	-0.1	0.2	-0.4	-0.1	3.4	-3.9	1.2	-2.6	1.66	1.45
	Ideal International Index Fund			-0.4	-0.4	-0.4	-0.4	-0.4	-0.4	-0.4	-0.4		
13	Yoko Ishibashi	Japan	6/00	-0.5	0.2	-1.2	-1.6		0.8	-1.5	-2.7	1.18	1.37

Select Funds (includes Real Estate and Utilities)

	Name	Current Funds	Start Month	FI Rating	Risk-Adj. Rel. Ret. Career	Front-Weighted Average	Relative Return Career	Relative Return 5 years	Relative Return 3 years	Relative Return 2 years	Relative Return 1 year	Index Volatility	Manager Volatility
1	Robert Lee	Food & Agriculture	6/04	9.9	8.7	11.1	10.5				11.6	1.27	1.16
2	Anmol Mehra	Automotive, Paper	2/04	8.8	3.5	14.1	10.6				17.7	2.53	1.78
3	Brian Kennedy	Brokerage	3/02	8.3	7.1	9.6	11.5		11.5	7.4	7.9	1.58	1.60
4	Jonathan Zang	Natural Gas	7/98	8.2	6.4	10.0	8.0	4.7	5.9	14.5	16.9	1.20	1.23
5	Kelly Cardwell	Software	7/01	5.2	6.4	4.1	9.4		6.8	1.0	-0.9	1.46	1.43
6	John Roth	Multimedia, Consumer	10/99	4.1	4.0	4.2	3.5	2.2	4.2	7.1	3.9	1.08	1.21
7	Aaron M Cooper	Leisure, Med Equip	6/04	4.1	3.5	4.6	5.0				4.1	1.39	1.41
8	James Morrow	Electronics, Tech	7/01	3.4	2.0	4.8	5.5		5.5	3.9	4.3	1.90	1.69
9	Douglas Simmons	Environment	2/04	2.3	1.2	3.4	2.4				4.3	1.59	1.85
10	Nathan Strik	Energy Services	6/04	2.2	1.4	3.0	2.7				3.2	2.42	2.41
11	Naved Khan	Computers	10/02	2.0	-1.9	5.9	1.4			9.3	7.0	1.29	1.58
12	Jody Simes	Industrial Materials	8/03	1.8	1.4	2.3	3.8				0.7	2.12	2.28
13	Matt Friedman	Chem,Cyc, Engy,Nat Rs	9/03	1.5	0.0	3.0	1.7				4.3	1.62	1.80
14	Brian Younger	Telcom, Wirels, UtilsGr	9/00	1.5	0.9	2.1	0.7		7.9	1.2	-1.2	1.85	2.07
15	Charles Hebard	Financial, Insurance	1/01	1.5	0.5	2.5	1.1		0.5	1.4	7.1	1.61	1.45
16	Valerie Friedholm	Home Finance	7/01	0.5	-0.6	1.6	-0.1		1.8	1.9	2.7	1.51	1.20
17	Dan DuPont	Gold	2/03	0.2	-1.3	1.7	-3.8				7.2	3.00	2.98
	Ideal Sector Index Fund			-0.4	-0.4	-0.4	-0.4	-0.4	-0.4	-0.4	-0.4		
18	Heather Lawrence	Banking	12/01	-1.6	-1.6	-1.6	-1.9		-0.8	-1.3	-2.3	1.23	1.10
19	Steve Buller	Real Estate	12/97	-1.9	-2.8	-1.1	-3.0	-0.4	-0.5	-1.0	-0.5	1.03	1.00
20	Charlie Chai	Dev Comm, Networking	5/03	-2.4	-2.5	-2.2	-4.0			-3.2	0.6	2.68	3.41
21	Chris Bartel	Ind Equip, Defense	2/02	-2.6	-2.3	-2.8	-4.3		-3.5	-1.2	-2.2	1.91	2.12

FIGURE 7.2   Map of Fidelity's managers

Return Index Career	Return Manager Career	Risk-Adj. Index Career	Risk-Adj. Manager Career
15.0	31.4	14.2	18.2
13.4	17.6	12.7	17.8
1.9	6.6	2.3	6.4
3.3	9.0	3.5	8.0
16.4	18.0	14.8	20.3
7.0	11.0	6.6	8.5
0.3	4.6	1.4	4.5
10.1	12.1	9.9	13.3
7.1	10.9	6.5	8.5
8.8	10.8	8.2	10.9
9.7	12.6	9.0	12.3
9.2	11.0	8.2	11.0
-2.5	-1.4	-0.6	0.3
7.4	8.5	8.0	9.2
1.1	4.3	2.5	4.1
8.5	10.5	8.4	10.6
9.7	12.7	8.3	10.8
0.1	-0.3	1.5	1.6
11.3	8.8	9.6	7.6
10.1	11.4	9.2	9.4
10.4	12.7	9.6	11.1
8.8	8.7	8.8	9.1
6.5	7.1	6.0	6.6
-1.2	3.5	1.3	3.7
10.1	9.4	10.1	10.6
5.3	6.1	4.9	5.3
7.0	9.8	5.7	7.5
10.2	9.9	10.9	11.0
-10.0	-10.4	-2.7	-2.6
4.8	3.2	5.0	3.1
11.8	11.4	11.6	11.1
-20.2	-16.5	-5.8	-7.6
10.1	8.2	11.1	9.1
21.8	20.3	25.0	20.7
11.6	8.6	10.3	8.2
14.0	11.5	13.5	12.4
13.9	12.1	14.8	11.7
12.1	9.7	10.8	8.4
7.7	4.6	8.0	4.7
0.6	-6.2	0.5	-4.0
12.4	15.6	12.0	10.2
10.8	5.5	10.0	5.3
14.4	11.8	15.3	9.5
0.8	9.8	1.3	8.1
21.2	30.1	15.5	18.9
31.8	43.4	28.2	36.0
-0.9	11.1	1.2	8.0
5.5	9.8	5.5	9.7
-0.7	3.3	1.3	3.6
17.3	19.7	10.1	10.8
0.3	3.0	0.7	3.1
29.0	30.1	23.7	25.0
6.0	7.5	6.4	7.7
7.0	8.0	7.2	7.4
7.2	7.1	5.9	6.2
-6.7	-8.2	-5.1	-4.9
0.2	10.7	1.0	9.8
-7.9	1.8	-0.7	2.8
-0.5	11.0	1.2	8.4
12.1	21.1	10.8	17.9
-1.6	7.7	0.2	6.6
-6.3	-3.0	-5.5	-1.8
3.9	9.1	3.9	7.6
-11.9	-7.0	-4.4	-2.5
4.9	7.4	4.6	5.9
46.4	50.4	21.5	23.2
28.1	29.9	22.7	20.4
16.5	21.0	9.9	11.5
21.7	23.7	14.9	15.0
-5.5	-4.9	-1.2	-0.3
0.1	1.2	1.6	2.1
1.2	1.1	2.2	1.6
11.0	6.8	6.3	4.9
5.9	3.9	5.6	3.9
15.3	11.8	15.0	11.8
21.1	16.2	10.4	7.6
9.0	4.4	6.6	4.2

FI Rating: The summation of a manager's record; the average of the next two numbers items below.

Risk-Adjusted Relative Return Career: A manager's return after factoring out both the fund's benchmark (e.g., the S&P/Barra 500 large-cap growth index) and the level of risk (Relative Volatility) the manager has taken on relative to that index. Any positive number would mean very successful active management. Industry-wide, managers will on average earn somewhat negative numbers due to fund expenses (often over 1.0%), brokerage commissions and bid-ask spreads.

Front-Weighted Average (Relative Return): The average of a manager's career (up to 10 years), 5-year, 3-year, 2-year, and 1-year performances relative to his benchmarks.

Relative Return Career: Simply a fund manager's annualized return over their career (up to 10 years) after subtracting out the return of a relevant benchmark index.

5-year Relative Return: A fund manager's annualized return over the last five years after subtracting out the return of a relevant benchmark index. 3-year, 2-year, and 1-year Relative Returns are similar, but, naturally, for 3-, 2-, and 1-year periods.

Index Relative Volatility and Manager Relative Volatility: Volatility is the uncertainty of a fund's return. A fund which goes up about the same each month (i.e., a money market) has very low risk, while a fund whose performance is more erratic has a higher relative volatility and is said to be more "risky." Relative Volatility is the standard deviation of monthly returns for a period (here, for the manager's career, up to 10 years), divided by the same standard deviation figure for the S&P 500 index.

Return Index Career and Return Manager Career: Simply the average annual return for the manager's benchmark indexes, and the manager's own funds, over the manager's career at Fidelity (up to 10 years).

Risk-Adjusted Index Career and Risk-Adjusted Manager Career: Figures that permit return comparisons between funds of varying levels of risk, by factoring out differences in volatility. A fund's risk-adjused return is the return one would obtain with a portfolio holding the fund and enough Cash Reserves or similar zero-volatility investment (or, for low-risk funds, enough margin) to maintain the risk level of the S&P 500. For a fund with a Relative Volatility of 1.25, a portfolio would be constructed of 80% of that fund, and 20% of a cash position, giving the hypothetical portfolio a volatility of 1.00. The returns for this hypothetical portfolio are that fund's Risk-Adjusted Return. For funds compared to an index other than the S&P 500, risk-adjusted return is also calculated for that index. (The risk-adjusted return for the S&P 500 is the same as its actual return, since its Relative Volatility is always exactly 1.00.) ∎

Changes in Fidelity managers require an investment decision about whether to continue with the fund vehicle and its new manager. Knowing the track record of the outgoing manager, and where that manager is going, as well as the track records of the incoming manager and pool of managers who fulfill the role of the departing manager's fund within your portfolio, is essential. If the incoming manager ranks poorly, you need to know that, and you need to know the range of potential managers in order to make an informed investment decision regarding who would be the best transitional and/or permanent manager for the position.

You should effect internal reviews of every manager in your portfolio and of the universe of potential managers for each niche role to provide in-depth analysis and ongoing monitoring of the pool and of the specific group of existing managers. To evaluate and monitor your existing lineup of managers intrinsically and against their extrinsic peers requires the establishment of objective and truly independent scales.

EIGHT

Fidelity's Growth Funds

Fidelity growth funds are the crème de la crème, the gold standard by which other growth funds have been, are, and will be measured. Of course, just like gold, the value of that standard can move up and down over any given time period. At times, Fidelity growth funds have had a rough (i.e., lagging) relationship with its peers. But over almost every meaningful time period since mutual funds began, Fidelity has been able to hold its banners higher, in more investment categories, than any of its competitors. Fidelity's growth funds are no exception to this rule.

Fidelity growth funds seek capital gains by buying stocks at one price and selling them (or just holding on) after a price rise. By definition, growth funds generally do not seek stock fund dividends (although they're often a nice extra tidbit); funds seeking a high level of dividend income are put in the growth and income category. Because growth stocks' values are, at least in the short term, especially subject to the whims of the market, they tend to have a higher volatility than stocks whose values are, like bonds, cushioned by a relatively high (and relatively fixed) dividend yield.

Magellan: The Untold Story

Fidelity is unquestionably best known, and rightly so, for its actively managed growth fund fleet. Unfortunately, that fleet—which is more diverse and well-captained than any other fund firm's growth fund fleet—is also almost always already tarred with its flagship's brush. The flagship? Magellan. The mighty Magellan! Not only does common investment wisdom lead most investors to think that as goes Magellan's performance, so goes all of Fidelity's funds' performances, especially its growth funds. But when asked to name an actively managed fund, you're going to almost always get one response: Magellan. Fidelity did such a remarkable job at marketing to Magellan's strengths (thanks to several successful managers, and one manager in particular, who hit rock star status, as you can see in the chart shown in Figure 8.1), that Magellan didn't simply become the flagship fund for Fidelity, it became the poster child for actively managed funds as such. Upshot: As went Magellan's performance, so went actively managed funds versus index funds.

The marketing power, the branding genius, and the asset-gathering prowess exhibited by what was once the largest mutual fund by a wide margin, often dwarfing with its assets the total assets of most fund firms, was inarguable—until Magellan's performance began to luff, then to actually lag its benchmark S&P 500 Index. In 1996, in a bid to stem both investor dissatisfaction and regulatory inquisitiveness into why a Magellan manager had suddenly placed nearly 18 percent of this model growth fund's assets into bonds, there was a manager change that looked right-minded at the time but wound up costing Fidelity (in terms of reputation, assets, market share, and revenue) more than Fidelity had likely ever bargained for.

As Magellan's performance began to consistently lag the performance of the S&P 500, assets began to trickle out, then flow on a regular basis, then flood out to the tune of $1 billion here and $1 billion there—in other words, *real money*. Magellan went from its apex asset total of more than $105 billion in 1999 to under $50 billion by midway through 2006. A simple expense ratio calculation, assuming an average expense ratio of 75 basis points, can tally that loss of revenue to upwards of $1 billion—a staggering sum that doesn't really do the damage assessment justice (in terms of Fidelity's tarnished image and lost market share).

Many misinformed or uninformed investors began to think that Fidelity managers as a whole were following in Magellan's underperforming footsteps, but the truth is that Fidelity's overall group of managers, and its growth fund managers in particular, were actually gaining strength in terms of delivering consistently more and better relative returns in comparison to both market benchmarks and peer competitors (see my risk/return scattergraph in Figure 8.3 at the end of this chapter).

Then Fidelity itself finally did the right thing (albeit painfully late in the

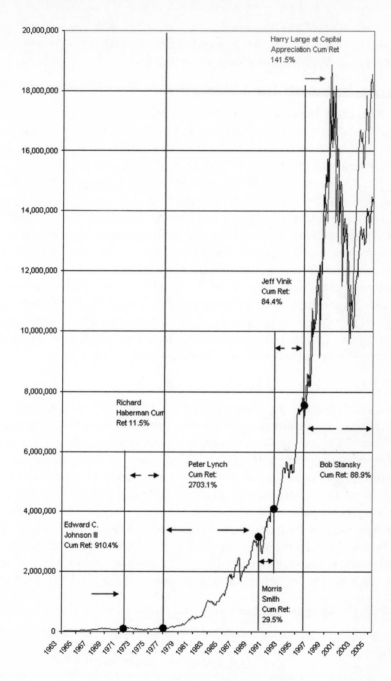

FIGURE 8.1   Manager changes at Fidelity Magellan

day) and replaced the underperforming manager, Bob Stansky, with the manager of another fund that benched against the S&P 500—Harry Lange, from Capital Appreciation. Please see Figure 8.1.

Fidelity's Growth Fund Strengths

On the seemingly endless punditry treadmill, which runs on pure mania for day trading and the onslaught of individual stock-picking braggarts, only to be followed by the doom-and-gloom soothsayers predicting that the markets will end tomorrow, it's more than nice to know that the Fidelity funds we invest in are managed by proven professionals who have been able to deliver relative calm in the face of the domestic and global markets' Sturm und Drang. No matter what you read, you can believe this: Fidelity is home to more than a handful of the world's most talented stock pickers, whose life, love, and daily bread come from beating the Street. Some are better than others. Some are more consistent than others. Some are weak kittens in the litter. But much like the full faith and credit underlying the aura of safety attending U.S. Treasuries, Fidelity's funds, with its flagship fleet of growth funds, are helmed by seasoned stock pickers whose know-how and talent (or lack thereof) are fully disclosed, day in and day out, over the span of their careers.

Fidelity's Large-Cap Growth Funds

These funds aim mostly to beat the S&P 500 Index. They can and often do differ from the index by concentrating on growth stocks or, conversely, on value stocks by making bets on various industry sectors; by picking individual stocks that will outperform their industry competitors; by weighting certain sectors over others and/or certain stocks more than others; by sticking to one capitalization range (i.e., large-cap stocks) or by wandering over wider pastures in pursuit of green (i.e., large-, mid-, and small-cap ranges); and by including foreign stocks. Most growth funds hold portfolios that lean more toward growth than value (the growth and income funds tend to hold stocks that, for the most part favor value stocks). But this is hardly enough of a rule to be able to distinguish exceptions.

Fidelity's Large-Cap Lineup

This section offers an overview of the large-caps funds available from Fidelity.

Aggressive Growth

Aggressive Growth invests primarily but not exclusively in domestic stocks. The fund seeks to buy companies that are achieving, or appear poised for, accelerated growth in earnings or revenue. In short, it is growthier than most other Fidelity growth funds and also holds a fair number of midsized companies (although it currently averages out as a large-cap fund). This fund has an uneven performance history, thanks to its frequent manager changes; although some have been stellar, others have been only okay, and one (Rob Bertelson), ranked rock bottom on my proprietary fund manager ranking system (see Chapter 7). Rob's been out of the driver's seat of this fund for several years, but this fund's performance history, which saw a gain of more than 100 percent in one year under one manager followed by a loss of nearly 83 percent under Bertelson, is instructive; as fund investors, we need to know whom we own as much as coming to terms with what we own. It's also instructive of another major fault line when it comes to investing in mutual funds: Morningstar gave this fund a five-star rating based on the stellar performance of the prior manager (Erin Sullivan), which led this fund (under Bertelson, the man I'm quoted in *Barron's* as saying was "the worst stock picker I've seen, bar none") to actually take in nearly $5 billion more in assets in 2000 (from about $15 billion when he took over to upwards of $22 billion) before plummeting, performance-wise and asset-wise, into the ground (when he left it had about $3.5 billion in assets). So much for a five-star rating's predictive powers; and caveat emptor when it comes to simply trusting Fidelity to get manager changes right every time.

For investors looking for aggressive growth investments, you can consider OTC or Growth Company or Fidelity's Nasdaq Tracker (OneQ), as well.

Blue Chip Growth (FBGRX)

As its name implies, Blue Chip Growth invests primarily in well-known, name-brand companies, although the definition of *blue chip* set forth in the fund prospectus is a rather outdated one—for the fund's purposes, a company qualifies for blue-chip status with a mere $1 billion market cap. This definition doesn't really exclude even true small-caps, and it still allows mid-caps as well as large-caps, the true "blue chips," by most definitions. But gone are the days when this fund was chock-full of the "blue chips of tomorrow." Current holdings (which haven't changed much in about a decade) are the usual suspects: Microsoft, GE, JNJ, AIG, Wal-Mart, Wyeth . . . you get the picture. The fund has had trouble competing with the large-cap defensive strengths of Dividend Growth when the going gets tough, as well as the large-cap offensive strengths of Contrafund, Growth Co, and the non-Fidelity QQQ (the exchange traded fund that holds the largest 100 stocks in the Nasdaq). But, it remains a fund

that is almost always well positioned to take advantage of a potential re-
bound in leadership large-cap growth stocks—a turn of events that happens about twice a decade.

Blue Chip Value (FBCVX)

Just as one would expect, the value side of the market's large-cap fence is
where this fund sows its stock seeds for greener pastures. Created as a
complement to Blue Chip Growth (see preceding), the fund tends to benefit mightily from recession lows through to the latter stages of a recovery. It has historically had some room to grow in the energy-infused
cycles, but can be prone to its benchmark's core holdings in interest
rate–sensitive financials; since the inception (June 2003), that stake has
been significantly underweight this benchmark's bias toward this one
sector.

Capital Appreciation (FDCAX)

Capital Appreciation (Cap App) can buy just about any type of stock (as
well as bonds). In practice, the fund generally has more than 95 percent of
its portfolio invested in equities, with whatever remains being held in
cash. Throughout its history, Cap App has maintained a well-diversified
mix of large- and mid-cap stocks with a relatively balanced blend of
growth and value issues. The fund can also invest globally and has often
done so in meaningful measure. With no necessary allegiance to any one
capitalization range, sector, or region, this fund is one of a handful of Fidelity funds (and only a handful of all mutual funds) that is a classic go-
anywhere fund; as such, I tend to like this fund in greater or lesser
portions for nearly any investor. After all, just because you can't cram it
into a style box doesn't mean that there isn't some great value to be had
by enabling managers to populate their portfolios with their best ideas—
regardless of the investment world's equivalent to political correctness
(i.e., style boxes).

Contrafund (FCNTX)

Contrafund is one of Fidelity's oldest and consistently best funds. Under
the stellar and unique stock-picking style born of an early, gifted, and
even quixotic manager, Leo Dworsky, the investment philosophy of this
fund helps it maintain its inimitable and always useful character: A contrarian is the sort of investor who looks for out-of-favor, unglamorous,
ugly-duckling stocks that the rest of the market is shunning or ignoring.
The fund has a history of living up to its contrarian credo—sometimes

being truly contrarian, other times letting its bets ride on the wave of market momentum. It shifts between growth, value, and a blend of the two, and like Capital Appreciation, it finds its home on any capitalization range with an natural bias toward large-cap stocks), as well as feeling fine when it comes to crossing the pond and adding some foreign stocks to its mix. Do expect it to often reflect contrary positions relative not only to the broader market weightings but also compared to the average Fidelity manager's weightings. Examples abound, but the consistent lever has been an inverse weighting of technology and financial services stocks (i.e., pro-tech, anti-finance, and vice versa).

Destiny I (FDESX)

This fund, which has a long history of mostly value-oriented investments, got caught short of the new economy's tech-driven surge in the late 1990s, but has nonetheless delivered a respectable, if not heart-pounding, long-term record. I recommend staying clear of this fund (and Destiny II) regardless of who is running it, how well its done, or how well you might think it will do, since both of the Destiny funds charge investors unjustifiably high fees for the privilege of participating in what is supposed to be a long-term disciplined investment plan (small amounts of money invested on a scheduled and automatic basis). While the Destiny sales plan might seem a good way to dollar-cost-average into the market for investors with small dollar amounts but a right-minded desire to invest in their financial future, the problem is that it charges a hefty up-front sales fee and locks investors into a commitment of 10 years or more. If you already own Destiny shares, you don't necessarily have to bail out just because it was probably a mistake to get into the fund. But I would.

Destiny II (FDETX)

Destiny II used to be a clone of Destiny I, but it has differentiated itself over the recent past enough to stand in its own portfolio's light; it's tends to be a somewhat more aggressive, growth-oriented portfolio. Trouble is, its portfolio is overshadowed by the same high charges and long-term commitment that I do not like. Given the expense structure of this fund, I still feel investors should give it a wide berth. (See my comments on Destiny I.)

Disciplined Equity (FDEQX)

Disciplined Equity invests primarily in domestic common stocks. Its "discipline" is that it doesn't make big sector bets, instead keeping industry weightings fairly close to the market's neutral weightings. The fund has historically been one of Fidelity's few heavily computer-aided, quantitatively enabled, funds; but it has not been a purely quant fund, typically preferring to wed its quant strengths to its analysis of fundamental factors such as earnings estimates. The fund has diverged over the past several years from its index-hugging S&P 500 course (its R^2 has been as high 96 percent with the S&P), but given its eschewal of big sector bets, the fund should continue to track the market index fairly closely. Still, Disciplined Equity is not an index fund; the fund's individual stock holdings have rarely exceeded 150 issues—a far cry from 500—and therein lies the performance potential or pitfalls of this fund. In 2000, this fund lost less than its benchmark S&P 500 Index; in 2005, it delivered more than double its benchmark returns. Although I prefer other funds in the large-cap camp to this one, it has consistently delivered a winning argument for considering it.

Discovery (FDSVX)

Formerly known as Contrafund II, this fund was created in 1998 to give contrarian investors who missed out on the original Contrafund (which closed) an opportunity to participate in a fund featuring their favored investment style. But, from the get-go, this fund differentiated itself from its namesake; its top 10 picks typically differed significantly from those of Contrafund. With the new name, the fund has clearly set a course all its own: trending toward a blend of value and growth on the growthier side of the balance sheet, concentrating more of the fund's assets in its top 10 holdings than most other Fidelity funds, and holding fewer (i.e., more concentrated) positions relative to most other Fidelity funds, too. All this sounds as though it should bode well for investors in his fund—or for investors seeking a more aggressive large-cap fund for their portfolio. It doesn't. At least not if you count performance among your investment criteria. Despite the earmarks of a fund that ought to be able to outperform its benchmark, it has rarely done so. Ironically, its best trait is a defensive one; rarely losing ground to its benchmark when the going gets tough.

Dividend Growth (FDGFX)

Dividend Growth concentrates on companies that seem likely to begin paying dividends or to boost current dividend levels in the expectation that such developments will cause their stock prices to rise. (In other words, fund performance is driven by capital gains, not dividend income.) The fund's portfolio is heavily oriented toward large-cap companies and holds a blend of value and growth stocks, with generally a slight lean toward value and almost always a large dose of health care names. The fund is a far cry from a closet index fund. It isn't afraid to make concentrated bets on favorite stocks. It's a focused portfolio that has rarely seen more than 100 issues populating the portfolio. The fund's low volatility and blue-chip holdings make it a solid choice as a core holding in most investors' portfolios. (I also believe most holders should complement this position with Growth Company or, for more aggressive investors, OTC.) But don't mistake this for a fund to invest in if you're looking for dividend income—it has rarely delivered more than the S&P 500's yield.

Export & Multinational (EXPX)

This fund primarily invests in U.S. companies that derive 10 percent or more of their annual revenues from sales of goods or services abroad, those that are involved in export-related businesses, or those that are multinational firms, which Fidelity defines as companies having a "substantial portion" of assets, sales, or profits overseas. But as interesting as this fund's charter may sound, the truth is that it is rather something of a marketing gimmick: In this global economy, so many U.S. companies meet Fidelity's criteria for being either exporters or multinationals that it renders such guidelines almost meaningless. But not quite. The fund has been all over the style map—from small-cap growth to large-cap value to large-cap blend to large-cap growth. While I think that a fund like Growth Company is probably a better choice given its more transparent objective, I wouldn't rule out this fund as one way to play the global marketplace—but I also would not mistake this as the one fund to own if you want to invest globally. That fund would be Fidelity's Four-In-One-Index fund (see Chapter 16 for my comments on this fund).

Fifty (FFTYX)

Fifty fund is what's known in the trade as a *concept fund*. As its name suggests, it eschews the level of diversification typical for equity funds in favor of a basket holding a few choice eggs. (Despite the name, it's usually closer to 60 than to 50.) While it normally seeks growth, the fund has not eschewed value stocks when they looked more appealing. Toward the end of 2000, then-manager John Muresianu (who left Fidelity to launch a hedge fund shortly thereafter) bet the ranch on energy and energy services stocks (58.7 percent of the fund) and a couple of gold stocks

(18.3 percent of the fund). The bets then didn't especially pay off—but the fund's 4.5 percent loss for the year was about half that of the large-cap stock market. *Losing less* than others is one mark of a solid stock picker—*gaining more* is the other. (In 1999, Muresianu's stock picking earned 45.8 percent.) But by 2006, under a new manager, the more radical sector bets and limited diversification gave way to a more industry-diversified (albeit still concentrated, holdings-wise) portfolio. This fund can make sense for aggressive investors looking for an active manager who will tell them which single stock plays he or she thinks make the most sense in any market environment—but enter at your own risk.

Focused (FTGGX)

Like Fifty above, Focused invests in a concentrated portfolios of names, typically under 50. This fund's names can and have represented virtually every industry and sector, but has traditionally excluded any significant foreign positioning. Large-cap in nature and bias, with a demonstrable tilt toward value stocks (financials, industrial, energy), this fund can play a niche role in most every portfolio leading to the obvious question: should it? The fund has historically lost significantly more than its market benchmark in downdrafts, and gained more on the upswings. That leaves it a bear market dropout but a bull market contender in my book.

Growth Company (FDGRX)

Growth Company invests primarily in stocks of domestic and foreign companies with above-average growth in earnings or sales. More aggressive than Fidelity's other growth funds, it still *trends* to be slightly less aggressive than, for example, Aggressive Growth. While large-cap growth stocks dominate the fund's portfolio, the manager has historically kept the door open for some of the right mid- and small-cap stocks. The fact that Growth Company is more aggressive than most other growth funds makes it an excellent choice as a complement or counterweight to a more conservative growth fund like Dividend Growth (see my previous comments) or a growth and income fund like Strategic Dividend & Income (see Chapter 9). True, this fund will take some lumps when the going gets tough, so its best suited for growth or aggressive growth investors (lionhearted ones, at that). While the fund's emphasis is large-cap growth (it has drifted into a "blend" positioning as an aberration from time to time), you'll almost always find some cherry-picked mid- and small-cap stocks in the mix (adding to both the volatility and return potential).

Independence (FDFFX)

Formerly known as Retirement Growth, this fund's charter, like that of Magellan, is extremely flexible—the fund can buy domestic and foreign common stocks, large or small, growth, value, or a blend of the above. This fund used to be slated for retirement-savings accounts, where tax efficiency isn't a concern, since its emphasis on capital gains leads to steady turnover. The fund has, over longer-term time periods and under successive managers, demonstrated an ability to deliver outperformance, albeit with added volatility and a higher-than-average turnover rate compared to its Fidelity growth fund counterparts. Growth investors with a very-long-term objective in mind might get a good view from this fund's hilltop, but I'd rather own another large-cap mountain like Contrafund or Growth Company.

Large Cap Growth (FSIGX)

Formerly known as Structured Large Cap Growth, this fund is set to replicate the best large-cap ideas among all of Fidelity managers. The resulting crossbred best-of-breed ideas portfolio is a uniquely interesting way to play the landscape (here, as in the other funds, Large Cap Value, Mid Cap Growth, and Mid Cap Value share this thematic). I like it as a diversifier and as a distiller of the best-of-breed ideas; but I think you'd really have to own all four funds that map to this "style" to get the best of all possible worlds. Even then, I'd want a single-minded manager to captain a ship in each capitalization range's sea.

Large Cap Stock

This fund invests primarily in domestic (and a few foreign) companies with market capitalizations greater than $1 billion at the time of purchase. By the most common definition, this market-cap rule includes all mid-caps as well as the large-caps, but this distinction is still important since, unlike almost every Fidelity growth fund, you won't find small-cap stocks in this portfolio. What you will find: a preponderance of stocks that adhere to its moniker (i.e., large-caps), companies with established growth records (if not actual earnings). And while it's true that the large-cap definition is typically $5 billion or higher, it's also true that many companies in the technology group, for example, break through the $1 billion and $5 billion barriers in quick succession. It has historically favored a large-cap blend leaning toward or in fact nearly ruling out value stocks in favor of growthier names. But that history can be subject to the current manager's revision, so check under its holdings hood before assuming that past growth inclinations are prologue for this fund. I'd avoid it in favor of Growth Company.

Large Cap Value (FSLVX)

This fund was formerly known as Structured Large Cap Value and built on the same underlying principle of stock selection as Large Cap Growth (see my previous comments).

Leveraged Company Stock (FLVCX)

The fund is uniquely diversified, focusing its assets in the leveraged stocks of junk-bond-status companies. As such, the risk here is getting the company's story wrong, as opposed to failing to be in one hot sector of the market or another. Investors often mistakenly think that this fund must be an even more aggressive bet on technology than, for example, Aggressive Growth or OTC. This is not so; technology typically accounts for less than one-fifth of the fund's overall assets. (Most technology companies are up-starts with no earnings on which to base and distribute debt instruments.) The lion's share of this fund's holdings trend toward value companies; en-ergy names have played a dominant role recently. When it launched, tele-com and industrial names were the heavy hitters. Look to this fund to trade around the most unloved and unwashed dirty debt laundry in any market's cycle—and come out on the upswing when the cycle spins in its favor. A great diversifier since no other fund company has a fund like it.

Low-Priced Stock (FLPSX)

Low-Priced Stock, which invests primarily in common stocks priced at or below $35 per share at the time of purchase (that price point has changed from $15 to $25 to now $35 since its 1989 inception), comes much closer to being a genuinely contrarian portfolio than Contrafund (see my previous comments on this fund). As its low-priced mandate encourages, but does not necessarily require, the fund has a longtime small-cap value orienta-tion. (Most low-priced stocks are small-caps, often "fallen angels" which are well off their highs, and cheap on a fundamental basis.) And while I try to refrain from talking about individual managers in this book (except in Chapter 7, ranking Fidelity's managers), this fund was the brainchild of one of the most gifted stock pickers of his or any generation. A scion of Peter Lynch's stock-picking tutelage, manager Joel Tillinghast has consis-tently delivered relative outperformance (i.e., his performance has con-sistently been better than that of his Russell 2000 Index). He clearly hits his stride against the tide. His value orientation, which had hurt him in the go-for-large-cap-growth-at-any-price days (namely, 1998 and 1999), helped him deliver in 2000 when the going got tough; but he's always at his best in a recovering economy where the vast majority of stocks fall under his $35 or less per share threshold, except maybe Big Blue. This enables this fund to stock up on low-priced stocks (whether small-, mid-, or large-cap) and ride them through the recovery cycle and almost all the way to the next bear market (there's always one around any bull market's corner). The reason: He doesn't have to sell at any price—just at the price he thinks best. Even if the unthinkable happens and Tillinghast leaves this fund's post anytime soon, the concept that drives this fund is one most investors would do well to get behind, not sidestep.

Magellan (FMAGX)

I've talked this one nearly to death. But in case you skipped my brilliant foreword and jumped right to this page, know that Fidelity's most legendary stock fund, which has among its most flexible investment guidelines (and so is free to invest in both domestic and foreign stocks, from large-cap to to small-cap, emphasizing either growth style or value style), failed to deliver big-time for nearly a decade beginning in 1996, but turned a corner in 2006 (a good argument for holding on as long as possible given potential capital gains taxes). The fund is now too large, in Fidelity's opinion, to admit new investors, but existing shareholders, as well as employees of companies whose 401(k) plans include Magellan, can still buy shares. The fund's size, as a practical matter, limits its ability to concentrate in small- or mid-caps and also prevents rapid changes in fund composition. Should such long-term shareholders hang onto Magellan? I would consider the following points. First, Magellan is once again like the fund it was when you bought it—it went through a large-cap growth/value blend as opposed to a growth fund orientation, and as such it played a more conservative role in your portfolio, basically aging along with you toward a more conservative approach to the markets. That's no longer the case; it's growth-pure and not so simple, since it's really a globally oriented growth fund and likely to remain so. As a result, Magellan should play the role in your current portfolio that you initially purchased it for years ago—or be set adrift in favor of more conservative funds like Dividend Growth; consider it for long-term capital appreciation as opposed to the modest market outperformance.

Mid Cap Growth (FSMGX)

One of Fidelity's few style-specific funds (its market benchmark is the Russell Midcap Growth Index), the fund is orchestrated along the lines of Large Cap Growth (see previous relevant comments).

Mid Cap Value (FSMVX)

Another of Fidelity's few style-specific funds (its market benchmark is the Russell Midcap Value Index), the fund is orchestrated along the lines of Large Cap Growth (see previous relevant comments).

Mid-Cap Stock (FMCSX)

Mid-Cap Stock's portfolio focuses on domestic companies with market capitalizations similar to those in the S&P MidCap 400. The fund's charter does allow management to hold onto companies that grow beyond, or shrink below, this capitalization, however. But unlike some other companies' mid-cap vehicles, Mid-Cap Stock has stuck to its knitting through successive manager changes, and it continues to provide investors seeking a mid-cap stake with a solid, clearly defined capital appreciation opportunity. It's not quite a biblical tale, but this fund often engages in a battle of epic proportions, wherein it is this fund versus the S&P 500 Goliath: David (as shown in Figure 8.2) typically wins. The fund's diversification, excellent record, and evenhanded approach to the overall stock selection (i.e., no big home-run swings) remain core reasons to like it. My sense: Long term, this fund provides both a reasonable defense and a good offense.

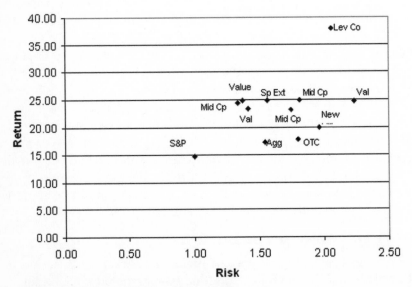

FIGURE 8.2   Mid-cap risk/return ratio

New Millennium (FMILX)

As you might expect from a fund named New Millennium, this fund's focus is on the future. When it began, back in 1992, the future didn't look particularly bright—but it looked a *helluva* lot better than the present. Then, the future, in the form of Y2K, became so bright that nearly every manager had to wear shades. (This fund delivered a whopping 109 percent return in 1999.) The ensuing sell-off of 2000 through 2002 saw this fund give up some ground, but hardly as much as it had recently gained. Since 2003, it's been gaining steam even as the market began to lose some momentum. Its charter is to invest in domestic (and some foreign) companies that look likely to benefit from the direction of social and economic change in order to achieve long-term capital appreciation. What will the next new millennium bring to this fund? While New Millennium's doors remain shut to most new investors, you can expect to find an open door to a technology emphasis complemented by a wide range of growth and value stocks in the fund—from electronics, PCs, and office supplies, to biotech, energy, industrials, communications, natural gas, and software. If you can stay the long-term course, New Millennium is an excellent, albeit more volatile, counterpart to Mid-Cap Stock. (If you can't invest in it, you can invest in OTC or Fidelity's Nasdaq Tracker (OneQ).)

Nasdaq Composite Index Fund (FNCMX)

I like the concept of this fund; a tracker of the broad basket of stocks representative of the whole Nasdaq, as opposed to OTC's focus on 200 or so stocks within it (and in contrast to the QQQ, the exchange traded fund that holds the largest 100 stocks in the Nasdaq). But I prefer to own the OneQ, Fidelity's sole exchange traded fund, which mirrors this index fund's mandate and holdings. Dubbed the "Nasdaq Tracker" by yours truly, there's simply no cost-, tax-, or trading-related advantage to owning the index fund version over the ETF. In fact, since there's an onerous 90-day redemption fee on the index fund, and none on the ETF, you'd have to be, how to put this delicately, more than a few cards shy of a full deck to opt for the index fund over the ETF. (If Fidelity gets its ETF act in order, and doesn't make the same mistake it made more than 30 years ago with regard to index funds—believing them to be a fad, which, as we now know, turned out to be a trillion-dollar mistake—and delivers more core market index ETFs as well as some active hybrids, I'd likely always side with the ETF over and above the index fund option. Note to Fidelity: Hey! Vanguard's already launched 14 ETFs; remember what happened when it launched 14 index funds—right, it built a trillion-dollar industry.)

Of course, that doesn't mean that you should buy either this index or ETF option unless there's a fundamental investment reason for doing so. For growth investors with a long-term investment horizon it makes sense to own a slice of the largest growth stock market on the planet. Expect tremendous volatility along the way relative to the stodgier S&P 500 Index, but relative to the QQQ or OTC, expect a slightly less lumpy ride. Typical top 10 holdings: Mr. Softy, Cisco, Intel, Amgen, Qualcomm, Google, Oracle, Dell, eBay, and Apple. While you'll also typically find 8 of these 10 in OTC and in the QQQ's top 10s lists, the fact that the tracker is significantly more diversified (more than 2,000 holdings versus 100, or in the case of Fidelity's OTC fund—see my comments that follow—just under 300), coupled with the fact that it has historically had no more than one-third of its assets in its top 10s lists, whereas the QQQ has nearly 40 percent, helps buffer that vehicle's higher volatility.

OTC Portfolio (FOCPX)

This fund invests primarily in over-the-counter (OTC) securities traded on the Nasdaq. But while small-caps accounted for much of the OTC market in the past, many of these companies are no longer so small—as far as their paper values are concerned, some are as big as they come. As a result, OTC Portfolio is now on average a large-cap growth fund. Unlike Fidelity's Nasdaq Tracker (which owns a broad basket of a few thousand stocks to replicate the performance behavior of the total Nasdaq market on any given day), and unlike the most heavily traded exchange traded fund, the non-Fidelity QQQ (which is a basket of the largest 100 stocks in the Nasdaq), OTC is an actively managed fund whose mandate is to outperform the Nasdaq. Historically, this fund has lived up to its mandate; but I prefer Fidelity's Nasdaq Tracker to it, or at the very least in tandem with OTC, to smooth out the overall volatility while at the same time making a long-term bet that the Nasdaq will continue to be the field where new companies are sown and grown.

Small Cap Growth (FCPGX)

This newish fund, launched in November 2003 together with Small Cap Value (see subsequent entry), invests primarily in what its name implies: small-cap growth stocks, in this case *technology stocks* (which tend to weigh more heavily in this small-cap fund than in the other Fidelity small-cap funds save one, Small Cap Stock). The fund defines *small-caps* as those companies that have market capitalizations similar to those found in the Russell 2000 and/or the Standard & Poor's Small Cap 600 Index. Among Fidelity's small-cap lineup, this fund will trend to be the

Table 8.1   Market Performance

	S&P 500	S&P 400	Russell 2000
YTD Cum	5.6	9.1	13.9
YTD Ann	1.8	3.0	4.4
1 Yr Cum	15.4	28.3	33.5
1 Yr Avg Ann	15.4	28.3	33.5
3 Yr Cum	50.8	89.3	98.5
3 Yr Avg Ann	14.7	23.7	25.7
5 Yr Cum	14.2	66.4	67.8
5 Yr Avg Ann	2.7	10.7	10.9

more volatile—but take a look at the long-term performance charts of small-cap stocks versus other market benchmarks (see subsequently). Long term, they're diamonds in the rough. The key is to find a company that has a long-standing history of being able to cultivate managers who know how to mine them. Hint: You don't have to look further than Fidelity; even if you do, you'll wind up looking back over your shoulder and returning to it. Please see Table 8.1.

Small Cap Independence (FDSCX) and Small Cap Retirement (FSCRX)

These two small-cap funds are run identically, unlike Small Cap Growth fund (see preceding), this fund's weighting can trend toward a blend of growth and value names, where you'll typically find a much bigger emphasis on health care, financials, and industrials, but not necessarily at the expense of technology. Like Small Cap Stock (following), these two funds can range across the growth and value style boundaries, but they have to stick to the small-cap corral as defined by companies with capitalizations similar to those found in the Russell 2000 Index. Note: Small Cap Retirement is intended only for qualified retirement accounts such as 401(k)s. Unlike Independence (formerly called Retirement Growth, see earlier), you can't just buy it in an IRA.

Small Cap Stock (FSLCX)

This fund tends to be distinctly different from Fidelity's other diversified small-cap funds in terms of its greater number of holdings and, typically, its greater sector weighting in technology names. Small Cap Stock invests in companies whose market capitalizations are similar to those in the Russell 2000 Index or the Standard & Poors Small Cap 600 Index. While this fund tends to be more growth-oriented than Fidelity's other small-cap offerings (even at times growthier than Small Cap Growth), it can and often has reverted to a "blend" of growth and value names. After doubling the return of the Russell 2000 Small-Cap Index in 1999 (42.6 percent versus 21.3 percent), it kicked assets again in 2000, ending the year up 11.8 percent while the Russell declined 3.0 percent. As the market recovered form its last recession, Small Cap Stock delivered a 45 percent return in 2003, but the Russell 2000 gained a bit more (up 47 percent), and the ensuing years saw it break about even with its benchmark. Still, I've liked this go-anywhere small-cap fund as one to buy (not watch) from day one.

Small Cap Value (FCPVX)

Since its November 2004 inception, the fund has earned its keep, besting the Russell 2000 Value Index. As expected, you'll find this fund weighted in financials, industrials, consumer, and energy names. The fund isn't afraid to make significant over- and underweightings against it above benchmark—this can add some volatility to the mix relative to it. Still, the fund will be unlikely to make a significant bet beyond its value box; but within it, technology is not off limits, just reduced versus the Russell 2000 Growth Index.

NOTE➤   Investors should be forewarned that Fidelity's small-cap stock funds have a 1.5 to 2 percent fee levied on the sale of shares held less than 90 days. Many Fidelity funds understandably impose short-term trading penalties, but I fail to see a legitimate reason to impose a minimum investment period on shareholders that is as long as this. Still, long-term investors would do well to consider this fund.

Stock Selector (FDSSX)

Stock Selector's charter gives its manager room to invest in common stocks of just about all shapes and sizes; what sets this fund apart from most other Fidelity growth offerings is its emphasis on computer-aided quantitative analysis, although old-fashioned fundamental analysis is also part of the management mix. Historically, this mix has been a blend of technical charting, quantitative analysis, and fundamentals. While the fund has marginally outperformed the market recently, it has lagged it noticeably in the past. As a result, Stock Selector has generally shown little reason to recommend itself in comparison with a Fidelity index fund (either Spartan 500 Index, my preferred Spartan Total Market Index, or Spartan Extended Market Index; see Chapter 16 for my comments on Fidelity's index fund lineup).

Tax-Managed Stock Fund (FTXMX)

Tax-Managed Stock Fund is a diversified growth stock vehicle with a special feature: It is designed to keep capital gains distributions, and thus the taxes incurred by shareholders, to a minimum. Launched in 1998, it had, for a while, a reasonable turnover rate of under 60 percent—not all that low, but suggesting that it was avoiding making capital gains distributions by not selling too many shares held for a gain. The fund also set out an onerous but rationalized way to discourage shareholder redemptions, levying a 1 percent fee on shares sold within two years of purchase (intended to reduce the need for the fund to sell shares). Trouble is, this fund hasn't taken its own medicine: Its turnover rate at the midpoint of 2006 was among the highest of any Fidelity growth fund—178 percent. Since this fund seeks to maximize after-tax returns, and some of its maneuvers (e.g., selling losing stock positions to offset winners) might not be ideal for maximizing nominal returns, it's obviously not intended for an IRA or other tax-deferred retirement account. Other disadvantages for this fund: The $10,000 minimum initial investment is four times the typical minimum for a non-Spartan Fidelity fund. The old adage, "Don't let the tax tail wag the investment dog," comes to mind.

Trend (FTRNX)

Trend fund is yet another Fidelity growth vehicle with the freedom to invest in all sorts of common stocks: large- to small-cap, growth to value, and even some foreign stocks (but mostly domestic). What sets Trend apart is its stated approach of momentum investing—the study of the speed and direction of company, industry, and marketwide price and earnings trends drives investment decisions. I prefer to invest in funds with either a fundamentally driven free hand or those with a specific investment style or capitalization range, rather than being left to the vague definition of what does and doesn't constitute a trend. Moreover, historically, this fund's performance hasn't *trended* to do well. Not that past performance is a guarantee of future results—but it sure looks like poor performance is this fund's trend.

Value (FDVLX)

Value fund invests mainly in U.S. companies whose stock prices appear cheap in comparison to the real worth of their assets, earnings, or cash flow. It has reliably remained in the mid-cap value to mid-cap blend style throughout its near 30-year history—but it can range afield of that cap range (higher or lower). While Value's commitment to "real" industries (those whose products go into the cars we drive, the objects we use, and the buildings that shelter us) feels solid and reassuring, its performance has generally been fair to middling, rarely besting its benchmark or losing to it by a meaningful number in any given year. I think this fund will experience some strong cycles, and as a core holding in the mid-cap camp it makes sense, but as a core long-term holding I'd opt for Spartan Extended Market Index or Value Discovery (see following).

Value Discovery (FVDFX)

The key distinction between this and Fidelity's other value funds is that it can wander in terms of capitalization range, growth and value picks, and concentrated or diluted bets. Historically, it's tracked between mid- and large-cap blend to growth ranges. But it's the mid-cap camp that it's most accurately tethered to. Still, a look at the fund's top 10 holdings at any given time since its inception tends to make it look larger-cap (JP Morgan, Pfizer, AIG, Altria, Verizon), but it has also typically held some mid-cap names in its top 10 list. Also, historically, the fund's top 10 holdings tend to represent under 20 percent of the fund's total assets. Top sector concentrations: Financials (but watch the weightings in this group versus that of its benchmark Russell 3000 value benchmark for signs of being bullish or bearish on this group), technology, health care, and energy names have been constants.

Value Strategies (FCPVX)

This fund has a wordy and fairly specific mandate: It focuses on stocks believed to be undervalued in relation to factors like assets, sales, earnings, or growth potential. Companies with lower-than-average price/book, price/sales, and/or price/earnings ratios fall into this fund's purview. The fund has hewed to a mid-cap value blend but is not restricted from owning larger- or smaller-cap stocks in equal or greater measure to its mid-cap holdings. This fund was closed to new investors for about a decade; then it suddenly reopened to them in the recovering phase of the 2003 market. But its longtime manager left the helm to one of Fidelity's tried-and-true value veterans, making the makeup of the fund increasingly indistinguishable from Value fund (see earlier entry). If this fund sees a manager change so that it is not cloned into an existing value-oriented fund's portfolio, consider it based on the merits of that change and the incoming manager's record. However, until that time, there's little to recommend it over and above Value.

The Fidelity Investor's Chart Room: Growth Funds

Please see Figure 8.3 and Tables 8.2 and 8.3.

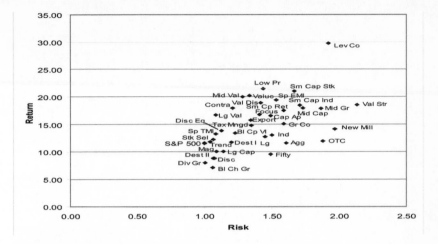

FIGURE 8.3   Fidelity growth funds risk/return chart

Source: www.fidelityinvestor.com

TABLE 8.2   Fidelity Growth Funds: Maximum Cumulative Loss, Maximum Time to Recovery

Fidelity Growth Funds

Maximum Cumulative Loss/Maximum Time to Recovery

	MCL	MTR
S&P 500	-44.7	NR
Blue Chip Growth	-51.9	NR
Blue Chip Value	-5.6	3
Capital Appreciation	-49.2	39
Contrafund	-33.2	21
Destiny I - class O	-52.6	NR
Destiny II - class O	-42.0	NR
Disciplined Equity	-41.1	42
Discovery	-42.9	NR
Dividend Growth	-32.5	38
Export & Multinational	-31.5	15
Fifty	-27.2	26
Focused	-57.1	NR
Growth Company	-68.4	NR
Independence	-54.0	NR
Large Cap Growth	-33.9	27
Large Cap Stock	-50.9	NR
Large Cap Value	-25.0	15
Magellan	-46.2	NR
Spart 500 Indx	-44.9	NR
Sp Total Mkt Idx	-44.1	43
Stock Selector	-46.7	NR
Tax Managed Stock	-46.7	NR
Trend	-45.1	NR

Source: www.fidelityinvestor.com

TABLE 8.3 Fidelity Growth Funds Correlation Table

	S&P 500	Blue Chip Growth	Blue Chip Value	Capital Appreciation	Contrafund	Destiny I - class O	Destiny II - class O	Disciplined Equity	Discovery	Dividend Growth	Export & Multinat'l	Fifty	Focused	Growth Company	Independence	Large Cap Growth	Large Cap Stock	Large Cap Value	Magellan	Spart 500 Indx	Sp Total Mkt Idx	Stock Selector	Tax Managed Stock	Trend	Aggressive Growth	Leveraged Co Stock	Low-Priced Stock	Mid Cap Growth	Mid Cap Value	Mid-Cap Stock	New Millennium	OTC	Spart Ext Mkt Idx	Value	Value Discovery	Value Strategies	Small Cap Inde	Small Cap Retire	Small Cap Stock
S&P 500	100	93	83	79	74	87	72	90	82	82	81	78	66	72	82	80	92	86	89	98	98	96	84	98	80	64	76	69	80	72	68	78	85	85	82	68	67	67	76
Blue Chip Growth	93	100	74	80	72	93	74	93	84	82	62	83	62	83	85	87	95	83	89	93	93	85	77	94	80	62	72	72	74	74	72	74	80	75	75	62	72	65	73
Blue Chip Value	83	74	100	67	67	76	62	81	67	83	63	74	73	57	79	72	70	82	81	83	82	81	78	84	59	61	71	64	80	68	67	67	67	85	77	53	63	60	67
Capital Appreciation	79	80	67	100	85	70	61	80	65	63	62	76	73	75	79	72	82	70	81	83	81	80	78	84	59	63	78	63	74	68	80	85	85	80	78	53	63	66	78
Contrafund	74	72	67	85	100	74	77	85	65	50	48	83	82	75	86	78	97	71	86	83	82	81	83	90	71	63	85	85	84	76	86	83	84	77	76	46	74	66	74
Destiny I - class O	87	93	76	70	74	100	84	83	60	65	50	72	73	54	81	77	91	66	84	77	77	72	71	80	55	53	74	46	54	52	47	75	57	61	57	42	50	51	56
Destiny II - class O	72	74	62	61	77	84	100	58	42	49	43	72	82	72	89	72	88	62	70	75	77	71	57	75	52	43	53	78	58	53	55	54	58	61	57	43	51	52	57
Disciplined Equity	90	93	81	80	85	83	58	100	67	65	65	83	84	89	86	89	94	82	88	82	82	83	62	87	70	76	84	69	84	70	48	75	80	82	91	48	51	52	79
Discovery	82	84	67	65	65	60	42	67	100	58	58	75	80	72	89	81	87	72	85	82	82	81	88	88	76	63	84	78	84	53	45	75	73	64	59	43	51	49	79
Dividend Growth	82	82	83	63	50	65	49	65	58	100	63	80	80	83	66	66	68	82	80	80	80	73	73	80	54	60	53	54	56	50	48	75	74	80	82	48	49	56	55
Export & Multinat'l	81	62	63	62	48	50	43	65	58	63	100	80	80	81	82	80	84	63	72	77	77	69	63	84	72	59	74	44	56	66	45	77	85	70	73	56	66	63	74
Fifty	78	83	74	76	83	72	72	83	75	80	80	100	97	94	97	86	88	75	84	87	89	83	83	87	70	71	74	78	82	79	79	80	82	80	82	70	75	73	74
Focused	66	62	73	73	82	73	82	84	80	80	80	97	100	83	82	80	81	73	80	82	86	86	83	86	71	66	69	80	80	73	75	80	85	80	77	73	73	66	72
Growth Company	72	83	57	75	75	54	72	89	72	83	81	94	83	100	89	90	94	72	89	92	92	82	78	97	83	66	72	78	73	78	79	82	79	73	70	56	71	67	80
Independence	82	85	79	79	86	81	89	86	89	66	82	97	82	89	100	86	88	75	86	83	84	81	83	89	77	67	81	87	88	86	89	79	81	83	80	66	70	73	82
Large Cap Growth	80	87	72	72	78	77	72	89	81	66	80	86	80	90	86	100	91	72	80	81	85	84	80	80	75	67	74	75	81	83	88	83	79	73	74	56	75	70	77
Large Cap Stock	92	95	70	82	97	91	88	94	87	68	84	88	81	94	88	91	100	80	91	90	90	84	80	94	80	65	76	83	82	84	86	79	82	80	78	60	67	67	78
Large Cap Value	86	83	82	70	71	66	62	82	72	82	63	75	73	72	75	72	80	100	86	86	83	84	87	83	64	60	64	67	68	66	58	67	67	85	78	58	72	73	77
Magellan	89	89	81	81	86	84	70	88	85	80	72	84	80	89	86	80	91	86	100	89	89	92	84	93	78	63	78	73	79	77	76	77	79	76	73	57	67	67	76
Spart 500 Indx	98	93	83	83	83	77	75	82	82	80	77	87	82	92	83	81	90	86	89	100	100	90	84	96	80	69	73	73	78	74	66	75	85	84	83	62	72	67	73
Sp Total Mkt Idx	98	93	82	81	82	77	77	82	82	80	77	89	86	92	84	85	90	83	89	100	100	96	86	98	84	69	80	79	86	82	75	79	89	83	83	65	77	70	84
Stock Selector	96	85	81	80	81	72	71	83	81	73	69	83	86	82	81	84	84	84	92	90	96	100	88	95	83	70	76	78	85	80	79	84	86	80	77	66	68	68	77
Tax Managed Stock	84	77	78	78	83	71	57	62	88	73	63	83	83	78	83	80	80	87	84	84	86	88	100	86	79	65	79	79	83	78	73	83	81	81	79	63	73	73	82
Trend	98	94	84	84	90	80	75	87	88	80	84	87	86	97	89	80	94	83	93	96	98	95	86	100	76	67	80	75	87	86	98	81	79	88	85	63	73	72	77
Aggressive Growth	80	80	59	59	71	55	52	70	76	54	72	70	71	83	77	75	80	64	78	80	84	83	79	76	100	53	87	86	88	70	78	86	84	73	70	53	79	77	77
Leveraged Co Stock	64	62	61	63	63	53	43	76	63	60	59	71	66	66	67	67	65	60	63	69	69	70	65	67	53	100	66	63	56	67	67	78	65	73	71	63	73	71	73
Low-Priced Stock	76	72	71	78	85	74	53	84	84	53	74	74	69	72	81	74	76	64	78	73	80	76	79	80	87	66	100	83	91	86	83	83	86	82	85	77	88	90	90
Mid Cap Growth	69	72	64	63	85	46	78	69	78	54	44	78	80	78	87	75	83	67	73	73	79	78	79	75	86	63	83	100	83	77	88	83	83	80	78	66	80	78	83
Mid Cap Value	80	74	80	74	84	54	58	84	84	56	56	82	80	73	88	81	82	68	79	78	86	85	83	87	88	56	91	83	100	82	80	88	86	75	83	79	88	79	79
Mid-Cap Stock	72	74	68	68	76	52	53	70	53	50	66	79	73	78	86	83	84	66	77	74	82	80	83	86	70	67	86	77	82	100	82	91	91	83	80	67	81	78	85
New Millennium	68	72	67	80	86	47	55	48	45	48	45	79	75	79	89	88	86	58	74	66	75	70	60	98	78	67	83	88	80	82	100	91	81	78	80	65	78	70	81
OTC	78	74	67	85	83	75	54	75	75	75	77	80	80	82	79	83	79	67	77	75	79	84	83	81	86	78	83	83	88	91	91	100	85	85	78	67	84	70	78
Spart Ext Mkt Idx	85	80	67	85	84	57	58	80	73	74	85	82	85	79	81	79	82	67	79	85	89	86	81	79	84	65	86	83	86	91	81	85	100	79	80	72	91	80	90
Value	85	75	85	80	77	61	61	82	64	80	70	80	80	73	83	73	80	85	76	84	83	80	81	88	73	73	82	80	75	83	78	85	79	100	94	77	80	73	84
Value Discovery	82	75	77	78	76	57	57	91	59	82	73	82	77	70	80	74	78	78	73	83	83	77	79	85	70	71	85	78	83	80	80	78	80	94	100	66	72	76	79
Value Strategies	68	62	53	53	46	42	43	48	43	48	56	70	73	56	66	56	60	58	57	62	65	66	63	63	53	63	77	66	79	67	65	67	72	77	66	100	72	75	73
Small Cap Inde	67	72	63	63	74	50	51	51	51	49	66	75	73	71	70	75	67	72	67	72	77	68	73	73	79	73	88	80	88	81	78	84	91	80	72	72	100	97	87
Small Cap Retire	67	65	60	66	66	51	52	52	49	56	63	73	66	67	73	70	67	73	67	67	70	68	73	72	77	71	90	78	79	78	70	70	80	73	76	75	97	100	87
Small Cap Stock	76	73	67	78	74	56	57	79	79	55	74	74	72	80	82	77	78	77	76	73	84	77	82	77	77	73	90	83	79	85	81	78	90	84	79	73	87	87	100

Source: www.fidelityinvestor.com

130

NINE

Fidelity's Growth and Income Funds

Fidelity's Growth and Income Funds Aren't Created Equal

G rowth.
  Income.
Growth *and* income.

Sounds like a right-minded approach to the dual-edged sword that all investors wield when they near or enter retirement.

And the fact that these two seemingly contradictory trajectories meet in one instrument—growth and income funds—sounds like a great deal.

After all, while the two objectives might appear to be at odds with one another, the truth is that, in tandem, they can actually serve to smooth out the rough patches in any given time period while at the same time enabling enough capital appreciation potential to coexist and grow your overall asset base.

But here's the catch: When investing in growth and income funds at Fidelity (or anywhere else), you should know that, for the most part, income is a secondary, and sometimes nonexistent, component of these funds.

Growth—income.

Income—growth.

What does growth plus income really equate to?

In fact, the vast majority of Fidelity's growth and income (G&I) funds, just like the vast majority of growth and income funds as a whole, have a

131

glaring hole when it comes to providing income. Instead, it's best to think of the "income" component of these funds as that piece of the mix that helps to reduce overall market risk. While it's true that some of Fidelity's funds offer an income component, they're the exception to the rule. Then again, most of Fidelity's growth and income funds offer investors a lower risk profile when compared to growth funds.

Fidelity Fund: The Fund that Launched 1,000 Ships

Fidelity's oldest fund, aptly named Fidelity, was launched in 1930; right into the teeth of the 1929 Crash. When the world was crashing around the American investor, Fidelity stepped up and launched its first of what would eventually become hundreds of its own fund ships. No small feat. No small fleet.

Ever since that bold and auspicious beginning, Fidelity has maneuvered to position itself wisely and well across U.S. markets and the world's markets. But while most investors correctly think of Fidelity as a growth fund shop, it's important to understand that at its heart, Fidelity is a Boston-based money management company that takes its fiduciary sensibility, stewardship, and shareholder accountability seriously. Seriously.

Today, Fidelity offers a wider range of growth and income funds to choose from than any of its competitors. Some are excellent. Some middling. A few really belong in the Select fund lineup (see Chapter 11). So, as in the case with every investment category covered in this book, be sure you look before you leap, since not all Fidelity's G&I funds are created equal, and some will be more appropriate than others for your particular objective.

Fidelity's growth and income funds run the gamut from the more aggressive, "pure" stock funds like Fidelity, Equity-Income, and Growth & Income (which invest the bulk of their assets in stocks but are classified as G&I funds due to their holdings' significant dividend income yield) to the less aggressive *balanced* funds, which invest in both stocks and bonds, like Balanced and Puritan. In fact, there's a G&I fund for nearly everyone, from younger investors who have more time than money on their hands to more conservative investors seeking moderate capital appreciation with reduced risk. But many investors overlook these funds altogether, mistakenly thinking that they're all either too aggressive or too conservative for their objectives and risk tolerance. This is rarely true.

But don't forget that the stock market isn't immune to declines, and growth and income funds don't always represent a safe alternative to growth funds. Like the stock market itself, growth and income funds, like any other category of funds, including bond funds, can hit pockets of turbulence that make you wish you'd never let your money leave the bank.

But while G&I funds may not be safe in the way banks, money markets, and mattresses are thought to be safe, they haven't exactly been risky, either. While many growth funds show double-digit losses in bear market years, and the most aggressive were down about equal with that of the S&P 500's own losses, the more conservative of Fidelity's G&I funds finished lost less than half that of market; in a loser's game, that's a win.

As with their growth fund siblings, the tale remains the same in the G&I group: The more aggressive the fund, the greater the risk and reward. Fidelity's most aggressive diversified G&I stock fund just so happens to be its oldest fund: Fidelity. In the trough of the most recent bear market it lost 22 percent in 2002. (Over that same time period, the S&P 500 lost 22 percent, too.) On the performance spectrum, Fidelity's more traditional growth and income funds, like Equity-Income (lost 17 percent in 2002) and, at the opposite end of the performance spectrum, Puritan (Fidelity's second-oldest fund and a balanced one at that), lost only 8 percent. The following year, when the market rose 28 percent, Puritan rose 22 percent, Equity Income rose 30 percent, and Fidelity rose 27 percent. Make no mistake, last year the defense of Equity-Income and Puritan has been a fundamentally better bet than the offense of Fidelity fund.

Balanced (FBALX)

Balanced does what its name implies; it's a diversified combination of stocks and bonds. As such, it's designed for the most conservative equity investors. In its "neutral" position, stocks comprise about 60 percent of the fund's portfolio and income securities (investment grade bonds and some cash) account for the remaining 40 percent. While it has some leeway to stray from these allocations, the bond/income component must remain at least 25 percent of fund assets. Balanced is just about as "aggressive" as Fidelity's other balanced fund, Puritan. The emphasis on risk aversion in both its equity and bond silos has made for a good risk-adjusted record, which in turn translates this fund into a sensible core holding for retirees and those nearing retirement.

Convertible Securities (FCVSX)

Convertible Securities is a moderately conservative way to invest in the equity market. It invests the bulk of its assets in, naturally enough, convertible securities. What is a convertible security? Simply put, it's a corporate bond or preferred stock that can be exchanged for a fixed number of shares of common stock in the issuing corporation. As such, its market performance tends to be midway between that of a bond and a stock. If the common stock goes down, the convertible is cushioned somewhat by its fixed, bondlike yield; if the stock goes up above the conversion price, the convertible goes up in value with the stock price. (Offsetting what would appear to be a best-of-both-worlds scenario, convertibles generally yield less than regular corporate bonds.) The fund has typically held converts from higher-growth, often mid-cap, companies in growing industries like technology, but has also always been capricious enough to move where the market's momentum lies, accounting for significant stakes in financial services names, when the interest rate environment is favorable to them, or energy names, when recovering economies place demand on supply. The result is that this seemingly staid fund can dance on the tabletops like the best of 'em; its relatively big tech weighting accounted for much of the fund's excellent 1999 return (44.1 percent)—as did it's energy weighting, which helped it surge 28 percent in 2003. When set against the backdrop of a bear market, the fund can also tap-dance its way to better returns: In 2000, the fund ended *up* 7.2 percent, while the S&P 500 *fell* 9 percent. The fund has historically been helped by timely moves out of media/leisure and into the health sector. Investors who can stomach a moderate dose of risk may want to hold on to this one.

Equity-Income (FEQIX)

Fidelity Equity-Income fund seeks to provide shareholders with a dividend yield higher than that generated by the stocks of the S&P 500. At least 65 percent of the fund's assets must consist of income-producing equity securities—generally large-cap value stocks—but the fund's charter gives management the freedom to invest the rest of the portfolio in all types of domestic and foreign securities, including bonds and lower-quality debt securities. In practice, however, Equity Income is essentially a stock fund; equities have virtually always accounted for over 90 percent of fund assets. Investors should note that this is a more conservative choice than the other "all stock" growth and income funds, with a pronounced emphasis on dividend-paying value stocks. The fund has basically tracked the market for large-cap value stocks with less risk than those stocks—and slightly less risk than the overall market. That's what I call value-added.

Equity-Income II (FEQTX)

Equity-Income II is similar to, but not an exact clone of, its namesake. Like its parent, the fund seeks to provide shareholders with a dividend yield above that generated by the stocks of the S&P 500. At least 65 percent of the fund's total assets must consist of income-producing common stock, but the fund's charter gives management the freedom to invest the rest of the portfolio in all types of domestic and foreign securities. Like Equity-Income, Equity-Income II is, in practice, essentially a stock fund, although the portion of the newer fund's portfolio holding equities has in the past few years been slightly lower, and its cash positions slightly larger, than that found in its elder sibling. This fund is a solid choice for many younger retirees, or to offset the risks of a near-retirement growth fund.

Fidelity (FFIDX)

Investors should realize that Fidelity fund is just as much a growth as it is a growth and income fund: Perhaps the only reason that it has been classified as a G&I fund is that its charter gives management leave to invest in bonds (including junk bonds). But the ground rules contain nothing regarding portfolio income, and it has been a long time since a significant portion of bonds have appeared in this portfolio. Guts and, over time, glory have been the hallmark of this fund. Launched in 1930, on the heels of the 1929 Crash, the namesake Fidelity fund has consistently proven to be a worthy choice. The fund has shown risks virtually identical to the S&P 500 Index, which makes Fidelity highly aggressive for a G&I fund but on the lower end of the risk spectrum for Fidelity growth funds. With a consistently high correlation to the S&P 500 and virtually identical returns, investors might want to consider Fidelity's index answer: the Spartan 500 Index fund (see Chapter 16 for my comments on this fund).

Growth & Income (FGRIX)

Fidelity's Growth & Income fund invests the majority of its assets in dividend-paying common stocks that show a potential for growth; its risk level is somewhat lower than that found in the Fidelity fund (see previous). This fund's charter sets no income requirement, but it does seek current income as well as capital appreciation. While in practice equities have long accounted for over 90 percent of its portfolio, Growth & Income tends to offer slightly more yield than Fidelity fund. Foreign stocks aren't typically foreign here (or in Fidelity fund, for that matter), but they're the blue chips of the established international markets of Europe and Japan and so have all the earmarks of the homegrown blue chips that populate its portfolio. This fund looks like a solid defensive choice, but I'd flip a coin, then opt for Dividend Growth (see page 116) or Strategic Dividend & Income (see following).

Growth & Income II (FGRTX)

Growth & Income II seeks high total return through a combination of current income and capital gains: Its portfolio is supposed to focus on dividend-paying common stocks that offer the potential for earnings growth. This younger sibling to Growth & Income (it was launched in December 1998, whereas it namesake broke ground in December 1985), due to its smaller size and slightly looser ground rules, has room to invest in debt instruments as well as non-dividend-paying stocks and smaller stocks with the potential for future income or capital gains. As a result, it can be the riskier of the two. That said, it still *trends* to a large-cap value or blend positions, typically with slightly more emphasis on the relatively conservative financial services sector and utilities and less emphasis on the growthier health care and technology sectors, but this has changed in the past and can change in the future.

Puritan (FPURX)

Fidelity's first balanced fund, Puritan is the second-oldest (1947) member of the Fidelity fund family and one of the nation's oldest balanced funds. Stocks and other equity securities form approximately 60 percent of Puritan's portfolio, with the remainder consisting of bonds and other fixed-income securities. The charter gives management leeway to diverge somewhat from this target, but the bonds and fixed-income securities mix must always account for at least 25 percent of total fund assets. Apart from just having different stock managers, this fund differs from Balanced primarily in that Puritan's bonds can be of somewhat lower investment quality (i.e., it can own some junk bonds). Puritan has been a solid choice for the most conservative equity investors for over 60 years—not a bad track record, and one few funds can boast. The fund, like Balanced (discussed earlier), is team-managed, dividing the responsibilities between stock and bond picking. While team-managed funds used to be a rarity at Fidelity, they're becoming more common in this group as well as in the international group (see Chapter 10). The fund has a solid history of eking out reasonable, but not market-matching returns while simultaneously eking out slightly higher yields without taking on measurably more risk. You can expect a less turbulent ride than on any of the all-stock equity-income funds, but you'll also have to give up a meaningful slice of their growth potential.

Real Estate (FRESX)

In my opinion, two of Fidelity's Select funds are masquerading as G&I offerings. One of these is Real Estate, a fund investing the bulk of its assets in the stocks of domestic and foreign companies involved primarily in the real estate industry. In practice, the fund mainly holds stock in equity real estate investment trusts (REITs), which are special property-holding companies that pass income through to shareholders without incurring taxes at the corporate level (much as mutual funds are corporations that pass through their income and gains to avoid corporate taxation). Most REITs have limited diversification, sticking to one sector (e.g., office buildings) or one geographic region, so it makes sense for most REIT investors to invest in a fund like this.

This relatively low growth, interest-rate-sensitive area was moribund while most stocks boomed in the late 1990s; then, when most stocks tanked, this fund sallied forth, delivering positive returns that knocked the socks off the stock market. In 2000, with many cities hitting historically low levels of office vacancy, Real Estate came back strong despite the early-2000 (i.e., pre-rate-cut) Fed policy. A friendly Fed tends to bode well for the area, but layoffs, consolidation, and recession tend to slam the door on this fund's profit potential. Still, it's worth revisiting the fund's recent past, which saw it buck the trend of a Fed that raised rates 16 times before this fund's performance cried uncle. That's because the Fed was trying to tame economic growth, something this fund tends to thrive on.

In 2000, when the S&P 500 fell 9 percent, this fund soared 31 percent. In 2001, when the market fell a further 12 percent, this fund gained 9.5 percent. In 2002, when the market crashed 22 percent, this fund continued to build, posting a 6 percent gain. And then, when the stock market soared 29 percent in 2003, this fund soared higher, up 34 percent. In 2004, when the market eked out an 11 percent gain, Real Estate turned in a 34 percent gain. In 2005, when the market gasped a last-breath gain of 5 percent, Real Estate finished up 15 percent. When do you not want to own this fund? In a slowing economy with rising rates or in a recession. But I still think for long-term investors, this fund makes sense—not simply because of its long-term return potential, but also because it's one fund where high yields aren't hard to find.

Strategic Dividend & Income

This fund is not only unique from an investment perspective, it's unique to Fidelity. No other fund family offers what can easily serve as the core or anchor fund for virtually any investor's portfolio. Mandated to hold 50 percent of its assets in stocks, typically large-cap value stocks, with the remainder divided among REITS (Real Estate Investment Trusts), convertibles (not the car, the security), and preferreds, this fund offers an excellent way to diversify your assets across four investment categories, the latter three of which tend to be underrepresented in most portfolios. With a short track record, it was launched in December 2003, the fund has already been able to demonstrate its strategic value. The fact that it has trended toward value stocks for its equity stake means that you'll need to see watch your portfolio's weighting in financials, which have been the lion share of this fund's past stock positioning and are typically the largest position in most large-cap value funds (which you may already own). It has been a core holding in my newsletter's G&I portfolio since its inception.

Utilities (FIUIX)

This is the other one of the two Fidelity Select funds that I think are masquerading as G&I offerings (see my previous comments on Real Estate). Utilities is a fund that invests the bulk of its portfolio in the securities of utility companies, ranging from cable service providers to gas companies to telephone companies. The fund seeks to buy utility companies offering the potential for capital gains in addition to their income stream. This is not your run-of-the-mill, plain-vanilla utilities fund, as the historical performance divergence between the Lipper Utilities Index and this fund's performance tend to show. In general, with sector funds, it's the sector, not the manager, that matters most. The tricky issue here is that this fund invests in the stocks of utility companies ranging from stodgier gas and electric to higher-growth cable and telephone companies. The fund's potential performance strength will likely switch on, thanks to its heavy telephone, and even cellular, company connections in growthy environments where the threat of rising rates is behind rather than ahead of it. Note: The yield, which many investors might mistakenly think would abound in this fund, has historically been little more than the yield of the S&P 500.

Fidelity's Asset Manager Funds

Fidelity's asset manager funds are created around two investment principles: team management and asset allocation. The former is self-explanatory. The latter, that performance is determined by the correct amount of allocation among the asset classes (stocks, bonds, cash), wherein managing that allocation is as important to the performance outcome as the underlying instruments, is a time-tested and proven thesis. This group, as a whole, represents a one-stop-shop approach to investing: Selecting one asset manager fund to meet your overall investment objectives is ostensibly all one need do. While this may sound overly simplistic, the factual truth is that these funds have a history of delivering. Their guiding asset allocation investment principle is notably different from the fund-of-fund approach used by the Freedom funds (discussed later in this chapter), which bank on the principle of fund selection and diversification.

Asset Manager Fund Lineup

Asset Manager: Income (FASIX)

Asset Manager: Income has a target portfolio mix of 20 percent in domestic and foreign stocks, 50 percent in bonds, and 30 percent in cash and short-term instruments. The fund's charter allows considerable room to maneuver, however. The weightings for stocks and bonds can move as much as 10 percent above or below their target allocations, while the cash/short-term portion can range as far as 20 percent above or below its benchmark. This fund is generally always already positioned defensively, but its current allocation can indicate a bullish or bearish belief by virtue of the more or less aggressive market sectors and bond types. The fund's longer-term performance has been, on balance, satisfactory for this type of vehicle, but I see little reason for investors, unless they are older retirees seeking current income, to own only this fund. Investors who have a specific short-term objective, like augmenting a college tuition fund that must be available within two or three years, should actually choose a more conservative investment (e.g., a short-term, high-quality bond fund or a Treasury note with the right maturity or, better still, Fidelity Cash Reserves). However, as a core diversifier for an income portfolio, this fund does have much to recommend it.

Asset Manager (FASMX)

Asset Manager has a benchmark portfolio mix of 50 percent in domestic and foreign stocks, 40 percent in bonds, and 10 percent in cash and short-term instruments. The fund's charter allows considerable room to maneuver, however. The weightings for stocks and bonds can move as much as 20 percent above or below their target allocations, while the portfolio's percentage in cash can dwindle all the way to 0 percent or grow to as much as 50 percent. Like other Asset Manager funds, this one can be positioned to be somewhat more defensive or offensive than its neutral benchmarks. The one-fund investment concept and team fund management work as well here as in the other Asset Manager funds. Still, outside of those few retirees who insist on keeping all their assets in a single fund, I don't think that many people can gain much by investing in this fund alone. However, as a core diversifier for a growth and income portfolio, this fund does have much to recommend it.

Asset Manager: Growth (FASGX)

Asset Manager: Growth has a benchmark portfolio mix of 70 percent in domestic and foreign stocks, 25 percent in bonds, and 5 percent in cash and short-term/money market instruments. The fund's ground rules allow considerable room to maneuver, however. Stocks can range from as little as 50 percent to as much as 100 percent of the portfolio, bonds can range from 0 percent to 50 percent, and cash and short-term/money market instruments can range from 0 percent to 50 percent. As a core diversifier for a growth portfolio, this fund does have much to recommend it.

Asset Manager: Aggressive (FAMRX)

Launched in September of 1999, Asset Manager: Aggressive was the newest and last addition to Fidelity's line of asset allocation one-fund-does-it-all product line. The fund's charter establishes a benchmark portfolio mix of 85 percent in domestic and foreign stocks and 15 percent in income investments (bonds, cash, and short-term instruments). The fund has considerable room to maneuver, however. Stocks can range from as little as 60 percent to as much as 100 percent of the portfolio. Among the Asset Manager group, this fund has the highest portion in stocks. But it's the mid-cap blend-to-growth orientation that is both unique (the other Asset Manager funds' stocks are large-cap issues with a value-to-blend orientation) and uniquely well positioned for growth environments. As a core diversifier for an aggressive growth portfolio, this fund has less to recommend it than the others; aggressive growth investors have plenty of other, more focused Fidelity growth funds to select from, including some Select funds.

Fidelity's Freedom Fund Lineup

Originally launched in 1996, with subsequent additions, the series of Fidelity's Freedom funds are a concept born of the times—the times in which most people want to have their retirement cake and eat it, too, without ever having to shop for the ingredients or learn how to cook. As an automatic retirement savings vehicle, you could fare far worse; each Freedom fund is made up of an array of Fidelity funds, typically numbering a baker's dozen or more of them. As such, they're a form of investing framed as a "fund of funds."

Funds of funds for everyone—the idea behind the Freedom series—offer investors who truly don't want to think about investing a way through the forest to the total return tree. But I remain generally skeptical about any fund family's own fund of funds. Since they're managed by the same company that runs the underlying funds, I think the tendency would be to pare down a holding rather than label one of their own a "sell"; and I don't think we'll ever see the day when Fidelity recommends that investors bale out of one of its funds based on the poor past record of an incoming manager. On the positive side, this group's expense ratio is extremely low—so low that if you tried to replicate the funds in any given Freedom fund of funds, you'd wind up paying nearly 1 percent more than what you'd be paying if you just opted for a Freedom fund.

The series runs in increments of five years; and the underlying investment assumption is that you select the one Freedom fund that fits your time line to retirement, and then stock with it through to the bitter end. Each fund is designed to become more conservative each and every year, thus to ensure that the one you select is the one you can ride into the golden sunset. At the risk of not wanting to be overly redundant, I'll review a few of the Freedom series' fund of funds next. You'll get the picture of the whole bridge from the following stepping stones.

Freedom Income (FFFAX)

Freedom Income offers a relatively fixed, conservative portfolio mix of approximately 20 percent in Fidelity stock funds, 40 percent in Fidelity fixed-income funds, and 40 percent in Fidelity money market funds.

The fund lineup chosen for the Freedom Income portfolio seems quite reasonable. For highly conservative, retired investors who want to own one fund, it may make a sensible choice. In 2000, Freedom Income gave shareholders an acceptable 6.3 percent, and its longer-term performance has been, on balance, satisfactory for this sort of bond-heavy vehicle.

Even for many retirees, however, I think that Freedom Income's allocation is just too conservative. Even a 70-year-old needs enough growth to meet his or her needs for at least 15 years, and that's certainly more than this fund offers. As for investors who have a specific short-term objective, like having funds available to pay college tuition bills that will be coming due in two or three years, they should actually choose a more conservative vehicle (e.g., a short-term, high-quality bond fund or a Treasury note with the right maturity).

Freedom 2000 (FFFBX)

Freedom 2000 was created in 1996 for investors planning on retiring in 2000. Granted, we are beyond that time line today, but it's instructive of the fund's charter. The allocation of the Fidelity funds comprising the portfolio continues to grow more and more conservative with the passage of time. Ultimately, at some point before 2010, Freedom 2000's portfolio allocation will eventually converge with that of Freedom Income, at which time the two funds will probably be merged. For folks who retired in 2000, however, I think that Freedom 2000's asset allocation is just too conservative to meet long-term needs. Someone who retires needs to have a portfolio that will grow sufficiently to provide a steady inflation-adjusted income for at least 25 years, and that's certainly more than this fund can offer. As for investors who have a specific short-term objective, like having funds available to pay college tuition bills that will be coming due in two or three years, they should choose a more conservative vehicle (e.g., a short-term, high-quality bond fund or a Treasury note with the right maturity, or my favored pick, Fidelity Cash Reserves).

Freedom 2010 (FFFCX)

Freedom 2010 is intended for investors planning on retiring in 2010. As provided for in the fund's charter, the allocation of the Fidelity funds comprising the portfolio is growing more conservative with the passage of time. Ultimately, at some point between 2015 and 2020, Freedom 2010's portfolio allocation will converge with that of Freedom Income, at which time the two funds will probably be merged. This fund may serve some purpose for investors who are dead set against buying more than one fund and who never want to give their portfolios a second thought. But is the fund really the best choice for investors retiring in 2010? As the years roll by, the equity proportion of the portfolio will dwindle away to about 20 percent, an overly conservative allocation, in my judgment, for most under-70 retirees.

Freedom 2020 (FFFDX)

Freedom 2020 is intended for investors planning on retiring in 2020; as such, it's a model for a growth portfolio. As provided for in the fund's charter, the allocation of the Fidelity funds comprising the portfolio will grow more conservative with the passage of time. Ultimately, at some point between 2025 and 2030, Freedom 2020's portfolio allocation will converge with that of Freedom Income, at which time the two funds will probably be merged. This fund may serve some purpose for investors who are dead set against buying more than one fund and who never want to give their portfolios a second thought. But is the fund really the best choice for investors retiring in 2020? For those investors with 10 or more years to go before they retire, it's okay.

Freedom 2030 (FFFEX)

Freedom 2030 is intended for investors planning on retiring in 2030; as such, it's a moderately aggressive growth portfolio. As provided for in the fund's charter, the allocation of the Fidelity funds comprising the portfolio will grow more conservative with the passage of time. Ultimately, at some point between 2035 and 2040, Freedom 2030's portfolio allocation will converge with that of Freedom Income, at which time the two funds will probably be merged. This fund may serve some purpose for investors who are dead set against buying more than one fund and who never want to give their portfolios a second thought. But is the fund really the best choice for investors retiring in 2030? While having 86 percent in stock funds seems appropriate now, as the years roll by their proportion of the portfolio will dwindle away to about 20 percent, an overly conservative allocation, in our judgment, for most under-70 retirees. I also think that many investors would do well to consider a multifund portfolio (e.g., Dividend Growth, Growth Company and International Value) for now.

Freedom 2040 (FFFFX)

Fidelity's model aggressive-growth fund, Freedom 2040, was launched in September 2000 and is intended for investors planning on retiring in 2040. As provided for in the fund's charter, the allocation of the Fidelity funds comprising the portfolio will grow more conservative with the passage of time. Ultimately, Freedom 2040's portfolio allocation will converge with that of Freedom Income, at which time the two funds will probably be merged. But that time is a long way down the road—and the question for retirement-oriented investors seeking a fund-of-fund solution to their retirement goals is whether this fund fits the bill. I think it does, given its long-term, equity-focused approach. But I also think that many investors would do well to consider a multifund portfolio (e.g., Dividend Growth, Growth Company, and International Value) for now.

The Fidelity Investor's Chart Room: Growth and Income Funds

Please see Figure 9.1 and Tables 9.1 and 9.2.

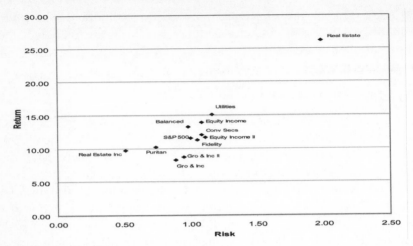

FIGURE 9.1   Fidelity growth & income funds risk/return ratios

Source: www.fidelityinvestor.com

Table 9.1   Fidelity Growth & Income Funds: Maximum Cumulative Loss and Maximum Time to Recovery

Fund	MCL	MTR
S&P 500	-44.7	NR
Balanced	-16.6	8
Convertible Securities	-28.2	17
Equity-Income	-29.7	16
Equity-Income II	-29.6	15
Fidelity Fund	-44.8	NR
Growth & Income	-34.1	NR
Growth & Income II	-34.3	40
Puritan	-16.6	13
Real Estate	-14.6	6
Real Estate Income	-3.6	4
Strat. Dividend & Inc	-3.9	5
Utilities	-61.6	NR

Source: www.fidelityinvestor.com

Table 9.2   Fidelity Growth & Income Funds Correlation Table

	S&P 500	Balanced	Convertible Securities	Equity-Income	Equity-Income II	Fidelity Fund	Growth & Income	Growth & Income II	Puritan	Real Estate	Real Estate Income	Utilities
S&P 500	100	83	60	93	92	92	90	83	87	23	12	34
Balanced	83	100	80	78	78	77	74	68	80	27	23	34
Convertible Securities	60	80	100	57	55	59	58	56	58	19	18	37
Equity-Income	93	78	57	100	93	89	89	80	95	18	11	37
Equity-Income II	92	78	55	93	100	86	84	81	87	20	13	41
Fidelity Fund	92	77	59	89	86	100	93	82	80	16	7	24
Growth & Income	90	74	58	89	84	93	100	81	84	23	14	35
Growth & Income II	83	68	56	80	81	82	81	100	70	20	7	32
Puritan	87	80	58	95	87	80	84	70	100	21	20	46
Real Estate	23	27	19	18	20	16	23	20	21	100	63	8
Real Estate Income	12	23	18	11	13	7	14	7	20	63	100	14
Utilities	34	34	37	37	41	24	35	32	46	8	14	100

Fidelity G&I Funds Correlation Table

Source: www.fidelityinvestor.com

TEN

Fidelity's International Funds

The World Is Fidelity's Oyster

Nowadays, it just about goes without saying that nearly every investor should have some portion of his or her portfolio invested in companies that are domiciled outside the United States. It's the only way to attain maximum diversification to protect your portfolio from those times when the U.S. stock market is in the tanks. But that's just the tip of the potential risk/return benefits we can get by crossing the pond.

International Funds Remain Key to Near- and Long-Term Growth

A global allocation in a growth-oriented portfolio, or for the growth portion of any portfolio, makes considerable sense, whether we're talking about the strategic opportunities offered by funds like International Small Cap and its sibling International Small Cap Opportunity offer, or the several reasons that have broadened my overall optimism for the global marketplace as such and in our ability to profit at home by investing wisely and allocating meaningfully abroad. Of course you'll need to keep a close watch on the risk/return relationship in each and every fund we own and in each and every region, sector, and capitalization range we're invested in, international funds included.

But guess what? Fidelity investors have a decided advantage when it comes to investing overseas. When it comes to international funds, nobody does it better than Fidelity.

Nobody.

Every single one of Fidelity's international fund managers outperformed its market benchmarks in 2005, and 9 out of 10 have done so year in and year out since they began managing our money. Credit Fidelity's commitment to its analysts and to analysis as such. In the inefficient capitalization ranges of established foreign markets, and in the inefficient marketplaces of the emerging markets, Fidelity's analysts rule the Street. Their better information, in the hands of the tech-savvy managers, leads to better execution, which in turn, time and again, has led to better performance. In fact, Fidelity had its first analyst on foreign soil when our forefathers were fixing bayonets, not portfolios. That kind of commitment pays off for investors like us.

This Globetrotter Remains Cautiously Optimistic

Aside from being confident about Fidelity's ability to navigate the often rocky shoals of the international markets, here are the chief factors contributing to my optimism about investing in international funds as such: the reemergence and emergence of a consumer class in Europe and Japan, across the Pacific Rim, and localized inside the borders of Latin America.

The growth of a consumer class, albeit in the early stages, looks familiar to our own—you just have to toss your head back more than 30 years to when we were transitioning from an industrial to a service-oriented economy, minting the largest consumer class in history and reaping the market-related benefits along the way. With cheap labor in high demand and increasingly more-efficient production commanding more manufacturing dollars from the United States, Europe, Japan, China, and the whole Pacific Rim look pitched to participate in the birth or rebirth of a global consumer class—whose demands for goods and services will not only increase the attractiveness of their respective domestic small-cap supply answers, but will also reverberate to our shores and our multinational companies' ability to answer the call.

But while I increasingly think that many investors, much of the time, should be diversified overseas, I don't think you have to or should spend a lot of time reading prospectuses for obscure Malaysian railroads and Russian pipe dreams. Indeed, unlike domestic larger-caps, individual investors generally have no business buying individual foreign stocks—at least not unless they're employees of a relevant firm or experts in a particular area or sector. Foreign markets' limited information, disclosure, tax

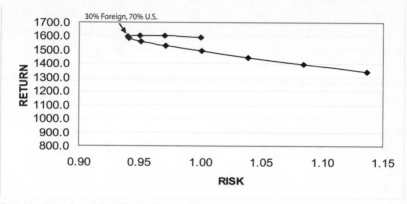

Shows risk and return for portfolios holding varying levels of U.S. (S&P 500) and foreign (Morgan Stanley EAFE) index investments.

FIGURE 10.1   Risk vs. return 1983–2006

Source: www.fidelityinvestor.com

Five-year returns: The EAFE Index of established markets (Morgan Stanley's Europe, Australasia, and Far East) up 58.9 percent, and the S&P 500 Index of large-cap U.S. stocks up 14.9 percent (and the Wilshire 5000 Index of all U.S. stocks up 23.6 percent). While you could argue that some of remarkable international gains versus our own domestic ones came from the foreign currencies' climb against the dollar, thinking that that was the sole or dominant cause for the outperformance would miss the fundamentally positive picture of the real capital appreciation that took, and is taking, place.

rules, political stability, and currency conversions continue to conspire against an amateur successfully dabbling in overseas stocks. For us, the active managers we invest in, supported as they are by their own experience and Fidelity's unrivaled analytical prowess, not only make for better prospects of gaining ground but also provide enough diversification to lose less when the going gets tough. Let's take a look at what I mean. Please see Figure 10.1.

The chart in Figure 10.1 illustrates that there are reasons to consider a solid weighting in this most efficient capitalization range, too. Chief among such reasons: A foreign position doesn't necessarily add to the risk of your stock portfolio. In fact, because foreign markets aren't closely correlated with the U.S. market, foreign positions of 30 percent or less almost always *reduce* risk.

Recessions, Like Gains, Are Global in Nature and Impact

Of course, it would be a mistake to think that there are no risks to investing abroad. In fact, it's also important to note the macro risk of recessions at home and their effect across the pond—and, increasingly, vice versa. The last recession (2000–2002) was global, hit most established foreign economies harder than the United States, and held a tougher grip on most established foreign economies even as we climbed (quite strongly) out of the recession. Lately, however, the established foreign economies have also been climbing out of their stagflation and recessionary holes— to the point where, just like at home, managing economic growth is where the risk lies.

Culture Shock Is a Good Thing

Confession: I was a general foreign-market skeptic, centered on the stodgy, bureaucratic, and overly government-controlled nature of most of the established markets (e.g., Europe and Japan), as I periodically illustrated with stories of thieving employees receiving bountiful severance payments and finance ministers skirting "rules" about spending.

But more recently (i.e., since 2000), it's been increasingly clear to me that the established markets of both Europe and Japan are showing sustained signs of overcoming their longer-term problems that stood to stifle growth. Indeed, their related fiscal, unemployment/welfare, and demographic/pension issues, while far worse than those we periodically voice worries about in the United States, remain a cloud on their horizons. But, much in the way major companies at home have had to undergo radical changes in the way they compensate employees and retirees, so, too, could you argue that countries like Japan and the United Kingdom in particular, and France far more reluctantly, are undergoing much the same form of weaning their citizens from government-subsidized jobs and retirement.

Orient Express

Japan, the world's second-largest economy, is, of course, a unified country (perhaps the most unified country on Earth), but its decade-plus of recession, weak recoveries, and weak political responses, followed by recession again, was a well-enough-established pattern to arouse skepticism over any predictions of radical improvement. But we're seeing radical improvement in Japan, throughout Asia, and across Europe in terms of growing or reinvigorating a consumer class, providing better and more transparent accounting methods and regulations, establishing regulatory bodies with real teeth and a willingness to bite, and witnessing governments inclined to promote economic growth in a measured and so potentially sustainable manner.

China's economic growth has been well documented and discussed. China currently consumes about 20 percent of world production in industrial metals, and its demand for metals and other commodities has grown about 50 percent over the past three years. Commodities, including oil, comprise the major area in which we've been seeing inflation over the past year, and China's growth, pretty much all by itself, explains that inflation.

Emerging Markets

If you can't drink the water, don't invest a dollar. Well, that may be a bit harsh, but I think it helps boil down to a common element regarding why any investor (myself included) who is wading in these very politically and economically volatile markets, had better have a very strong stomach. The areas I like best: Korea, Brazil, and South Africa. I think that when it comes to emerging markets, the Pacific Rim's growth looks far more sustainable than that of Latin America, where dictators continue to determine the course of political, human, and capital destiny.

Fundamentals

In short, foreign stock markets remain generally cheaper than the U.S. market relative to current fundamentals (like earnings); there are still some bargains in Europe's and Japan's basements; and many inefficient markets exist in which a good manager can outperform the averages with wise overseas stock selection relative to wise domestic stock selection. Indeed, Fidelity's international fund managers are quite consistently able to beat their market benchmarks; remember that they have a consistent history whereby every single Fidelity international fund manager (or nearly every one) bests his or her market benchmark.

Not All Fidelity International Funds Are the Same

International funds are largely named and defined by their geographic divisions. Still, a few funds have significant set style deviations from a straight benchmark (e.g., International Small Cap, Japan Smaller Companies, and Aggressive International, the latter's growth style being less notable than that of several funds on the domestic side), and one fund also holds bonds (Global Balanced), but there are no Fidelity international sector funds or even the sort of really aggressive leanings we see among some domestic growth funds (like OTC fund, which still has almost half of its assets in technology shares). There used to be four currency funds— they've been history for about a decade. And there are a few single-country or narrowly drawn regional funds like Canada and Nordic countries. We'll get to these exceptions to the rule, as well as the normative international funds, in short order.

Upshot

Before we turn to the individual funds, let me reiterate that I think that international diversification isn't simply a good thing for growth investors—I think it's a necessary ingredient for successful, long-term investing. True, in the 1990s, the U.S. market handily outperformed the international ones. But, if you look back over the history of the global markets, one fact stands out: That was the only decade in which relative outperformance was exhibited (and let's not forget that that performance was enhanced by the steroid of cooked books that led to a swift and sudden recession at the outset of this decade). If you were structuring a portfolio now that for some reason you couldn't touch for the next 20 years, you'd be wise to put, say, 20 to 30 percent in foreign stock funds. Such a move would be expected to slightly increase expected return while slightly decreasing expected volatility/risk (see Figure 10.1 which illustrates this point).

In recent years, being invested outside the United States has paid off even more handsomely. While the S&P 500 Index cranked out an average annualized return of 9.23 percent over the three-year period ended June 30, 2006, the EAFE Index (which is a composite of European, Australian, and developed Far Eastern markets) jumped by a whopping 21.13 percent.

Performance aside, investing outside the United States is also the only way to make sure you're filling your portfolio with the best companies. After all, the U.S. stock market accounts for only about 40 percent of the world stock market capitalization. Like it or not, America does not have a monopoly on fast-growing companies.

For most investors, the best way to invest in foreign companies is through a mutual fund.

Global stock funds (also known as *world stock funds*) invest in a combination of foreign and U.S. stocks. I generally avoid these funds. That's because it seems to make more sense to own a U.S. stock fund and an international fund rather than a fund that purports to rule in two very different markets.

International stock funds invest only overseas, in the stocks of several companies or regions. If you truly believe the economy is going global (as I do!), then you want to invest in an international fund.

Emerging-market funds invest in companies in countries that have not yet attained "developed" status. Some, in fact, invest in companies in countries that barely qualify as underdeveloped. While the returns can be good, they can also be bad—very bad. Be prepared for a bumpy ride.

Single-country funds invest in the stocks and bonds of companies domiciled in one country. The risk and volatility of these funds depends primarily on the country they invest in. While investing in a fund that focuses on Japan—which has well-established markets, industries, and accounting practices in place—may allow you to sleep peacefully at night; putting your money in a fund that focuses on Iraq is recipe for insomnia.

International bond funds invest in foreign government or corporate bonds. Since I am not a fan of debt, in particular foreign debt, I avoid these funds like the plague.

International Funds

Investing in a country-specific fund may sound too risky. As a result, many investors own a diversified option. As I've said before, this makes things simplest for us, and it gives the fund manager the most leeway to make stock-by-stock choices from the broader countries' menu. However, it eliminates our flexibility to choose areas because we are bullish on their prospects. And it may be close to impossible for a single fund manager to really understand all the companies he or she would be holding all over the world.

At the other extreme, we could own a bunch of single-country funds. This would give us maximum flexibility and leave the fund managers with relatively simple tasks. However, it would also increase fund expenses and increase the number of decisions we would have to make, and we'd be giving up any value-added we'd get from the fund manager's ability to pick countries. Further, the manager of, for example, a France or a Nordic fund may feel that he or she would have to own a company just because it dominates that country's stock market.

More conservative investors should generally hold more diversified international funds (if any), whereas more aggressive investors should take the middle ground of holding regional funds. For Europe, especially since it is an increasingly integrated economy, it really makes sense to buy a Europe-wide fund and to let the manager study the region and make his or her country bets. In the case of the Pacific Basin, we have a situation where one country (Japan) dominates the economy and also headquarters most of the region's multinationals. We can tweak our options: If we want only blue chips, we hold Japan; if we find the country's small-caps to have more growth potential, we buy Japan Small Companies; and if we're willing to move further afield, we choose Pacific Basin. Choosing a Southeast Asian fund in this area is far more radical than choosing Germany within the European area; it's a bet I might make in the future, but only with a small portion of assets and only for more aggressive investors.

Our model portfolios in Chapter 18 reflect the current foreign allocation and individual fund selection I like best for each portfolio's objective. But before you flip to Chapter 18, let's take a look at all the arrows in Fidelity's stellar international fund lineup. (No, Fidelity is not paying me to crow about its international funds. In fact, those who know me well know well enough that I've been clamoring for Fidelity to focus more on marketing to this group's core strength.)

Fidelity's International Fund Lineup

Fidleity's lineup of international funds is the best in the business, not just in quantity (number), but in terms of quality (performance). Let's take a look.

Aggressive International (FIVFX)

This fund seeks growth primarily from the common stock of foreign companies. In February 2000, the fund was renamed from International Value, reflecting the fact that it really hadn't been concentrating in value stocks. (Fido-philes will no doubt note that in 2006, Fidelity launched a new fund named International Value; see below for my subsequent comments under "International Value.") This fund, which tends to make significant sector and country bets and which tends to run with a concentrated portfolio of less than 100 names, is far from being a closet indexer. (In 1999, Aggressive International's then-heavy stake in Japan helped it to generate a 58.9 percent return, more than double the 27.2 percent of the benchmark EAFE Index.) Heading into the future, I like this fund for its unusually nimble and concentrated portfolio wherein even small-cap purchases can make a return impact.

Canada (FICDX)

Investing primarily in the common stocks of Canadian issuers, Canada fund's top sectors at the end of last year were finance, energy, and technology. Canada—whose market is about one-tenth the size of that in the United States—is *not* an insignificant economy and *is* the largest trading partner of the United States, but for this reason acts more like a part of the American economy, albeit more heavily affected by natural resources. Canada's whole economy is more linked than ours to the global natural resources markets, especially forest products, natural gas, and metals. This fund's cyclical play can often pay off as a short-term defense. Longer term, in a recovering economic cycle (both domestically and globally), the fund offers advantages similar to Select Natural Resources (see Chapter 11); choose this international fund for its tangential cyclical connection. (You could also buy this fund to bet on a surge in the Canadian dollar or some other major, most likely politically related, factor unique to Canada.) But I wouldn't.

China Region (FHKCX)

This "one-country, two-systems" fund, formerly called Hong Kong & China, now at least has a name that falls under one sun. Nevertheless, it still concentrates on firms based in Hong Kong, with mainland China taking a backseat to Taiwanese and even British-domiciled companies. As such, it isn't really a play on China's growth as much as a speculative bet on Taiwan's longevity. Since its inception, this fund has closely tracked Southeast Asia fund (discussed later in the chapter), in terms of both monthly movements (as shown by the two funds' R^2 relative to each other) and annual returns (see the Chart Room at the end of this Chapter for details).

Enter the volatility dragon. After losing 5.3 percent in the economic turmoil of 1998, in 1999 this fund shot up 84.9 percent. Then in 2000 it lost 17.6 percent; in 2001 it lost 10.5 percent; in 2002 it gave up 15 percent; in 2003 it surged 46 percent; in 2005 it finished up 11.5 percent; and 2005 saw it rise 14.5 percent. You get the picture. If you're looking for a money roller coaster, this might be your pick, but while I am a clear advocate of global investing, I remain skeptical of the fund—not because of the manager, or even because of the troubles of the multiparous political entities known as China, but because of the fund's misleadingly and narrowly defined regional focus.

Diversified International (FDIVX)

This fund normally invests most of its assets in foreign common stocks. While the fund can also hold a few U.S. companies, in practice virtually all of its stocks are based in Japan and the established markets of Europe. (The U.S. position is mostly just cash and equivalents.) As the fund's name implies, its portfolio tends to be significantly more diversified than that of, say, Aggressive International. Rarely does it hold less than several hundred issues.

The fund has a solid record of beating the EAFE (Morgan Stanley's Europe Australasia and Far East Index) benchmark of established foreign markets, not despite but precisely because of its successful lineage of its managers. In fact, the fund has *trended* to outperform the EAFE most years, with slightly less risk—that's a recipe for investment success in any language.

Emerging Markets (FEMKX)

You read my earlier quip: Don't invest in a country where you can't drink the water. But, truth be told, I don't drink the tap water here, either. (Poland Springs is my thirst quencher.) Emerging Markets invests primarily in companies in countries with emerging stock markets or in those that are classified by the World Bank as being either "developing" nations or ones possessing low- to middle-income economies. Fidelity has several ways to invest (or dare I say, *speculate*) in emerging markets. Dancing to a different beat, consider Pacific Basin (predominantly Japan, but with a smattering of the rest of Asia). Investing in the most promising emerging markets stocks wherever you find 'em—in Southeast Asia, Eastern Europe, and the Middle East—will pay off from time to time, but history has taught us that consistency and reliability aren't to be had for love or money in the Latin American markets. Hence, I prefer to invest where I can understand the inherent risks of the potentially more lucrative (i.e., mid- and small-cap) side of the world's established international markets.

Emerging Markets' country diversification helps buffer some of the single-country blowups that are par for its course. But here's a caveat prologue: There was no emerging marketplace safe harbor from the 2000 decline, the year in which this fund lost 33 percent of its value. In 1998 it lost even more: down 41 percent. And in a matter of weeks in 2006, it lost more than 20 percent. Okay, the upside is that in 2003 it soared 49 percent; in

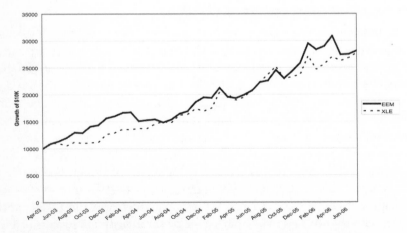

FIGURE 10.2   Emerging markets correlate to energy markets

Source: www.fidelityinvestor.com

2004 it climbed 23 percent; and in 2005 it soared another 44 percent. I still prefer solid ground to potentially submerging markets. While I always reserve the right to change my mind as market and economic conditions change, I am likely to do that far sooner for Japanese and/or European investments than for emerging markets, as healthy capital flows and wise government policies are far likelier to appear in the former areas. One other note: Emerging markets (and this Fido fund) trends with the price of oil and oil stocks. A look at the chart in Figure 10.2 helps illustrate this often-overlooked point. I mention it because when oil prices are rising, this fund ought to give you a multiple play on that price; ditto for the downside.

Europe (FIEUX)

Europe fund invests primarily in the common stocks of Europe, primarily the economically mature areas of Western Europe (including outlying Iberia, the United Kingdom, and Scandinavia)—but it can also invest in the postcommunist emerging markets of Eastern Europe and the geographically Eastern, but Western-oriented, Greece and Turkey. As Europe (the region) is attempting to unify, so this fund saw Fidelity's regional French, German, and U.K. funds roll into its fold in July 2000. (Why? With a total of just $50 million in assets and expense ratios of about 2.0 percent—which would be higher if not capped and paid for by Fidelity—the funds were money losers for Fidelity and far from ideal choices for investors.) Although Europe is the older of the two Fidelity Europe funds, its blue-chip portfolio oriented toward the United Kingdom can in fact lead to a higher beta profile compared to Europe Cap App.

While Europe can play a role in your portfolio as a way to hedge the U.S. market and capitalize on the broadening consumer base on the continent, I typically prefer a one-shop diversified international fund stop like Diversified International, International Discovery, or Overseas to cover my Europe and Japan bases.

Europe Capital Appreciation (FECAX)

Like Europe fund, Europe Capital App invests primarily in the economically mature areas of Western Europe. While there was initially some talk of this fund holding positions in Eastern Europe, it hasn't had any significant stakes there (on the whole, a fortunate thing for the fund's investors). While its name implies that Europe Capital App is a generally more aggressive alternative to Europe, it no longer shows significantly higher risk scores. All in all, the two Europe funds are broadly similar: The differences that do distinguish them stem almost entirely from the individual preferences of their particular fund managers. While this is a common enough situation among domestic growth funds, these two funds are the only regional choices on Fidelity's international side where this has held true.

Global Balanced (FGBLX)

Global Balanced fund invests in a mix of stocks and bonds (including lower-quality bonds). Bonds and other income securities always account for at least 25 percent of assets. The fund aims for a diversified selection of countries, including the United States (recently close to half of assets). The fund has done a creditable job of corralling solid risk-related returns in the past, and has held to this mark in the present, boding well for its future. But I think investors would do well to avoid this fund in favor of owning a straightforward international stock fund (e.g., Diversified International, International Discovery, or Overseas), a domestic stock fund or two, and, if desired, a plain-vanilla U.S. bond fund. I'm generally skeptical of the value of holding foreign bonds, and I'd certainly rather hold such components separately so I can have more control over my portfolio. If you have your money in Global Balanced and decide you want to sell out of one of its asset classes, you have little option but to sell out of the entire position and buy other funds separately.

International Discovery (FIGRX)

This fund was formerly called International Growth & Income (known affectionately as "IGI" among us Fido-philes). It invests primarily in foreign stocks. (While it used to keep about a quarter of its assets in foreign bonds, that changed when manager William Bower took over the fund in mid-1998. Under Bower's stewardship, the fund moved into an all-equity focus, which led to the name change to more accurately reflect its mission.) The fund's equity holdings still focus on somewhat more conservative, value-oriented, dividend-paying stocks than those found in, say, Overseas fund (just as Dividend Growth differs from Capital Appreciation, see Chapter 8.) This fund also seeks stocks with the potential for capital appreciation. The fund guidelines, and its diversified stock picks, make this venerable fund less vulnerable to the choppy international markets than, for example, Aggressive International.

International Small Cap (FISMX)

This fund is focused on real companies with real earnings and real consumers in their respective backyards of Europe and Asia, where consumer classes are emerging. With the bulk of the fund's assets invested in consumer discretionary and industrial names, and to a lesser extent with technology and energy-related names, *theoretically* this fund offers both a solid defense and a solid offense, as well as a diversification hedge against our own market's volatility.

International Small Cap Opportunities (FSCOX)

This is a new fund (launched in August of 2005 to capture the assets that were no longer able to rush into the closed International Small Cap), but like its sibling this fund focuses on the small-cap stocks in the established markets of Europe and Japan. If the first year is any indication of its lifespan, this fund will tend to be more volatile than its sibling not by virtue of preferring growth stocks over value stocks, but by virtue of the (fewer) number of holdings and greater concentration in its top 10 names. Like its sibling, I think this fund ought to play a growth role in nearly any investor's portfolio, with allocation being the guide; for an investor with 30 years to go before he or she retires, a 20 percent allocation ought to serve them well.

International Real Estate (FIREX)

This is a newish fund (launched in 2004) that seeks a novel way to approach the growing global existence of consumers who are willing and able to drive their local economies. In such an environment, all of the following will be in demand: offices, malls, construction, housing, and land.

International Value

A newer fund launched to widen Fidelity's global encompassment of investment ideas, this fund will focus on finding value where the manager sees it; don't be surprised to find both growth and value stocks in its mix. Its playing field is the international markets, but it will stick to the pitches of the established ones (Europe and Japan) for the lion's share of its capital appreciation pursuits. While it's too early to tell whether this fund adds value to the overall international lineup, it's not too early to think that it will cast its eye on mostly larger-cap names for its makeup.

Japan (FJPNX)

Japan fund, naturally enough, invests primarily in the stocks of Japanese companies.

In 1999, Japan fund rocketed to a 146.1 percent return, more than double the 61.8 percent return of the Morgan Stanley Japan Index. Then-manager Brenda Reed achieved these results by concentrating on blue-chip Japanese companies like Sony, Toyota, and Fujitsu. But 2000 turned out quite a bit differently. Suddenly, without warning, Japan's prime minister (and leading reformer) suffered a catastrophic stroke in April and died in May. The resulting political tension and uncertain future of reform have served to exacerbate an overall tough economic condition. The fund lost 37 percent.

Since the world's second-largest economy has been the victim of many starts and fits over the past decades, the key question remains Japan's ability to sustain its current recovery (economic, political, and regulatory) trajectories. Japan remains a question mark due to another factor: Its aging population demographics favor conservative saving over equity investing, and the uncertainties that attend restructuring tend to dampen consumers' willingness to spend. Still, there's more than enough reason to presume optimism. And while some of it stems from China's resurgence and Japan's role as the gateway for most exporters heading into China, there's a fundamental reason for better days. In early 2006, the Japanese savings rate began to dip—and for all the ballyhoo about the benefits of saving, the dip in the world's second-largest economy revealed that consumers were once again spending. In early 2006 we also saw the Japanese market take a company that had been falsifying its financial statements, Livedoor, down; a decade ago that scandal would have been swept under one keiretsu's rug or another. The regulators let the free market reign—exactly the kind of reformation we want to see. Finally, this fund has a consistent history of hunting for, and finding, good companies, good management, and good disclosure.

Japan Smaller Companies (FJSCX)

Japan Smaller Companies fund, naturally, invests primarily in the common stock of smaller Japanese companies. In 1999 this fund did even better than Japan fund, gaining an astounding 237.4 percent. Unfortunately, what goes up can come down just about as fast, and this fund lost 50.2 percent in 2000. In 2005 it rose 41 percent. But halfway through 2006 it had shed more than half of that gain. The caveats and reasons for optimism mentioned previously apply here in general, but this fund will be significantly more volatile by virtue of its cap-range focus and predilection for technology names. That latter point is not a small one; this fund can offer you a multiple play on our own homegrown Nasdaq—for good or ill.

Latin America (FLATX)

This regional fund invests primarily in the common stock of companies based in Latin America, especially Mexico and Brazil, and also Argentina, Chile, Colombia, Ecuador, Panama, Peru, and Venezuela. I think it's too tough to tell who's on first in Latin America. Investing in such emerging markets stocks will pay off from time to time. But history has taught me that consistency and reliability aren't to be had for love or money in these markets. Hence, I still prefer to invest where only metaphorical, not actual, blood is running in the streets—and where I can understand the inherent risks of the more speculative and potentially more lucrative (i.e., mid- and small-cap) side of the world's established markets. While I always reserve the right to change my mind as market and economic conditions change, I am likely to do that far sooner for Japanese and/or European investments than for emerging markets, as healthy capital flows and wise government policies are far likelier to appear simultaneously in the former areas, whereas Latin America remains historically prone to the vagueries of one dictator's version of socialism or another's.

New Markets Income (FNMIX)

Interest rate risk. Credit risk. Call risk. Political risk. There's one reason why I'd typically prefer not to own this fund: I don't like investing in foreign debt, especially in less-developed countries. But the fact that typically most of the fund is in foreign debt that's denominated in U.S. dollars means there's virtually no currency risk. And the fund's high current yield may continue to reward over and against its market risks. Just remember that there are other ways to invest in high yield without going abroad: Capital & Income (see Chapter 12) and the newer Leveraged Company Stock (which owns stock in the kinds of companies that issue high-yield bonds, see Chapter 8) look ripe for investing in when in a recovering economy. I continue to think that most investors will be better served in the more liquid equity markets of established international marketplaces rather than by loading their portfolios with debt-related instruments, especially those from emerging markets. But for the aggressive investor, this limb looks less shaky than it has in the past. Climb at your own risk.

Nordic Countries (FNORX)

This regional fund invests primarily in the common stocks of companies based in Denmark, Finland, Norway, and Sweden. The fund has fared relatively better than its benchmarks FT/S&P-A-Nordic Index). Despite its volatile performance, there's little question that Nordic fund has done quite well since its 1995 inception. But can Scandinavia continue to show higher growth than the rest of Europe? Prudence suggests that most investors would be better off in a more diversified, and less volatile, Europe fund. But aggressive investors looking for a way to energize their portfolios might consider this fund, especially since it has a telecom focus (Nokia, Ericsson, etc.) that's likely to plug back into profits whenever telecom can patch into them.

Overseas (FOSFX)

Overseas fund normally invests primarily in foreign common stocks, with a diversified mix of mostly established-market countries. While Europe populates this fund's landscape, Japan tends to be the largest single country position. The fund has historically bested its benchmark EAFE Index, largely explainable by its modest overweighting in Japan. While Overseas still seeks growth, the fund is a more diversified and tends to be a slightly less risky alternative to Aggressive International (discussed earlier in the chapter). Because it pretty much sticks to the established markets, it makes a solid choice for many investors for one-stop international shopping. As a diversified global portfolio, it would also be a good foil to a regionally concentrated fund. With a 20-plus-year history to its name, Fidelity's original international fund has rewarded, and is likely to continue to reward, investors reasonably well.

Pacific Basin (FPBFX)

This regional fund, the broadest-based of Fidelity's Asian offerings, invests primarily in the common stocks of companies based in Japan, Australia, and New Zealand and the emerging countries found in Southeast Asia fund (Hong Kong, Indonesia, South Korea, Malaysia, China, Philippines, Singapore, Taiwan, and Thailand). While Japan has always been the fund's biggest holding, the position can actually fluctuate considerably year by year. The fund has had remarkable up and down years, but has always stayed ahead of its Morgan Stanley Pacific benchmark. Heading into the future, the key question for investors in Asia remains whether the Japanese economy can continue to overcome deep-seated structural problems and sustain the trajectory of its current recovery and whether China maintains its market-based case: As goes Japan and China, so goes the Pacific Basin.

Southeast Asia (FSEAX)

This regional fund invests primarily in the common stocks of companies based in Hong Kong, South Korea, Taiwan, Singapore, and Malaysia, and has also held smaller positions in Thailand, India, and Indonesia. In 1999, Southeast Asia fund experienced a fantastic turnaround. After losing money for two consecutive years it shot up 91.5 percent in 1999, beating its benchmark (the Morgan Stanley Far East Free ex-Japan Index) by almost 30 percent. All in all, 1999 must have seemed like a vindication to veteran manager Allan Liu, who has headed the fund since its 1993 inception. The euphoria was short-lived. In 2000, the fund fell 30.4 percent. On the other hand, its benchmark declined 36.8 percent in 2000, and so Liu once again showed market-beating returns. (In other words, we can't blame the manager for the decline.) In the recovery of 2003–2005, Liu repeated his pattern of outperforming his benchmark by a wide margin. This region has the potential for superior economic growth, and its future likely is bright. But investors must always keep in mind that this is a volatile market, subject to numerous political and economic risks—not the least of which is the fact that Japan, while not literally a part of the fund, is a heavy driver of these markets.

Spartan International Index (FSIIX)

Just as Spartan 500 Index fund tracks the S&P 500 Index, Spartan International Index fund tracks the Morgan Stanley Capital International EAFE (Europe, Australasia, and Far East) Index. This is basically all of the world's established markets outside of North America. To keep transaction costs down, this fund doesn't track every stock in the index as closely as Spartan 500 Index fund tracks the 500 stocks in the S&P Index, but it still has an R^2 (correlation) of 97 percent against the EAFE Index. Investors who are not put off by the fund's $15,000 minimum investment may find this low-cost vehicle (its expense ratio is capped at 0.35 percent) attractive. But if you're going to invest at Fidelity, whose strength resides in its deep pool of active-management talent, why buy an index fund? I think Fidelity's managers will continue to provide above-average returns over the long run. However, since this is a low-turnover index fund, it will probably continue to have relatively low taxable distributions. That may tip the scales in its favor if you're investing in a taxable (not an IRA or other retirement) account.

Worldwide (FWWFX)

Worldwide fund invests in the common stocks of companies based all over the world. As a global fund, Worldwide naturally has a very high U.S. position compared to most of Fidelity's other international offerings. Unlike Fidelity's other global fund, Global Balanced, Worldwide does not put significant assets in bonds. However, I still prefer the greater flexibility that comes from owning separate domestic and foreign positions. To my mind, combining, say, Dividend Growth with Aggressive International (both of which were discussed earlier) makes for a better play than owning just one (e.g., this) fund.

ELEVEN

Fidelity's Select Funds

Sector Funds for Active Traders and Long-Term Investors

Fidelity's Selects are undoubtedly its riskiest collection of funds. Because each Select fund invests in a *single sector or industry* grouping, and companies within the same industry often move together, most of the Select funds show much more volatility than both the market as a whole and Fidelity's diversified growth funds. However, this risk can be tamed, and these funds are suitable for many investors seeking longer-term growth.

In the first place, like the stock market itself, a diversified portfolio of Selects can have a lower volatility than any of its component holdings. That's because the various Select funds do not all closely track each other; often, when one is going down, others are going up. Of course, while it's possible to re-create the market as a whole by buying all the sectors that make it up, there would be little point in doing so when you can buy Spartan Market Index. However, Selects can prove useful in many circumstances.

First, you can build a portfolio primarily of Select funds, which is more diversified than any one fund (i.e., with enough diversification to bring down risk). By using Selects, you can tailor the portfolio to hold the sectors you like and avoid the sectors you dislike. (Of course, you have to have some confidence in your sector-picking abilities for such a strategy to make sense.)

Second, you can use one or a few Selects to diversify a portfolio that is otherwise overly skewed in a certain way. Perhaps much of your money is tied up in stock options in the company you work for, or you hold some funds or stocks that are heavily weighted in a certain industry or industries. If you're looking for a fund to add to your portfolio, you may want to be sure to buy a fund or funds that will not be adding even more to the areas you are overweighted in.

In either case, owning Select funds is really a substitute for picking individual stocks rather than a substitute for holding well-rounded portfolios. The question of whether to buy Selects then comes down to whether you have the time and expertise to pick your own stocks and whether the Select funds will have lower loads and expenses than a portfolio of individual stocks bought in a brokerage account. In many cases, unless you're a very knowledgeable investor with a large portfolio and a low-turnover trading strategy, Select funds will prove the smarter option.

Moreover, some Selects make sense for most growth portfolios: Electronics, Developing Communications, Health Care, and Utilities Growth chief among them. In fact, the latter two funds provide lower-risk ways to profit from long-term growth stories.

My Map of the Markets

Fidelity's no-load Select fund universe can also be used as a map of the market, reflecting both investment pitfalls and opportunities.

Of course, Fidelity's uniquely diversified sector fund lineup also presents the fledgling management track records of the managers we track. Although these funds are tied to their market sectors, and the managers have limited ability to overweight or underweight stocks or go outside their "sector box" (making the fund's sector at least as important as knowing who's running it, unlike with diversified growth funds), there's no doubt that Fidelity's Select fund managers, on the whole, add value. In fact, 7 out of 10 Select fund managers consistently beat their benchmarks; last year that number was 8 out of 10.

Are Sector Funds for Everyone?

Yes and no. No, most sector funds aren't for everyone, with their generally high volatilities and often high expense ratios. But yes, one sector fund, Health Care could be owned by any buy and hold investor, no matter what his or her risk tolerance or investment objective. As for the others, any one of them could be suitable for growth-oriented investors who might otherwise be considering individual stocks; and for investors looking to add diversification to a portfolio notably lacking in one or more sector, it makes sense to consider one or more of Fidelity's 41 Select funds.

Fidelity Sector Funds Go Global

There's one "sector" that has become a still silent but increasingly important ingredient to most Select funds: foreign stocks. Even Health Care has an 11 percent allocation to foreign stocks, Food & Agriculture is over 23 percent, and Gold is over 80 percent. Why bring this up? Select fund managers are, like us, pursuing growth on a global as opposed to a local scale, and in doing so, investors in such funds are actually building toward a global portfolio.

Closer to home, there's one Fidelity Select fund that many investors often overlook; but when exchanging in and out of Select funds, it's worth keeping in mind: Fidelity Select Money Market (FSLXX). This fund was specifically designed as a parking place for cash exchanged out of a Select fund. (For rules on exchanging Fidelity funds, see Chapter 2.)

Now, let's roll out Fidelity's Select fund map.

Air Transportation (FSAIX)

Select Air Transportation invests the bulk of its assets in national and regional airlines as well as foreign carriers. The fund can also hold stock in related businesses like express delivery firms and air cargo carriers, aviation training and service-related firms, manufacturers of aircraft and aircraft components, defense and aviation-related electronics, and communications service equipment.

Automotive (FSAVX)

Select Automotive invests the bulk of its assets in domestic and foreign auto manufacturers and auto parts firms dealing in new and aftermarket components, but it can also invest in auto parts retailers, tire and battery manufacturers, truck body and engine builders, and automotive-related machine-tool manufacturers.

Banking (FSRBX)

In the past two years, this fund has changed its name—it formerly did business as Regional Banks—and changed managers thrice. Select Banking invests in regional banks, national money center banks, and some foreign banking institutions, and it also holds some credit and finance company stocks.

Biotechnology (FBIOX)

Select Biotechnology invests primarily in biotechnology companies, but because most biotech firms are highly speculative ventures whose stock prices often ride on the fate of a single highly anticipated new treatment, it can also own more established pharmaceuticals like Schering-Plough to act as an anchor to windward. The fund tends to go its own way, with extremely low correlations against the market, reflecting the speculative nature of these stocks. Especially this past year, Biotech has actually tracked the technology funds more closely than it has tracked the thematically similar Select Health Care. The future for this sector looks healthy: Earnings are coming to light; buyout candidates abound; the completed map of the human genome means more potential drugs to be crafted; and patented medications remain the most lucrative way to profit from the longest-term growth story we have—our aging population. The caveat: Government price control schemes could dampen the trend to newer and more-specialized drug treatments. The cure: long-term investing.

Brokerage & Investment Management (FSLBX)

The stocks of many Fidelity competitors can be found in the portfolio of Select Brokerage & Investment Management, a fund that invests primarily in securities and commodities broker/dealers, mutual fund companies, and other investment-related firms. The fund also holds some insurance and other financial services companies. The number of American investors is likely to keep growing well into the new century: In the long run, the forces at work in the sector should make it more efficient and profitable.

Business Services & Outsourcing (FBSOX)

Select Business Services & Outsourcing invests primarily in companies providing services like payroll processing, computer services, credit and other human resources services, reservations and order taking, and consulting. Traditionally performed in-house, these tasks are increasingly likely to be outsourced. Because most of these companies make heavy use of computer databases to manage information and service, Business Services is considered a technology-related fund. However, while this fund holds firms that *use* computers and software to help businesses work more efficiently (e.g., Paychex does corporate payrolls, and IMS Health does data processing for health companies), all of the other technology funds concentrate in firms that *make* software, electronics, peripherals, and computers. Consequently, Business Services tends to move on its own and with much less volatility, whereas the other technology funds all move together.

Chemicals (FSCHX)

Select Chemicals invests in firms designing, manufacturing, and/or marketing a variety of chemical products ranging from commodity petrochemicals, industrial gases, fertilizers and pesticides, plastics, and resins and adhesives to more-specialized products such as food additives, paint, cleaning supplies, photographic supplies, and even pharmaceuticals. The low-P/E, dividend-paying nature of many of these stocks may continue to look attractive to tech-shy investors.

Computers (FDCPX)

Select Computers invests in producers of computers, naturally, but also in semiconductors, electronic components, data communications and telephone equipment, and software. This is another Select fund that is loosely tethered to its ostensible sector—it can also invest in *users* of computer technology (e.g., telephone and data services firms, even airlines). The fact of the matter is that it can be somewhat difficult to make clear distinctions between the portfolios of Select Computers, Developing Communications, Electronics, Technology, and even Software. Further, these funds (i.e., all of Fidelity's technology-related funds except for Business Services) all move up and down closely together.

Construction & Housing (FSHOX)

Select Construction & Housing invests in just about anything related to the built environment. The fund invests in general contracting, architectural, and engineering firms involved in domestic and commercial construction and civil engineering projects. It holds stock in modular and mobile home manufacturers, producers and sellers of building materials ranging from concrete to lumber, and manufacturers of earth-moving equipment, building tools, and other machinery. It invests in furniture, home furnishings, carpet, and appliance manufacturers. It can even invest in home-finance-related firms, notably Fannie Mae.

Consumer Industries (FSCPX)

With half of the American economy tied to consumer spending, it's hardly surprising that Consumer Industries is the most broad-based Select fund and has among the highest correlations (R^2) to the overall market. Indeed, it is debatable whether this can be considered a real sector fund at all. The fund can invest in any of the sectors held by the other consumer-related Selects: agriculture; food, beverages, and tobacco;

cosmetics; apparel; toys; sporting goods; small appliances and other consumer nondurables; advertising, broadcasting, publishing, and other media concerns; hotels, casinos, restaurants, and other entertainment and leisure firms; consumer services, retailing, and wholesaling companies; and even durables manufacturers like automakers, although these have usually accounted for only a modest portion of fund assets.

Cyclical Industries (FCYIX)

Cyclical Industries is, along with Consumer Industries, the most diversified member of Fidelity's Select lineup. It can invest in a broad range of industries (many of which have dedicated Select funds): air transportation, automotive, chemicals, construction and housing, defense and aerospace, environmental services, industrial equipment, industrial materials, paper and forest, and transportation. Despite its broad-based holdings, this relatively new (inception in 1997) fund has a small asset size and is rather hampered by its resulting expense ratio. (See Table 11.1 at the end of this chapter.) Cyclicals are by definition those stocks most susceptible to the economy's cycles. The stodgy, dividend-paying nature of many of these stocks may continue to look attractive to tech-shy investors.

Defense & Aerospace (FSDAX)

Select Defense & Aerospace can invest in firms manufacturing weapons and ammunition; ships and ship parts; aircraft, jet engines, and airplane parts; missiles, space vehicles, and satellites; electronics related to defense, avionics, and communications; training equipment; and satellite communications and other defense- and aerospace-related services. While this is sometimes considered a technology area, Fidelity puts it in the cyclical category. While the defense component of this sector appears to be mature, given the increasing mobility of the people around the globe the air travel side should continue to grow, although fierce competition within the industry will no doubt hurt individual players. Note that this fund has often shared several holdings with Select Air Transportation.

Developing Communications (FSDCX)

Select Developing Communications invests in the more-high-tech end of the media spectrum—companies involved in cable broadcasting, the Internet, software development, satellite services, and cellular phone services. The fund also holds manufacturers of data communications and computer networking equipment, TV and radio hardware, telephone equipment, computer equipment, and general electronics. In other words, it can buy just about any of the stocks held by the other technology firms, but it does have more of an emphasis on high-tech media (e.g., AOL), cellular (Nokia), and networking stocks. In the first three months of 2000, Dev Com joined the tech group's last-gasp rally. Then reality set in. The dot-coms were running out of money, and while market bubbles can inflate on nothing but hot air, they do have trouble ignoring impending layoffs and impending bankruptcies. Dev Com wasn't invested in the more insane Internet ideas, but the tech decline was painted with a broad brush, and like the rest of the sector, this fund slogged along through the spring and most of the summer, then fell apart in the fourth quarter. History lesson: Investors must remember that Developing Communications is a highly volatile, high-octane fund that can plug into *and* unplug from profits.

Electronics (FSELX)

Necessary parts. Necessary parts. Necessary parts. That's been the mantra for profiting in technology, and it will probably continue to be more profitable than, say, ideas for selling dog toys or groceries over the Internet. Select Electronics invests primarily in manufacturers of the electronic components used in products like computers and communications devices. It also holds some stocks in the manufacturers of finished products, creating some overlap between this fund and Select Computers (and others). The main difference between the two funds is that Electronics has a greater emphasis on manufacturers of components like semiconductors. But don't overlook the fact that this fund can leave you feeling giddy one day and depressed the next—witness 2000, the end of which saw a slowing economy and a bloated tech market crunching the blue chips, along with the rest of the sector. Still, the rumors of the PC's death are greatly exaggerated, as are any rumors that this fund is over and done.

Energy (FSENX)

Select Energy invests primarily in the major players in the business of extracting, refining, and marketing petroleum and petroleum-related products, especially gasoline and fuel oil. The fund also invests in gas pipeline companies, drilling and exploration concerns (companies that make up the bulk of Select Energy Services' portfolio), and related engineering firms. It can also hold producers of other fuels, like coal. (Clinton's mid-2000 intervention in what should have been a free oil market did diddly to cure the long-term issue of demand outstripping supply. While I like government intervention about as much as having a tooth filled, I thought it was particularly unconscionable to wield what is essentially a military reserve for politicking. And, by the way, the 30-day, 30 million–barrel deposit was sopped up quickly—and well in advance of the hardest winter months for the Northeast. To boot: The move didn't do much in the way of encouraging OPEC to self-regulate—we lost that battle a few year's back.) Bush hasn't made the same mistake, but the energy crunch has obviously accelerated. This is one way to fight back.

Energy Services (FSESX)

I call it the Levis Strauss approach: Sell picks and shovels to the miners and make your profit whether or not they strike gold. In this case, we're talking about black gold. Select Energy Services invests primarily in firms engaged in oil and gas exploration and drilling. It also invests in firms supplying oil field equipment and has some holdings in other energy-related firms. They're a volatile mix. In fact, it's one of the most volatile funds you can own (2.91 times riskier than the overall market, in fact). The reason: Energy prospecting is far more speculative than operating a major integrated oil company. Energy prospecting, while far more speculative than operating a major oil company, can be profitable. Bottom line: You want oil, you have to drill for it. You want to drill, you have to build for it. You want to build, you have to pay for it. Prospecting alone won't foot the bill. But tight supply, high demand, and three-fourths of the drills getting recommissioned will. Long term, this group provides a way to capitalize on global economic expansion when it gets back on track. Near-term, it's the supply/demand story that continues to brew a strong mug of Texas tea.

Environmental Services (FSLEX)

Despite its name, Select Environmental Services is not strictly speaking a "green" fund. It does invest in companies that clean up or mitigate pollution, recycle waste, and develop and/or manufacture equipment used in those undertakings. And it can also hold stock in just about any firm that has a cleaner way of doing business than its competition. But Environmental Services also invests in conventional trash haulers and waste-disposal firms. The case of Environmental Services is a classic example of Fidelity being all too willing to create a fund for every fad—the over-hyped sector it covers has been disappointing in almost every regard. Why? The 1980s "shortage" of landfill space turned out to be a temporary and mostly political problem. Landfill owners have not been able to reap monopoly profits, and waste removal has remained just another competitive low-tech business. Recycling also has largely proven unprofitable, as increasing supply led to much lower prices for recycled material. Still, cleaner energy is a powerful new trajectory that this fund, in small measure, can plug into.

Financial Services (FIDSX)

Select Financial Services invests in all types of financial services companies. This includes brokers and investment managers, insurance companies of all types, banks and savings and loans, and credit and finance companies. Banks continue to account for a large portion of the portfolio, with names like Citigroup and Bank of America typically found in the fund's top 10 holdings. Financial services firms will lag the market due to rising inflation and interest rates. Conversely, in a declining- or stable-rate environment this group can soar. Softening credits on personal and business loans may weaken the banking sector. Still, I like this area's defensive characteristics, as well as the potential for profit from interest rate cuts and/or industry consolidation.

Food & Agriculture (FDFAX)

Think defense. Besides the agricultural and food-processing businesses, Select Food & Agriculture can also hold stocks in beverage and tobacco companies as well as in restaurants and food retailers. (Historical perspective: In the go-go days of 1999, Food & Ag sank like a hard biscuit, ending the year down 20.5 percent, but when the froth blew off in 2000, this fund leavened 29.8 percent.) Food stocks ought to be the ultimate defensive investment, since we all have to eat no matter what the economy is doing. But even though the received wisdom is that these companies perform best in a recession, over the past 15 years packaged food firms have shown profit growth mostly by pushing through price increases. There's a limit to how far that trend can go, as generics and upstart brands can try to pick off market share by undercutting prices. I think this fund can play a role in most investors' portfolios. From here on out, I think there's some shelf space for total return improvement—but the real investment here is the defensive one.

Gold (FSAGX)

Formerly known as Select American Gold, this fund is something of an apartheid-era relic: Created as a "no South Africa" alternative to Precious Metals fund, Select American Gold invested in Canadian, American, and Latin American miners and refiners of gold, silver, and other precious metals. Now the need for South African investment to mitigate a moral dilemma has thankfully passed into history (Precious Metals was merged into this fund in early 2000). Gold has traditionally been seen as the ultimate defensive play, the reasoning being that should some global catastrophe throw us back into an economic Middle Ages, gold and silver will again be the only reliable media of exchange. A certain level of such fear occasionally brings big profits to shorter-term speculators, but if events really did put us back into a medieval economy, I doubt that owning shares in any sort of mutual fund would do anyone much good. And despite increased inflation coming from the energy markets, I wouldn't advocate putting gold stocks in your bomb shelter, either, although that would at least be more consistent with ultrapessimistic "gold bug" fears.

Health Care (FSPHX)

Select Health Care invests primarily in pharmaceutical companies, but it can also invest in biotechnology and in manufacturers of medical equipment and supplies, as well as health care providers such as hospital chains, nursing homes, and HMOs. Production of health care products is a high-growth sector that's relatively immune to a slowing economy. So the area is helped by: (1) good values after cyclical weakness; (2) high growth rates as the other major high-growth area—computer-related technology—was hemorrhaging assets; and (3) fears of recession (as well as higher energy prices and interest rates) limiting enthusiasm for more traditional sectors. In the past few years, HMO cost-control efforts have cut into the profit margins on many medications, but since new drugs are protected by patents, price competition in this area is much less important here than in other industries. Health plan administrators are also well aware that drugs are usually cheaper than surgery, long-term psychotherapy, or complications from chronic illness. The only major threat, overbearing government intervention, seems less likely or priced in. Still, for all the known reasons, not least of which is the aging boomer's desire to stay active longer, this would be my choice for the one Select fund to own if you could own only one.

Home Finance (FSVLX)

Select Home Finance invests in savings and loans, banks (including, despite the fund's name, commercial banks), and other credit and finance companies. It differs from Select Banking primarily in that it perennially has big positions in the government finance companies Freddie Mac and Fannie Mae, and it can also hold mortgage real estate investment trusts (REITs). Financial services firms typically lose ground to inflation and rising interest rates. But when rising rates are already factored into stock prices, and when the rate increases stop, this fund typically takes off. That, the sector's defensive characteristics, and industry consolidation will help the fund, but softening credits on personal and business loans likely limit any potential gains. Home prices are perhaps unsustainably high; home buyers are likely tapped out; and home financers are deeply in debt. Still, I like this area's defensive characteristics, as well as the potential for profit from future interest rate cuts and industry consolidation.

Industrial Equipment (FSCGX)

Select Industrial Equipment invests in the manufacturers of a broad range of electrical and mechanical equipment, including aircraft, autos, engines, and related accessories, especially for trucks; construction, oil field, and agricultural equipment; industrial and agricultural chemicals; electrical machinery, electronics, computers, and software; metal forgings and stampings; and pumps, tools, and office equipment. Value-oriented investors should take a look at this fund when the cycle is right. This fund would be a short-term play on a recovering near-term economy, but in the overall late stage of an economic recovery, this fund wouldn't make much sense.

Industrial Materials (FSDPX)

Select Industrial Materials invests in the producers and transporters of a variety of basic materials and semifinished goods with industrial uses. These include producers of petroleum products, chemicals and plastics, building materials, steel and other metals and their ores, containers and other paper and forest products, and the railroads that ship them. The fund has not held big positions in energy stocks (although fuel is certainly as much a basic industrial material as are metals and forest products), mostly because Fidelity has other options covering this area (i.e., Natural Resources, Energy, and Energy Services). This fund tends to lag from higher petroleum costs (which especially hit chemical producers) and higher interest rates (which hurt all cyclical and industrial sectors), but recover quickly once the negatives are priced in. The fund should benefit most when the world economic cycle turns to early-stage economic growth (rather than the near-term economic recovery fueled by Fed-lowered interest rates). When the former happens, this fund will be right on track.

Insurance (FSPCX)

Select Insurance invests in all types of insurance companies—its portfolio contains life insurers, property and casualty insurers, accident and health insurers, multiline insurers, and reinsurers. Fueled by, among other things, increased numbers of aging buyers who want to protect everything under the sun for themselves and for their kith and kin, this interest-rate-sensitive fund tends to be cowed by continued rate increases from the Federal Reserve Board. Flip side: When the rate hikes stop it tends to rally strongly. Rather than batten down the hatches, I'd still lift up this fund's prospectus. I like this area's defensive characteristics, as well as the potential for profit from interest rate cuts. The fundamentals are strong, and consolidation in the industry was and is a positive. It's a more defensive play than Brokerage—but combined, you could create your own financial services fund.

Leisure (FDLSX)

Select Leisure invests in all sorts of companies whose products and services play a part in our leisure-time activities. Most obviously, it holds stock in companies involved in lodging, gambling, amusement parks, restaurants, and travel services. The fund also invests in a variety of media companies whose businesses include Internet enterprises, broadcast and cable television, movie production and distribution, radio, advertising, and publishing. It also buys companies that manufacture items like sporting goods, toys, consumer electronics, and photographic film. Pushing the concept of leisure stock to the limit, Leisure even buys stock in retailers and cellular phone companies. Clearly, this is a sector ideally placed to benefit from good economic times. But beware Fed tightening and slower economic growth. Among consumer sectors, Leisure represents more discretionary outlay than food and other nondurables, so naturally, weakening consumer confidence turns into, say, less travel and less holiday shopping well before families cut back on the grocery budget. (In fact, retail is often considered a cyclical sector.) Media companies are somewhat less affected by consumer confidence. Slower economic growth doesn't bode well for revenue enhancement through advertising. Greater economic growth does.

Medical Delivery (FSHCX)

Select Medical Delivery invests in health care providers like hospital chains, nursing homes, detox centers, and HMOs and other health insurers. It also invests in other medical services, drug distributors and drugstores, and has held very small positions in other health-related areas, such as pharmaceuticals. Health care is a sector that's relatively immune to a slowing economy. The area was helped by (1) good values after previous market weakness, (2) assets fleeing the computer-related technology sectors, and (3) fears of recession (as well as higher energy prices and interest rates) limiting enthusiasm for more traditional sectors. Currently, the United States has more hospital beds than are needed, and both private and public payers are increasingly reluctant to subsidize empty beds, teaching hospitals, free care for the poor, and inpatient care for arguably ambulatory patients. Many major hospitals and HMOs are deeply in debt, with few prospects for climbing out of the holes they've dug for themselves. And there's always the prospect of the leaden hand of government overregulating this industry back into the ground. Still, HMOs that survived the bleak years of the late 1990s are leaner, meaner, and more profitable than before.

Medical Equipment & Systems (FSMEX)

Select Medical Equipment & Systems invests in companies that specialize in the research, development, manufacture, distribution, supply, or sale of medical equipment, devices, and related technology. The fund's portfolio generally combines a bunch of large-cap pharmaceutical firms that have substantial R&D divisions with the expected smaller and growthier manufacturers of surgical and other medical devices. Production of health care products is a high-growth sector that's relatively immune to a slowing economy. The area was helped by (1) good values after 1999's weakness, (2) high growth rates as the other major high-growth area (computer-related technology) was hemorrhaging assets, and (3) fears of recession (as well as higher energy prices and interest rates) limiting enthusiasm for more traditional sectors. I like this fund's concentration in the necessary parts of our medically intensive future. While near-term volatility is always a concern, I expect this area to produce profits for years to come.

Multimedia (FBMPX)

Lately, of course, even our cars might be considered to be media stations instead of old-school wagons. Select Multimedia invests in a wide array of media companies whose businesses include advertising, publishing, film production, cable and broadcast television, radio, Internet services, software development, satellite services, and even cellular phone services. This is a very interesting area of the market. Its holdings overlap to a considerable degree with Select Leisure (the two funds have an R^2 correlation with each other of 94 percent) and somewhat with Developing Communications (R^2 of 59 percent). True, with a beta measured at 1.06, this fund is not nearly as risky as the thematically similar but more speculative Developing Communications, but it is more aggressive than most nontechnology sectors, and is certainly not a defensive area. Media companies are, in general, moderately affected by consumer confidence, but can track more closely with technology stocks.

Natural Gas (FSNGX)

Select Natural Gas invests in firms engaged in natural gas exploration, drilling, pipelines, delivery, and/or retail sales as well as the manufacture or provision of related supply equipment or services. Although Fidelity puts this Select fund in its Utilities group, a good argument could be made for putting it in the Natural Resources group along with Energy and Energy Services. (Natural Gas has an R^2 correlation of 92 percent with Energy, but only 16 percent with Utilities Growth.) As with utility companies, the stock prices of firms engaged solely in the transmission or distribution of natural gas tends to move in the opposite direction from interest rates and winter temperatures. On the other hand, shares of companies that explore, drill for, or own gas deposits tend to move in the same direction as oil prices (and oil company stocks), in part because many exploration firms drill in fields containing both gas and oil, and many commercial customers have some flexibility in terms of consuming either gas or oil. Energy resources have been running low of late, and that's what an investor likes to hear: Tight supply. Sky high demand. Explosive returns.

Natural Resources (FNARX)

Select Natural Resources can invest in a wide variety of natural resources stocks and the firms that transport or market these products, but it has tended to emphasize the energy-related issues that form the biggest part of this market. In fact, you could often hold a mirror up to this fund's top 10 holdings and those of Energy and you'd swear you were looking at a fraternal, if not identical, twin. While this theoretically "broad-based" fund can invest in all kinds of natural resources stocks, it is basically an energy fund, with 66 percent in energy (down from 82 percent in midyear 2000); 15 percent in basic industries (e.g., Alcoa aluminum and International Paper); 12 percent in utilities (they are, after all, deliverers of energy in the form of electricity or natural gas); and just 1 percent in precious metals. I don't always rate this fund the same as Select Energy, despite the fact that it tends to hold many of the same stocks and is run by the same manager. Basically, I don't see the point of combining these sectors just because they all come from the earth, and when I like energy, I'd rather be a pure energy buyer.

Networking & Infrastructure (FNINX)

Launched on September 25, 2000, Networking & Infrastructure came out at a very tough time for technology and especially Internet-related stocks. The fund plummeted from the get-go and finished the year down 40.7 percent. Select Networking & Infrastructure concentrates on firms that make, sell, or distribute products and services that support the flow of electronic information, including voice, data, images, and transactions. These include telecommunications and network equipment; data storage systems; software; servers, routers, and switches; data encryption and other security software and hardware; Internet hosting; fiber optics; satellites, and cable equipment. The fund naturally has a lot of overlap with the other technology-related funds. I think that this relatively new kid on the Select fund block (the other is Wireless) is well positioned to capitalize on one of the strongest trends in the new economy. For long-term, aggressive investors, this fund is one to watch.

Paper & Forest Products (FSPFX)

Select Paper & Forest is one of Fidelity's more focused and obscure sector funds. It invests in firms that grow, cut, and/or process trees for lumber, paneling, paper and paperboard, and containers. It can also move a bit away from this sector to buy stock in makers of wood-harvesting equipment. Indeed, a clause allowing management to buy stock in companies using paper in their core businesses has in the past allowed the fund to invest in enterprises as far removed from the paper and forest products sector as newspaper publishers. Looking ahead, the performance of the paper and forest products sector will be shaped by a variety of countervailing forces. For example, while stricter environmental policy leads to increasing restrictions of logging on federal lands, those companies owning timber holdings should then be able to realize higher prices. Also, this group is up against a slowing economy and declining newspaper circulations (partly due to the Internet and increased TV options). However, falling interest rates may ameliorate damage to the housing sector, and the cheap, dividend-paying nature of this mature industry may continue to make it attractive to investors who've been burned by the Internet sector.

Pharmaceuticals (FPHAX)

Launched in June 2001, this fund differentiates itself from the diversified Health Care (see earlier entry) by virtue of its focus on drug companies, mainly large, but midsize and small, too. The fact that this fund weeds out everything but pharmas might be viewed as a weakness for long-term-growth investors who, naturally enough, ought to consider biotech, HMOS, and medical systems and equipment companies, too (which of course you can do either by owning Health Care or by owing the individual Select funds bearing the same names of each subsector). I like this fund's emphasis on what once was the darling of the growth investors' portfolios but has really been a dog for about a decade, meaning that these real companies, with real products, real market share, and real profits and earnings, offer both good value and positive growth potential. Investors should note that this fund's global profile is nearly 50/50 between U.S. and foreign stocks. (Another plus in my long-term-growth book.)

Retailing (SRPX)

Retailing invests in a variety of retail and wholesale companies: firms selling apparel, hardware and lumber, toys, car parts, books, jewelry, drugs, and general merchandise. The fund also holds convenience and grocery stores and even some restaurants (e.g., Wendy's). While Fidelity lists Retailing as a consumer sector, it's just as much a cyclical sector—and certainly more susceptible to economic cycles than, say, Food & Agriculture. The big retailing story continues to be the rise and fall of Internet shopping concepts, but this fund's holdings have included few Internet retailers. Weakening consumer confidence can hurt this fund for obvious reasons, and even bad weather can; a cold November and December tends to prevent holiday-shopping rebounds. Why buy this fund? The biggest persistent problem is that there are just too many retailers and too much retail in cyberspace competing for the same customers. There's also spiraling consumer debt. So, where will you find opportunity at a discount? Consolidation plays and increased profitability in the survivor's Web-cased packages.

Software & Computer Services (SCSX)

Software & Computer Services invests primarily in the publishers of prepackaged software. It also holds computer service firms as well as some manufacturers of computers, data communications equipment, semiconductors, and other electronics. While this fund is slightly less volatile than the more-hardware-oriented technology Selects, it will take its lumps when tech sells off. Whether it sticks to its knitting (pure software firms) or puts a few more assets into the manufacturers of computers (Sun), data communications equipment, semiconductors, and other electronics, this fund likely won't see smooth short-term sailing, but will likely see solid long-term results. The fund's fortunes almost always rest on better fourth- and first-quarter buying sprees from big business all the way down to the homely PC.

Technology (FSPTX)

Select Technology is the most broadly based of Fidelity's technology-related sector funds, although none of them have really restrictive portfolios.

Technology invests in producers of electronic equipment, including semi-conductors, computers and computer parts, voice and data communications equipment (including cellular telephones), and software publishers. Fund policies also allow management to invest in computer technology users like telephone companies, data service providers, and aerospace firms. The fund can range even further afield, buying stock in biotech and pharmaceuticals firms, areas in which Fidelity's other technology sector funds do not participate. Note, however, that this added bit of diversification does essentially nothing to reduce the fund's risks; its volatility is the highest in the Technology group (and behind only Gold and Energy Services). True, the technology story isn't just beginning. But, you and I know that the technology story is also far from over.

Telecommunications (FSTCX)

In addition to holding stock in long-distance companies and the regional Bells, Select Telecommunications invests in the sort of higher-tech concerns found in Developing Communications' portfolio, companies involved in cable broadcasting, the Internet, software development, satellite services, and cellular phone services. This fund also holds stock in manufacturers of voice and data communications equipment, television and radio hardware, computers, electronics, and software. Going forward, telecom will be shaped by the twin forces of convergence and competition, as the old distinctions between local and long-distance phone companies and between phone companies and cable and Internet access providers continue to erode. But while many of these companies are likely to fall victim to trends they cannot control or exploit, as a whole the sector looks poised for growth in our ever-more-connected world.

While this fund does invest in the sort of higher-tech concerns found in Developing Communications (cable, Internet, software, satellite, cellular, computers, and electronics), it also holds the traditional phone utilities. The deflationary environment, slowing product sales, and saturation have all been present and accounted for in current price levels. Going forward, as a whole, I think telecom stocks will redial profits in our increasingly inter- and Internet-connected world.

Transportation (FSRFX)

Select Transportation invests in transportation companies such as freight and delivery services, truckers, railroads, and airlines as well as in builders and manufacturers of transportation equipment, including trucks and automobiles, aircraft, ships, and railroad cars. The fund also holds stock in companies producing components that go into these vehicles, including jet engines, airframe parts, and truck and automobile parts. Transportation is still a stodgy, relatively low margin and low-growth sector. There are times when I'd rather own the companies that are producing what these companies are transporting. Note that the fund's relative emphasis on railroads (about as mature an industry as you can find) has kept it on a profitable track for several years.

Utilities Growth (FSUTX)

There are two Fidelity utilities funds: Select Utilities Growth and plain-old Utilities, which is grouped with its growth and income funds (see Chapter 9). While Select Utilities Growth is among Fidelity's lowest-risk Select funds, it is nevertheless somewhat more aggressively positioned than its non-Select sibling, which holds more electric companies. Select Utilities Growth invests in the whole range of utilities, including power, natural gas, and telephone companies, but the fund's portfolio has long been biased toward the higher-growth telephone and communications companies. Long term, Utilities Growth is plugged into solid, risk-adjusted profit potential. But the fund's telecommunications emphasis, which helped it to handily beat the industry average for utilities funds some years, can hurt it in others. I think that the same factors affecting Select Telecommunications (both negatively and positively) rule this fund's future.

Wireless (FWRLX)

Select Wireless concentrates on firms that make, sell, or distribute wireless communications services or products, including cellular communications, paging, mobile radio, wireless LANs, microwave transmissions, personal communications devices and networks, and related software. The fund has a lot of overlap with the other technology Select funds, especially Developing Communications. One of two newer kids on the Select block (the other being Networking & Infrastructure, discussed earlier in the chapter), Wireless opened to investors on September 25, 2000, a tough time for any tech fund to come out. The fund finished the year down 16.7 percent, in the process actually showing the second-best technology performance, after Business Services, for that year's fourth quarter. To catch the waves of our communications future—in cellular, wireless, and microwave communication devices and networks—plug this fund into a long-term growth portfolio.

The Fidelity Investor's Chart Room: Select Funds

Please see Figure 11.1 and Tables 11.1 and 11.2.

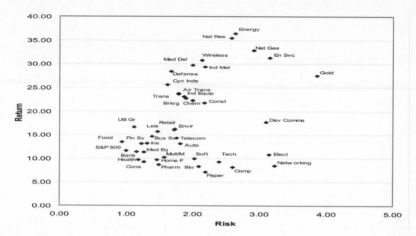

FIGURE 11.1 Fidelity select funds risk/return ratios

Source: www.fidelityinvestor.com

Table 11.1 Fidelity Select Funds: Maximum Cumulative Loss and Maximum Time to Recovery

Fund	MCL	MTR
S&P 500	-44.7	NR
Consumer Industries	-30.5	29
Food & Agriculture	-31.5	10
Leisure	-41.6	27
Multimedia	-45.4	38
Retailing	-38.7	21
Air Transport	-45.5	29
Automotive	-27.8	5
Chemicals	-18.4	8
Constrctn & Housing	-26.8	14
Cyclical Industries	-28.6	10
Defense & Aerospace	-26.5	8
Environmental Services	-36.7	65
Industrial Equipment	-39.9	20
Industrial Materials	-25.8	11
Paper & Forest	-23.2	15
Transportation	-28.8	13
Banking	-29.3	11
Brokerage	-38.3	16
Financial Services	-24.9	13
Home Finance	-30.5	7
Insurance	-28.7	5
Biotechnology	-66.0	NR
Health Care	-33.1	38
Medical Delivery	-36.3	12
Medical Equipment	-12.5	9
Pharmaceuticals	-33.5	40
Energy	-29.0	21
Energy Services	-47.9	38
Gold	-35.5	15
Natural Resources	-29.4	17
Business Services	-38.6	27
Computers	-80.2	NR
Devel Comms	-84.2	NR
Electronics	-79.5	NR
Networking	-88.1	NR
Software	-61.6	NR
Technology	-81.5	NR
Wireless	-77.8	NR
Natural Gas	-35.0	20
Telecommunications	-80.3	NR
Utilities Growth	-62.7	NR

Source: www.fidelityinvestor.com

Table 11.2   Fidelity Select Funds Correlation Table

Fidelity Select Funds Correlation Table

	S&P 500	Consumer Industries	Food & Agriculture	Leisure	Multimedia	Retailing	Air Transport	Automotive	Chemicals	Constr & Housing	Cyclical Industries	Defense & Aerospace	Environmental Svcs	Industrial Equipment	Industrial Materials	Paper & Forest	Transportation	Banking	Brokerage	Financial Services	Home Finance	Insurance	Biotechnology	Health Care	Medical Delivery	Medical Equipment	Pharmaceuticals	Energy	Energy Services	Gold	Natural Resources	Business Services	Computers	Developing Comm	Electronics	Networking	Software	Technology	Wireless	Natural Gas	Telecommunications	Utilities Growth
S&P 500	100	72	43	66	49	45	55	50	59	79	52	61	77	51	56	48	60	67	60	65	26	47	17	26	23	21	16	16	14	15	23	66	64	56	58	53	47	66	64	14	64	37
Consumer Industries	72	100	54	79	69	78	45	47	36	60	34	51	57	36	52	44	60	51	40	49	23	45	15	20	14	10	10	4	5	10	7	66	64	48	54	48	59	65	51	6	54	23
Food & Agriculture	43	54	100	40	40	61	28	30	34	33	19	35	28	24	30	29	15	20	11	18	7	23	13	18	9	5	11	4	5	9	7	24	14	22	18	20	14	17	15	9	17	18
Leisure	66	79	40	100	67	61	50	53	45	51	41	44	60	40	40	26	49	59	46	55	30	44	20	23	12	10	12	7	7	9	11	55	60	56	44	47	50	58	44	10	56	20
Multimedia	49	69	40	67	100	50	21	28	28	31	25	36	56	28	26	26	30	41	43	40	27	29	14	19	8	5	7	3	5	9	6	44	46	43	35	34	42	43	35	6	46	19
Retailing	45	78	61	61	50	100	36	51	28	55	29	31	49	25	28	20	30	43	30	42	19	28	15	18	7	6	8	4	5	7	4	49	40	40	30	33	41	43	29	4	41	13
Air Transport	55	45	28	50	21	36	100	36	29	51	29	51	44	44	35	38	74	38	30	31	15	31	10	12	7	5	6	5	7	4	5	47	35	29	31	29	35	37	29	5	40	13
Automotive	50	47	30	53	28	51	36	100	31	51	31	28	41	29	36	35	48	42	30	42	19	28	16	17	9	6	8	3	5	11	5	31	22	21	24	18	19	24	18	5	26	12
Chemicals	59	36	34	45	28	28	29	31	100	45	53	41	49	43	56	49	35	25	21	26	13	27	9	12	7	5	5	11	13	14	19	28	18	21	25	15	11	24	18	14	21	14
Constr & Housing	79	60	33	51	31	55	51	51	45	100	43	51	57	36	48	36	56	75	49	66	32	44	13	19	10	7	10	1	1	10	6	45	30	32	27	24	30	34	30	6	34	24
Cyclical Industries	52	34	19	41	25	29	29	31	53	43	100	33	48	45	63	61	35	20	17	21	12	24	15	20	7	5	5	13	15	24	21	27	27	27	27	24	21	31	23	15	23	22
Defense & Aerospace	61	51	35	44	36	31	51	28	41	51	33	100	56	55	50	44	66	30	25	28	13	37	13	17	8	6	3	2	2	6	5	40	32	27	29	24	27	31	26	4	39	22
Environmental Svcs	77	57	28	60	56	49	44	41	49	57	48	56	100	44	50	33	50	44	35	38	20	39	20	25	8	5	8	5	5	13	8	44	40	40	28	25	37	41	36	5	46	18
Industrial Equipment	51	36	24	40	28	25	44	29	43	36	45	55	44	100	52	42	42	20	17	18	8	32	11	13	5	4	4	5	3	20	11	35	23	15	30	24	18	31	24	14	26	15
Industrial Materials	56	52	30	40	26	29	35	36	56	48	63	50	50	52	100	64	40	26	23	30	15	35	21	17	10	7	7	7	9	18	23	30	28	24	29	23	21	34	23	17	27	13
Paper & Forest	48	44	29	26	26	20	38	35	49	36	61	44	33	42	64	100	30	20	18	20	11	29	17	18	9	5	5	2	3	14	18	26	23	24	25	18	17	27	19	15	24	14
Transportation	60	60	15	49	30	30	74	48	35	56	35	66	50	42	40	30	100	42	32	38	18	40	11	16	7	6	5	5	7	2	6	52	37	29	30	25	30	37	31	6	41	17
Banking	67	51	20	59	41	43	38	42	25	75	20	30	44	20	26	20	42	100	80	74	50	63	6	10	2	4	5	2	1	2	5	48	30	28	20	15	23	30	29	5	30	16
Brokerage	60	40	11	46	43	30	30	30	21	49	17	25	35	17	23	18	32	80	100	78	50	50	7	12	2	2	2	1	2	8	13	48	35	43	30	20	30	44	30	5	40	18
Financial Services	67	49	18	55	40	42	31	42	26	66	21	28	38	18	30	20	38	74	78	100	63	63	12	15	6	7	3	3	2	5	8	48	36	46	34	21	43	46	40	6	43	16
Home Finance	26	23	7	30	27	19	15	19	13	32	12	13	20	8	15	11	18	50	50	63	100	42	6	10	3	3	2	3	1	14	17	39	20	27	20	10	20	28	20	4	33	18
Insurance	47	45	23	44	29	28	31	28	27	44	24	37	39	32	35	29	40	63	50	63	42	100	8	11	4	5	4	4	5	15	14	44	33	30	28	11	24	36	36	6	42	15
Biotechnology	17	15	13	20	14	15	10	16	9	13	15	13	20	11	21	17	11	6	7	12	6	8	100	45	43	68	41	0	2	6	7	14	20	20	17	15	14	20	11	2	15	17
Health Care	26	20	18	23	19	18	12	17	12	19	20	17	25	13	17	18	16	10	12	15	10	11	45	100	60	60	60	2	2	2	1	11	6	7	7	7	5	8	7	2	6	11
Medical Delivery	23	14	9	12	8	7	7	9	7	10	7	8	8	5	10	9	7	2	2	6	3	4	43	60	100	30	30	0	5	2	2	13	6	13	7	7	17	20	6	2	18	12
Medical Equipment	21	10	5	10	5	6	5	6	5	7	5	6	5	4	7	5	6	4	2	7	3	5	68	60	30	100	41	0	1	5	5	26	24	24	21	23	21	28	16	5	12	18
Pharmaceuticals	16	10	11	12	7	8	6	8	5	10	5	3	8	4	7	5	5	5	2	3	2	4	41	60	30	41	100	6	0	7	7	8	2	3	2	1	6	6	8	12	12	13
Energy	16	4	4	7	3	4	5	3	11	1	13	2	5	5	7	2	5	2	1	3	3	4	0	2	0	0	6	100	96	8	89	7	2	12	6	8	2	10	8	90	8	16
Energy Services	14	5	5	10	5	5	7	5	13	1	15	2	5	3	9	3	7	1	2	2	1	5	2	2	5	1	0	96	100	8	89	6	3	10	5	6	0	12	7	85	6	13
Gold	15	10	9	7	9	7	4	11	14	10	24	6	13	20	18	14	2	2	8	5	14	15	6	2	2	5	7	8	8	100	33	17	5	15	9	12	10	13	4	20	5	8
Natural Resources	23	7	7	11	6	4	5	5	19	6	21	5	8	11	23	18	6	5	13	8	17	14	7	1	2	5	7	89	89	33	100	11	6	15	10	8	4	12	10	90	14	10
Business Services	66	66	24	55	44	49	47	31	28	45	27	40	44	35	30	26	52	48	48	48	39	44	14	11	13	26	8	7	6	17	11	100	56	52	56	56	59	67	44	10	40	10
Computers	64	64	14	60	46	40	35	22	18	30	27	32	40	23	28	23	37	30	35	36	20	33	20	6	6	24	2	2	3	5	6	56	100	78	91	80	64	88	67	10	33	8
Developing Comm	56	48	22	56	43	40	29	21	21	32	27	27	40	15	24	24	29	28	43	46	27	30	20	7	13	24	3	12	10	15	15	52	78	100	64	93	69	85	75	10	58	10
Electronics	58	54	18	46	35	30	31	24	25	27	27	29	28	30	29	25	30	20	30	34	20	28	17	7	7	21	2	6	5	9	10	56	91	64	100	69	46	88	67	10	33	8
Networking	53	48	20	47	34	33	29	18	15	24	24	24	25	24	23	18	25	15	20	21	10	11	15	7	7	23	1	8	6	12	8	56	80	93	69	100	71	80	75	7	48	6
Software	47	59	14	50	42	41	35	19	11	30	21	27	37	18	21	17	30	23	30	43	20	24	14	5	17	21	6	2	0	10	4	59	64	69	46	71	100	68	52	4	44	12
Technology	66	65	17	58	43	43	37	24	24	34	31	31	41	31	34	27	37	30	44	46	28	36	20	8	20	28	6	10	12	13	12	67	88	85	88	80	68	100	76	11	46	10
Wireless	64	51	15	44	35	29	29	18	18	30	23	26	36	24	23	19	31	29	30	40	20	36	11	7	6	16	8	8	7	4	10	44	67	75	67	75	52	76	100	11	61	22
Natural Gas	14	6	9	10	6	4	5	5	14	6	15	4	5	14	17	15	6	5	5	6	4	6	2	2	2	5	12	90	85	20	90	10	10	10	10	7	4	11	11	100	12	17
Telecommunications	64	54	17	56	46	41	40	26	21	34	23	39	46	26	27	24	41	30	40	43	33	42	15	6	18	12	12	8	6	5	14	40	33	58	33	48	44	46	61	12	100	54
Utilities Growth	37	23	18	20	19	13	13	12	14	24	22	22	18	15	13	14	17	16	18	16	18	15	17	11	12	18	13	16	13	8	10	10	8	10	8	6	12	10	22	17	54	100

Source: www.fidelityinvestor.com

TWELVE

Fidelity's Bond Funds

Fidelity's Hidden Strength

B onds.

James's bonds.

Fidelity's bond funds . . . or yours.

Let's face it, there's nothing particularly sexy, elegant, or exhilarating about bonds and the funds that invest in them. At least, not on the surface.

But like Yeats' swan, whose elegance above the surface is propelled by a tremendous amount of churning energy beneath it, bond fund managers are among the most active managers you'll encounter. Nowhere is this more true, and more valuable to you, than at Fidelity.

That's ironic, right, given that by and large, bonds are a conservative type of investment and therefore offer very limited potential for growth? Well, that's a stale definition of bonds and bond funds, many of which aren't as safe as you think, some of which are downright misleading. So the old saw that says that investors ought to invest their age in bonds and that they're generally more suited to retirees than to young (or young*ish*) can be quite easily stood on its head. As our model portfolios in Chapter 18 suggest, bond funds can play a role in any investor's portfolio— whether it's aggressive growth or pure income. The trick is to know which bond funds suit your portfolio's objective, and how.

If bonds and the funds that invest in them operate under a cloud of un-knowing, then it behooves us to disperse that cloud at the outset. Bottom line: We can all benefit from knowing a thing or two about investing in bonds. After all, you won't stay young forever. And as you get older—or as you get within a few years of shelling out big bucks for your first home or your seventh child's college education—you will want to inject a dose of diversification into your portfolio by investing in different types of bond funds that relate to your objective.

Remember, a bond fund's role in your overall portfolio doesn't have to be restricted to the income stage; some bond funds can add some total return value, too. Adding a bond fund (of any type) can help diversify your portfolio and, depending on the type of bond fund you select, can help smooth out the bumps on risky road of investing in stock funds.

As we go about our bonds' myth-busting course, there's another mistake many investors make: They think Fidelity isn't a bond fund shop or that the bond fund shop at Fidelity doesn't produce durable goods. The truth is just the opposite. Among Fidelity's hidden strengths, bond funds loom large. Its bond fund managers know no equal—whether we're talking about plain-vanilla Treasury-based bond funds or the ever-more-volatile high-yield (a.k.a. junk-bond) funds. In fact, Fidelity's bond fund group has a campus all its own—separate not only from the equity group by investment type, but geographically removed (to Digital Computer's old campus outside of Merrimac, New Hampshire).

The bond group members not only consistently earns their keep the hard way (by outperforming their relevant market benchmarks), they do so in a state-of-the-art environment created by and for them. It's the most advanced bond floor I've ever seen, right down to all the bond fund teams having their own live ITY specialist so that they can provide new analytical twists in real time (rather than sending a request to an IT department and drubbing their fingers on the desk for three weeks to get a response). As with every aspect of money management at Fidelity, no dime was spared in getting these bond managers what they want when they want it. After that, they're on their own.

But before we get ahead of ourselves, let me return to the basics and explain what a bond fund is. A bond fund is nothing more than a mutual fund that invests in bonds in companies or governments as plentiful and diverse as the stocks that stock funds invest in.

That was easy.

Now you're probably wondering what a bond is. That gets a little more complicated. But, not much.

Simply put, a bond represents an IOU issued by a public company or a government. Companies and governments issue bonds when they're looking for outside investors to help grow their business or pay for the construction of a bridge or highway, fund a school building, dam a river, or change a landscape (as with Boston's "Big Dig"). Most bond agreements require that the borrower make periodic interest payments and, on a specified date, repay the entire loan amount. When you buy a bond, you are essentially lending money to the entity issuing the bond. As such, you are entitled to interest and the eventual repayment of the loan amount (also known as the *face value*). Being able to reap the interest rewards, while at the same time safeguarding the principal value of your initial investment, is music to many investors' ears.

However, some bonds run the risk of default (inability to pay back the initial sum), and these bonds are cleverly monikered "high-yield" bonds (they're junk bonds)—since they do in fact issue eye-catchingly higher yields relative than the plain-vanilla and ultrasafe Treasuries. But their higher yield comes with the heightened risk of default. That risk can be mitigated by a junk-bond fund that diversifies away the default risk of a single issue by owning a basket of 100 or more junk bonds, while still delivering the higher yield. Smart move. And the good news is that Fidelity has some of the oldest and best junk-bond funds in the business (more on this in a moment).

Like a share in a public company, a bond is a negotiable financial instrument and may be bought and sold by investors right up until the time it is paid off. The price at which you are able to sell a bond depends on three things: the annual interest payments, the amount of time the issuer has to pay off the principal (known as the *maturity*), and the creditworthiness of the issuer. As a result a bond has a *face value*, which is the principal loan value, and a *market value*, which is what the bond is worth on the street, so to speak. While a bond's face value (also known as its *par value*) remains constant, its market value goes up and down depending upon whether the issuer's credit rating has changed or what has happened to market rates of interest since the bond was first purchased. Therefore, it's entirely likely you can buy a corporate bond for $800, even though it has a face value of $1,000. While knowing you're guaranteed to collect $1,000 when that bond matures may make it sound like the deal of the century, there's probably a very good reason it's selling at a discount. For example, current bond issuers may be paying higher interest rates. Or maybe the issuer was late on some other loan payments and, as a result, its credit rating lowered.

Like a stock fund, a bond fund offers the benefits of diversification. Since bond funds are portfolios of dozens—and sometimes hundreds—of bonds, if one of the issuers goes belly-up, it is unlikely to wreak havoc on your portfolio.

Bonds, bond funds, and investing in the fixed-income markets can be confusing. In fact, once you get beyond the bond buy-in rational (i.e., "they're safe," which, by the way, isn't true for reasons we'll get into), bond market investing is more than a mystery for most people. Truth be told, I think it's simpler to understand bond funds and the major factors that affect how they act than it is to understand stock funds and the myriad inputs that impact pricing every day. After reading this, I think you'll agree with me.

Bond Basics

The U.S. bond market, at more than $20 trillion, is about 50 percent larger than the U.S. stock market. As a consequence, there are plenty of factors that go into pricing bonds of all stripes, every minute of every day. And I don't pretend to understand them all, nor would I try to explain them all. I don't think anyone could do that, short of writing a Ph.D. thesis—and no doubt thousands of such theses have already been written. I will say, though, that I've been more than impressed with the depth of knowledge among Fidelity's top bond fund managers. That doesn't make them teachers, however. Frankly, I don't think that Fidelity has done an adequate job of educating its investors on bonds in general or on its own bond funds. If they have, well, people still don't get it.

Bond Yields Affect Bond Prices

It's likely that we've already passed the inflection point of record-low interest rates, meaning that rates are more likely to rise than to fall. But not all rates. You have to remember that rates at the short end of the maturity spectrum and those at the long end are affected by different factors. Long-term bonds, such as the benchmark 10-year Treasury and other longer-maturity bonds that you'll find in funds like Long-Term Treasury or Long-Term Corporate (see my upcoming commentary on these funds), for example, take their cues from inflation. When inflation is rising, yields begin rising (and bond prices begin falling)—and vice versa.

On June 13, 2003, the 10-year Treasury's yield fell to a low of 3.11 percent. At the time, consumer inflation was running just slightly over 1 percent. Producer inflation appeared to be negative, or actually deflationary. Then inflation began to come back. By mid-2006, the 10-year Treasury's yield had risen to 5.25 percent. The Treasury's yield will almost certainly continue to rise in periods when the economy strengthens and inflation continues to show itself. (The inverse is true, too.)

At the short end of the maturity spectrum are the three-month Treasury bills and various other short-term debt instruments. You would find the shortest of these in money funds and slightly longer-maturity securities in short-maturity bond funds like Short-Term Treasury or Short-Term Bond Index (see my upcoming comments on these funds). Because these securities are issued and redeemed over very short periods of time, or else they have aged to the point where they are about to be redeemed within months rather than years, inflation is not so much of a concern. But Fed policy is. And it's Fed policy that dictates where yields on short, short securities trade.

Bond Prices Effect Bond Yields

Understanding the basics on bond yields is as important as understanding the basics on bond prices. Interest rates and bond prices move *inversely*. If rates go up, bond prices go down, and vice versa. Why? Here's a simple way to think about it. Widget, Inc., issues a 10-year bond with a yield of 4.00 percent. Three months later Widget decides to sell some more 10-year bonds. But with the economy having grown, demand up, prices for raw materials rising a bit, labor costs up, and myriad other factors causing an increase in inflation, investors demand a bit more yield because inflation has made their dollars worth a bit less, so Widget issues its new bonds at 4.50 percent. Obviously, the new bonds are more valuable since they pay a greater yield. Owners of the older, 4.00 percent bonds would see their price decline, since their 4.00 percent coupon yield isn't worth as much as the new 4.50 percent yield. How much would the price drop? Taking time and other minor issues out of the equation, the price of the old bonds would sink to a level where that 4.00 percent coupon would generate a 4.50 percent yield based on the new, lower price. Remember, the yield is based on the interest being paid out divided by the price of the security. For the old bonds to have a yield that approximates the new 4.50 percent coupon yield on the new bonds, its price has to decline.

Beyond Bond Basics: Bond Investing

I had to get those basics out of the way before tackling the meat of the issue: how this affects you and your bond fund investments.

The way I'd like to approach this is to think about two types of investors—the person I'll call the "income" investor and the person who is the "total return" investor. Again, I don't expect to be able to cover every conceivable question you may have—but I should cover a lot of them.

The income investor is someone who wants monthly income from their bond funds and is not reinvesting any of that income back into the funds. The total return investor owns one or more bond funds as a diversification move. A certain percentage of total return investors' money is allocated to the bond market, in the same way that a portion of their money may be allocated to foreign stocks, cash, small-caps, or maybe REITs.

I think the biggest confusion, particularly at times when the bond market is making big moves, lies with the income investor. The reason is that the income investor often has investment objectives that are in direct conflict with one another. Remember what I said about prices and interest rates moving inversely? While income investors want that monthly income, they also don't like to see their capital lose value. When their income falls but prices are going up, income investors are unhappy because their income is down. When their income begins rising but the price of their bond fund shares are falling, income investors are unhappy again. The problem is that you can't have your cake (all the income you want) and eat it, too (never see your principal erode).

Most income investors own a fixed number of shares in a bond fund, established when they first bought into the fund. They aren't reinvesting any of their distributions, so the number of shares they own remains the same, year in and year out. As interest rates move up or down, their monthly income will move up or down. Most of the time, the changes are small. But after big moves in the bond markets, the impact can be felt for a while. Meanwhile, the value of that fixed number of shares is changing every day.

Even though income investors care almost entirely about their monthly income, they become uncomfortable with the fluctuations in their bond fund's price. But really, this should be a secondary consideration if your objective is income. Unfortunately, as I hear way too often, these income seekers don't like their principal to show a loss in value even if they're receiving the income they need.

If you are an income investor, you need to determine whether it's income you want, capital preservation, or some combination of the two. If the fund you are invested in today generates enough income for your needs, will you reinvest the "excess" as its monthly yield rises? If so, you should be able, over time, to maintain some capital equilibrium, or possibly generate some gains, because each dollar you reinvest will buy you more shares, which will pay you more income, the excess of which you can reinvest, and so on. But if you simply spend the additional income rather than reinvest it, then your capital will decline. There is no such thing as a free lunch.

Diversify Me

The "gains" or "total return" investor is in a different situation. This investor owns one or more bond funds to satisfy the desire, or need for, diversification. The level of diversification differs from investor to investor.

The question for the total return investor is not only which fund to own for balance, diversification, and total return, but how much. Here, investors have to make a judgment call on just how much risk they are willing to assume, balancing the desire for a greater total return with the desire for reduced loss in the event of a market drop.

However, this doesn't mean jumping into a money market fund when interest rates are rising and bond prices are falling. I'd love to be able to say this is easy to do, but this is nothing more than market timing. You've heard me say again and again that timing the stock market is a losing proposition. Well, the same can be said for the bond market. Yes, you could sit in a money market fund and use that as your fixed-income allocation, but what would it earn you? Over most periods a money market fund will earn far less than even a very short term bond fund. Of course, when rates rise and the bond fund loses money, the money market remains at its fixed price of $1 per share, paying out its tiny monthly dividend as regular as clockwork.

Rather than settle for the tiny return on a money market fund, you and I take measured risks by investing in bond funds where the risks are not as great as the potential returns. When I think interest rates are going to rise, I'll reduce exposure to long-term bond funds and increase exposure to short-term bond funds and maybe add some cash to the mix. But I won't simply sell everything and go to cash. We could miss a rally. And even if we didn't, at some point the bond market would settle down, or maybe turn up, and you and I would be sitting in cash trying to time our entry back into the fray. It just can't be done.

Bonds or Bond Funds?

Now, one last question arises. I'm often asked about whether it's better to own bond funds or simply to buy bonds and hold them to maturity. Much could also be written about bonds versus bond funds, but suffice it to say that owning bonds other than straight Treasuries means having a very large portfolio that allows diversification among many issues of many different maturities. You simply can't do that without committing a lot of money, time, and research into what you're buying. Plus, if you've ever bought bonds through a broker, you may have thought you were getting a good deal, but in all likelihood the broker was earning a nice commission from the sale, taking it straight out of your principal. You didn't see the charge, because it's hidden in the price you paid for the bond. (And try looking up the price to verify it. You can't.) I would much prefer that a Fidelity manager negotiate on my behalf with his or her multi-billion-dollar buying power. And for that, plus the diversification I achieve in a bond fund, I'll gladly pay the nominal operating expense.

That said, in 2005, Fidelity launched the only authentic supermarket for buying and selling individual bonds from several different shops; until then, you had to basically buy whatever your brokerage had on its shelves. Not only did this create a far more efficient mode of transaction, Fidelity also lowered the price of each transaction so dramatically that it simply no longer makes sense to do your bond bidding elsewhere.

Also, owners of bonds forget three things. First, while their interest payments will never go down, they will also never rise. Second, those interest payments need to be reinvested somewhere. You may have enough money to buy several individual bonds, but will your interest payments provide enough cash to buy another one without having to look for some odd-lot type of security? Third, while a bond's principal will be returned, intact, at maturity, that principal will be worth less due to inflation. The $10,000 bond you buy today, which matures in 10 years, isn't going to be worth the same $10,000 in 2014. If I'm using a bond fund and reinvesting my distributions, there's a good chance that I'll come out ahead of the straight bond portfolio over time.

As I said, there's plenty more to think about when it comes to investing in the bond market. But the basics are simple. Price and yield move in opposite directions. The more income (or even total return) that you want from your bond fund, the more risk to principal you'll have to take. You can cut your apparent principal risk and earn a stable yield by buying a bond rather than a fund. But inflation will take a toll—a toll that could be considerable on a 10-year bond.

Considering all the these factors, but before you take a look at the bonds or bond funds in your portfolio and make your own determination about where you think your money should be invested, we need to review your Fidelity bond fund options. As with Fidelity's stock funds, its bond funds come in many, many flavors:

Short-term bond funds invest in a mix of government and corporate bonds with maturities of one to five years. They are good if you are looking for a little income with very limited exposure to interest rate risk.

Intermediate-term bond funds generally hold a mix of government and corporate bonds with maturities of 5 to 10 years. They're good if you are looking to earn a little more income than you would with a short-term bond fund.

Long-term bond funds invest in a mix of government and corporate bonds with maturities of 15 to 30 years. They're okay if what you are after is a steady source of income.

High-yield bond funds (also known as junk-bond funds) invest in bonds below investment-grade quality that offer potentially high profits as a reward for taking more risk. Obviously, these can be fairly volatile. But they are also an excellent way to generate higher-than-average yield and some pretty decent returns.

Municipal bond funds (better known as "munis") invest in bonds of state and local governments. The main benefit of these funds is that they offer a tax-free income stream.

Single-state bond funds invest in bonds from only one state. Since interest earned from these funds is free of state (and often local) as well as federal income taxes, single-state funds often provide the highest tax-equivalent yields.

Foreign bond funds invest in a mix of established and emerging market debt instruments; some focus exclusively on established foreign market debt, others exclusively on emerging market debt.

In general, owning a broad mix of all the preceding types of funds makes more sense than placing all your chips on only one. This is even more true today with the advent of the global economy; long-lived as a rumor, it has finally become an economic reality—and the funding of global growth will, in large measure, come about thanks to the issuance of many types of debt instruments (a.k.a. bonds). In short, if you're investing in the foreign stock markets, it makes sense to consider owning the underlying debt of those markets as well.

Should You Invest in a Muni?

Basically, the answer to whether or not you should invest in a muni comes down to just one thing: your tax status.

If you pay a relatively low federal tax rate, it's probably best to avoid munis and look for some other fixed-income investment promising a higher return. If you are in a high tax bracket (say 31 percent or higher), you are likely to end up with more dividends in a muni fund than in a taxable bond fund.

Of course, that means you have to know your tax rate. Please see Tables 12.1 through 12.4.

Table 12.1   Single Individuals—2006

Taxable Income Over	But Not Over	Marginal Tax Rate
$0	$ 7,550	10%
7,550	30,650	15%
30,650	74,200	25%
74,200	154,00	28%
154,000	336,550	33%
336,550	—	35%

Table 12.2   Married Filing Separate Returns—2006

Taxable Income Over	But Not Over	Marginal Tax Rate
$0	$ 7,550	10%
7,550	30,650	15%
30,650	61,850	25%
61,850	94,225	28%
94,225	168,275	33%
168,275	—	35%

Table 12.3   Married Filing Joint Returns—2006

Taxable Income Over	But Not Over	Marginal Tax Rate
$0	$15,100	10%
15,100	61,300	15%
61,300	123,700	25%
123,700	188,450	28%
188,450	336,550	33%
336,550	—	35%

Table 12.4   Head of Household—2006

Taxable Income Over	But Not Over	Marginal Tax Rate
$0	$10,750	10%
10,750	41,050	15%
41,050	106,000	25%
106,000	171,650	28%
171,650	336,550	33%
336,550	—	35%

Here's a formula that will allow you to compare returns from a tax-exempt and taxable bond fund:

Tax equivalent yield = tax-free yield ÷ 1 – tax rate

Let's take a closer look at how this works. Suppose you have a choice of investing in a taxable bond fund that provides a return of 8 percent and a tax-free muni fund that generates a 6 percent return. If you pay federal taxes of 33 percent, the 6 percent municipal bond fund would provide a return that is comparable to a taxable return of 8.95 percent. Because the municipal bond's tax equivalent yield is higher than the return you would earn on the taxable bond fund, the muni fund makes more sense (8.95 percent versus 8 percent).

Now, if you pay federal taxes of 15 percent, the 6 percent municipal bond fund would provide a return that is comparable to a taxable return of 7 percent. Because the municipal bond's tax-equivalent yield is lower than the return you earned on the taxable bond fund, it would make more sense to invest in the taxable bond fund (8 percent versus 7 percent).

Fidelity's Taxable Bond Funds

Capital & Income (FAGIX)

Capital & Income invests mainly in lower-quality bonds, but may also hold preferred stock (which is actually more like a nonmaturing bond than common stock) and some common stock. Virtually all the bonds in this portfolio have below-investment-grade ratings or are simply unrated. In other words, Capital & Income is a junk-bond fund. While junk bonds come with much greater credit risk than investment-grade bonds do, investors can put that risk level into better perspective by looking at them as substitutes for stocks. And Capital & Income has lower risk scores than any stock fund except for the balanced growth and income funds, which also hold a lot of bonds. Investors should realize that the presence of "deferred interest" bonds in Capital & Income's portfolio means that the fund's effective yield is higher than its stated yield, assuming the issuers of these bonds make good on their interest payment obligations.

Floating Rate High Income (FFRHX)

A relatively new addition to the fund lineup, and a welcome one to the junk-bond fund niche, Floating Rate High Income parks at least 80 percent of its assets in floating-rate loans (lower-quality paper based on junk-bond securities), both domestic and foreign. The result: a beehive of risks (political, economic, and currency). But before you run in the opposite direction, consider the fact that if you know how to handle a beehive you can extract the honey without getting stung. Here, the beekeeper tends to smoke out a remarkable yield with less risk than Fidelity's other junk-bond fund offerings, with about half the turnover rate. (There is a redemption fee of 1 percent on shares held less than 60 days.)

Focused High Income (FHIFX)

Fidelity's addition of this junk-bond fund (in September 2004) rounded out its suite of junk-bond fund offerings and, in so doing, left virtually no stone unturned in the junk pile. This fund differentiates itself from the others in its junk-bond fund class by virtue of its focus on securities rated BB by Standard & Poor's, Ba by Moody's, or comparable ratings by other agencies (or, if unrated, assessed to be comparable quality by Fidelity). The caveats that apply to all junk-bond funds (Fidelity's and beyond) apply to this as well, but you can expect this one to fall between Floating Rate High Income (on the lower end of the junk-bond risk spectrum) and Capital & Income (on the higher end). Still, given that the biggest risk to junk bonds is default; the fact that every Fidelity fund is not only well diversified but well managed means that one or two blowups aren't going to make a dent in the fund.

Ginnie Mae (GNMA)

This fund invests primarily in mortgage-backed securities issued by the Government National Mortgage Association (GNMA). (In May of 1999, assets of the similar Spartan GNMA fund were merged into this fund.) In some ways, GNMAs, which pay a higher yield than U.S. Treasuries, resemble other high-credit-quality bonds. But that extra yield comes at a cost. Unlike Treasuries, GNMA bonds do come with some, albeit very low level, credit risk attached. Also, their interest payments are taxable at the state and local levels. Most problematic, however, is the fact that mortgage-backed bonds expose investors to the risk that, should interest rates decline, the holders of the underlying mortgages will refinance, leaving bondholders stuck with cash. (In 2007 we could be heading into a rate-cut environment (after more consecutive rate hikes in the prior two years than any time in history.) And just as maturities shorten when rates fall, refinancings slow and maturities lengthen when rates increase (again, just the opposite of what shareholders would like to see). In my opinion, the higher yields that GNMAs offer in comparison to Treasuries do not generally make up for this prepayment risk and the other disadvantages that these securities have compared to Treasuries. So, why invest in GNMA? When bond markets have been strong for long periods of time, which typically means rates have gotten as low as they have been in a while, significant capital appreciation in any bond sector is unlikely; yield becomes the advantage. To pick up a decent yield without too much risk of losing capital tends to favor this fund.

Government Income

Government Income invests primarily in U.S. government securities and related instruments. This fund holds U.S. Agency as well as U.S. Treasury securities, but since it holds fewer mortgage-backed securities than Ginnie Mae fund, it is not subject to that fund's significant prepayment risk. In addition, income from this fund's nonmortgage securities is mostly free of state and local income taxes. This and Spartan Government Income are virtually identical funds, often sharing the same manager. In a benign interest rate environment, shareholders can reap the benefits rather than the wrath of interest-rate risk. The Spartan fund, with slightly higher yields due to lower expenses, is the better choice for those who can meet that fund's $25,000 minimum.

High Income

High Income invests mainly in lower-quality (junk) bonds but may also hold preferred stock (which is actually more like a nonmaturing bond than like common stock) and some convertible securities. Virtually all the bonds in this portfolio have below-investment-grade ratings or are simply unrated. In other words, High Income is a junk-bond fund. While junk bonds come with much greater credit risk than investment-grade bonds do, investors can put that risk level into better perspective by looking at them as substitutes for stocks. And High Income has lower risk scores than any stock fund except for the balanced growth and income funds, which also hold a lot of bonds. While I tend to prefer Capital & Income, largely for its stable fund management, High Income's 0.73 percent expense ratio is quite low for a fund in its category, and it's a reasonable choice for many investors.

Intermediate Bond

Intermediate Bond invests in U.S. dollar–denominated investment-grade bonds (medium to high quality) while maintaining an average maturity of 3 to 10 years. As its name implies, the fund thus avoids extremes of quality and maturity, holding investment-grade bonds (rated from AAA to BBB) with a duration usually close to its current 3.3 years. The fund does have almost a quarter of assets in bonds rated BBB (the lowest investment grade), but a third of the fund is rated AAA. When the Fed is cutting rates, it will help bonds almost across the board, and this fund would be no exception. When the Fed is raising rates, this will be among the least affected among the bond fund group.

Intermediate Government Income

Intermediate Government Income invests primarily in U.S. government and related securities while maintaining an average maturity of 3 to 10 years. Shareholders will find most fund income, except for that generated by mortgage-backed securities, exempt from state and local taxes. (In April 1999, the assets of Spartan Short-Intermediate Government fund were merged into this fund.) As with Government Income, Intermediate Government Income's portfolio is heavily invested in U.S. Agency securities. A typically low duration of three years makes Intermediate Government Income one of the Fidelity bond funds with the lowest interest-rate risk.

Investment Grade Bond

Investment Grade Bond normally invests in U.S. dollar–denominated investment-grade (rated BBB or better) bonds. In practice, the portfolio holds a fixed-income smorgasbord of corporate bonds, mortgage-backed bonds, Treasuries, and U.S. dollar–denominated foreign bonds. Compared to Intermediate Bond, this fund has a slightly higher average credit quality, with 16.3 percent of the fund in bonds rated BBB and 56.3 percent rated AAA. Investment Grade does tend to have a longer duration than Intermediate, but not by much.

Mortgage Securities

Mortgage Securities invests primarily in high-quality mortgage-related securities, such as GNMAs and FNMAs. Mortgage securities pay a higher yield than U.S. Treasuries. But that extra yield comes at a cost. Unlike Treasuries, GNMAs and other mortgage securities do come with some, albeit very low level, credit risk attached, while their interest payments are taxable at the state and local levels. Most problematic, however, is the fact that mortgage-backed bonds expose investors to the risk that, should interest rates decline, the holders of the underlying mortgages will refinance, leaving bondholders stuck with lower-yielding cash. And just as maturities shorten when rates fall, refinancings slow and maturities lengthen when rates increase (again, just the opposite of what shareholders would like to see). The higher yields don't make up for this prepayment risk and the other disadvantages that these securities have in comparison to Treasuries.

Short-Term Bond

Short-Term Bond primarily holds investment-grade bonds, with an average maturity of three years or less. The fund's short average maturity translates into low interest-rate risk. (In June of 1999, the assets of Spartan Short-Term Bond were merged into this fund.) As of now, the fund is halfway between Intermediate and Investment Grade in terms of credit rating, but has a much shorter duration (1.5 years), meaning less risk from increases in interest rates (generally the most important risk component in this category), although that also means it shouldn't benefit nearly as much as its longer-duration counterparts in a rate-cut environment.

Spartan Government Income

Since late 1998, Spartan Government Income has essentially been the Spartan version of Government Income fund, and both funds are often managed by the same manager. This Spartan fund, with slightly higher yields due to lower expenses, is the better choice for those who can meet that fund's $25,000 minimum. Spartan Government Income invests primarily in U.S. government and related securities. The fund holds U.S. Agency as well as U.S. Treasury securities, but since it holds fewer mortgage-backed securities than Ginnie Mae fund, it is not so subject to that fund's significant prepayment risk. In addition, income from this fund's nonmortgage securities is generally free of state and local income taxes.

Spartan Investment Grade Bond

This Spartan fund is typically run very similarly to Investment Grade Bond. The funds invest almost exclusively in investment-grade (rated BBB or better) bonds. In practice, the portfolio holds a fixed-income smorgasbord of corporate bonds, mortgage-backed bonds, Treasuries, and U.S. dollar–denominated foreign bonds. Mortgage-backed securities can figure prominently in the portfolio. On the credit front, the fund moves from about a quarter of the portfolio in the lowest investment-grade rating to about a tenth of its assets there. But investment-grade issues and the fund's longish duration prove to be most successful in a stable or rate-cutting environment. This fund's return is also typically slightly better than the fund's non-Spartan equivalent posted, almost exactly the same as the difference due to this Spartan fund's lower expense ratio.

Spartan Intermediate Treasury Index, Spartan Short-Term Treasury Index, Spartan Long-Term Treasury Index

Fidelity's Spartan lineup of Treasury funds simplifies the process of laddering maturities for the sake of interest-rate risk while enabling the holder to diversify the yield in these plain-vanilla, plodding, predictable bond issuances. If I wanted to create a position in an income portfolio that held Treasuries, and I could meet the Spartan minimum of $10,000, I'd maneuver among these three.

Strategic Income

The fund is a mix of lower-quality debt instruments, including high-yield (i.e., junk-bond) securities, U.S. and investment-grade securities, emerging-market securities, and foreign developed-market debt. Strategic Income invests in four major types of debt with the following benchmark portfolio allocations: 40 percent in junk bonds, 30 percent in U.S. government securities and investment-grade corporate bonds, 15 percent in emerging-markets securities, and 15 percent in foreign developed-markets securities. This fund stands alone in its diversification, but I generally consider it closest to the junk-bond funds since it's riskier than the conventional corporate (not to say the government) funds. It also can share its manager and some holdings with International Bond and New Markets Income, which are discussed in Chapter 10 (international funds), not here with the other bond funds. For investors willing to take on junk-bond or stock market risks, this is a fund to consider in virtually any portfolio.

Strategic Real Return

This fund invests in four income asset classes: inflation-protected debt, floating-rate loans, commodity-linked notes and related investments, and real estate investment trusts (REITs) or real estate–related investments. Not to be confused with a commodity-based fund, this fund is designed to behave like one—benefiting when commodities are benefiting and stubbing its toes when they're not. The fund was created to answer both a gap in the overall bond fund lineup and to capitalize on the cyclical interest in commodities. Unique among Fidelity bond funds, but not unique to Fidelity (PIMCo has one, too), the time to buy this fund as a diversifier is in the early stages of an economic recovery.

Total Bond

Sometimes, the less said the better. To wit, this is Fidelity's diversified (investment-grade, high-yield, emerging-market debt) answer to the question: If you could own only one bond fund, which one would it be? You might answer, "This one."

Fidelity's Municipal Bond Funds

Municipal Bonds

These funds' interest-rate-risks vary considerably. But as is expressed by the funds' duration measures, most of these funds have more interest-rate risk than any of Fidelity's taxable offerings. While none of these funds has the high credit risk of the taxable junk-bond funds Capital & Income and Spartan High Income, the funds do carry varying amounts of credit risk.

All of these funds are free from regular federal income taxes. However, many may distribute a portion of income subject to the federal alternative minimum tax (AMT), and those funds that don't have the name of your state in the title are generally subject to your state's income taxes on the bulk of their income.

These funds are a terrible choice for investors in the 15 percent tax bracket, and generally marginal for those in the 28 percent bracket, but income investors with taxable (non-IRA, etc.) accounts who are in the 28 percent or higher bracket should compare tax-equivalent yields for municipal funds (including any state-specific fund) to comparable taxable funds. For the latest yields (and tax-equivalent yields), check *The Fidelity Investor* (www.fidelityinvestor.com) or call Fidelity Customer Service.

Note that capital gains distributions are subject to income taxes, but these are usually a small portion, if any, of these funds' total return.

As on the taxable side, muni bond prices move inversely with interest rates, and rates are mostly driven by expectations of inflation.

Spartan Intermediate Municipal Income

Spartan Intermediate Municipal Income primarily invests in investment-grade municipal debt securities whose interest payments are exempt from federal income tax. A portion of fund income may be subject to the infamous federal alternative minimum tax (AMT). With most of its assets invested in muni bonds rated A or better by S&P, Spartan Intermediate Municipal Income is well insulated against credit risk. Despite the "Intermediate" in the fund's name, its duration, however, is another matter—it has typically exposed shareholders to a considerable level of interest-rate risk.

Spartan Municipal Income

Spartan Municipal Income primarily invests its portfolio in investment-grade municipal debt exempt from federal income tax. A portion of fund income may be subject to the infamous federal alternative minimum tax

(AMT). With most of its assets invested in muni bonds rated A or better by S&P, Spartan Municipal Income is well-insulated against credit risk. Its duration, however, is also (as with Spartan Intermediate Muni Income) another matter—it tends to expose shareholders to a considerable level of interest-rate risk (higher, indeed, than any of Fidelity's taxable funds carry). When a rising interest-rate table turns, this fund looks downright attractive, as do all of Fidelity's munis.

Spartan Short-Intermediate Municipal Income

Spartan Short-Intermediate Municipal Income primarily invests in investment-grade municipal debt securities with an average maturity of two to five years. A portion of fund income may be subject to the infamous federal alternative minimum tax (AMT). With most of its assets invested in muni bonds rated A or better by S&P, Spartan Short-Intermediate Municipal Income was well insulated against credit risk last year. And with its typically short duration, this fund takes less interest-rate risk than any other Fidelity municipal security vehicle except a money market fund. Even this fund should make money when interest rates decrease, and investors who are looking for tax-free income with essentially no risk to principal should consider it.

Spartan Single-State Municipal Income Funds

Fidelity's lengthy list of single-state muni bond funds primarily invest in investment-grade municipal securities whose income is free from federal, state, and often city income taxes. (The Florida fund is exempt from that state's intangible tax.) Higher-income investors should be aware that a portion of fund income may be subject to the infamous federal alternative minimum tax (AMT), and some may even be subject to some state taxes.

With the vast majority of their assets invested in muni bonds carrying at least an A rating, the single-state funds are fairly well insulated against credit risk. However, a statewide disaster could eventually cause problems in such a portfolio, even if it doesn't directly hold bonds in, say, bankrupt electric utilities. While other funds could have slight exposure to this unfolding story, California Spartan clearly has the potential for a larger blackout if the situation worsens. California Spartan holders might want to consider Spartan Muni Income for the interim, keeping in mind that such a move would mean paying state income taxes.

SINGLE-STATE MUNICIPAL BOND FUNDS

Arizona Spartan

California Spartan

Connecticut Spartan

Florida Spartan

Maryland Spartan

Massachusetts Spartan

Michigan Spartan

Minnesota Spartan

New Jersey Spartan

New York

Ohio Spartan

Pennsylvania Spartan

The average duration of these funds exposes shareholders to a considerable level of interest-rate risk—indeed, more than any of Fidelity's taxable funds carry. When a rising interest-rate table is turned, such long maturities will look downright attractive.

The Fidelity Investor's Chart Room: Bond Funds

Please see Figure 12.1 and Tables 12.5 and 12.6.

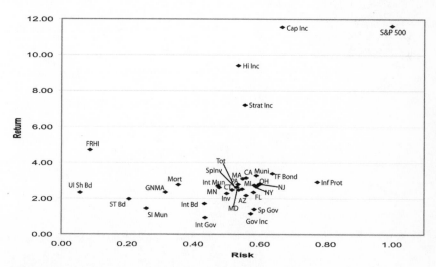

FIGURE 12.1   Fidelity bond funds risk/return ratios

Source: www.fidelityinvestor.com

Table 12.5   Fidelity Bond Funds: Maximum Cumulative Loss and Maximum Time to Recovery

Fidelity Bond Funds

Maximum Cumulative Loss/Maximum Time to Recovery

Fund	MCL	MTR
S&P 500	-44.7	NR
Capital & Income	-29.2	9
Floating Rate Hi Inc	-0.6	1
Focused High Inc	-3.0	3
GNMA	-1.8	2
Gov't Income	-5.0	7
High Income	-25.8	15
Inflation-Protected	-5.7	5
Intermediate	-2.8	5
Interm Gov't Inc	-3.2	7
Investment Grade	-3.5	5
Mortgage Secs	-1.8	2
Short-Term Bond	-1.3	3
Spartan Gov't Inc	-5.1	7
Spartan Int Treas Idx	-1.8	NR
Sptn Invest Grade	-3.5	5
Spartan LT Treas Idx	-5.3	NR
Spartan ST Treas Idx	-0.1	1
Strategic Income	-3.5	3
Strategic Real Return	-2.1	3
Total Bond	-3.8	5
Ultra-Short Bond	-0.1	1
Int Muni	-3.3	2
Muni Income	-4.4	5
Sht-Int Muni	-1.9	3
Tax-Free Bond	-4.9	4
AZ Muni	-4.6	5
CA Muni	-4.4	5
CA S-I Muni	-0.3	2
CT Muni	-4.3	5
FL Muni	-4.8	5
MD Muni	-4.0	5
MA Muni	-4.1	5
MI Muni	-4.2	5
MN Muni	-3.9	5
NJ Muni	-4.5	5
NY Muni	-5.0	5
OH Muni	-4.6	5
PA Muni	-3.9	5

Source: www.fidelityinvestor.com

Table 12.6   Fidelity Bond Funds Correlation Table

Fidelity Bond Funds Correlation Table

	S&P 500	Capital & Income	Floating Rate Hi Inc	GNMA	Gov't Income	High Income	Inflation-Protected	Intermediate	Interm Gov't Inc	Investment Grade	Mortgage Secs	Short-Term Bond	Spartan Gov't Inc	Sptn Invest Grade	Strategic Income	Total Bond	Ultra-Short Bond	Int Muni	Muni Income	Sht-Int Muni	Tax-Free Bond	AZ Muni Inc	CA Muni Inc	CT Muni Inc	FL Muni Inc	MD Muni Inc	MA Muni Inc	MI Muni Inc	MN Muni Inc	NJ Muni Inc	NY Muni Inc	OH Muni Inc	PA Muni Inc
S&P 500	100	31	20	2	2	28	0	2	3	1	0	2	2	7	7	1	1	2	2	3	2	2	1	2	2	2	2	2	2	2	2	2	2
Capital & Income	31	100	65	12	8	92	4	13	8	14	16	10	8	14	63	21	0	11	12	9	11	10	11	10	11	11	12	10	11	11	11	11	12
Floating Rate Hi Inc	20	65	100	1	0	61	0	0	0	2	2	0	0	2	26	5	0	1	1	0	1	0	0	0	0	1	0	1	1	1	1	0	1
GNMA	2	12	1	100	86	11	72	87	85	91	96	78	84	91	56	89	10	83	83	78	83	83	82	82	81	84	85	83	84	83	82	83	82
Gov't Income	2	8	0	86	100	7	87	96	97	97	90	89	100	97	56	94	19	90	92	71	90	91	90	93	92	92	92	92	92	90	91	91	91
High Income	28	92	61	11	7	100	8	13	8	13	15	8	11	14	64	20	0	12	12	10	11	11	11	11	11	11	12	11	12	12	11	11	12
Inflation-Protected	0	4	0	72	87	8	100	80	81	81	88	72	84	87	48	76	10	76	77	71	77	77	77	79	77	78	78	78	78	75	76	77	78
Intermediate	2	13	0	87	96	13	80	100	99	97	94	95	90	96	64	96	20	90	92	86	91	92	90	93	92	92	92	93	92	90	89	90	91
Interm Gov't Inc	3	8	0	85	97	8	81	99	100	96	88	94	96	96	56	96	23	89	90	86	89	89	87	92	91	91	90	90	90	89	89	89	90
Investment Grade	1	14	2	91	97	13	81	97	96	100	94	89	97	99	60	94	16	92	93	81	93	93	90	92	92	92	92	93	92	92	91	91	92
Mortgage Secs	0	16	2	96	90	15	88	94	88	94	100	83	89	94	64	93	12	85	86	79	85	85	83	87	85	86	86	84	84	86	85	82	85
Short-Term Bond	2	10	0	78	89	8	72	95	94	89	83	100	88	89	56	89	32	82	83	84	82	82	79	84	82	83	81	84	81	81	81	82	84
Spartan Gov't Inc	2	8	0	84	100	11	84	90	96	97	89	88	100	97	57	90	17	90	92	82	91	91	90	92	92	92	91	91	90	90	91	90	90
Sptn Invest Grade	7	14	2	91	97	14	87	96	96	99	94	89	97	100	65	94	16	93	93	86	92	89	93	94	94	94	94	93	93	93	91	93	93
Strategic Income	7	63	26	56	56	64	48	64	56	60	64	56	57	65	100	72	5	60	61	53	60	59	59	60	59	61	60	59	60	60	59	59	61
Total Bond	1	21	5	89	94	20	76	96	96	94	93	89	90	94	72	100	14	89	90	87	90	90	90	90	90	90	90	90	90	89	90	89	89
Ultra-Short Bond	1	0	0	10	19	0	10	20	23	16	12	32	17	16	5	14	100	22	21	25	21	20	22	22	20	20	20	22	21	20	21	21	22
Int Muni	2	11	1	83	90	12	76	90	89	92	85	82	90	93	60	89	22	100	99	95	99	99	98	99	93	99	92	99	99	99	99	99	98
Muni Income	2	12	1	83	92	12	77	92	90	93	86	83	92	93	61	90	21	99	100	92	99	99	99	99	92	99	99	99	99	99	99	99	99
Sht-Int Muni	3	9	0	78	71	10	71	86	86	81	79	84	82	86	53	82	25	95	92	100	91	88	89	93	92	89	89	93	90	89	91	92	93
Tax-Free Bond	2	11	1	83	90	11	77	91	89	93	86	82	91	92	60	90	21	99	99	91	100	99	98	99	93	99	99	99	99	99	99	99	99
AZ Muni Inc	2	10	1	83	91	11	77	92	90	93	85	82	91	89	59	90	22	99	99	88	99	100	98	99	92	99	99	93	99	99	99	99	99
CA Muni Inc	1	11	0	82	90	11	77	90	87	91	83	79	90	93	59	90	21	98	99	89	98	98	100	99	99	98	99	98	98	98	98	98	98
CT Muni Inc	2	10	0	82	93	11	79	93	92	92	86	85	92	93	60	90	22	99	99	93	99	99	99	100	99	99	99	99	99	99	99	99	99
FL Muni Inc	2	11	0	81	92	11	77	92	91	92	85	82	92	92	59	90	20	99	99	92	99	92	99	99	100	99	99	99	99	99	99	99	99
MD Muni Inc	2	11	1	84	92	11	78	92	91	92	86	83	92	94	60	90	20	99	99	89	99	99	99	99	99	100	99	99	99	99	99	99	99
MA Muni Inc	2	12	0	85	92	12	78	92	90	92	86	83	92	94	61	90	20	99	99	89	99	99	99	99	99	99	100	99	99	99	99	100	99
MI Muni Inc	2	10	1	83	92	11	78	93	90	93	84	84	92	93	59	90	22	99	99	93	99	93	99	99	99	99	99	100	99	99	99	100	99
MN Muni Inc	2	11	1	84	92	12	78	92	90	92	84	81	92	94	60	90	21	99	99	90	99	99	98	99	99	99	99	99	100	99	100	100	99
NJ Muni Inc	2	11	1	83	90	12	75	90	89	92	86	81	90	93	60	89	20	99	99	89	99	99	98	99	99	99	99	99	99	100	99	99	98
NY Muni Inc	2	11	1	82	91	11	76	89	89	91	85	81	91	91	59	90	21	99	99	91	99	99	99	99	99	99	99	99	100	99	100	100	99
OH Muni Inc	2	11	0	83	91	11	77	90	89	91	82	84	90	93	59	89	21	99	99	92	99	99	98	99	99	99	100	100	100	99	100	100	99
PA Muni Inc	2	12	1	82	91	12	78	91	90	92	85	84	90	93	61	89	22	98	99	93	99	99	98	99	99	99	99	99	99	98	99	99	100

Source: www.fidelityinvestor.com

THIRTEEN

Fidelity's Money Market Funds

From These Small Acorns Grow Mighty Oaks

Whether you're saving money for a rainy day or just looking for a place to park some spare dollars between investments, Fidelity's money market funds provide you with some of the highest-yielding safe choices available, as well as extraordinary convenience when it comes time to use your money.

You can write checks on most money market funds (with minimums as low as $0 on FDIT). If you desire, dividends and interest (and even capital gains) earned on other Fidelity funds can be automatically deposited into your money market for easy access.

Contrary to some, I think that having a money market fund is a *smart investing move*. But there's more to Fidelity's money market funds than meet the untrained eye—or even the trained eye. Most reports that rank mutual fund firms based on their underlying assets don't rule in money market fund assets. Doing so invariably leads to the mistaken assumption that Fidelity's asset size may be smaller than that of other firms whose bond funds are included in the mix. But the three legs to the investment stool are stocks, bonds, and cash—and at Fidelity, money market assets have always been about twice as large as its bond fund assets, accounting for an average of 24 percent of its overall assets (bonds account for, on average, about 11 percent of its total assets, and stock funds make up the lion's share).

Fidelity's history in the money market business is part of the original DNA of money markets (see Chapter 1 for details). For the best present uses of Fidelity's broad array of taxable and tax-free money market funds, read on.

Cash May Not Make You a King, but It Is Often King

First, if you decide to get out of some other investment, it's good to have a money market account set up to trade into. Second, though the check-writing option is available on a host of other Fidelity funds, you should avoid, at all costs, using any fund other than a money market as your checking account. The reason: Any time you write a check on a fund you are, in effect, selling shares in the fund to cover the amount of your check. Write a check for $1,000, and when it is cashed Fidelity will sell as many shares as necessary to cover the amount. And each time shares are sold, it's a taxable event whose gain or loss will have to be calculated and re-ported to the Internal Revenue Service. This problem does not exist in a money market. Since money market funds are always priced at exactly $1.00 per share, there is no profit or loss on the transaction.

True, money market yields can look relatively low or seductively high at any given time (Fidelity's taxable money markets were up about 5 per-cent in 2006). In a rising-rate environment, they tend to tie or beat bond funds, too (except for junk bonds).

Money market funds invest your dollars in very, very short-term bank, corporate, and government debt securities. Because of the nature of these short-term securities, the price of a share in a money market mutual fund changes only infinitesimally from day to day, so your money market shares remain priced at a constant $1.00. Only the interest rate paid on your money market assets changes. Your principal investment never grows or shrinks in value. However, your interest is constantly being paid out and reinvested in your money market account. While the resulting increase in your shares is only apparent in your stated balance at the end of each month, in fact Fidelity tracks it (and effectively credits it) on a daily basis.

One of the great things about Fidelity money market funds is that you have virtually instantaneous access to your cash through check-writing privileges. Or you can wire money from your money market account throughout the U.S. banking system.

Fidelity's money market managers can't buy anything yielding much more than a three-month Treasury bill. They aren't allowed, on average, to go out longer than 90 days because that would imperil their "fixed" $1.00 share price if rates went up. And they can get only a little more in yield (certainly not more than 1 percent) by going to corporates, since they have to stick to AAA-quality corporates with almost all (95 percent) of their assets.

So Fidelity money market fund managers have little leeway in building a better, higher-yielding mousetrap by being smarter investors. The only way to safely boost yields above the average is to cut fund expenses. At Fidelity, that means going to Spartan funds, where expenses are 0.5 percent or less per year on taxable money markets. However, Spartan expenses aren't all that much lower than non-Spartans' nowadays; for example, Cash Reserves' expense ratio is down to 0.43 percent). Further, you have to weigh yield against Spartan's higher fund minimums ($20,000 for Spartan taxables and $25,000 for Spartan munis) and Spartan fees ($2 per check and $5 for most other transfers out, waived on accounts over $50,000).

Even if there were no fund expenses and the money markets yielded a half percent or so more, many investors would want still higher yields. That shouldn't mean jumping into longer-term bond funds, especially in today's climate, with the Fed still probably not finished raising rates. The risks associated with investing in long-term bond funds is well beyond what most investors would consider appropriate for their cash reserves.

Money Market Risks

With your share price virtually locked at $1, and interest being paid every day, that doesn't mean that money market funds are completely risk-free—no mutual fund is. The two biggest risks to any income fund are interest-rate risk and credit risk (neither being a major concern when investing in a Fidelity money fund).

Interest-rate risk describes the impact of rising and falling interest rates on the value of the securities held in your money market fund's portfolio. The level of this interest-rate risk is set by an income fund's average length of maturity. Despite a money market's very short average maturity, a sudden, severe rise in interest rates, if combined with heavy shareholder redemptions, could have an impact on your money market fund's portfolio value. However, it would take an extraordinary event to push interest rates high enough and fast enough to cause a problem. If the 3 percent rise in rates experienced in 1994 didn't cause a problem for Fidelity's funds, it's a good bet that nothing so dramatic will occur anytime soon. Given the conservative management of Fidelity's money funds, I don't think this problem is worth losing any sleep over. You can be sure that before any Fidelity fund was forced to price its shares below $1.00, many other fund complexes and banks would already have failed.

Credit risk can be a bigger problem for some money market funds. Credit risk involves the possibility that the issuer of one or more of the securities held in your fund would default on that security and be unable to pay it off at maturity. During the 1980s one well-publicized corporate default did force a couple of mutual fund complexes to dip into their own reserves to keep their money market investors from losing a couple pennies on their $1.00 shares. But again, Fidelity's conservative management makes the possibility of a default among its portfolios extremely remote. Of course, by investing in a government-only money market fund, such as Spartan U.S. Treasury, you can eliminate virtually any possibility of credit risk.

In short, money market funds are some of the safest and most convenient places to park your cash, and they can also help you avoid an accounting nightmare when income taxes are due. So, why would anyone want to try to earn a higher yield? Because the long-term gain in yield and return often is worth the additional volatility (short-term risk) that you take.

Enhance Your Yield

The first and most conservative step in boosting money market rates is to make sure you own the right money market. In taxable (i.e., not IRA or other retirement) accounts, look at your tax-equivalent yield. If you're invested in a taxable money market fund like Cash Reserves or Spartan U.S. Government, and you're in the 28 percent or higher federal tax bracket, consider one of Fidelity's municipal money market funds. Spartan Municipal Money invests in securities whose interest payments are exempt from federal income taxes. (In some cases, a portion of the fund's income may be exempt from state taxes as well.) And investors in Arizona, California, Connecticut, Florida, Massachusetts, Missouri, New Jersey, New York, Ohio, and Pennsylvania should consider a state-specific tax-free money market fund, whose interest is exempt from federal, state, and sometimes city taxes.

(Self-serving note: Every month, www.fidelityinvestor.com reports tax-equivalent yields for all of Fidelity's municipal funds. If the yield on the general municipal money fund or the money fund for your state is higher than the yield on your taxable money fund, make the switch.)

Some investors may feel insecure about investing in a single-state money fund. Given the 1994 default by Orange County, you may be inclined to stay away from single-state money funds, but Fidelity's conservative money market policies make this a fairly minor issue. Fidelity's California and Spartan California money markets rode through the Orange County debacle unscathed.

FOURTEEN

Fidelity's VIP Funds

Variable Insurance Products from Fidelity

For years, Fidelity Investments has been quietly staking its claim on a lucrative turf long dominated by insurance companies: *annuities*. But before I get to the good news about investing in Fidelity's variable insurance products (VIPs), I want to review the bad and the ugly.

Are You VIP Material?

Variable annuities and variable life insurance can be an attractive option for tax-deferred investing. But let's look before you leap, since investing in an annuity is really a contractual relationship with the product.

For one thing, although Fidelity Retirement Reserves' annual annuity charge has been reduced over time from 1.0 percent to 0.8 percent to 0.25 percent (that's remarkably inexpensive compared to any competitor), that 0.25 percent is still more than you'd pay in an IRA or other retirement plan. Annuities also have fewer fund options. (There are 38 annuity portfolios managed by Fidelity, including seven sector-focused VIPs, whereas you can choose from over 200 Fidelity retail options—not counting money markets—in your IRA.) Annuities' expenses can also overwhelm any tax advantage; further, annuities can complicate estate planning and can even diminish what's left after estate and other taxes.

Like traditional IRAs, exchanges within your annuity are not taxed, but withdrawals are subject to taxes (and often, before age 59½, a 10 percent penalty). In addition, Fidelity charges annuity redemption fees in the first five years.

I think that most investors should maximize other tax-deferred retirement plans first, such as 401(k)s and IRAs (especially the Roth IRA). If you've maximized these options, then a variable annuity or variable life insurance plan could make sense for you.

If you're like most people, most of your fund (or stock) investing throughout your life has been made with your retirement and/or old age in mind. After all, no one wants to be impoverished or a burden in his or her old age. But once you get to the point where you do not expect to spend all your money, you probably have in mind leaving what's left to family heirs. When they inherit from you, their cost basis will be the shares' value on the day you die. No matter how cheaply you bought the shares, your heirs get the higher stepped-up basis, and no one owes any taxes on the gains made while you were alive.

VIP Tax Warning

Many retirement investors know this, but what does it mean in terms of making investment decisions? Simply that that portion of your assets that you're fairly sure you will be leaving to your family can be invested in tax-efficient funds (especially an index fund like Spartan Total Market Index) or in individual stocks, and you'll pay very little in taxes on them (mostly some stock dividends) and your heirs won't pay gains taxes, either. As long as you're a buy-and-hold-forever investor of the right kinds of stocks or stock funds, this money can grow virtually tax-free without being held in a tax-deferred vehicle, and thus you have little reason to use potentially expensive sheltering arrangements, such as variable annuities, for this money. What happens if your investment is held in a tax-advantaged annuity? If you leave the annuity to anyone but your spouse, the appreciation of the annuity is taxed as income! Note that estate planning gets a lot more complicated than this and really requires an expert (unless you don't mind your estate paying a lot in extra taxes, perhaps on the grounds that the federal government is as worthy a charity as any). You should consult a qualified (and neutral) estate planner, accountant, or attorney, especially if you expect to leave an estate of more than $600,000.

VIPs the Fidelity Way

With the bad and the ugly behind us, let's get to the VIP goods.

When you buy an annuity through Fidelity (or more precisely, the insurance company owned by Fidelity), you are entering into a contract.

Essentially, you agree to hand over a wad of money in return for a check every month for the rest of your life. Like life insurance, annuity contracts are based on the principal of risk pooling. While life insurance protects you against premature death, an annuity will protect you against living longer than expected and running out of money. In other words, the burden of not knowing how long you will live is shifted from you to Fidelity.

For a price, of course.

The downside of annuities is that they tend to be expensive. In addition to an annual annuity charge, you also pay the fees and expenses associated with any underlying mutual funds linked to the annuity. While Fidelity's annuities are known for being relatively cheap, the annuity and fund management charges may still easily consume upwards of 3 percent of your investment dollars each year.

While there are nearly as many varieties of annuities as there are garden tomatoes, most fall into one or two camps: fixed and variable.

Fixed annuities are savings plans that pay interest at a guaranteed rate that is adjusted periodically. These periodic payments may last for a definite period, such as 20 years, or an indefinite period, such as your lifetime or the lifetime of you and your spouse.

Variable annuities, meanwhile, are linked to an underlying stock or bond fund. While variable annuities offer the potential for higher returns than do fixed annuities, they can also lose money—unless, of course, you buy one that contains guarantees against investment losses.

Annuities can be part of an IRA, part of a qualified retirement plan such as a 401(k) or 403(b), or they can be purchased with after-tax dollars as part of a nonqualified personal retirement account.

With nearly $2 trillion in assets, annuities are one of the most popular retirement savings vehicles in the United States. But, for all their popularity, few investors really understand annuities. And who can blame them? For years, financial services companies have been launching one feature-laden annuity after another. It's gotten to the point where even the financial pros can't make sense out of all the extraneous bells and whistles attached to annuities or the seemingly onerous charges associated with them.

Of course, it doesn't help that in recent years, annuities (in particular, variable annuities) have received a torrent of bad publicity because of unsavory sales practices and high fees.

True to form, Fidelity Investments is using the industry's travails to steal market share.

In September 2005, the company unveiled the Personal Retirement Annuity, a variable annuity that promises nothing but tax-deferred savings and the ability to deliver a steady stream of income after retirement. The annuity comes with a $5,000 initial investment minimum, which is low by industry standards.

Fidelity recently added four funds to its variable insurance products (VIP) lineup to go along with the Personal Retirement Annuity. Each of the four funds invests in a combination of retail and VIP funds to achieve more or less exposure to equities. Of course, you may also choose a fund from Fidelity's assortment of VIP funds, which are essentially clones of its retail funds, as well as a handful of non-Fidelity funds.

Fidelity's annual annuity charge is 0.25 percent for the Personal Retirement Annuity, well below the industry average of 1.4 percent. That annuity charge does not include any fees associated with your annuity's underlying funds, which may run as high as 2.19 percent.

In addition Fidelity also launched Fidelity Freedom Lifetime Income, a variable-income annuity aimed at those approaching or already in retirement. When you invest in Fidelity Freedom Lifetime Income, which has a $25,000 investment minimum, you have the option of investing in one of three so-called life-cycle funds. It pays a guaranteed amount in retirement and has an annual management fee of 0.6 percent, compared with an industry average of 1.12 percent. Fund management fees, however, will add anywhere from 0.78 percent to 0.92 percent on top of that.

Needless to say, others saw what Fidelity was doing and are scrambling to keep up. As this book was going to press, for example, Raymond James Financial Inc. was getting ready to take the wraps off a lineup of simplified variable annuities that feature lower commissions and underlying fees.

Fidelity also offers Fidelity Income Advantage, which comes with more bells and whistles, such as a guarantee period to ensure that a surviving spouse or heir will continue to receive income payments from the annuity for up to 45 years. That fund, which comes with a $25,000 investment minimum, has a 1 percent annual annuity charge, not including the underlying expenses of the underlying funds.

VIP Contrafund

VIP Contrafund invests mainly in equity securities whose value, its manager believes, has been underestimated by the investing public. This includes stock in companies experiencing positive fundamental change, companies whose earnings potential has increased, companies that have temporarily and undeservedly fallen out of favor with the marketplace, and companies whose stock seems underpriced in relation to their industry peers. In other words, this is supposed to buy ugly-duckling stocks. But generally, Contrafund's main emphasis has been on companies with strong earnings growth trading at moderate price-to-earnings multiples.

However, its 2006 end-of-year growth orientation means it's not currently holding stocks that are cheap or undervalued by the standard measures. Given the limited choices in the VIP lineup, I often favor this fund and will likely continue to do so well into the next millennium.

VIP Growth

VIP Growth fund invests mainly in the common stock of companies that have the potential for substantial growth in earnings or revenue. It has no close retail fund equivalent, and its manager typically does not run any retail funds. Despite the fund's name and its current large-cap growth style, it sometimes has a large-cap blend, or even value orientation. I think this is a suitable core holding for many VIP investors, especially those with an investment time line of 10 years or more.

VIP Growth Opportunities

This fund seeks capital appreciation by investing primarily in common stocks. Despite the fund's name, don't confuse it with a true growth vehicle. The fund continues to have a value or blended style to its mostly large-cap stocks. I like the orientation toward the predominantly large-cap, value-oriented stocks of companies engaged in the manufacture and distribution of goods for consumers around the world. But I still think there are better ways to participate in these markets in VIP land.

VIP Mid-Cap

VIP Mid-Cap invests primarily in stocks with "medium" market capitalizations, that is, capitalizations within the range of the S&P 400 mid-cap index, at the time of purchase. (The fund can hold on to positions that grow into large-caps due to market appreciation.) VIP Mid-Cap has often shared its manager and virtually all of its positions with the retail Mid-Cap Stock fund. I like the mid-cap arena in general, and think most VIP investors should give this fund strong consideration. The only caveat is the fund's risk level; although it is well diversified, it is suitable only for aggressive, growth-oriented investors.

VIP Index 500

VIP Index 500 fund seeks to mirror the performance of the celebrated S&P 500 Index, which of course consists of essentially (not precisely) the 500 U.S. companies with the biggest market capitalizations. I strongly prefer active management—at least as it has been practiced at Fidelity—but I must concede that this fund is not a bad choice for investors who want to buy a fund and hold it for the next 20 years. The VIP Index 500 could also serve as a solid complement to VIP Growth. But if you aren't yet a VIP investor, and know you want to make an index fund investment, consider a retail index fund like Spartan 500 Index or Spartan Total Market Index instead. Index funds have very low taxable distributions, and their gains are thus largely tax-deferred even without putting them in an annuity or IRA-type tax-deferred shell.

VIP Asset Manager

This balanced fund invests in a diversified mix of domestic and foreign stocks, bonds, and short-term instruments. VIP Asset Manager's neutral mix is set at 50 percent stocks, 40 percent bonds, and 10 percent short-term/money market instruments. As such, VIP Asset Manager is similar in risk and holdings to the retail Asset Manager fund. While this fund's asset allocation may be appropriate for certain highly conservative individuals who want to own just one fund, I think that most VIP investors could fare better by creating a portfolio composed of several funds, such as the Growth, High Income, and perhaps Money Market options, or by using VIP Asset Manager in conjunction with such funds, or to reduce risk in a portfolio composed primarily of other stock funds.

VIP Asset Manager: Growth

This balanced fund invests in a diversified mix of domestic and foreign stocks, bonds, and short-term instruments. VIP Asset Manager Growth's neutral mix is set at 70 percent stocks, 25 percent bonds, and 5 percent short-term/money market instruments. As such, VIP Asset Manager: Growth is similar in risk and holdings to the retail Asset Manager: Growth fund. While I don't recommend putting all your money in a single fund, even a diversified option like this one, VIP Asset Manager: Growth could make sense for most investors in 2001 as a part of a portfolio that includes other funds, such as the Growth, High Income, and perhaps Money Market options.

VIP Balanced

This balanced fund holds a diversified portfolio of equity and fixed-income securities bought for their current income and potential for income growth and/or capital appreciation. The fund's benchmark "neutral" mix calls for a core of approximately 60 percent in stocks and 40 percent in income investments (bonds and cash). The fund has some flexibility to deviate from this ratio, but it must keep at least 25 percent of assets in income securities. If you could own only one VIP fund and are a very conservative investor, this could be the one. With its emphasis on safety, I think that growth and income VIP investors would find it a good match. Unlike most VIP funds, which are basically clones of retail equivalents, this VIP choice can be a somewhat more aggressive than retail Balanced, but the stock holdings are, of course, well tempered by the high-quality bonds.

VIP Equity-Income

VIP Equity-Income fund primarily invests in income-producing common stocks, aiming to produce a yield higher than the S&P 500 while still taking advantage of opportunities for capital appreciation. It can invest in foreign securities and bonds, but is basically a domestic stock fund. VIP Equity-Income is a close clone of the retail Equity-Income fund, which has historically held almost exactly the same holdings. VIP Equity-Income can certainly be a more aggressive vehicle than either VIP Balanced or VIP Asset Manager. Still, the fund's equity holdings are concentrated in larger, value-oriented, dividend-paying stocks. Of course, in today's low-dividend market, a stock with a P/E of 20 and a yield of 2 percent (which once would have been considered an "aggressive growth" stock) would readily qualify as a candidate for this portfolio. Even so, VIP Equity-Income's orientation should make it less risky than the broader market.

VIP Growth & Income

VIP Growth & Income fund invests mainly in the common stock of companies that pay current dividends and offer potential for earnings growth, but may include, at the behest of the fund's managers, non-dividend-paying stocks that appear to have good prospects for future income or capital appreciation and also some bonds. Note that the fund tends to share similar holdings and managers not with retail Growth & Income, but with Growth & Income II. While the fund charter sets no set income requirement, it generally provides a yield in the neighborhood of that produced by the S&P 500—which isn't much these days. For individuals seeking risk-adjusted capital appreciation, this fund could be a solid VIP choice.

VIP Overseas

VIP Overseas fund primarily invests in foreign stocks. As the only international stock fund choice for VIP investors, this offering might be worthwhile strictly for the reduction in diversification risk it could provide.

Fortunately, with an impressive 10-year history to its credit, this fund is anything but an also-ran.

VIP High Income

This fund invests primarily in higher-yielding, lower-rated, fixed-income securities. While high current income is management's main priority, capital gain opportunities are considered as well. In plain English, this is a junk-bond fund. Attractive values and yields mean strong total returns can be had—but remember that they come at a cost. VIP High Income shareholders are exposed to a much greater level of credit risk than are investors in plain-vanilla bond funds like VIP Investment Grade. Even so, I remain partial to junk bonds because I think the risks will be well worth the rewards, especially in a recovering economy.

VIP Investment Grade Bond

This fund invests in a broad range of investment-grade, fixed-income securities (i.e., bonds rated BBB or better by S&P) to generate current income while preserving capital. VIP Investment Grade Bond has held a wide variety of mortgage-backed, corporate, and government bonds of varying maturities. The fund's yield relates to its typically lengthy duration, meaning that it ought to be near the 10-year Treasury. As such, it is exposed to a degree of interest-rate risk that VIP Money Market (see next) simply isn't.

VIP Money Market

VIP Money Market is, like all money markets, basically an extremely short-term bond fund (with maturities on the order of two months, not the five years or more of most bond funds without the word *short* in their name). The VIP accrual accounting means this funds doesn't have a fixed $1.00 share price; instead, income is added to the share price every day, as VIP funds don't make the distributions that regular mutual funds are required to (so that shareholders pay taxes on their income). But despite the lack of a fixed price, VIP Money Market is every bit as safe as Cash Reserves and other retail money market offerings. You're extremely unlikely to lose money in this or any money market. I generally recommend money markets only for offsetting the risks of more aggressive funds, for meeting short-term needs, or for other short-term purposes (e.g., as a parking place between other investments or to reflect an investor's bearish stance).

The Fidelity Investor's Chart Room: VIP Funds

Please see Figure 14.1 and Tables 14.1 and 14.2.

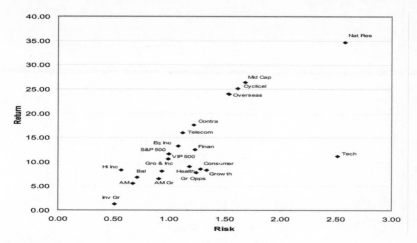

FIGURE 14.1   Fidelity VIP funds risk/return ratios

Source: www.fidelityinvestor.com

Table 14.1   Fidelity VIP Funds: Maximum Cumulative Loss and Maximum Time to Recovery

Fidelity VIP Funds

Maximum Cumulative Loss/Maximum Time to Recovery

Fund	MCL	MTR
S&P 500	-44.7	NR
VIP Aggressive Growth	-8.4	NR
VIP Contrafund	-34.1	22
VIP Dynamic Cap App	-18.3	10
VIP Disc Small Cap	0.0	
VIP Growth	-57.2	NR
VIP Growth Opps	-51.0	NR
VIP Growth Stock	-7.8	NR
VIP Mid-Cap	-19.3	5
VIP Index 500	-45.9	NR
VIP Value	-3.0	NR
VIP Value Leaders	-4.0	NR
VIP Value Strategies	-13.5	3
VIP Asset Manager	-25.3	38
VIP Asset Mngr. Growth	-40.0	NR
VIP Balanced	-22.7	34
VIP Equity-Income	-30.3	17
VIP Growth & Income	-34.7	42
VIP Real Estate	-14.5	4
VIP Freedom 2005	-1.8	NR
VIP Freedom 2010	-1.7	NR
VIP Freedom 2015	-2.1	NR
VIP Freedom 2020	-2.5	NR
VIP Freedom 2025	-2.6	NR
VIP Freedom 2030	-2.9	NR
VIP Freedom Income	-0.7	1
VIP FundsMngr 20% Port	0.0	
VIP FundsMngr 50% Port	0.0	
VIP FundsMngr 70% Port	0.0	
VIP FundsMngr 85% Port	0.0	
VIP Int'l Cap App	-6.0	NR
VIP Overseas (x)	-55.6	37
VIP Overseas class R	-55.6	37
VIP Consumer Ind	-23.8	12
VIP Cyclical Industries	-27.6	10
VIP Financial Services	-21.2	13
VIP Health Care	-22.4	27
VIP Natural Resources	-23.7	15
VIP Technology	-52.0	39
VIP Telecom & Utilities	-45.5	34
VIP High Income	-38.9	NR
VIP Investment Grade	-3.7	6
VIP Strategic Income	-1.9	3

Source: www.fidelityinvestor.com

Table 14.2 Fidelity VIP Funds Correlation Table

	S&P 500	VIP Contrafund	VIP Growth	VIP Growth Opportunities	VIP Mid-Cap	VIP 500	VIP Asset Manager	VIP Asset Manager: Growth	VIP Balanced	VIP Equity-Income	VIP Growth & Income	VIP Overseas	VIP Overseas class R	VIP Consumer Industries	VIP Cyclical Industries	VIP Financial Services	VIP Health Care	VIP Natural Resources	VIP Technology	VIP Telecom & Utilities	VIP High Income	VIP Investment Grade
S&P 500	100	74	86	84	65	100	74	82	70	93	82	64	63	71	79	67	25	24	63	37	20	1
VIP Contrafund	74	100	75	79	88	74	58	66	62	67	65	68	68	62	72	47	12	46	69	20	12	3
VIP Growth	86	75	100	83	65	86	57	65	58	71	72	56	56	72	69	59	17	17	85	19	11	3
VIP Growth Opportunities	84	79	83	100	64	84	73	82	69	75	76	61	61	66	69	59	22	28	70	22	12	1
VIP Mid-Cap	65	88	65	64	100	65	48	54	58	65	56	69	69	47	74	42	5	57	60	20	18	1
VIP 500	100	74	86	84	65	100	74	82	70	93	82	64	63	71	79	67	25	24	63	37	20	1
VIP Asset Manager	74	58	57	73	48	74	100	97	77	75	62	64	63	51	47	53	31	31	42	36	39	5
VIP Asset Manager: Growth	82	66	65	82	54	82	97	100	77	82	71	67	67	60	57	57	31	31	44	34	32	1
VIP Balanced	70	62	58	69	58	70	77	77	100	72	79	68	68	43	68	52	31	41	44	34	21	1
VIP Equity-Income	93	67	71	75	65	93	75	82	72	100	79	66	66	59	80	61	21	34	45	37	24	1
VIP Growth & Income	82	65	72	76	56	82	62	71	79	79	100	61	61	54	66	59	23	28	52	30	11	3
VIP Overseas	64	68	56	61	69	64	64	67	68	66	61	100	100	42	50	49	12	34	49	15	28	0
VIP Overseas class R	63	68	56	61	69	63	63	67	68	66	61	100	100	41	50	49	12	35	49	15	28	0
VIP Consumer Industries	71	62	72	66	47	71	51	60	43	59	54	42	41	100	58	51	9	8	60	22	11	1
VIP Cyclical Industries	79	72	69	69	74	79	47	57	68	80	66	50	50	58	100	43	8	35	50	26	14	9
VIP Financial Services	67	47	59	59	42	67	53	57	52	61	59	49	49	51	43	100	10	6	44	16	15	0
VIP Health Care	25	12	17	22	5	25	31	31	31	21	23	12	12	9	8	10	100	2	6	13	6	0
VIP Natural Resources	24	46	17	28	57	24	31	31	41	34	28	34	35	8	35	6	2	100	16	19	12	3
VIP Technology	63	69	85	70	60	63	42	44	44	45	52	49	49	60	50	44	6	16	100	11	7	7
VIP Telecom & Utilities	37	20	19	22	20	37	36	34	34	37	30	15	15	22	26	16	13	19	11	100	30	20
VIP High Income	20	12	11	12	18	20	39	32	21	24	11	28	28	11	14	15	6	12	7	30	100	20
VIP Investment Grade	1	3	3	1	1	1	5	1	1	1	3	0	0	1	9	0	0	3	7	20	20	100

Source: www.fidelityinvestor.com

FIFTEEN

Fidelity Advisor Funds

Broker-Sold Funds for Everyone, Fidelity Style

I t's as if Mark Felt, also known as "Deep Throat," had whispered the words "follow the money" in the ear of Ned Johnson, Fidelity Investment's long-standing chairman and chief executive.

After rising to the top of the mutual fund heap after decades of encouraging investors to think and invest for themselves, Fidelity Investments suddenly began pushing a family of load funds through stockbrokers, financial planners, banks, and insurance companies. Indeed, with the launch of the Fidelity Advisor group of funds in the early 1990s, Fidelity made clear its determination to win the war for mutual fund sales no matter where that battle had to be fought.

Believe it or not, that wasn't the first time around the block with advisers for Fidelity. In fact, the company spent its first 33 years as a load fund family, selling exclusively through brokers. Then, in 1979, it switched to selling directly to investors, and the rest, as they say, is history.

Fidelity's renewed focus on load funds would prove to be yet another testament to its ability to look ahead and adapt. More and more mutual fund shareholders are buying funds through some sort of financial intermediary, whether that intermediary takes the form of a 401(k) plan, a brokerage firm, a financial planner, a bank, or an insurance company. In 2003, individual investors owned 85 percent of their mutual fund assets through an intermediary, up from 72 percent in 1980 and 80 percent in

1990, according to the most recent data available from the Investment Company Institute, the fund industry's main trade group.

Increasingly, investors are turning to professional financial advisers for help in managing their assets. In fact, the push toward adviser-sold funds really gained momentum after the bear market of 2000 to 2002 rattled the confidence of many investors to invest for themselves.

To be sure, the bulk of Fidelity's mutual fund assets still come directly from individual investors. At the end of April 2005, Fidelity's retail stock and bond funds comprised $710.6 billion in assets, versus $94.1 billion for its stock and bond funds sold through intermediaries.

Of course, Fidelity is not the only fund company to recognize investors' rising dependence on advisers. Over the past few years, such fund companies as T. Rowe Price Group Inc. and Invesco have followed Fidelity's lead and either abandoned the no-load market altogether or added funds with loads.

Today, Fidelity offers 80 adviser-sold funds. Most of those funds are clones of existing funds. The main difference is that the adviser-sold funds come with loads, which is nothing more than a sales commission charged to and deducted from your account. They also come with a 12b-1 fee, which is a charge deducted from the funds' overall assets to meet costs associated with marketing or to pay what is called a *trail* to brokers.

Those charges make it more expensive to own an adviser-sold fund. The annual cost of owning Fidelity Advisor Aggressive Growth, for example, ranges from $1.33 to $2.09 for every $100 invested, depending upon which share class you purchase. Meanwhile, its no-load counterpart, Fidelity Aggressive Growth, charges just 79 cents for every $100 invested.

Don't underestimate the impact of that cost differential on your investment performance. Since annual fees are deducted from a fund's assets, they act as a drag on performance. Fidelity Advisor Aggressive Growth, for example, is up 8.64 percent on average over the past three years compared with a 9.43 percent gain for Fidelity Aggressive Growth.

Given the difference it costs, it's no wonder Fidelity Aggressive Growth has amassed nearly $4 billion in assets, while its adviser-sold counterpart is barely scraping by with $40 million in assets.

Let's take a closer look at how the Fidelity Advisor Funds are priced. Basically, the funds come in four classes: A, B, C, and T.

1. *Class A* shares generally charge a front-end sales load at the time of the purchase as a percentage of the sales price. This share class also often has a 12b-1 fee, although the fee is usually smaller than with other share classes. The Class A shares on the Fidelity Advisor equity

funds cost up to 5.75 percent, depending on how much is invested. The shares also come with a 12b-1 fee of 0.25 percent. The fixed-income funds, meanwhile, come with a maximum sales charge of 4.75 percent and a 0.15 percent 12b-1 fee.

2. *Class B* shares typically do not have a front-end sales load. Instead, Fidelity pays the brokers their commission from its own coffers. It recoups that commission, however, by charging you a higher 12b-1 fee. Fidelity, for example, charges a 1 percent 12b-1 fee on its adviser-sold stock funds and 0.90 percent for its bond funds. The funds also come with a contingent deferred sales load (CDSL), which is triggered if the shares are redeemed before seven years of ownership. The CDSL decreases the longer the shares are held, and the shares automatically convert to Class A shares after seven years.

3. *Class C* shares, like B shares, also generally do not have a front-end load. Unlike with B shares, the contingent deferred sales load disappears if the shares are held for more than a year. Also, the shares never convert to Class A shares, which means you will pay the higher 12b-1 fee for as long as you own them. In addition, Class C shares come with an annual commission. Fidelity, for example, charges an annual 1 percent commission and a 1 percent 12b-1 fee on its adviser-sold stock and bond funds.

4. *Class T* shares are designed to reimburse retirement plan administrators. They come with a maximum front-end sales load of 3.50 percent for both stock and bond funds, a 0.50 percent 12b-1 fee on stock funds, and a 0.25 percent 12b-1 fee on bond fund. See Table 15.1.

While most brokers and planners work hard to select shares that are most appropriate for their clients, you should be aware of unscrupulous practices in this area. Since B and C shares carry higher expenses, and part of those fees go straight to the broker each year, some brokers have put clients in those shares regardless of whether they are suitable. As a result, some fund shops have stopped selling B shares altogether.

To help ensure that you get into the right share class for your needs and time horizon, you should ask your broker why he or she is recommending a certain share class and know what assumptions he or she is making about your holding period.

Also be sure to ask whether your total investment with a given fund family qualifies you for a discounted sales charge. At Fidelity, these break points kick in when your total investment reaches $50,000 or more, and they can save you substantial amounts of money.

Table 15.1   What Shares Are Best for You

Class A	Class B	Class C	Class T
• Long-term investors who are comfortable with traditional front-end loads • Large-volume purchasers who want to take advantage of quantity discounts • Investors concerned with higher ongoing fees	• Long-term investors who prefer not to pay a front-end sales load • For investors who may want to own Class A shares without paying a front-end load, by keeping their Class B shares through conversion to Class A • Investors who are not planning to redeem shares in the short term	• Long-term investors who prefer not to pay a front-end sales load • Investors in a managed account wrap program • Investors who have a shorter or uncertain time horizon	• Long-term investors who are not comfortable with traditional front-end loads • Large-volume purchasers who want to take advantage of quantity discounts • Investors who want to spread some of their sales charge expense over time

Source: Fidelity Investments.

Advise or Dissent?

I continue to believe that investors making their own investment choices should opt for the no- or low-load retail Fidelity fund options, but others, who are getting the personalized attention of a stockbroker or other professional, will necessarily be limited to Advisor mutual funds for their Fidelity mutual fund assets.

What's in a Name?

As with Fidelity's VIP funds, many Advisor funds and Fidelity retail funds sound alike, and you may wonder whether they are exactly the same fund. Some of the Advisor funds have names similar to a Fidelity retail fund, but have different managers. In that case, you can't expect the Advisor fund to have the same holdings and performance as the similar retail fund. In other cases, the Advisor and retail versions are both managed by the same person, and the funds' holdings and performances are very similar. In a few other cases, some funds are available only under the Advisor banner (e.g., Advisor Korea), or sound that way, such as Advisor Emerging Asia, which in fact resembles the retail Southeast Asia (see Chapter 10) but has tended have a different manager and somewhat different holdings.

As with all Fidelity funds, once you know what you can own, you need to determine what you want to own. Sorting the Advisor fund wheat from the chaff is my next step.

Advisor Growth Funds

Advisor Aggressive Growth (FGVTX)

This mid-cap growth fund is virtually the same as its retail counterpart, Aggressive Growth (see Chapter 8 for my comments on this fund). Like any aggressive growth fund, this one is at its best when the last bull market gains have been wrung out of the growth sectors of the market.

Advisor Dividend Growth (FDGTX)

This primarily large-cap, value-to-blend fund is basically an identical twin of the retail fund, Dividend Growth (see Chapter 9 for my comments on this fund), often with the same manager and virtually identical portfolios. Buy the retail version if you can—if not, by all means, consider this fund as a core defensive growth fund; risk is moderate. While the fund has begun to correlate more closely to the market, outperformance has occurred.

Advisor Dynamic Capital Appreciation (FRGTX)

This "flexible" growth fund is able to invest in growth and value stocks and across capitalization ranges, although it trends toward a large-cap blend fund.

Advisor Equity Growth (FAEGX)

This fund holds mostly large-cap stocks, often leaning toward growth. Top sectors have tended to be technology and health care. But despite the name, the fund is not always oriented toward growth. It is a suitable core holding for many Advisor investors.

Advisor Equity Value (FAVTX)

This fund has tended to be virtually identical to its retail counterpart, Equity-Income II fund (see my comments on this fund in Chapter 9), and it has posted a strong record of outperformance. This fund bears watching for investors who need a lower-risk stock fund option. Like Equity-Income II, this fund will have a large-cap, value-to-blend style. It is not as focused on dividends, value stocks, or large-caps as the original retail Equity-Income (or VIP Equity-Income), and it has a relatively higher turnover rate but it is more conservative and has held up better to the bear market than most equity funds. The fact that Advisor places this fund with other "Equity" funds, not with its "Growth & Income" funds, while the identical retail fund is in the G&I category, shows the somewhat arbitrary nature of the categories, and this fund's position lies right on that line.

Advisor Fifty (FFYTX)

This is a close clone of retail Fifty fund, similarly holding 50 to 60 stocks, with virtually identical holdings and typically the same manager. While the fund has ranged from the large-cap value to large-cap growth style, it hasn't really strayed below its large-cap orientation.

Advisor Growth Opportunities (FAGOX)

This fund is misnamed. Don't infer the presence of smaller-cap stocks with great growth opportunity here; it is a large-cap fund with a diversified value-to-blend style emphasis.

Advisor Large Cap (FALGX)

This is a twin of retail Large Cap Stock, a large-cap, blend-to-growth stock offering sharing sectors. I like the capitalization range, just not this corral, which has lagged the market despite closely correlating with it.

Advisor Leveraged Company Stock (FLSTX)

This is another twin of its retail namesake, investing in the very same list of stocks. It holds stocks in leveraged companies, those that have issued a lot of debt, to the extent that their debt is, or is equivalent to, junk-bond status. The fund fared surprisingly well in the face of the last protracted economic downturn, and it benefited even more from the recent economic recovery. Its mostly mid-cap holdings have ranged from value to growth, but it does have a history of making one or two very significant sector bets.

Advisor Mid-Cap (FMCAX)

In contrast to many of the preceding funds listed, this fund isn't a clone of the retail namesake—typically thanks to being run by a different manager, leading to totally different top holdings, weightings, and so forth. It has generally shown a blend-to-growth, mid-cap orientation. All this could change if the manager of this fund becomes identical to the retail one.

Advisor Mid-Cap II (FITIX)

This fund is an example of an Advisor fund that is unique to Fidelity's overall mid-cap lineup. The fund has consistently outperformed its peer group and the S&P 500—but has not had to wend its way through a bear market (it was launched in mid-2004 on an upward slope). It has, in its brief lifespan, rarely drifted beyond the growth side of the mid-cap fence; but it has, as its name implies, stuck to its capitalization range. While mid-cap value stocks tend to provide some bear market defense, the same can't be said of the growth stocks in this cap range. As a result, this fund isn't a substitute for either a mid-cap blend or mid-cap value fund but could complement both, especially for more growth-oriented investors.

Advisor Small Cap (FSCTX)

Not surprising, this fund concentrates on the kinds of stocks found in the small-cap Russell 2000 Index—those not among the 1,000 largest in the United States. Although not required to do so, the fund has generally emphasized growth over value, which helped it in 1999, then hampered performances over the ensuing three-year sell-off, only to help bolster it to market-beating results when the recovery took hold. The fund has undergone a recent manager change; former manager Harry Lange is the man Fidelity moved to manage Magellan's listing ship. Look for changes to bring a holdings pattern similar to that of the retail Small Cap Stock.

Advisor Small Cap Growth (FCTGX)

See my comments on the retail Small Cap Growth fund (Chapter 8).

Advisor Small Cap Value (FCVTX)

See my comments on the retail Small Cap Value fund (Chapter 8).

Advisor Strategic Growth (FTQTX)

This typically mid- to large-cap, blend-to-growth (listing toward large-cap growth) fund used to be called Advisor TechnoQuant Growth and relied on technical charting methods to pick stocks based on such things as market trends. But in late 2001 (when retail TechnoQuant Growth became Focused Stock, which bears little resemblance to this fund), this fund changed its name and gave up the charts in favor of more fundamentals-based, computer-aided, quantitative methods (looking at factors such as earnings and dividends).

Advisor Tax Managed Stock (FTSMX)

Like its retail twin, with which it typically shares its manager, this is really a large-cap blend fund in a tax-efficiency wrap. There's not much to recommend it, but I would note that the very high turnover rate found in mid-2006 is a reflection of a manager change and not necessarily indicative of future turnover rates or tax-inefficiency. In fact, after the sudden sell-off in the domestic and global markets in 2006, the incoming manager likely had plenty of losses to harvest and offset the gains.

Advisor Value (FTVFX)

This mid-cap value tilting fund has been run along the same lines, with the same holdings and sector weightings as Fidelity Value (FDVLX) fund (see Chapter 8 for my comments on this fund).

Advisor Value Leaders (FVLTX)

An excellent choice for those investors seeking an actively managed large-cap blend of value and growth stocks with a tilt toward value. This fund has consistently outperformed its market benchmark with a bit less risk. But while you can look for the fund to tilt toward value more often than not, that doesn't mean, as in the case of some other funds, that this fund eschews growth names. It doesn't. But, the growth names it lists have rarely included much in the way of technology; the clear preference is for pharmaceuticals when seeking an injection of growth.

Advisor Value Strategies (FASPX)

Despite its stated objective of focusing on medium-sized value stocks, this has often been a small-cap value fund; more recently, it has mapped as a mid-cap blend fund. (See my comments on its retail counterpart in Chapter 8.)

Advisor Growth & Income Funds

Advisor funds run the fund universe gamut, from growth to income. The following funds combine the best of both those worlds.

Advisor Asset Allocation (FAATX)

If you're looking for one fund for any market, this could be it. The fund allocates its assets with an average, or "neutral," mix of 70 percent stocks, 25 percent bonds, and 5 percent cash. As such, it's actually the Advisor equivalent of the retail Asset Manager: Growth. (See my comments under that entry in Chapter 9.) The funds (Advisor versus retail) have in the past held significantly different holdings and have had differing sector weightings within their overall allocation allotments—something that tends to smooth out over time.

Advisor Balanced (FAIGX)

This is the most conservative G&I offering in the Advisor fund group, with a "neutral" mix of 60 percent stocks and 40 percent bonds. The fund's manager has tended to also run the retail Growth & Income II and VIP Growth & Income. (See my comments on these funds under their respective headings in Chapter 9.) That said, even when these funds have shared the same manager, they have considerably different individual holdings. (While this Advisor fund's stocks are almost purely large-caps, the retail version has had close to half its assets in mid-caps.) While I believe that most investors should take control of their own asset allocation, holding stock and bond funds to the extent set by their own objectives (which tend to become more conservative over time, especially after retirement), this fund is certainly appropriate for conservative investors looking for one-stop diversification.

Advisor Equity-Income (FEIRX)

Like its retail counterpart (Fidelity Equity-Income), this fund seeks to provide shareholders with a large-cap value portfolio sporting a dividend yield higher than that generated by the stocks of the S&P 500. (Of course, with the index sporting a yield under 2 percent, even an equity-income fund isn't going to get all that large a return component from dividends.) The two funds have had different holdings and managers in the past, but both funds have held up reasonably well in the last bear market, and have even handily beaten their value benchmark, with the Advisor version slightly better than retail Equity-Income over the longer-term time periods.

Advisor Growth & Income (FGITX)

This fund is basically a slightly more conservative alternative to the growth fund group, although its risk profile could pair it with Advisor Dividend Growth. The fund has quite closely tracked the retail Growth & Income II (see Chapter 9 for details) recently; the past performance divergence between these two funds could largely be explained by whether the fund has been managed by the same manager or by different managers. In today's market, dividend income is not a major component of return for any diversified stock fund, but funds holding dividend-paying stocks still tend to be less volatile than funds holding growth stocks. I'd prefer Advisor Dividend Growth over this correlated option, but wouldn't invest in either for the sake of their dividend stream.

Advisor Real Estate (FHETX)

This fund tends to map Real Estate (see Chapter 9); and hews to a mid-cap blend style box—but that box contains nothing but REITs inside.

Advisor Strategic Dividend & Income (FTSDX)

This unique and uniquely advantageous fund tends to map its retail namesake (see Chapter 9).

Advisor Freedom Funds

Fidelity's Advisor series of lifestyle or life-cycle funds are perfect clones of their retail series of the same name.

Advisor Freedom Income (FTFAX), Freedom 2005 (FFTVX), Freedom 2010 (FCFTX), Freedom 2015 (FFVTX), Freedom 2020 (FDTFX), Freedom 2025 (FTTWX), Freedom 2030 (FTFEX), Freedom 2035 (FTFEX), Freedom 2040 (FTFFX)

See my comments on Fidelity's Freedom fund lineup in Chapter 9.

Advisor International Funds

At last count there were 14 Fidelity Advisor international funds. Most of them share a name, manager, virtually identical portfolios, and returns similar to those of Fidelity's retail international funds. (The exceptions, most of which are merely a matter of name differences, appear in the list that follows.) For foreign country funds, as for sector funds, the fund's named area of investment tends to trump any consideration of fund manager or exact holdings, because the bulk of the variance in returns is defined by the fund's investment universe. Consequently, these funds tend to be rated the same as their retail counterparts, although sometimes a fund will be rated one notch higher here, given the limited alternative options.

Advisor International Capital Appreciation closely resembles, in holdings and returns, the retail Aggressive International fund.

Advisor Emerging Asia is not a clone of retail Southeast Asia fund, typically having a different manager, but its country and sector breakdown is, naturally enough, very similar, as are its returns and holdings.

Advisor Emerging Markets Income is a close sibling of the retail New Markets Income: Typically, it has the same manager with very similar holdings and returns.

Advisor Global Equity generally invests a bit over half its assets in the United States and the rest overseas. Because it is fully invested in stocks (no bonds), it more closely resembles the retail fund

Worldwide than retail Global Balanced. But it does tend to have a different manager, and hence different holdings and returns.

Advisor Japan has typically been run by a different manager than the one running the retail Japan fund; but the manager of this Advisor fund has, in the past, run other retail funds, like Pacific Basin (but not Japan), at the same time.

Advisor Korea is the one international Advisor fund with no retail counterpart (and its manager typically doesn't run a retail Fidelity fund).

Advisor Focus Funds

Fidelity's Advisor group has 10 Focus, or sector, funds. All but one is a clear carbon copy of an existing Select fund, most sharing managers and virtually identical portfolios and ratings (see my Select fund reviews in Chapter 11). The one apparent exception, Advisor Focus Telecommunications & Utilities Growth, is in fact a close clone of Select Utilities Growth, typically sharing a fund manager and an almost even mix of telecommunications services and more traditional (electric and gas) utilities.

Advisor Income Funds

The Advisor bond funds are also generally clones of retail funds, with similar holdings in line with the funds' names, and generally the same managers (not that active management makes much of a difference at a bond fund, except for junk-bond funds).

Advisor High Income (FHITX) and Advisor High Income Advantage (FAHYX)

These are the two Advisor junk-bond funds. High Income Advantage is the far more aggressive choice by virtue of the types and amounts of distressed debt that it holds. The environment for investing in distressed companies is always about as good as it's likely to get in the trough of a recession, when the thought of economic recovery is considered to be little more than a pipe dream.

Advisor Floating Rate High Income (FFRTX)

This fund is similar to retail Floating Rate High Income, with which it has tended to share a manager. On one hand, as its name suggests, this is a unique kind of junk-bond fund. On the other hand, because of the inherent low interest-rate risk from floating-rate bonds, this fund has so far shown only as much volatility as, for example, Advisor Short Fixed-Income. However, if higher rates or a double-dip recession were to put a credit squeeze on issuing firms, this fund's credit risk may make it by far the riskier option.

The Fidelity Investor's Chart Room: Advisor Funds

Please see Figure 15.1 and Tables 15.2 and 15.3.

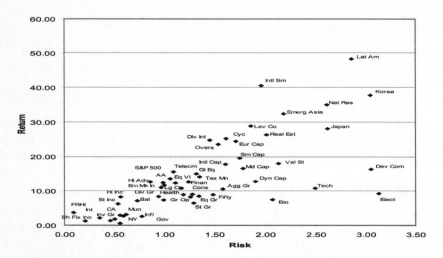

FIGURE 15.1   Fidelity Advisor Funds risk/return ratios

Source: www.fidelityinvestor.com

Table 15.2   Fidelity Advisor Funds: Maximum Cumulative Loss and Maximum Time to Recovery

Fidelity Advisor Funds
Maximum Cumulative Loss/Maximum Time to Recovery

Fund	MCL	MTR	Fund	MCL	MTR
S&P 500	-44.7	NR	Europe Capital App	-43.9	23
Aggressive Growth	-47.0	NR	Global Equity	-41.8	36
Dividend Growth	-32.4	40	Int'l Capital App	-50.5	37
Dynamic Capital App	-57.0	NR	Int'l Discovery	-5.1	NR
Equity Growth	-57.0	NR	Int'l Small Cap	-7.9	NR
Equity Value	-26.9	13	Int'l Small Cap Opp	-7.3	NR
Fifty	-23.6	15	Int'l Value	0.0	
Growth Opportunities	-51.3	NR	Japan	-64.1	NR
Large Cap	-51.1	NR	Korea	-64.0	46
Leveraged Co Stock	-31.2	9	Latin America	-53.8	24
Mid Cap	-34.3	15	Overseas	-53.7	34
Mid Cap II	-7.7	3	Biotechnology	-58.9	NR
New Insights	-5.4	2	Consumer Industries	-29.5	22
Small Cap	-42.7	21	Cyclical Industries	-27.1	9
Small Cap Growth	-8.3	2	Developing Comms	-67.9	NR
Small Cap Value	-6.8	2	Electronics	-66.6	NR
Strategic Growth	-58.8	NR	Financial Services	-24.7	14
Tax Managed Stock	-30.6	26	Health Care	-33.5	40
Value	-4.5	2	Natural Resources	-28.8	17
Value Leaders	-5.6	3	Technology	-79.8	NR
Value Strategies	-35.9	8	Telecom & Utils	-66.7	NR
Asset Allocation	-34.7	34	Floating Rate High Inc	-1.7	4
Balanced	-22.5	27	Gov't Investment	-5.1	8
Equity Income	-27.2	15	High Income	-10.7	12
Growth & Income	-41.8	NR	High Inc Advantage	-29.0	7
Real Estate	-14.4	4	Inflation-Protected	-5.6	5
Strategic Div & Inc	-4.0	5	Intermediate Bond	-3.0	5
Freedom Income	-1.6	5	Investment Grade	-3.6	6
Freedom 2005	-3.0	4	Mortgage Securities	-1.9	3
Freedom 2010	-2.9	4	Short Fixed-Income	-1.3	3
Freedom 2015	-3.6	4	Strategic Income	-3.4	2
Freedom 2020	-4.0	4	Strategic Real Return	-2.2	3
Freedom 2025	-4.4	4	Total Bond	-3.0	3
Freedom 2030	-4.7	3	Ultra-Short Bond	-0.1	1
Freedom 2035	-4.9	3	Intermediate Muni	-1.3	NR
Freedom 2040	-5.1	3	Municipal Income	-4.7	5
Diversified Int'l	-33.2	10	Short-Interm Muni	-1.9	3
Emerging Asia	-54.7	48	CA Muni Income	-4.4	5
Emerging Markets	-13.1	4	NY Muni Income	-4.7	5
Emerging Markets Inc	-10.8	5			

Source: www.fidelityinvestor.com

Table 15.3 Fidelity Advisor Funds Correlation Table

	S&P 500	Aggressive Growth	Dividend Growth	Dynamic Capital App	Equity Growth	Equity Value	Fifty	Growth Opportunities	Large Cap	Leveraged Co Stock	Mid Cap	Small Cap	Strategic Growth	Tax Managed Stock	Value Strategies	Asset Allocation	Balanced	Equity Income	Growth & Income	Real Estate	Diversified International	Emerging Asia	Emerging Markets Inc	Europe Capital App	Global Equity	International Capital App	International Small Cap	Japan	Korea	Latin America	Overseas	Biotechnology	Consumer Industries	Cyclical Industries	Developing Communications	Electronics	Financial Services	Health Care	Natural Resources	Technology	Telecomm & Utilities Growth	Floating Rate High Income	Government Investment	High Income	High Inc Advantage	Inflation-Protected	Intermediate Bond	Investment Grade	Mortgage Securities	Short Fixed-Income	Strategic Income	Municipal Income	CA Muni Income	NY Muni Income
S&P 500	100	68	81	61	86	91	78	84	67	64	75	77	79	84	66	82	71	96	82	23	56	46	8	58	80	57	37	7	40	41	63	17	71	79	57	59	67	26	23	62	38	19	3	19	36	0	2	2	1	1	6	2	2	2
Aggressive Growth	68	100	52	70	80	57	79	78	77	51	77	80	81	70	72	65	58	62	57	22	55	41	4	45	77	53	41	12	30	34	56	35	62	56	69	66	48	23	23	77	17	11	2	9	26	0	1	1	0	1	2	2	2	2
Dividend Growth	81	52	100	48	64	70	66	68	75	45	64	56	69	61	48	70	57	79	63	18	42	30	9	42	61	41	24	10	29	23	48	21	60	56	42	30	49	41	13	42	38	24	0	26	46	0	0	0	0	0	9	0	0	0
Dynamic Capital App	61	70	48	100	75	52	81	66	73	64	68	70	66	76	69	63	45	58	47	12	46	35	5	53	63	42	27	3	25	36	47	10	52	50	66	69	36	13	32	80	17	11	1	11	27	0	1	1	1	1	4	1	1	1
Equity Growth	86	80	64	75	100	75	80	83	90	59	71	85	80	78	63	68	59	79	72	23	46	46	2	48	72	49	34	7	38	29	55	21	72	69	78	80	56	17	17	84	20	12	6	10	25	1	4	4	3	3	1	5	4	4
Equity Value	91	57	70	52	75	100	72	76	77	62	67	73	70	81	62	75	73	91	81	21	58	52	11	56	77	60	39	7	40	51	65	12	62	81	46	53	59	18	34	54	41	22	4	25	36	1	2	2	1	1	8	3	2	3
Fifty	78	79	66	81	80	72	100	84	87	58	78	78	80	83	70	74	67	77	71	17	57	45	8	50	77	57	34	11	42	44	58	18	69	69	60	60	49	17	33	74	27	15	2	12	28	1	2	2	1	1	3	3	3	3
Growth Opportunities	84	78	68	66	83	76	84	100	88	55	73	70	82	78	62	74	70	79	77	21	58	46	6	46	84	59	39	13	42	45	59	16	67	67	58	61	58	23	28	70	23	14	2	12	25	0	1	2	1	1	3	3	2	2
Large Cap	87	77	75	73	90	77	87	88	100	52	73	76	82	79	68	75	65	82	81	24	52	41	3	51	76	53	34	9	39	36	58	23	71	69	65	62	68	23	20	73	21	15	5	12	27	2	3	4	3	2	2	4	4	4
Leveraged Co Stock	64	51	45	64	59	62	58	55	52	100	76	68	59	79	63	68	48	67	45	10	60	45	10	64	70	50	51	7	26	41	61	0	45	61	48	52	29	7	47	54	34	32	0	31	52	0	0	0	0	0	18	0	0	0
Mid Cap	75	77	64	68	71	67	78	73	73	76	100	75	80	80	66	82	62	73	64	15	66	38	12	62	82	56	49	12	25	41	63	12	61	68	59	51	43	18	37	83	40	30	0	27	49	0	0	0	0	0	12	0	0	0
Small Cap	77	80	56	70	85	73	78	70	76	68	75	100	76	84	84	72	50	75	57	23	51	48	4	50	73	51	41	10	36	34	58	19	67	74	69	67	47	12	27	73	25	19	6	17	34	2	4	4	2	4	4	5	4	5
Strategic Growth	79	81	69	66	80	70	80	82	82	59	80	76	100	77	69	71	61	74	66	19	57	49	7	48	81	52	43	12	41	38	60	24	60	64	65	61	50	28	24	69	27	22	3	14	37	1	2	2	0	2	3	3	2	3
Tax Managed Stock	84	70	61	76	78	81	83	78	79	79	80	84	77	100	73	86	61	87	64	19	62	48	11	62	82	58	44	8	37	54	63	9	63	78	53	64	52	15	45	66	33	18	2	19	35	0	1	1	1	1	7	2	1	1
Value Strategies	68	72	48	69	83	62	70	62	68	63	66	84	69	73	100	62	42	64	46	21	43	43	5	39	61	45	34	9	33	29	54	14	70	61	73	76	46	6	14	79	13	15	3	18	31	0	2	2	1	2	3	3	3	3
Asset Allocation	82	65	70	63	68	75	74	74	75	68	82	72	71	86	62	100	63	82	63	23	62	46	20	60	79	61	40	8	38	51	64	10	70	69	42	48	63	20	33	53	36	23	0	32	46	0	0	0	0	0	17	0	0	0
Balanced	71	56	57	45	59	73	67	70	65	48	62	50	61	61	42	63	100	71	81	26	71	57	17	62	78	69	51	12	45	56	67	11	45	54	40	43	52	20	40	45	37	18	0	22	35	1	1	1	1	2	12	0	1	0
Equity Income	96	62	79	58	79	91	77	79	82	67	73	75	74	87	64	82	71	100	78	18	59	48	8	60	80	59	40	8	41	45	64	13	67	82	48	53	61	23	34	54	35	20	3	21	37	1	2	2	1	1	6	2	2	2
Growth & Income	82	57	63	47	72	81	71	77	81	45	64	57	66	64	46	63	81	78	100	21	57	48	4	52	74	59	39	8	44	45	60	17	54	65	46	49	58	24	27	52	33	15	6	10	21	1	4	4	3	2	1	4	4	4
Real Estate	23	22	18	12	23	21	17	21	24	10	15	23	19	19	21	23	26	18	21	100	16	10	19	11	18	16	9	5	7	21	18	13	13	12	24	19	36	8	2	23	10	4	4	9	7	10	7	6	7	9	14	4	5	4
Diversified International	56	55	42	46	46	58	57	58	52	60	66	51	57	62	43	62	71	59	57	16	100	58	18	78	87	88	81	32	41	64	92	5	33	46	37	39	41	13	51	43	20	20	0	24	35	2	1	0	1	1	18	0	0	0
Emerging Asia	46	41	30	35	46	52	45	46	41	45	38	48	49	48	43	46	57	48	48	10	58	100	12	46	59	67	60	14	73	47	64	7	36	42	31	44	35	8	31	34	13	14	3	15	23	0	1	1	0	0	6	1	1	1
Emerging Markets Inc	8	4	9	5	2	11	8	6	3	10	12	4	7	11	5	20	17	8	4	19	18	12	100	10	13	10	10	6	5	42	12	0	4	2	3	1	15	1	10	3	22	14	49	44	23	46	54	56	57	54	71	49	49	48
Europe Capital App	58	45	42	53	48	56	50	46	51	64	62	50	48	62	39	60	62	80	52	11	78	46	10	100	73	65	62	6	27	48	72	3	33	45	43	37	41	14	45	41	30	24	0	26	42	0	0	0	0	1	18	1	1	1
Global Equity	80	77	61	63	72	77	77	84	76	70	82	73	81	82	61	79	78	80	74	18	87	59	13	73	100	79	66	20	47	58	82	13	53	66	52	56	53	23	46	60	30	20	0	22	38	0	0	0	0	0	11	0	0	0
International Capital App	57	53	41	42	49	60	57	59	53	50	56	51	52	58	45	61	69	59	59	16	88	67	10	65	79	100	73	35	53	53	93	7	41	45	33	43	46	13	36	42	15	16	1	20	29	0	0	0	0	0	10	1	1	1
International Small Cap	37	41	24	27	34	39	34	39	34	51	49	41	43	44	34	40	51	40	39	9	81	60	10	62	66	73	100	45	35	44	77	3	21	31	30	32	28	5	36	31	13	25	0	21	32	0	0	0	1	0	13	0	0	0
Japan	7	12	10	3	7	7	11	13	9	7	12	10	12	8	9	8	12	8	8	5	32	14	6	6	20	35	45	100	17	9	34	2	4	5	4	5	7	1	5	7	0	7	0	8	8	2	1	1	3	2	5	0	0	1
Korea	40	30	29	25	38	40	42	42	39	26	25	36	41	37	33	38	45	41	44	7	41	73	5	27	47	53	35	17	100	35	47	7	34	36	20	35	33	9	16	25	4	7	6	6	13	2	4	4	2	3	1	5	5	5
Latin America	41	34	23	36	29	51	44	45	36	41	41	34	38	54	29	51	56	45	45	21	64	47	42	48	58	53	44	9	35	100	54	2	20	33	22	32	42	6	51	32	20	16	1	21	19	4	2	2	3	4	20	2	2	1
Overseas	63	56	48	47	56	65	58	59	58	61	63	58	60	63	54	64	67	64	60	18	92	64	12	72	82	93	77	34	47	54	100	6	42	50	43	45	48	12	37	49	16	25	1	28	42	0	0	0	0	0	15	1	1	1
Biotechnology	17	35	21	10	21	12	18	16	23	0	12	19	24	9	14	10	11	13	17	13	5	7	0	3	13	7	3	2	7	2	6	100	15	10	16	11	16	43	1	13	2	0	2	0	1	2	2	2	1	1	2	3	2	3
Consumer Industries	71	62	60	52	72	62	69	67	71	45	61	67	60	63	70	70	45	67	54	13	33	36	4	33	53	41	21	4	34	20	42	15	100	58	49	54	51	10	7	60	23	10	3	11	25	1	2	2	1	2	1	2	2	2
Cyclical Industries	79	56	56	50	69	81	69	67	69	61	68	74	64	78	61	69	54	82	65	12	46	42	2	45	66	45	31	5	36	33	50	10	58	100	37	49	43	9	35	48	26	15	14	13	25	9	12	11	7	9	1	12	10	10
Developing Communications	57	69	42	66	78	46	60	58	65	48	59	69	65	53	73	42	40	48	46	24	37	31	3	43	52	33	30	4	20	22	43	16	49	37	100	63	46	7	9	82	15	15	1	9	24	0	0	0	0	0	4	0	0	0
Electronics	59	66	30	69	80	53	60	61	62	52	51	67	61	64	76	48	43	53	49	19	39	44	1	37	56	43	32	5	35	32	45	11	54	49	63	100	38	5	19	84	8	5	6	3	12	0	6	5	3	5	0	6	5	5
Financial Services	67	48	49	36	56	59	49	58	68	29	43	47	50	52	46	63	52	61	58	36	41	35	15	41	53	46	28	7	33	42	48	16	51	43	46	38	100	11	6	43	16	6	0	14	16	1	0	0	1	1	9	0	0	0
Health Care	26	23	41	13	17	18	17	23	23	7	18	12	28	15	6	20	20	23	24	8	13	8	1	14	23	13	5	1	9	6	12	43	10	9	7	5	11	100	2	7	14	7	0	4	13	0	0	0	0	0	1	0	0	0
Natural Resources	23	23	13	32	17	34	33	28	20	47	37	27	24	45	14	33	40	34	27	2	51	31	10	45	46	38	36	5	16	51	37	1	7	35	9	19	6	2	100	15	19	9	0	13	17	0	0	0	0	0	9	0	0	0
Technology	62	77	42	80	84	54	74	70	73	54	63	73	69	66	79	53	45	54	52	23	43	34	3	41	60	42	31	7	25	32	49	13	60	48	82	84	43	7	15	100	12	12	4	7	21	0	3	3	2	3	1	4	3	3
Telecomm & Utilities Growth	38	17	38	17	20	41	27	23	21	34	40	25	27	33	13	36	37	35	33	10	20	13	22	30	30	15	13	0	4	20	16	2	23	26	15	8	16	14	19	12	100	21	4	32	37	5	4	5	5	4	24	5	6	6
Floating Rate High Income	19	11	24	11	12	22	15	14	15	32	30	19	22	18	15	23	18	20	15	4	20	14	14	24	20	16	25	7	7	18	25	0	10	15	15	5	8	7	9	12	21	100	0	62	67	0	2	2	3	1	27	1	1	1
Government Investment	3	2	0	1	6	4	2	2	5	0	0	6	3	2	3	0	0	3	6	4	0	3	49	0	0	1	0	0	6	1	1	2	3	14	1	6	0	0	0	4	4	0	100	14	5	82	96	98	89	90	52	93	91	92
High Income	19	9	28	11	10	25	12	12	12	31	27	17	14	19	16	32	22	21	10	9	24	15	44	26	22	20	21	8	6	21	28	0	11	13	9	3	14	4	13	7	32	62	14	100	78	7	23	21	20	21	70	18	17	16
High Inc Advantage	36	26	48	27	25	36	28	25	27	52	49	34	37	35	31	46	35	37	21	7	35	23	23	42	38	29	32	8	13	19	42	1	25	25	24	12	16	13	17	21	37	67	5	78	100	2	9	8	8	7	48	7	6	6
Inflation-Protected	0	0	0	0	1	1	1	0	2	0	0	2	1	0	0	0	1	1	1	10	2	0	46	0	0	0	0	2	2	4	0	2	1	9	0	0	1	0	0	0	5	0	82	7	2	100	77	82	78	71	44	76	77	76
Intermediate Bond	2	1	0	1	4	2	2	1	3	0	0	4	2	1	2	0	1	2	4	7	1	1	54	0	0	0	0	1	4	2	0	2	2	12	0	6	0	0	0	3	4	2	96	23	9	77	100	97	89	96	63	91	87	88
Investment Grade	2	1	0	1	4	2	2	2	4	0	0	4	2	1	2	0	1	2	4	6	0	1	56	0	0	0	0	1	4	2	0	2	2	11	0	5	0	0	0	3	5	2	98	21	8	82	97	100	94	90	60	94	92	93
Mortgage Securities	1	0	0	1	3	1	1	1	3	0	0	2	0	1	1	0	1	1	3	7	1	0	57	0	0	0	1	3	2	3	0	1	1	7	0	3	1	0	0	2	5	3	89	20	8	78	89	94	100	85	59	84	83	83
Short Fixed-Income	1	1	0	1	3	1	1	1	2	0	0	4	2	1	2	0	2	1	2	9	1	0	54	1	0	0	0	2	3	4	0	1	2	9	0	5	1	0	0	3	4	1	90	21	7	71	96	90	85	100	59	65	81	82
Strategic Income	6	2	9	4	1	8	3	3	2	18	12	4	3	7	3	17	12	6	1	14	18	6	71	18	11	10	13	5	1	20	15	2	1	1	4	0	9	1	9	1	24	27	52	70	48	44	63	60	59	59	100	56	54	53
Municipal Income	2	2	0	1	5	3	3	3	4	0	0	5	3	2	3	0	0	2	4	4	0	1	49	1	0	1	0	0	5	2	1	3	2	12	0	6	0	0	0	4	5	1	93	18	7	76	91	94	84	85	56	100	98	99
CA Muni Income	2	2	0	1	4	2	3	2	4	0	0	4	2	1	3	0	1	2	4	5	0	1	49	1	0	1	0	0	5	2	1	2	2	10	0	5	0	0	0	3	6	1	91	17	6	77	87	92	83	81	54	98	100	99
NY Muni Income	2	2	0	1	4	3	3	2	4	0	0	5	3	1	3	0	0	2	4	4	0	1	48	1	0	1	0	1	5	1	1	3	2	10	0	5	0	0	0	3	6	1	92	16	6	76	88	93	83	82	53	99	99	100

Source: www.fidelityinvestor.com

SIXTEEN

Fidelity Index Funds

Fidelity Investment's forte is stock picking.

That said, in the never-ending battle between actively managed mutual funds—which are funds run by portfolio managers aiming to beat a market index—and the stock market indexes themselves, Fidelity clearly hedges its bets. Of the more than 300 mutual funds run by Fidelity, nearly 20 are passively managed, meaning they are more or less run by a computer programmed to invest exactly as their target indexes.

The argument for investing in passively managed funds, otherwise known as *index fund investing*, is pretty convincing.

Over the five-year period ending December 31, 2005, the Standard & Poor's 500 Index beat 61.9 percent of large-cap funds, the Standard & Poor's MidCap 400 Index beat 70.4 percent of all mid-cap funds, and the Standard & Poor's SmallCap 600 outperformed 71.4 percent of all small-cap funds. Similarly, over the same five-year period, the indexes beat 65.4 percent of large-cap funds, 81.3 percent of mid-cap funds, and 72.4 percent of small-cap funds.

What's more, the average expense ratio for index funds is dropping. In part, that's because Fidelity and Vanguard Group, dueling to become the provider of the lowest-cost index funds, recently lowered fees associated with their index funds.

Indeed, the average large-cap index fund sported a 0.39 percent expense ratio in 2005, down from 0.41 percent in 2004. The average mid-cap index fund, meanwhile, cost 0.55 percent, and the average small-cap index fund charged 0.54 percent, down from 0.60 percent and 0.55 percent, respectively, in 2004, according to Standard & Poor's Corporation.

On many of its index funds, Fidelity runs two classes of shares: Advantage Class and Investor Class. Investors able to invest at least $100,000 in the fund can purchase the Advantage Class shares, which come with a 0.07 percent expense ratio on stock funds and a 0.10 percent expense ratio on bond funds. Investors unable to meet the $100,000 minimum may invest in the Investor Class shares, which come with an expense ratio of 0.10 percent for stock funds and 0.20 percent for bond funds.

Let's take a closer look at what Fidelity has to offer.

Passive Funds for Active Investors

Fidelity Four-in-One Index Fund invests in a combination of four Fidelity stock and bond index funds using an asset allocation strategy designed for investors seeking a broadly diversified, index-based investment. The fund's target asset allocation is approximately 55 percent in Spartan 500 Index Fund, 15 percent in Spartan Extended Market Index Fund, 15 percent in Spartan International Index Fund, and 15 percent in Fidelity U.S. Bond Index Fund.

Target index: N/A
Investment category: Large-cap blend
Expense ratio: 0.21 percent

Fidelity Nasdaq Composite Index Fund aims to invest at least 80 percent of its assets in common stocks included in the Nasdaq Composite Index. It uses a sampling technique based on quantitative analytic procedures to create a portfolio of securities listed in the index that have a similar investment profile to the entire index.

Target index: Nasdaq Composite Index
Investment category: Large-cap growth
Expense ratio: 0.45 percent

Spartan 500 Index Fund-Advantage (FSMAX) seeks results corresponding with the total return of common stocks as represented by the S&P 500 Index. The fund normally invests at least 80 percent of its assets in equity securities of companies included in the index. Assets are allocated among common stocks in approximately the same weightings as the index.

Target index: S&P 500 Index
Investment category: Large-cap blend
Expense ratio: 0.07 percent

Spartan 500 Index Fund-Investor Class (FSMKX) seeks results corresponding with the total return of common stocks represented by the S&P
500 Index. The fund normally invests at least 80 percent of its assets
in equity securities of companies included in the index. Assets are
allocated among common stocks in approximately the same weightings as the index.

Target index: S&P 500 Index
Investment category: Large-cap blend
Expense ratio: 0.10 percent

Spartan Extended Market Index Fund-Advantage (FSEVX) seeks total returns that match those of the Dow Jones Wilshire 4500 Completion
Index, which represents the performance of stocks of mid- to small-
capitalization U.S. companies.

Target index: Wilshire 4500 Index
Investment category: Mid-cap blend
Expense ratio: 0.07 percent

Spartan Extended Market Index Fund-Investor (FSEMX) seeks total returns that match those of the Dow Jones Wilshire 4500 Completion
Index, which represents the performance of stocks of mid- to small-
capitalization U.S. companies.

Target index: Wilshire 4500 Index
Investment category: Mid-cap blend
Expense ratio: 0.10 percent

Spartan International Index Fund-Advantage (FSIVX) aims to match the
total return of the foreign stock markets. It invests at least 80 percent
of its assets in stocks that are included in the Morgan Stanley Capital
International Europe, Australasia and Far East (MSCI EAFE) Index.
It does not invest in emerging market countries. The fund may invest
a significant portion of its assets in Japanese companies.

Target index: MSCI EAFE
Investment category: Foreign large-cap blend
Expense ratio: .07 percent

Spartan International Index Fund-Investor (FSIIX) aims to match the total
return of the foreign stock markets. It invests at least 80 percent of

its assets in stocks that are included in the Morgan Stanley Capital International Europe, Australasia and Far East (MSCI EAFE) Index. It does not invest in emerging market countries. The fund may invest a significant portion of its assets in Japanese companies.

Target index: MSCI EAFE
Investment category: Foreign large-cap blend
Expense ratio: 0.10 percent

Spartan Total Market Index Fund-Advantage (FSTVX) seeks to match the total return of the Dow Jones Wilshire 5000 Composite Index, which represents the performance of a broad range of U.S. stocks.

Target index: Dow Jones Wilshire 5000 Composite Index
Investment category: Large-cap blend
Expense ratio: 0.07 percent

Spartan Total Market Index Fund-Investor (FSTMX) seeks to match the total return of the Dow Jones Wilshire 5000 Composite Index, which represents the performance of a broad range of U.S. stocks.

Target index: Dow Jones Wilshire 5000 Composite Index
Investment category: Large-cap blend
Expense ratio: 0.10 percent

Spartan U.S. Equity Index Fund-Advantage (FUSVX) seeks results corresponding with the total return of common stocks represented by the S&P 500 Index. The fund normally invests at least 80 percent of its assets in equity securities of companies included in the index. Assets are allocated among common stocks in approximately the same weightings as the index. This fund is generally available only to institutional and retirement plan investors.

Target index: S&P 500
Investment category: Large-cap blend
Expense ratio: 0.07 percent

Spartan U.S. Equity Index Fund-Investor (FUSEX) seeks results corresponding with the total return of common stocks represented by the S&P 500 Index. The fund normally invests at least 80 percent of its assets in equity securities of companies included in the index. Assets are allocated among common stocks in approximately the same weightings as the index. This fund is generally available only to institutional and retirement plan investors.

Target index: S&P 500
Investment category: Large-cap blend
Expense ratio: 0.10 percent

Bond Index Funds

Fidelity U.S. Bond Index Fund (FBIDX) aims to replicate the price and interest performance of the debt securities in the Lehman Brothers Aggregate Bond Index.

Target index: Lehman Brothers Aggregate Bond Index
Investment category: Intermediate-term bond
Expense ratio: 0.32 percent

Spartan Intermediate Treasury Bond Index Fund-Advantage (FIBAX) invests at least 80 percent of its assets in bonds included in the Lehman Brothers 5–10 Year U.S. Treasury Bond Index. It normally maintains a dollar-weighted average maturity between 3 and 10 years.

Target index: Lehman Brothers 5–10 Year U.S. Treasury Bond Index
Investment category: Broad market bond
Expense ratio: 0.10 percent

Spartan Intermediate Treasury Bond Index Fund-Investor (FIBIX) invests at least 80 percent of its assets in bonds included in the Lehman Brothers 5–10 Year U.S. Treasury Bond Index. It normally maintains a dollar-weighted average maturity between 3 and 10 years.

Target index: Lehman Brothers 5–10 Year U.S. Treasury Bond Index
Investment category: Broad market bond
Expense ratio: 0.20 percent

Spartan Long-Term Treasury Bond Index Fund-Advantage (FLBAX) invests at least 80 percent of its assets in bonds included in the Lehman Brothers Long U.S. Treasury Bond Index. Normally maintains a dollar-weighted average maturity of 10 years or more.

Target index: Lehman Brothers Long U.S. Treasury Bond Index
Investment category: Broad market bond
Expense ratio: 0.10 percent

Spartan Long-Term Treasury Bond Index Fund-Investor (FLBIX) invests at least 80 percent of its assets in bonds included in the Lehman

Brothers Long U.S. Treasury Bond Index. Normally maintains a dollar-weighted average maturity of 10 years or more.

> Target index: Lehman Brothers Long U.S. Treasury Bond Index
> Investment category: Broad market bond
> Expense ratio: 0.20 percent

Spartan Short-Term Treasury Bond Index Fund-Advantage (FSBAX) invests at least 80 percent of its assets in bonds included in the Lehman Brothers 1–5 Year U.S. Treasury Bond Index. Normally maintains a dollar-weighted average maturity of three years or less.

> Target index: Lehman Brothers 1–5 Year U.S. Treasury Bond Index
> Investment category: Broad market bond
> Expense ratio: 0.10 percent

Spartan Short-Term Treasury Bond Index Fund-Investor (FSBIX) invests at least 80 percent of its assets in bonds included in the Lehman Brothers 1–5 Year U.S. Treasury Bond Index. Normally maintains a dollar-weighted average maturity of three years or less.

> Target index: Lehman Brothers 1–5 Year U.S. Treasury Bond Index
> Investment category: Broad market bond
> Expense ratio: 0.20 percent

Fidelity Investor Chart Room

Please see Figures 16.1 through 16.3.

Fund	MCL	MTR
S&P 500	-44.7	NR
Sp 500 Idx	-44.9	NR
Sp Tot Mkt Idx	-44.1	43
Nasdaq Idx	-11.6	3
Sp Ext Mkt Idx	-47.6	34
4in1 Idx	-36.8	34
Sp Intl Idx	-48.5	30
ONEQ	-11.7	3

FIGURE 16.1 Fidelity Index Funds: Maximum cumulative loss and maximum time to recovery

Source: www.fidelityinvestor.com

	S&P 500	Sp 500 Idx	SpTot Mkt Idx	Nasdaq Idx	Sp Ext Mkt Idx	4in1 Idx	Sp Intl Idx	ONEQ
S&P 500	100	100	98	77	76	95	59	77
Sp 500 Idx	100	100	98	77	76	95	59	77
SpTot Mkt Idx	98	98	100	84	88	97	60	84
Nasdaq Idx	77	77	84	100	87	77	39	99
Sp Ext Mkt Idx	76	76	88	87	100	84	49	86
4in1 Idx	95	95	97	77	84	100	74	76
Sp Intl Idx	59	59	60	39	49	74	100	39
ONEQ	77	77	84	99	86	76	39	100

FIGURE 16.2   Fidelity Index Funds correlation table

Source: www.fidelityinvestor.com

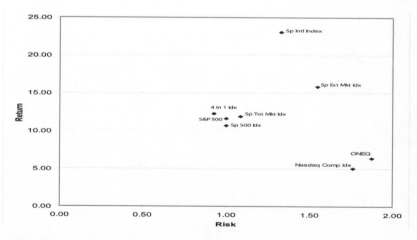

FIGURE 16.3   Fidelity Index Funds risk/return ratios

Source: www.fidelityinvestor.com

SEVENTEEN

Exchange Traded Funds

Fidelity's Playing Catch-Up, or Not

"ETFs, Benjamin" might be the words whispered in Dustin Hoffman's ear in *The Graduate,* were it being filmed today instead of the 1960s.

Thanks in part to their low fees as well as increasing demand from financial advisers eager to distinguish themselves from competitors by offering something new and different, exchange traded funds (ETFs) are the fastest-growing segment of the mutual fund industry.

ETF assets have soared to $322 billion, up from $226 billion at the end of 2004 and a mere $70 billion in 2001. While ETFs are still nipping at the heels of the nearly $9 trillion mutual fund industry, the 29 percent annual growth rate of the ETF industry is nearly three times that of the mutual fund industry.

As a firm believer in active management, Fidelity Investments seems content to play a relatively minor character in the unfolding story of ETFs—at least for now. Trouble is, for those of us who know Fidelity's history, there's a fad that it took Fidelity 30 years to believe in: index funds. In the process of hemming and hawing, Fidelity ceded a trillion-dollar industry to Vanguard. If it's not careful, Fidelity is likely to cede the next trillion-dollar industry, exchange traded funds, to Barclays and, to a lesser but no less stinging extent, Vanguard.

Fidelity launched its one and only ETF, the OneQ, in October of 2003. Despite being late to the table, the OneQ was the first ETF to track the

Nasdaq Composite Index, one of the most widely watched indexes in the world.

Today, OneQ, which trades on the Nasdaq (of course!) under the symbol ONEQ, has more than $85.6 billion in assets. Please see Figure 17.1.

So, what exactly is an ETF? Good question. At its core, an ETF is an investment vehicle that trades like a stock but is diversified like a fund.

ETFs are a great way to participate in the broader markets at a lower cost and greater tax efficiency than provided by a mutual fund that invests in the same index. Today, there are more than 200 ETFs to choose from. You can purchase the Standard & Poor's 500 Index using something nicknamed the "Spider" (the ticker for this investment vehicle is SPY) or buy the Dow Jones Index using something dubbed the "diamonds" (the ticker for this investment vehicle is DIA). Then there's the "cube" (ticker QQQ), which invests in the top 100 stocks of the Nasdaq Composite Index.

ETFs can also be more "imaginative" (read: risky) and invest in very specialized sectors such as alternative energy companies or commodities.

While the rate at which money is flowing into ETFs (not to mention the rate at which fund companies are cranking out new ETFs) certainly suggests there is a faddish quality to the new investment vehicle, ETFs are here to stay. Here's why.

FIGURE 17.1   ETF Asset Growth

- *Diversification:* ETFs combine the strengths of mutual fund diversification, both broad indexing and more narrowly focused sector participation, with the day-to-day control of individual stock investing.

- *Low cost:* ETFs are consistently cheaper than actively managed mutual funds, including most index funds. The expense ratio of Fidelity's OneQ, for example, is 0.30 percent, compared to 0.45 percent for the Fidelity Nasdaq Composite Index Fund.

- *Tax efficiency:* Turnover, a measure of how much trading of securities takes place within a portfolio, is relatively low on ETFs. Since shareholders foot the bill for trading costs, low turnover translates into lower costs.

- *Flexibility:* Unlike actively managed and index mutual funds, ETFs trade throughout the day and can be bought and sold at the click of a button.

- *Sophistication:* On the surface, ETFs appear to a relatively straightforward investment vehicle. But they may also be used in conjunction with a number of complex investment techniques, including covered call writing, cash management, hedging, tax-loss repositioning, and the so-called core-and-explore style of investing.

Of course, there are reasons not to invest in ETFs.

- *Passive investing:* While there is a lot of scuttlebutt about the creation of actively managed ETFs, right now you are pretty much limited to passively managed ETFs.

- *Trading costs:* ETFs are usually subject to commissions on the same or a similar schedule as individual stocks. At Fidelity, you can make online stock trades for $19.95. But at that price, a monthly purchase of shares translates into $239.40 a year in commissions. Generally speaking, for monthly dollar cost averagers with accounts under $100,000, it's cheaper to invest in an index than a similarly managed ETF.

Fidelity has found another way to tap into the popularity of ETFs. About a year after launching the OneQ, it unveiled a service that assists its brokerage account holders to build and trade portfolios of ETFs. That tool is called Fidelity ETF Portfolio Builder.

Before discussing how Fidelity may be useful in assembling a portfolio of ETFs, let's take a closer look at how ETFs work and what makes them different from other classifications of mutual funds.

ETFs: What Are They and How Do They Work?

Much like closed-end mutual funds, ETFs are baskets of stocks that are themselves traded like stocks. While most ETFs trade on the American Stock Exchange, they're also traded on the New York Stock Exchange and Nasdaq. Since they're traded like stocks, they are priced continually throughout the day and can be shorted or bought on margin—many even have put and call options.

To understand how ETFs work, it helps to compare them to open- and closed-end mutual funds.

Open-end funds are bought from and sold back to the fund manager, generally at the fund's net asset value, or NAV. Sometimes additional fees are levied in the form of sales loads or redemption fees. Without a doubt, open-end funds are the most common form of mutual funds.

Meanwhile, closed-end funds are bought from and sold back to investors and brokers. Unlike an open-end fund, which issues new shares with each new purchase, a closed-end fund sells a fixed number of shares in its portfolio of securities. Like ETFs, closed-end funds trade on the major U.S. exchanges, and their market value is determined by the good-old-fashioned laws of supply and demand. As a result, the price of their shares can go far—often 20 percent or more—above or below net asset value.

The vast majority of closed-end funds trade at a discount to NAV. That said, the management of a closed-end fund does have some control over market prices. If a fund's market price falls too far below net asset value, management has the option to buy back shares. For most fund companies, however, that is a measure of last resort. That's because a share buyback means a smaller fund and lower management fees. Managers can also add closed-end shares in a secondary offering, which they are somewhat more likely to do if the fund is popular enough to trade at a premium.

One of the biggest advantages of closed-end funds is that they tend to hold more illiquid securities. Free from the worry about shareholder redemptions, closed-fund managers tend to load up on thinly traded, micro-cap, or foreign securities, including those based in emerging markets.

Now Come ETFs

Basically, you should think of an ETF as the beautiful love child of open- and closed-end mutual funds. Indeed, ETFs have most of the advantages of closed-end funds and most of the advantages of open-end mutual funds with few of the disadvantages of either.

For the most part, transactions involving ETFs involve a broker. While fund companies don't continually buy and sell shares, they will trade large blocks of shares, called Creation Units, primarily to institutions engaged in arbitrage. If the market price of an ETF falls *below* net asset value, arbitrageurs can buy up a block of the ETF, sell it to the fund company, and in return get the ETF's component stocks, plus a small amount of cash, mostly from recent stock dividends. The arbitrageur can then sell the individual stocks for a profit. If an ETF's market price *exceeds* net asset value, arbitrageurs can buy a basket of the requisite stocks and exchange them to the fund company for newly created ETF shares, again for a profit.

While the arbitrage profit is pretty much guaranteed, it is never a large one. That's because arbitrageurs generally keep the price of an ETF from getting too far out of whack with net asset value. Consequently, prices for the more heavily traded ETFs typically stay within a half percent of NAV.

How Are the ETFs' Prices Set?

Most ETFs have their net asset values set as a relatively even portion of the relevant index. Even so, NAVs will vary slightly due to index rebalancings and distributions.

Cubes: QQQQ = 1/40 of the Nasdaq 100 Index

Spiders: SPY = 1/10 of the S&P 500

Diamonds: DIA = 1/100 of the Dow Jones 30 Industrials Average

Costs

While ETFs are generally cheaper than other mutual funds, they do come with stock commissions. If you make frequent purchases, such as in a dollar cost averaging plan, you will probably find ETFs more expensive than traditional funds.

Still, it's important to remember that many fund companies (Fidelity included) discourage frequent trading—either by charging redemption fees or putting a limit on the number of trades involving a particular fund over a certain time period. If that's the case, paying ETF commissions may be preferable to paying redemption fees or getting frozen out of a mutual fund account.

It's also worth noting that besides commissions, you may have to "pay" a bid/ask spread when trading ETFs. These spreads vary from zero for SPDRs and QQQ under normal market conditions to close to 1 percent for the least-liquid sector offerings, and even close to 4 percent for the most illiquid foreign markets, like the iShares MSCI Brazil Index.

Taxes and ETFs

A fully invested mutual fund is required to sell stocks whenever investors make significant net redemptions from the fund. Meanwhile, an index fund has to sell its positions proportionately. In other words, it can't just sell the positions being held for a loss.

But ETF shareholders mostly buy and sell among themselves. Even when ETFs are broken up, the fund company delivers individual stocks, not cash, so there is no capital gain or loss realized.

While ETFs do sometimes have capital gains distributions, those distributions are generally limited to the extent that they have sold stocks to account for changes in their underlying index benchmark. Even then, any previous ETF turnover via Creation Units would already have allowed the ETF to get rid of its lowest-cost-basis shares, and thus reduced the taxable gain realized from later selling a stock.

Spiders and Vipers and Cubes . . . Oh My!

If you are the kind of person who has a difficult time remembering names, be prepared to cringe. Generally, the names given to ETFs reflect the company that is sponsoring the ETF and the index the ETF follows. Following is a list of some of the most popular ETFs:

> *SPDRs* (pronounced spiders) is an acronym for Standard & Poor's Depositary Receipts. SPY tracks the S&P 500 Index; the Mid Cap SPDRs, or MDY, track the S&P 400 mid-cap index. Sector SPDRs track the broader sector groupings within the S&P 500.

> *CUBEs*, or the QQQ, tracks the tech-heavy Nasdaq 100 Index, which essentially consists of the 100 largest nonfinancial stocks in the Nasdaq Composite and is thus almost a pure technology index, albeit one not including IBM and other NYSE-listed firms.

> *DIAMONDs* tracks the Dow Jones Industrial Average, a benchmark of 30 blue-chip stocks.

> *iShares.* Barclays Global Investors has numerous domestic-style ETFs, tracking Russell and S&P value, growth, and combined indexes, and also the broader Dow Jones sectors, Goldman Sachs technology subsectors, and also a Cohen & Steers Realty sector. Its Morgan Stanley Capital International foreign stock offerings run the gamut, from the broad-based EAFE Index of foreign established markets to individual country ETFs, including some emerging markets.

> *VIPERs* (pronounced vipers), an acronym for Vanguard Index Participation Receipts, are share classes of existing Vanguard open-end

funds. (Note: Vanguard is toying with the idea of renaming its VIPERs "ETFs"—there's some real creative genius for you. But, by the time you read this, don't be surprised if Vanguard VIPERs are wearing ETF clothing.)

HOLDRs (pronounced holders) is an acronym for Holding Company Depository Receipts. These Merrill Lynch products track such relatively narrow sectors as biotechnology and the Internet.

StreetTRACKS are State Street Global Advisors' lineup of ETFs, which track the Dow Jones–style and global indexes, Morgan Stanley technology indexes, and three financial services indexes offered by Keefe, Bruyette & Woods.

Fidelity ETF Portfolio Builder

Essentially, this tool allows you to customize and trade a portfolio of ETFs based on one of seven so-called lenses. Each lens falls into one of three groupings.

1. *Sector lenses* allow you to view market by sectors, such as energy or biotechnology.
   a. Dow Jones Sector iShares
   b. S&P 500 Sector Spiders

2. *Capitalization lenses* allow you to view market by a company's market capitalization.
   a. Russell iShares
   b. S&P iShares

3. *Style/capitalization lenses* allow you to view the market based on growth or value opportunities.
   a. S&P Barra iShares
   b. Russell iShares
   c. Morningstar iShares

Using Fidelity ETF Portfolio Builder

1. *Select a market lens.* After you select a market lens, Fidelity ETF Portfolio Builder will provide you with a list of the ETFs in that lens, set to their default share price and weighting.

2. *Enter an investment amount.* The Fidelity ETF Portfolio Builder defaults the investment amount to $10,000, but the amount can be changed at any time. Note: To buy an ETF portfolio there must be at least two ETFs and an investment amount of $2,000.

3. *Adjust your portfolio.* Select one of three options: Weighting, Dollars, or Shares. Selecting Lock will fix an entry. All other weightings will automatically recalculate and adjust proportionally, based on whole shares and the investment amount.

You must name and save your ETF portfolio before you can buy it.

Word to the Wise

Remember, ETFs trade like stocks. That means you should expect to pay a commission for each ETF you purchase. If you decide to replicate the Dow Jones Sector iShares portfolio, for example, you could find yourself buying 10 ETFs, which would cost you $199.50 at Fidelity's standard $19.95 rate for each purchase.

PART FOUR

Securing Your Financial Future Using Fidelity's Funds

EIGHTEEN

Model Portfolios

Getting a Return on Your Investment in Fidelity

The following model portfolios represent four specific investment objectives, which range from the potentially more volatile Aggressive Growth and Global Growth portfolios to the more moderate, risk-adjusted Growth & Income to the conservative Income portfolios. (See the Chart Room at the end of this chapter for model portfolio holdings.)

Each portfolio is distinct in terms of investment objective, asset allocation, holdings, capitalization range, regional concentration, industry weightings, diversified total holdings (the total number of stocks and/or bonds represented in each portfolio), investment styles, capital gains exposure, yield, and risk. The industry concentration, turnover rate, average P/E ratio, and capital gains exposure will likely be significantly higher in my more aggressive portfolios. The yields will tend to be highest where you'd expect them to be: in the portfolios with the name *income* in them.

While each portfolio is designed as a buy-and-hold model portfolio, a lot can happen in 15 minutes, let alone 15 years. Actively monitoring and managing your own assets remains key to ensuring your financial engine will get you where you want to go.

The Aggressive Growth Portfolio

This portfolio's objective is *total return* over a 15-year or greater time span. This is not a day trader portfolio, but, over time, you could expect this to have the highest turnover rate relative to the other four portfolios if you were actively managing it. As such, the trading fees for this portfolio could be significantly higher or lower (which is the price you pay for trying to outpace the market in short-term moves), while its tax efficiency could be demonstrably lower or higher based on the amount of trading you might do with it. This portfolio is most suitable for investors who are willing to take on more risk than the market in order to tap into potentially bigger gains, and it is best suited to tax-advantaged accounts such as an IRA. While I'm not an advocate of short-term trading or market timing (at least for most investors), I do believe in active management of investment instruments relative to your objective. As a result, this Aggressive Growth portfolio is designed for investors who are also comfortable with fairly active trading—who are willing to make meaningful trades on a monthly basis but who are comfortable with making no trades if they are riding a strong wave of performance on their existing holdings.

The Global Growth Portfolio

This portfolio's objective is designed for today's growth investor—someone with a minimum of 10 years to go before he or she needs to even consider taking a dime out of the portfolio and who can benefit from the clearest long-term trend in the markets today: globalization. (As such, it really replaces what I would call a typical "growth" model portfolio.) It can invest as much as 80 percent of its assets in non-U.S. markets, which could have volatility above and beyond the Moderate Growth Portfolio that follows.

The global economy and global marketplace is a reality that many U.S. investors continue to ignore, compromising their risk management and total return benefit. I continue to believe that every investor can benefit from a non-U.S stake (see Chapter 10 for my take on the global marketplace and Fidelity's unique international fund lineup and strengths).

While it's hard to imagine for some, the fact is that over half the stock market value in the world is outside the United States. And the growth rate of the non-U.S. markets is significantly faster, and for the most part the average price per share is cheaper than the United States. Yes, there are risks (some greater, some smaller) depending on the region. Emerging markets in Latin America are distinctly different from those in Eastern Europe and Asia. Even within each subregion, you need to tread carefully. Mexico and Venezuela look downright problematic from both a political and socioeconomic standpoint and through a market valuation lens. In contrast, Brazil seems solid. In the established markets of Europe and Japan, there are correlation issues to contend with in the large-cap space and inefficiencies to profit from in the mid- and small-cap ranges.

As Scott Offen, manager of the Fidelity Value Discovery Fund (FVDFX), told me in a recent interview, "In every single decade but one, the rest of the world outperformed the U.S.—including the '50s which was considered one of the greatest bull markets of all time. The only exception was the '90s, but if you take the bubble years out of the '90s, the rest of the world outperformed, too. And it's not that we're failing as a country, it's just that when people start from a lower base it's easier to grow more quickly. We already have the highest standard of living in the world, and it's much easier for people to catch up than it is for us to keep powering ahead." To a measured extent, I agree.

Growth & Income Portfolio

The objective of this portfolio is reasonable capital appreciation with less risk than the stock market and reasonable yield with less interest-rate and/or credit risk than the bond market. While the portfolio is naturally weighted in bond funds, it's not exclusively a bond portfolio—not by a long shot. That's because income-oriented investors need to keep their eye on the capital appreciation ball, too. Why? With an all-bond portfolio, inflation (even the historically low inflation rates that we have been experiencing for the past several years) would take its toll on the purchasing power of your principle. Looked at from another angle, bonds just aren't likely to show returns as high as the stock market over any period of more than a few years, and those few years may be behind us.

Income investors may think that yield is the most important thing to attain when it comes to this portfolio. But high yields typically signal undue risks. In the recent bull market and robust economy, investors have enjoyed some fairly reliable rewards for their yield-related risk taking. When looking for short-term, plain-vanilla bond funds, Fidelity has several to choose from (see Chapter 12), which is fine, since the one I like owns a basket of blue-chip short-term U.S. Treasury bonds.

Capital & Income Portfolio

This portfolio is best suited for the retirees who want to preserve the value of their nest egg while generating a reasonable level of income, those who want to reduce the level of investment risk to a minimum, those who have no need to grow their capital assets in order to maintain their lifestyle. This portfolio could also serve as a complement to a Moderate Growth or Growth & Income portfolio—especially for investors looking to safeguard a portion of their asset base. It can also be used as a hedge for the more aggressive growth-oriented portfolios.

The Fidelity Investor's Chart Room

Please see Figure 18.1.

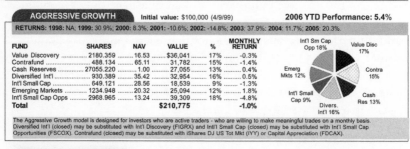

AGGRESSIVE GROWTH — Initial value: $100,000 (4/9/99) — **2006 YTD Performance: 5.4%**

RETURNS: 1998: NA; 1999: 30.9%; 2000: 8.3%; 2001: -10.6%; 2002: -14.8%; 2003: 37.9%; 2004: 11.7%; 2005: 20.3%.

FUND	SHARES	NAV	VALUE	%	MONTHLY RETURN
Value Discovery	2180.359	16.53	$36,041	17%	-0.3%
Contrafund	488.134	65.11	31,782	15%	-1.4%
Cash Reserves	27055.220	1.00	27,055	13%	0.4%
Diversified Int'l	930.389	35.42	32,954	16%	0.5%
Int'l Small Cap	649.121	28.56	18,539	9%	-1.3%
Emerging Markets	1234.948	20.32	25,094	12%	1.8%
Int'l Small Cap Opps	2968.965	13.24	39,309	18%	-4.8%
Total			**$210,775**		**-1.0%**

The Aggressive Growth model is designed for investors who are active traders - who are willing to make meaningful trades on a monthly basis. Diversified Int'l (closed) may be substituted with Int'l Discovery (FIGRX) and Int'l Small Cap (closed) may be substituted with Int'l Small Cap Opportunities (FSCOX). Contrafund (closed) may be substituted with iShares DJ US Tot Mkt (IYY) or Capital Appreciation (FDCAX).

GROWTH — Initial value: $100,000 (1/1/98) — **2006 YTD Performance: 6.3%**

RETURNS: 1998: 14.3%; 1999: 41.7%; 2000: 11.3%; 2001: -8.8%; 2002: -16.8%; 2003: 35.5%; 2004: 15.2%; 2005: 15.8%.

FUND	SHARES	NAV	VALUE	%	MONTHLY RETURN
Value Discovery	2337.070	16.53	$38,632	15%	-0.3%
Contrafund	433.884	65.11	28,250	11%	-1.4%
Low-Priced Stock	613.218	42.40	26,000	10%	-1.2%
Strategic Dividend & Inc	2468.684	12.67	31,278	12%	0.7%
Diversified Int'l	1006.235	35.42	35,641	13%	0.5%
Int'l Small Cap	709.568	28.56	20,265	8%	-1.3%
Emerging Markets	1185.338	20.32	24,086	9%	1.8%
Int'l Small Cap Opps	1543.974	13.24	20,442	8%	-4.8%
Cash Reserves	38207.461	1.00	38,207	14%	0.4%
Total			**$262,802**		**-0.4%**

The Growth model looks to deliver capital appreciation for most longer term investors: Most suitable for investors with 10 years or more to retirement. Low-Priced (closed) may be substituted with Value (FDVLX). Diversified Int'l (closed) may be substituted with Int'l Discovery (FIGRX) and Int'l Small Cap (closed) may be substituted with Int'l Small Cap Opportunities (FSCOX). Contrafund (closed) may be substituted with iShares DJ US Tot Mkt (IYY) or Capital Appreciation (FDCAX).

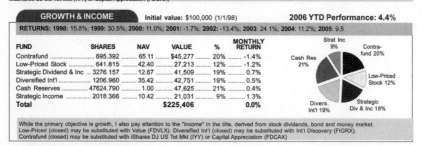

GROWTH & INCOME — Initial value: $100,000 (1/1/98) — **2006 YTD Performance: 4.4%**

RETURNS: 1998: 15.8%; 1999: 30.5%; 2000: 11.0%; 2001: -1.7%; 2002: -13.4%; 2003: 24.1%; 2004: 11.2%; 2005: 9.5

FUND	SHARES	NAV	VALUE	%	MONTHLY RETURN
Contrafund	695.392	65.11	$45,277	20%	-1.4%
Low-Priced Stock	641.815	42.40	27,213	12%	-1.2%
Strategic Dividend & Inc	3276.157	12.67	41,509	19%	0.7%
Diversified Int'l	1206.960	35.42	42,751	19%	0.5%
Cash Reserves	47624.790	1.00	47,625	21%	0.4%
Strategic Income	2018.366	10.42	21,031	9%	1.3%
Total			**$225,406**		**0.0%**

While the primary objective is growth, I also pay attention to the "income" in the title, derived from stock dividends, bond and money market. Low-Priced (closed) may be substituted with Value (FDVLX). Diversified Int'l (closed) may be substituted with Int'l Discovery (FIGRX). Contrafund (closed) may be substituted with iShares DJ US Tot Mkt (IYY) or Capital Appreciation (FDCAX).

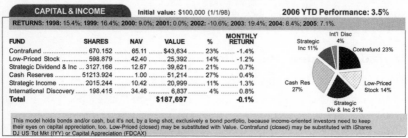

CAPITAL & INCOME — Initial value: $100,000 (1/1/98) — **2006 YTD Performance: 3.5%**

RETURNS: 1998: 15.4%; 1999: 16.4%; 2000: 9.0%; 2001: 0.0%; 2002: -10.6%; 2003: 19.4%; 2004: 8.4%; 2005: 7.1%.

FUND	SHARES	NAV	VALUE	%	MONTHLY RETURN
Contrafund	670.152	65.11	$43,634	23%	-1.4%
Low-Priced Stock	598.879	42.40	25,392	14%	-1.2%
Strategic Dividend & Inc	3127.166	12.67	39,621	21%	0.7%
Cash Reserves	51213.924	1.00	51,214	27%	0.4%
Strategic Income	2015.244	10.42	20,999	11%	1.3%
International Discovery	198.415	34.46	6,837	4%	0.8%
Total			**$187,697**		**-0.1%**

This model holds bonds and/or cash, but it's not, by a long shot, exclusively a bond portfolio, because income-oriented investors need to keep their eyes on capital appreciation, too. Low-Priced (closed) may be substituted with Value. Contrafund (closed) may be substituted with iShares DJ US Tot Mkt (IYY) or Capital Appreciation (FDCAX).

FIDELITY INVESTOR · AUGUST 2006 · 1-800-718-8291 · WWW.FIDELITYINVESTOR.COM

FIGURE 18.1 Model portfolio vital statistics

Source: www.fidelityinvestor.com

NINETEEN

Fidelity Hot Hands Funds

Chasing Performance Can Work

You've read this book with an eye toward getting a return on your investment in it.

If you've read each chapter sequentially, you know there's a wealth of information.

This section is designed to unequivocally provide that return on your investment—both in a measured, model portfolio manner (see Chapter 18) and right here in an exclusive trading strategy that works singularly well for investors in Fidelity funds.

Hot Hands 101

Let me cut right to the performance chase.

While most investment experts tell you that chasing performance is to investors what chasing cars is to dogs—a one-way ticket to a dirt nap—I'm here to tell you that *chasing performance can work*.

Yes. It can.

Buying last year's best-performing fund cuts against the grain of consensus opinion and conventional wisdom. Yet this simple maneuver has consistently rewarded Fidelity fund investors—that is, specifically, investors in Fidelity funds.

This Fidelity fund–based (as opposed to manager-based) investing concept is called *Hot Hands*. The concept is simple: Basically, buying whichever Fidelity fund has performed best in the previous year has, in fact, turned out to be a winning ticket.

The rewards, as demonstrated by more than 20 years of data, are ample and compelling.

But before I get to the Fidelity Funds Hot Hands details, let me cast some rational cold water on this strategy.

For starters, let me emphasize this nonstarter: This strategy does not beat the market every year. (But it does reveal a very healthy long-term result, which I'll get to in a moment.)

Further, I do not advocate sinking your entire stash into the latest Fidelity Hot Hands fund. That would foolishly fly against the fully diversified, risk-adjusted investment approach that I personally practice and professionally preach.

Now for the good news: I believe that many growth-oriented investors could improve their performance by putting a portion (10 percent or so) of their money to work following the Fidelity Hot Hands strategy.

Why?

Simply put, within the Fidelity family of funds there is strong evidence that top fund performance persists, that repeat winners can stay ahead of the masses. Or, simply put: At Fidelity, Fidelity Hot Hands stay hot.

This cuts against the grain of fund industry dogma that "past performance is no guarantee of future results." Well, it isn't a guarantee, *but I think it is a meaningful predictor*.

My model portfolios in my multiple-award-winning, independent advisory newsletter (www.fidelityinvestor.com) have strongly outperformed the markets for a few reasons, but probably the most important single reason is the linchpin of our proprietary manager ranking system (see Chapter 7 for details on this system). Our success shows that managers with consistent career records of outperformance are better bets than managers with consistently weak or inconsistently good records. Natch.

And, as it happens, looking back over the past 20 years, Fidelity Hot Hands has shown very similar outperformances to my newsletter's Growth model portfolio (more on that in a moment).

System Failure

On the face of it, the fact that one year's top-performing fund ought to continue to perform well sounds reasonable (but also like the kind of language that would be nixed by a Securities and Exchange Commission lawyer if a fund company put it in its advertising). Interestingly, *this strategy doesn't work for all fund families or for all funds*. Some "persistence of performance" investors have had their heads handed to them over the years. I tried it with Janus limited funds' lineup, Putnam's, and T. Rowe Price's excellent universe of funds, and it failed. The one other fund family where this system consistently pans out rather than pans: Vanguard!

One reasons that Fidelity Hot Hands works at Fidelity, but not at many other fund families, is that Fidelity managers do what they do, and keep doing it, no matter how the markets change around them—and they eschew groupthink.

It's interesting to see how a simple system—and you can't get much simpler than "buy last year's winner"—can beat the market and most professional managers.

Dogs Don't Have Their Day

Using the prior year's performance as a guide for selecting Fidelity funds is highly profitable. And ignoring it, or going with the "dogs," as some investment advisers who use a contrarian approach like to suggest, can lead Fidelity investors to market-lagging, and even negative, returns.

Consider, for instance, 2000's dog fund, Aggressive International. Had you bought it in 2001, after the dismal 31.0 percent loss it suffered in 2000, you'd have lost another 8.9 percent. In 2001, the dog was Aggressive Growth, and I probably don't have to tell you it was the worst fund in 2002, down 41.2 percent. Yes, Aggressive Growth was again the 2002 dog . . . and then gained 33.4 percent in 2003, but that's not particularly impressive given how many funds gained more than that. Dogs are dogs for a reason. They may be man's best friend, but they're an investor's nightmare.

Gaming the System

Enter the Hot Hands winners. Here are the ground rules for the strategy. First, I looked at all of Fidelity's retail diversified stock funds for each year between 1983 and 2006. I excluded single-sector (Select, Real Estate, Utilities) funds and balanced funds (those with significant bond positions). On the international side, I did include the diversified internationals, but (analogous with excluding sector funds) I excluded the geographically nondiversified (single-country) international funds.

The methodology isn't complicated.

But does it work?

You betcha.

For example, by following a Fidelity Hot Hands investment strategy at Fidelity from the end of 1983, putting your money into Magellan, through the end of 2005, putting your money into International Small Cap Stock, you would have bested the market by a wide margin. Playing the contrarian and buying the previous year's worst fund, however, has proven to be an awful idea. Since 1983 the strategy would have netted the investor index-lagging returns. See Figure 19.1.

FI Funds Hot Hands History			
Year	Hot ETF Held	12 Mo Ret	S&P 500
1984	Magellan	2.0	6.2
1985	Equity-Income	25.1	31.6
1986	Overseas	69.2	19.2
1987	Overseas	18.4	5.1
1988	Capital Appreciation	37.6	16.5
1989	Capital Appreciation	26.9	31.8
1990	Contrafund	3.9	-3.1
1991	Contrafund	54.9	30.5
1992	Aggressive Growth	8.4	7.6
1993	Low-Priced Stock	20.2	10.1
1994	Overseas	1.3	1.3
1995	Blue Chip Growth	28.4	37.6
1996	New Millenium	23.2	23.0
1997	Export & Multinational	23.7	33.4
1998	Disciplined Equity	21.8	28.6
1999	Aggressive Growth	103.0	21.0
2000	New Millenium	-6.0	-9.1
2001	Mid-Cap Stock	-12.8	-11.9
2002	Low-Priced Stock	-6.2	-22.1
2003	Fifty	20.4	28.7
2004	Leveraged Company Stock	24.5	10.9
2005	International Small Cap	29.5	4.9
	Cumulative	6743.0	1237.8
	Annualized	21.2	12.5
*as of 12/30/2005			

VIP Funds Hot Hands History			
Year	Hot ETF Held	12 Mo Ret	S&P 500
1993	VIP Equity-Income	16.8	10.1
1994	VIP Overseas	0.5	1.3
1995	VIP Equity-Income	33.8	37.6
1996	VIP Contrafund	20.1	23.0
1997	VIP Index 500	31.4	33.4
1998	VIP Index 500	27.3	28.6
1999	VIP Growth	36.3	21.0
2000	VIP Overseas	-19.8	-9.1
2001	VIP Investment Grade	7.6	-11.9
2002	VIP Investment Grade	9.5	-22.1
2003	VIP Investment Grade	4.4	28.7
2004	VIP Technology	-1.0	10.9
2005	VIP Real Estate	14.2	4.9
	Cumulative	380.0	265.8
	Annualized	12.8	10.5
*as of 12/30/2005			

FIGURE 19.1   Hot Hands Hot Returns

On an annualized basis that's 21.2 percent for Fidelity Hot Hands versus 12.5 percent for the market and just 9.5 percent for the worst-fund contrarian strategy. Hot Hands outperformed the market by 8.7 percent per year.

As it happens, this is almost exactly the outperformance shown by my Model Growth Portfolio. For the six years through mid-2006 since I launched www.fidelityinvestor.com, my Model Growth Portfolio has shown an annualized return of 7.1 percent, while the S&P 500's annualized return has been 2.1 percent. That's a 5.0 percent per year average outperformance.

This would appear to be a statistical tie, but it's a lot easier to beat the market in a strong up market (the past 20 years) than it is in a virtually flat one (the past six years), especially if you're taking on more risk than the market. Compared to Fidelity Hot Hands, for example, www .fidelityinvestor.com's Model Growth Portfolio's outperformance has been relatively consistent, and its volatility, or risk, has been considerably lower than the market's risk, while Fidelity Hot Hands has been considerably more risky (as you'd expect for a single-fund portfolio) and has shown big differences from the market's return—sometimes down, but mainly on the up and up.

Still, it's humbling to see that the investment equivalent of a tic-tac-toe-playing pigeon can do so well over time, especially given that putting together my Growth model has been a lot more work than just buying the latest year's winner.

As I said before, buying the Fidelity Hot Hand fund doesn't guarantee you are going to beat the index every year. In fact, the Hot Hand fund beat the index in only 13 out of 22 years.

But that's not the point.

It's the accumulation of market-beating returns that really makes the difference. (To put it another way, the good years were better than the bad years were poor.) Over the long haul, this strategy soars like an eagle when most other simple strategies fall like, well, turkeys.

How can you make use of this Fidelity Hot Hands phenomenon? First, as I've said, this isn't meant to be an all-or-nothing strategy. I certainly don't recommend that you put all of your money into one fund and switch it each year. A method that's generally worked in the past isn't a sure thing, and with just one holding at a time, you'll take on much more risk than you need to. We need to use our heads as well as our computers.

But make no mistake, this Fidelity Hot Hands strategy leads to funds that can serve as a niche performance piece for a well-rounded, smartly diversified portfolio.

TWENTY

Your Own Fidelity Mutual Fund

Fidelity's Top 100 Holdings

Okay.
    This is not a no-brainer like the prior chapter's strategy.

Still, with a little bit of Web legwork, you can track and, if the spirit moves you, create your own Fidelity fund using some searchable information about Fidelity's funds' holdings.

Not to be confused with front-running any individual fund, this approach is one based on ferreting out the top 100 holdings owned by all of Fidelity's funds as a way to create a total market portfolio using Fidelity's funds' largest holdings as your guide. Think of it as an equivalent to one of the most heavily traded exchange traded funds, the "Cube" (QQQQ): The Cube holds the top 100 stocks in the Nasdaq. Here, you'll have what we can dub the "IQ," which is Fidelity's managers' know-how in sorting the top 100 holdings' wheat from the total markets' chaff.

Does it make sense to attempt to do so? Let's look at three key considerations: (1) meeting the minimum investment amount required, (2) upholding the diversification principle, and (3) delivering performance.

1. From an investment minimum standpoint, it does. If you have $10,000 or more, plenty of time, and relatively good research and Excel formatting confidence (if not outright experience), it can.

2. From a diversification standpoint, yes, it does, since the names (see following) reflect Fidelity's funds' largest holdings, you get plenty of expected large-cap names in the mix, but you also net some mid-cap, small-cap, and foreign stocks to boot.

3. From a performance perspective, it works as well.

Getting Started

The best place to begin is with a self-test of your Excel formatting skills and interests. If you flip back to Chapter 4, where we discussed the construction of a Fidelity Daily tracking sheet, you'll quickly get a sense of whether pursuing this strategy makes sense or will be of practicable interest for you. From that vantage, you can begin to survey the Web's landscape for the reliable sources of data that you'll need to be able to rebalance our Fidelity IQ portfolio on a quarterly basis.

To find top holdings for Fidelity, go to the following link (www.sec.gov/cgi-bin/browse-edgar?action=getcompany&CIK=0000315066&owner=include) and look for Form 13F-HR (Quarterly report filed by institutional managers, Holdings). The other ways is to start at Edgars's home page (www.sec.gov/edgar.shtml) and go to "Search Company Filings" and click on "Companies and Other Filers." Type in FMR CORP in "Company Name" space or the number 0000315066 in the CIK space and then look for Form 13F-HR.

Index Debate

There are many different ways to construct an index of holdings, using so many different modes, nodes, and methods that it hardly makes sense to delve into the deep end of the debate in this chapter.

For our purposes, know that there are basically two types of index constructionist camps: *equal-* and *capitalization-*weighted indexers. Those in the latter camp weight their indexes in accordance with the capitalization size of the listed instruments accounted for in the weightings of each position in the index. The S&P 500 is the best example of this approach, which basically means that larger companies not only account for a greater portion of any given index, but that the percentage amounted to each company within such an index is also determined by the size of the company. Another example would be the Cube mentioned earlier, wherein you'll find the largest 100 companies in the Nasdaq.

Equal-weighted indexers use whatever filer they choose to sift the number of companies they want to have represented in their index and then weight those holdings equally—no matter what the size of the company is. Doing so lets the current market activity determine the future value of each holding in relationship to all others in the index. It's my preferred approach, but that doesn't mean it's the best or only one—it just means that I think it is!

Here, we can benefit from the best of both worlds; with a meta-incorporation of our predetermined Fidelity filter to determine Fidelity's funds' largest 100 holdings. Not to be conflated or confused with Fidelity's funds' largest company holdings (although that would also be an interesting index to track), this index will account for a range of large-, mid-, and even a few small-cap companies and then equal-weight them: 1 percent in each of the 100 holdings.

Creating Our Fidelity IQ Fund

Here's what a portfolio of Fidelity's Top 100 stocks would have looked like as of June 30, 2006. Please see Figure 20.1.

Fidelity Top 100 Holdings as of 3/31/2006

1 American International Group	51 Amgen Inc
2 General Electric	52 America Movil SA
3 Google Inc	53 Novartis AG
4 Johnson & Johnson	54 Verizon Communications
5 Microsoft	55 Clear Channel Communications
6 UnitedHealth Group	56 Colgate Palmolive Co
7 Schlumberger Ltd	57 ConocoPhillips
8 Bank of America	58 Federal Natl Mtg Assn
9 Wal-Mart Stores	59 Goldman Sachs Group Inc
10 Exxon Mobil	60 Disney Walt Co
11 Genentech Inc	61 Hartford Finl Svcs Group Inc
12 Home Depot	62 Bellsouth Corp
13 AT&T Inc	63 BP Plc
14 Wyeth	64 Peabody Energy Corp
15 Apple Computer Inc	65 UBS AG
16 Qualcomm Inc	66 Baxter Intl Inc
17 Honeywell Intl Inc	67 St Jude Med Inc
18 Merrill Lynch & Co Inc	68 Avon Prods Inc
19 Valero Energy Corp New	69 Golden West Finl Corp
20 Halliburton Co	70 Motorola Inc
21 Pfizer Inc	71 3M Co
22 Wells Fargo & Co	72 United Technologies Corp
23 Cardinal Health Inc	73 Intel Corp
24 Sprint Nextel Corp	74 Seagate Technology
25 Best Buy Inc	75 Qwest Communications Intl
26 Hewlett Packard Co	76 Baker Hughes Inc
27 Encana Corp	77 Network Appliance Inc
28 Altria Group Inc	78 Burlington Northn Santa Fe
29 Wachovia Corp	79 SLM Corp
30 Citigroup Inc	80 Research in Motion Ltd
31 Nokia Corp	81 Symantec Corp
32 American Express Co	82 ACE Ltd
33 JP Morgan Chase & Co	83 Corning Inc
34 Total SA	84 Gilead Sciences Inc
35 Cisco Sys Inc	85 Merck & Co Inc
36 Yahoo Inc	86 Prudential Finl Inc
37 Procter & Gamble Co	87 Target Corp
38 Dell Inc	88 Newmont Mining Corp
39 Staples Inc	89 Canadian Natl Ry Co
40 Marvell Technology Group Ltd	90 Starwood Hotels & Resorts Wrld
41 Celgene Corp	91 First Data Corp
42 Berkshire Hathaway Inc	92 Royal Dutch Shell PLC
43 Monsanto Co	93 Talisman Energy Inc
44 CVS Corp	94 GlobalSantaFe Corp
45 Canadian Nat Res Ltd	95 Safeway Inc
46 Ebay Inc	96 State Str Corp
47 Oracle Corp	97 National OilWell Varco Inc
48 Aetna Inc	98 Dr Horton Inc
49 Pepsico Inc	99 Metlife Inc
50 Allergan Inc	100 Weatherford International LT

FIGURE 20.1   Fidelity top 100 holdings as of 3/31/2006

Source: www.fidelityinvestor.com

Tracking Our Fidelity IQ Fund

Plugging the information into your Fidelity Daily (see Chapter 4 for details) will mean that you can keep a running record of how this portfolio is performing relative to the major total market indexes and benchmarks. While it's not rocket science, and while the returns might not be rocketing, the ability to create your own Fidelity Fund based on a clear and consistent manner and method is one way to take a step closer to feeling what it's like to be a Fidelity manager in your own right.

The Fidelity Way

As we've come to see throughout this book, Fidelity is more verb than noun—the more you view it as such, the more you'll be able to use it to your financial advantage.

By *verb* I mean that Fidelity is not simply a static mutual fund company. Nor is it a staid financial services conglomerate. Nor is it (yet) a dynamic processing empire. It's all three and then some, offering some of the most innovative tools, products, and platforms for the novice and sophisticated investor alike, all at steeply discounted prices when compared with full-service brokerages, and none at discounted quality.

In the near future, I'd look to Fidelity to become a cross between Automatic Data Processing (ADP), which processes nearly one out of every four 401(k) account statements and is deeply embedded in everything to do with payroll solutions for businesses of nearly every size; Wal-Mart, which offers multiple lines of products from several competing producers at discounted prices; and a private bank, which delivers goods and services to its clientele ranging from insurance to income distributions to capital preservation and appreciation strategies, trust, and charitable giving.

I expect Fidelity to combine all three for the benefit of its own overall bottom line, taking pennies on trillions of dollars rather than dimes on billions, and I expect Fidelity investors to benefit from the multitude of services in three distinct ways: comprehensive breadth of offerings, dis-counted cost of services, and ease of use.

That's no small order for any company, but Fidelity's not a place where thinking small (unless it's thinking small-caps) or staying inside the box goes unchallenged. Fidelity transformed the investment world by suc-cessfully delivering expert and low-cost portfolio management, in the form of mutual funds, to Main Street. Fidelity's next step was to apply the discount brokerage model it had executed so well in money management to the whole financial services industry, from insurance soup to bond-trading nuts. These days, Fidelity has its eye on its next $1 trillion indus-try, applying its discount prices but full-service quality to everything to do with you financial life.

But don't think that you don't have your work cut out for you. The de-gree to which you'll benefit from your relationship with Fidelity depends upon how much you're willing to put into it—at least initially.

Reading this book is one step in that direction.

As with any business, Fidelity has its glitches and shortcomings. But from the top down and the bottom up it's not a place that has ever rested on its laurels. Instead, it has always sought to compete at the highest level, in the highest orders, and win. For the most part, thanks to the steward-ship of the family that owns and oversees it, it has been not simply a suc-cessful competitor, but a respected leader and innovator—not simply reactive to others' better business ideas, but inventive of them.

Of nearly 40,000 people who are currently employed by Fidelity and an-other several hundred thousand who have at some point parked their ca-reers at the curb on Devonshire Street, no one who has worked at Fidelity in any capacity would discount the caliber of the people who work there. Human capital is equally as esteemed and valued as investment capital; new ideas don't just sprout of their own accord, nor does the process of nurturing those ideas through to their harvest in real-world practice, with-out many knowing hands tending the garden.

Now that Fidelity has so many fields to tend, the onus is on upper man-agement to grow their core businesses reasonably well, while at the same time nourishing the almost entrepreneurial zeal and feel of the place.

When I last cashed a Fidelity paycheck, back in 1992, I left feeling much the way I felt when I received my diplomas from the sundry high-minded colleges I attended prior to landing my Fidelity job; never once did I not feel that Fidelity was itself a high-minded place, where ideas mattered as much as their execution, and both mattered more than any office politick-ing or the realpolitik of NBC's *The Office*. Never.

In a world where flip-flopping has become mainstay, I remain un-equivocal: The Fidelity way is one that I believe in and one that I person-ally as well as professionally invest in. Credit for my belief in Fidelity is based on what I know about the company, its management, and its man-agers' success, which is in turn, I know, based in part on Fidelity's unique way of hiring, training, culling, promoting, and supporting the overall mission of financial services excellence at low cost. Fidelity grows its own talent unlike any other firm in the business. That's been good news for Fidelity investors in the past, and it will remain good news for the future of Fidelity investors!

Fidelity Investor Centers

Unless otherwise noted, hours are Monday through Friday, 8:00 a.m. to 5:30 p.m. To confirm addresses and hours, or for directions, call one of the local numbers listed or 1–800–544–9797.

ARIZONA

Scottsdale
Scottsdale Center, 7373 N. Scottsdale Rd., Suite 182A,
Scottsdale, AZ 85253
800–352–9793

CALIFORNIA

Brea/Orange County
815 E. Birch Street, Brea, CA 92821
800–526–7251

Glendale
527 North Brand Blvd., Glendale, CA 91203
800–638–0620

Irvine—Newport Beach
The Atrium, 19200 Von Karman, Suite 150, Irvine, CA 92612
800–331–5829

Los Angeles—Century City
10100 Santa Monica Blvd., Los Angeles, CA 90067
800–544–5853

Palo Alto
251 University Ave., Palo Alto, CA 94301
800–742–1566

Sacramento
1760 Challenge Way, Sacramento, CA 95815
800–635–3441

San Diego
7676 Hazard Ctr. Dr., Suite 210, San Diego, CA 92108
800–635–0472

San Francisco
8 Montgomery St., San Francisco, CA 94105
800–462–5450

San Jose
851 East Hamilton Ave., Suite 100, Campbell, CA 95008
800–544–4180

San Rafael
950 Northgate Drive, Suite 101, San Rafael, CA 94903
800–990–1139 or 415–472–0955

Walnut Creek
1400 Civic Drive, Suite 100, Walnut Creek, CA 94596
800–544–8235

Woodland Hills
Warner Center/Trillium Complex, 6300 Canoga Avenue, Suite 1001, Woodland Hills, CA 91367
800–544–7602

COLORADO

Denver
World Trade Center, 1625 Broadway, Suite 110, Denver, CO 80202
800–543–5219

CONNECTICUT

Greenwich
Pickwick Commons, 48 West Putnam Avenue, Greenwich, CT 06830
800–833–3349

New Haven
One Century Tower, 265 Church Street, New Haven, CT 06510
800–243–4549

Stamford
300 Atlantic St., Stamford, CT 06901
800–882–8255

West Hartford
Town Center, 29 S. Main Street, Suite A02, West Hartford, CT 06107
800–458–6665

DISTRICT OF COLUMBIA

Washington, D.C.
1900 K Street NW, Suite 110, Washington, DC 20006
800–854–2832

DELAWARE

Wilmington
PNC Bank Center, 222 Delaware Avenue, Suite 5, Wilmington, DE 19801
800–201–5380

FLORIDA

Boca Raton
Tower Shoppes, 4400 N. Federal Hwy, Suite 150, Boca Raton, FL 33431
800–544–8237

Coral Gables
90 Alhambra Plaza, Coral Gables, FL 33134
800–552–7389

Fort Lauderdale
4090 North Ocean Blvd., Ft. Lauderdale, FL 33308
800–535–9051

Naples
8880 Tamiami Trail North, Naples, FL 34103
800–544–6761

Orlando
Longwood Village, 1907 West State Road 434, Longwood, FL 32750
800–451–7690

Palm Beach Gardens
The Harbour Shops, 2401 PGA Blvd., Palm Beach Gardens, FL 33410
800–553–3292

Sarasota
8065 Beneva Road, Sarasota, FL 34238
800–237–8826

Tampa
1502 N. Westshore Blvd., Tampa, FL 33607
800–248–2710

GEORGIA

Atlanta—Buckhead
3445 Peachtree Road NE, Suite 125, Atlanta, GA 30326
800–543–2158

Atlanta—Dunwoody
1000 Abernathy Road, Northpark Town Center, Building 400,
Lobby Level, Atlanta, GA 30328
800–526–7169

ILLINOIS

Chicago—North Franklin
One North Franklin Street, Ground Floor, Chicago, IL 60606
800–621–9222

Oak Brook
Oak Brook Regency Towers, 1415 West 22nd St., Suite 100,
Oak Brook, IL 60523
800–526–7260

Schaumburg
Prudential Bldg., 1700 E. Golf Rd., Suite 150, Schaumburg, IL 60173
800–521–5650

Wilmette
Edens Plaza, 3232 Lake Avenue, Suite 155, Wilmette, IL 60091
800–325–1105

INDIANA

Indianapolis
4729 East 82nd Street, Indianapolis, IN 46250
800–343–2575

MAINE

Portland
3 Canal Plaza, PO Box 4910, Portland, ME 04101
800–521–3018

MARYLAND

Bethesda
7401 Wisconsin Ave., Bethesda, MD 20814
800–531–2419

Towson
Towson Commons, 1 West Pennsylvania Ave., Suite 180
Towson, MD 21204
800–451–2620

MASSACHUSETTS

Boston—Back Bay
801 Boylston St., Boston, MA 02116
800–445–9448

Boston—Congress Street
155 Congress Street, Boston, MA 02109
800–343–2140

Boston—State Street
27 State Street, Boston, MA 02109
800–343–3548

Braintree
Executive Plaza Ctr., 300 Granite Street, Braintree, MA 02184
800–356–2854

Burlington
44 Mall Road, Suite 100, Burlington, MA 01803
800–526–7172

Worcester
416 Belmont Street (Route 9), Worcester, MA 01608
800–521–3026

MICHIGAN

Birmingham
280 Old N. Woodward Ave., Birmingham, MI 48009
800–682–4746

Southfield
Franklin Plaza, 29155 Northwestern Hwy., Southfield MI 48034
Mail to: P.O. Box 5037, Southfield, MI 48086
800–343–9631

MINNESOTA

Minneapolis
7600 France Avenue South, Suite 110, Edina, MN 55435
800–543–2165

MISSOURI

Kansas City
The Plaza Steppes, 700 West 47th St., Suite 120
Kansas City, MO 64112
800–633–8703

Ladue
Schnuck's Ladue Crossing, Suite One, 8885 Ladue Road
Ladue, MO 63124
800–777–1910

NEW JERSEY

Millburn
150 Essex Street, Millburn, NJ 07041
800–545–0323

Morristown
56 South Street, Morristown, NJ 07960
800–622–0281

Paramus
Garden State Plaza, 501 Route 17 South
Paramus, NJ 07652
800–722–0438

NEW YORK

Garden City
1055 Franklin Ave., Suite 100, Garden City, NY 11530
800–233–0117

Melville
999 Walt Whitman Road, Melville, NY 11747
800–526–7252

New York City—Downtown
61 Broadway, Street Level, New York, NY 10006
800–348–3030

New York City—Midtown
350 Park Avenue, New York, NY 10022
800–662–6008

New York City—Rockefeller Center
Rockefeller Center, 1271 Avenue of the Americas
New York, NY 10020
800–275–8354

NORTH CAROLINA

Charlotte
Two Coltsgate, 4611 Sharon Road, Suite 125
Charlotte, NC 28211
800–275–6799

OHIO

Cincinnati
600 Vine St., Convergys Center, Suite 108, Cincinnati, OH 45202
800–634–5574

Woodmere Village
Eton Collection, 28699 Chargrin Blvd.
Woodmere Village, OH 44122
800–432–8359

OREGON

Portland—Tigard
16850 SW 72nd Avenue, Tigard, OR 97224
800–922–4307

PENNSYLVANIA

Philadelphia
One Mellon Bank Ctr., 1735 Market Street, Philadelphia, PA 19103
800–722–0437

Pittsburgh
Union Trust Building, The Pine Tree Shops, 12001 Perry Highway
Wexford, PA 15090
800–272–7567

RHODE ISLAND

Providence
Providence Place Mall, 47 Providence Place, Providence, RI 02903
800–742–1567

TENNESSEE

Memphis
Regalia Center, Suite 110, 6150 Poplar Avenue, Memphis, TN 38119
800–452–9936

TEXAS

Austin
The Arboretum, 10000 Research Blvd., Lobby, Austin, TX 78759
800–544–7815

Dallas
Plaza at Preston Center, 4017 Northwest Parkway, Dallas, TX 75225
800–358–5204

Houston—Highland Village
2701 Drexel Drive, Houston, TX 77027
800–367–7516
Hours: M–F: 8–4:30.

Houston—North
19740 IH-45, North Spring, TX 77373
800–822–4816
Hours: M–F: 8–4:30.

Houston—Memorial Drive
12532 Memorial Drive, Houston, TX 77024
800–572–7011
Hours: M–F: 8–4:30.

Irving—Las Colinas
400 E. Las Colinas Blvd., Suite 120, Irving, TX 75039
800–526–7249

San Antonio
Pacific Plaza, 14100 San Pedro, Suite 110, San Antonio, TX 78232
800–272–7569

UTAH

Salt Lake City
Parkside Tower, 215 South State Street, Suite 130, Salt Lake City, UT 84111
800–544–5586

VIRGINIA

Tyson's Corner
1861 International Drive, McLean, VA 22102
800–543–8736

WASHINGTON

Bellevue
One Bellevue Center, 411 108th Avenue NE, Bellevue, WA 98004
800–344–1783

Seattle
1518 6th Ave., Seattle, WA 98101
800–543–2162
Hours: M–F: 7:30–4:30.

WISCONSIN

Milwaukee
Cannon & Dunphy Law Building, 595 North Barker Road,
Suite 400, Brookfield, WI 53045
800–992–3130

Fidelity's 2006 Fund Manager Map

Buy the manager, not the fund!

That's what I'm constantly exhorting investors like you to do (see Chapter 7 for details). And Fidelity's vaunted research team has turned on its share of bright lights during the past decades. But the people in charge of your money at most of these funds aren't famous. Indeed, managers seem to come and go at Fidelity before you have time to know them.

No longer.

The following biographies will help you get to know the fundamentals of the Fidelity managers who are currently running the show. While these managers will change funds from time to time, at least the following map will help you better know those you currently "own."

Fidelity managers earn money for you the new-fashioned way: through intensive, in-depth fundamental analysis on a comprehensive scale, which enables each manager to zero in on potential opportunities in particular industries and companies. When it comes to such research, nobody does it better. But both internally at Fidelity and relative to their peers, some managers are simply better than others.

That's why I keep close tabs on manager changes—it's important for you to know as much as you can about your managers, old and new. Knowing what funds he or she has managed will help you decide whether to stick with your fund(s). It's also important to know where your old manager has moved, since it may be in your best interest to move in tandem. While this section doesn't give you individual commentary on each fund (the fund pages in this book do that), it does help you gain a better understanding of the experience and skill sets that each manager brings to the table.

Fidelity's 2006 Manager Map

Ken Anderson manages Retirement Money Market and the Money Market funds. He received his BS from Northeastern University in 1988.

Paul Antico has managed Small Cap Stock fund since its March 1998 inception. He joined Fidelity in 1991 as a portfolio assistant for the Equity-Income II and Balanced funds. Also working as an analyst, he followed the restaurant, computer equipment, office equipment, and electrical equipment industries. Funds managed include Select Leisure (1/97–1/98), Select Consumer Industries (1/97–8/97), Select Industrial Equipment (3/96–2/97), and Select Developing Communications (12/93–8/96). Antico received his BS from MIT in 1991 and is also a Chartered Financial Analyst (CFA).

Ramin Arani has managed Trend since May of 2000. Arani joined Fidelity in 1992 as a research associate covering defense electronics and was promoted to analyst in 1995. Arani previously managed Select Health Care (8/99–5/00) and Select Retailing (1/97–8/99). He covered Real Estate Investment Trusts through 1996. He received his BA from Tufts in 1992.

John Avery has managed Fidelity Fund since February 2002. Prior to this he managed VIP Balanced, Advisor Growth & Income Fund, and Advisor Balanced Fund. He joined Fidelity in 1995 as a research analyst following the chemical industry. Funds managed include Select Banking, then called Regional Banks (9/96–1/98), and Select Chemicals (7/95–6/97). He worked at Putnam Investments from 1993 to 1994. He received his BA from Harvard in 1986 and his MBA from the Wharton School in 1993.

Chris Bartel manages Select Chemicals, Select Cyclical Industries, Select Industrial Equipment, Select Paper and Forest Products, and he has co-managed Select Transportation with Lindsay Connor since April 2006. He previously managed Select Defense and Aerospace (3/04–11/05) and Select Networking and Infrastructure (2/02–2/03). He received a BA from Dartmouth College in 1994 and an MBA from the Wharton School in 2000.

Justin Bennett has managed Select Paper and Forest Products since March 2006. He received his BA from Middlebury College in 1996 and his MBA from the Wharton School in 2005.

Brent Bottamini has managed Latin America Fund since April 2005. He received a BBA from the University of Massachusetts in 1998.

William Bower has managed Diversified International since April 2001. Previously, he ran International Discovery (formerly International Growth & Income) from May 1998 through April 2001. He has also managed Select Construction & Housing (12/94–7/96). Bower joined Fidelity in 1994 as an analyst; he followed building materials, housing, recreational vehicle, and manufactured housing industries. Before Fidelity, he worked as a commercial real estate loan officer for Michigan National Bank from 1989 to 1992. He received his BA from Western Michigan University in 1989 and his MBA from the University of Michigan in 1994.

Steve Buller has managed Real Estate since October of 1998. Previously, he managed Select Environmental Services (12/97–9/98). He joined Fidelity in 1992 as an analyst in the fixed-income group, where he focused on distressed and bankrupt securities. He received his BA from the University of Washington in 1990 and his MS from the University of Wisconsin in 1992.

Steven Calhoun has managed Aggressive Growth since June 2005. Prior to this he managed Mid-Cap Stock (3/05–10/05), Select Health Care (1/02–2/04), Select Medical/Equipment Systems (1/02–2/04), and Select Retailing (8/99–2/02). He joined Fidelity's research department in 1994, covering specialty chemicals and other cyclical industries, and became director of associate research in 1997. Calhoun earned his BA from Dartmouth College in 1994.

Kelly Cardwell has managed Select Software and Computer Services since January 2003. Prior to this he managed Select Automotive (7/01–1/03). He received a BS from Bradley University in 1997.

Harlan Carere has managed Select Pharmaceuticals since January 2005 and has managed Select Health Care since March 2005. Prior to this he managed Select Air Transportation (1/04–1/05), Select Biotechnology (10/04–10/05), and Select Transportation (1/04–1/05). He received his BA from McGill University in 1993, and he received an MBA from Harvard Business School in 2000.

John Carlson has managed New Markets Income since joining Fidelity in June of 1995. He managed Strategic Income from May 1998 through

June 2001. He was the lead manager of International Bond from February 1998 through June 2001. He was also manager of Emerging Markets (5/01–12/03). Prior to working for Fidelity he was an executive director of emerging markets at Lehman Brothers International in London. He received his BS from Wayne State University in 1973 and his MS from the University of Michigan in 1975.

Jim Catudal took on Stock Selector in October 2001 and Growth & Income II in October 2005. He managed Select Financial Services (and Advisor Financial Services) from February 2000 through October 2001. He has also managed Select Energy Services (1/98–1/00) and Select Industrial Materials (8/97–8/98). He joined Fidelity in 1997 as a research analyst following North American nonferrous metals firms. Prior to joining Fidelity, Catudal worked for State Street Research as an equity analyst following banks, thrifts, and REITs. He received his BS from the University of Connecticut in 1983 and his MBA from the Amos Tuck School in 1995.

Charlie Chai currently manages Select Developing Communications (since 5/03) and Select Networking and Infrastructure (since 7/04). He received a BA from Dartmouth College in 1997.

Ren Cheng has comanaged the Freedom funds since their October 1996 inception. He has also managed Unique College Investing Plan, Delaware College Investment Plan, the U.Fund College Investing Plan, and Trust accounts for Fidelity Management Trust Company. Prior to joining Fidelity, Cheng spent nine years at Putnam Investments. He earned a BA from National Taiwan University in 1979 and an MA from Brown in 1983, where he was a Ph.D. candidate.

Timothy Cohen has managed Growth & Income since October 2005. He previously managed Export and Multinational (2/02–10/05), Select Insurance (2/99–9/00), Utilities (9/00–2/02), and Select Telecommunications (9/00–2/02). Prior to joining Fidelity, Cohen was a senior associate at Coopers & Lybrand's business assurance group, and he interned with Fidelity in the summer of 1995. Cohen earned a BS from the University of Vermont in 1991 and an MBA from the Wharton School in 1996.

Lindsay Connor has been comanager of Select Transportation with Chris Bartel since April 2006. She joined the firm as a research analyst in 2004. Previously, she was an associate and founding employee for Edgemont Capital Partners in New York. She received her BA from Duke University in 2000 and her MBA from the Amos Tuck School in 2005.

Matthew Conti has managed Focused High Income since 2001. He has previously managed Asset Manager (6/00–11/04), Asset Manager:

Aggressive (6/00–11/04), Asset Manager: Growth (6/00–11/04), and Asset Manger: Income (6/00–11/04). Conti joined Fidelity in 1995 as a high-yield bond analyst covering a number of industries. He received a BS from Carnegie Mellon University in 1998, an MSE from Rensselaer Polytechnic Institute in 1992, and an MBA from Columbia Business School in 1995.

Aaron Cooper has managed Select Medical Equipment and Systems since March 2005. Prior to this he managed Select Leisure (6/04–10/05). He received a BA from Harvard University in 2000.

Nora Creedon has managed Select Construction and Housing since February 2006. She graduated with a BS from Georgetown University's School of Foreign Service in 2000.

William Danoff has managed Contrafund since October of 1990 and VIP Contrafund since its January 1995 inception. He joined Fidelity in 1986, managing Select Retailing (10/86–1/90). Danoff also served as assistant manager of Magellan from 1989 to 1990. He was previously employed by Furman Selz as an analyst, as well as by Steinhardt Partners. Danoff earned a BA from Harvard in 1982 and an MBA from the Wharton School in 1986.

Bruce Dirks currently manages Large Cap Value and Mid Cap Value. He has managed these funds since February 2005. He received a BA from Amherst College in 1981 and an MBA from the University of Chicago in 1992.

John Dowd has managed Select Energy Service since December 2005. He is comanager of Select Natural Resources (5/06–present) with Matthew Friedman. He received a BS from Carnegie Mellon University in 1990.

Andrew Dudley has managed Short-Term Bond since February of 1997. He has managed Ultra-Short Bond since August 2002. Prior to this he managed Intermediate Government Income (12/98–6/02). He also managed the Spartan and regular Short-Intermediate Government (12/98–4/99) and Spartan Short-Term Bond (2/97–6/99). Prior to joining Fidelity, Dudley worked for Putnam Investments from 1991 to 1996. He received his BA from Yale in 1987 and his MBA from the University of Chicago in 1991.

Stephen DuFour took on Equity-Income II at the end of January 2000. He has also managed the equity portion of Balanced (7/97–1/2000), Convertible Securities (1/97–6/97), Select Energy (10/96–1/97), Select Transportation (12/94–1/97), and Select Multimedia (7/93–1/96). He joined

Fidelity in 1992 as an analyst covering media firms. DuFour previously worked at PaineWebber as a financial analyst. He earned a BA from Notre Dame in 1988 and an MBA from the University of Chicago in 1992.

Daniel Dupont has managed Select Gold since February 2003. He received a Bachelor of Communications from McGill University in 2001.

Bahaa Fam manages Large Cap Growth (2/04–present) and Mid Cap Growth (2/04–present). Prior to this he managed Asset Manager: Aggressive (5/00–11/02) and Focused Stock (10/01–2/04). He received a BS from Johns Hopkins in 1979 and an MS from Johns Hopkins in 1980.

Jeffrey Feingold has managed Worldwide since January 2006. Prior to this he managed Home Finance (1/01–5/04), Financial Services (10/01–4/04), Air Transportation (2/00–1/01), Defense & Aerospace (10/98–1/01), and Transportation (2/00–8/00). He joined Fidelity in 1997 as an equity analyst following the footwear, apparel, and textile industries. Before joining Fidelity, he worked with Morgan Stanley in M&A and venture capital from 1992 to 1995. Feingold received his BA from Brown University in 1992 and his MBA from Harvard in 1997.

Rich Fentin has been managing Value since March of 1996. He started managing Value Strategies in June 2005. He has also managed Puritan (4/87–3/96), Growth Company (1/83–3/87), Select Precious Metals (7/81–12/83), and an earlier stint at Value (4/92–12/92). Prior to joining Fidelity in 1983, Fentin was employed by Peoples' Bank & Trust as a loan officer. He earned a BA from Emory University in 1976 and an MBA from Harvard in 1980.

George Fischer manages Spartan Municipal Income (since 1/98), Government Income (since 1/03), Intermediate Government Income (since 6/02), and Mortgage Securities (since 1/03). Prior to this he managed the Connecticut, Maryland, Ohio, New Jersey, New York, and Michigan Spartan muni bond funds (since 5/96, 1/98, 4/97, respectively, taking on the last three in 7/00, and managing them all until 6/02), as well as the Advisor High-Income funds. He previously managed Spartan Insured Muni Income (8/95–8/98), Spartan Aggressive Muni Income (1/98–8/98), and Spartan Bond Strategist (9/93–12/96), all of which have been merged into other funds. Prior to joining Fidelity, Fischer was a product specialist at Abbott Laboratories. He received his BA from Boston College in 1983 and his MBA from the Wharton School in 1989.

Valerie Friedholm has managed Select Home Finance since May 2004. Prior to this she managed Select Construction and Housing (1/02–8/02), Select

Environmental (7/01–2/02), and Select Food and Agriculture (2/03–6/04). She received a BA from Colgate University in 1994 and an MBA from Harvard University in 2000.

Matt Friedman has managed Select Energy since June 2004. He is comanager of Select Natural Resources (since 6/04) with John Dowd. He previously managed Select Chemicals (5/04–1/06), Select Cyclical Industries (5/04–11/05), Select Multimedia (9/03–5/04), and Select Natural Gas (6/05–10/05). He received a BS from Emory University in 1994 and an MBA from the University of Chicago in 2000.

Matthew Fruhan has managed Large Cap Stock since May 2005. Prior to this he managed Select Food & Agriculture (11/99–1/01), Select Defense and Aerospace (1/01–10/03), Select Cyclical Industries (8/02–5/04), Select Air Transportation (1/01–7/02), and Select Financial Services (4/04–5/05). Fruhan first joined Fidelity as an equity research associate in 1995; he has covered specialty retailers, automotive suppliers, transportation, international phone carriers, and the food industry. Fruhan received a BA in 1995 and an MBA in 1999, both from Harvard University.

Robert Haber has managed Focused Stock since February 2004. Prior to this he managed Balanced (11/86–3/87 and 3/88–3/96), Canada (7/98–9/99), Convertible Securities (1/87–12/88), Global Balanced (2/93–12/93 and 1/94–12/94), and Select Electronics (1/86–3/87). He received a BS from Tufts University in 1979, an MS from Tufts in 1980, and an MBA from Harvard University in 1985.

Dick Habermann has been lead manager of the Asset Manager and VIP Asset Manager funds since March of 1996. Since joining Fidelity in 1968 as an analyst, he has held many positions, including manager of Magellan (1/72–5/77), Trend (6/77–8/82), Select Energy (9/82–6/87), Select Energy Services (12/85–6/86), director of research from 1982 to 1989, and director of international research after that. In 1996 he became joint chief investment strategist for Portfolio Advisory Services (19964/97). Habermann was appointed senior vice president of FMR in 1993. Prior to joining Fidelity, he was a lieutenant in the U.S. Navy. He received his BA from Yale in 1962 and his MBA from Harvard in 1968.

Brian Hanson took on Blue Chip Growth in April 2005. Prior to this he managed Select Consumer Industries (3/02–12/02), Select Electronics (2/00–2/02), and Select Retailing (2/02–12/02). Hanson joined Fidelity in 1996 as an equity analyst following health care and technology stocks. He earned his BS from Boston College in 1996.

Lionel Harris has managed Small Cap Growth since April 2005. He received a BA from Dartmouth College in 1989 and an MBA from the Wharton School in 1995.

Ian Hart has managed Overseas since January 2006. Prior to this he managed Europe Capital Appreciation (4/00–12/05). He earned a BS from the London School of Economics in 1988 and an MS there a year later.

Andrew Hatem currently manages Select Air Transportation (since 1/05) and Select Defense and Aerospace (since 12/05). He received a BA and a BS from Boston College in 1994 and an MS from the Carroll Graduate School at Boston College in 1998.

Charles Hebard currently manages Select Brokerage and Investment Management (since 3/06) and Select Financial Services (since 5/05). Prior to this he managed Select Insurance (6/04–2/06), Select Energy Service (2/02–6/04), and Select Leisure (1/01–2/02). He received his BA from the University of Pennsylvania in 1992 and an MBA from the Wharton School in 1999.

Thomas Hense has managed Small Cap Value since March 2006. He received a BA from the University of St. Thomas in 1986 and an MBA from the University of Chicago in 1993.

Stephen Hermsdorf has managed Select Insurance since March 2006. He received a BA from Harvard University in 1995 and an MBA from the University of Chicago in 2004.

Ben Hesse has managed Select Business Services and Outsourcing since March 2006. He received a BA from Michigan State University in 1999 and an MBA from Columbia Business School in 2005.

Adam Hetnarski has managed Discovery since February of 2000. He previously managed Export and Multinational (3/98–2/00) and Select Technology (3/96–7/98). Hetnarski joined Fidelity in 1991 as a member of the Fidelity Investments Institutional Services training program. In 1992, he became a structured equity analyst. Before joining Fidelity, he was a management consultant for Andersen Consulting. Hetnarski earned his BS from the University of Rochester in 1986 and his MBA from the Amos Tuck School in 1991.

Frederick D. Hoff Jr. has managed High Income since June of 2000. Hoff joined Fidelity in 1991 as a portfolio assistant and high-yield analyst following the aerospace and defense, general industrial, and automotive sectors. From 1996 to 2000, he managed the high-yield portions of a number of Fidelity's asset allocation funds, also managing high-yield funds available exclusively to Japanese and Canadian investors. Before Fidelity, Hoff was a credit analyst for Bankers Trust Company and a corporate loan officer for Chemical Bank. He received a BA from Lafayette College in 1986 and an MBA in finance and international business from Columbia University in 1991.

Brian Hogan has managed Blue Chip Value since inception in June 2003. Prior to this he managed Select Construction and Housing (4/99–12/00), Select Cyclical Industries (2/00–12/00), and Strategic Income (5/98–11/98). He received a BS from James Madison University in 1986 and an MBA from the University of North Carolina at Chapel Hill in 1990.

Tim Huyck manages Institutional Money Market: Treasury Only Class I (since 4/02), Institutional Money Market: Government Portfolio Class I (since 3/04), Institutional Money Market: Treasury Portfolio Class I (since 4/02), Government Money Market (since 9/03), Money Market Trust: Retirement Government Money Market (since 9/03), U.S. Government Reserves (since 9/03), Institutional Money Market: Government Portfolio Class II (since 3/04), Institutional Money Market: Government Portfolio Class III (since 3/04), Institutional Money Market: Government Portfolio Select Class (since 3/04), Institutional Money Market: Treasury Only Class II (since 4/02), Institutional Money Market: Treasury Only Class III (since 4/02), Institutional Money Market: Treasury Only Select Class (since 4/02), Institutional Money Market: Treasury Portfolio Class II (since 4/02), Institutional Money Market: Treasury Portfolio Class III (since 4/02), Institutional Money Market: Treasury Portfolio Select Class (since 4/02), Treasury Fund—Advisor B Class (since 4/02), Treasury Fund—Advisor C Class (since 4/02), Treasury Fund—Capital Reserves Class (since 4/02), and Treasury Fund—Daily Money Class (since 4/02). He received a BS from Babson College in 1987 and an MBA from Southern Methodist University in 1994.

William Irving manages Ginnie Mae (since 11/04), Spartan Long-Term Treasury Bond Index Fund—Fidelity Advantage Class (since 12/05), Spartan Long-Term Treasury Bond Index Fund—Investor Class (since 12/05), Spartan Intermediate Treasury Bond Index Fund—Fidelity Advantage Class (since 12/05), Spartan Intermediate Treasury Bond Index Fund—Investor Class (since 12/05), Spartan Short-Term Treasury Bond Index Fund—Fidelity Advantage Class (since 12/05), Spartan Short-Term Treasury Bond Index Fund—Investor Class (since 12/05), Inflation-Protected Bond Fund (since 11/04), Advisor Government Investment Fund: Class A (since 11/04), Advisor Government Investment Fund: Class B (since

11/04), Advisor Government Investment Fund: Class C (since 11/04), Advisor Government Investment Fund: Class I (since 11/04), Advisor Government Investment Fund: Class T (since 11/04), Advisor Inflation-Protected Bond Fund: Class A (since 11/04), Advisor Inflation-Protected Bond Fund: Class B (since 11/04), Advisor Inflation-Protected Bond Fund: Class C (since 11/04), Advisor Inflation-Protected Bond Fund: Class T (since 11/04), and Advisor Inflation-Protected Bond Fund: Institutional Class (since 11/04). He received a BS from MIT in 1987 and a Ph.D. from MIT in 1995.

Yoko Ishibashi has managed Japan since June of 2000. She earned her BA from Tsuda Women's college in 1987 and her MBA from Columbia Business School in 1994.

Mike Jenkins has managed Aggressive International since January 2006. He received a BA from Western Michigan University in 1981 and an MBA from University of Michigan in 1984.

Sonu Kalra currently manages OTC Portfolio (since January 2005). He previously managed Select Computers (12/02–1/05), Select Networking and Infrastructure (1/02–2/02), and Select Technology (2/02–1/05). He received a BS from Penn State University in 1993 and an MBA from the Wharton School in 1998.

Rajiv Kaul has managed Select Biotechnology since October 2005. He managed this same fund from June 1998 to January 2000. In the interim, he managed Select Developing Communications (2/00–6/01) and Aggressive Growth (11/02–6/05). Kaul joined Fidelity in 1996 as an equity research associate following the health care sector, moving up to research analyst in 1998. He received a BA from Harvard in 1995.

William Kennedy has managed International Discovery since October 2004. Prior to this he managed Pacific Basin (9/03–10/04 and 12/98–9/02). He joined Fidelity in 1994, covering investment opportunities in India and the regional power sector. Kennedy also served as director of research for Southeast Asia from 1996 through January 1998. He earned his BA from Notre Dame in 1990 and is a Chartered Financial Analyst.

Adam Kutas currently comanages Latin America with Brent Bottamini (since 4/05). He received a BA from University of Western Ontario in 1992.

Harry Lange has managed Magellan since October 2005. Prior to this he managed Capital Appreciation (3/96–10/05), Select Computers (5/92–3/96), Select Electronics (1/94–3/95), and Select Technology (10/93–3/96). Lange also managed Select Capital Goods (now a component of Select Industrial Equipment) in 1988. Prior to joining Fidelity in 1987, he was employed as a vice president at Wellington Management. Lange has also worked at Chevrolet and at Idanta Partners. He earned a BSE from the General Motors Institute in 1975 and an MBA from Harvard in 1983.

Heather Lawrence has managed Select Computers since April 2006. She has also managed Select Air Transportation (8/02–12/03), Select Banking (3/04–1/06), and Select Transportation (12/01–12/30). She received a BS from the Wharton School in 1994 and an MBA from Columbia Business School in 2001.

K. C. Lee has managed China Region since June 2005. He received a bachelor's degree in social science from the University of Hong Kong.

Robert Lee currently manages Select Food and Agriculture (since June 2004). He received a BS from Babson College in 1995 and an MBA from the Wharton School in 2001.

Maxime Lemieux has managed Canada Fund since November 2002. She received a Bachelor of Communications from McGill University in 1996.

Matthew Lentz has managed International Real Estate since January 2006. He received a BA from the College of William and Mary in 1996.

Norm Lind manages CA AMT Tax-Free Money Market, CA Municipal Money Market, MA AMT Tax-Free Money Market, MA Municipal Money Market, and Municipal Money Market. Previously, he managed AMT Tax-Free Money Fund (5/01–8/03), the Connecticut, Massachusetts, New Jersey, and Ohio muni funds and the Arizona, Connecticut, Florida, Massachusetts, and New Jersey Spartan muni funds from July 2000 to September 2001, Spartan Intermediate Municipal Income (1/98–7/00), Spartan Short-Intermediate Muni (10/95–7/00) as well as the Michigan, New Jersey, and New York muni funds (1/98–7/00, 4/97–7/00, and 10/93–7/00, respectively), Spartan Muni Income (6/90–9/95), and two other New York funds (which were merged into the remaining New York fund). Lind joined Fidelity in 1986 as a municipal research analyst and later served as a municipal-research group leader. He earned a BA from the University of Washington in 1980 and an MBA from Cornell in 1986.

Bob Litterst manages Cash Reserves and Select Money Market. Prior to these he managed U.S. Government Reserves MM (4/97–8/03), Spartan U.S. Government MM (4/01–8/03), and Spartan U.S. Treasury MM (4/97–3/02), and many institutional money markets (all since 4/97), as well as Cash Reserves (1/92–3/97) and VIP Money Market (1/92–3/97). Before joining Fidelity in 1991, Litterst was a vice president and senior portfolio manager for Prudential Securities' Money Markets Group and a senior auditor at Touche Ross & Company. He earned a BA from Temple University in 1981 and an MBA from Stern/NYU in 1989.

Allan Liu has managed Southeast Asia since its April 1993 inception. He is director of Fidelity Investments in Hong Kong. Since joining Fidelity in 1987, Liu has also managed a number of Fidelity funds for foreign investors. Liu previously worked for Chase Manhattan Bank as a business analysis officer in their Hong Kong office. He earned a BS in 1983 and an MBA in 1986 from the Chinese University of Hong Kong.

Charles Mangum has managed Dividend Growth since January of 1997. Prior funds managed: OTC (6/96–1/97), Convertible Securities (2/95–5/96), Select Medical Delivery (2/91–2/93) and Select Health Care (2/92–2/95). Prior to joining Fidelity in 1990, Mangum was employed by Eppler, Guern and Turner as a corporate finance analyst. He earned a BA from Southern Methodist University in 1986 and an MBA from the University of Chicago in 1990.

Mike Marchese manages Municipal Money Market (since 10/01), Massachusetts Municipal Money Market (since 7/06), Massachusetts AMT Tax-Free Money Market (since 7/06), Connecticut Municipal Money Market (since 9/02), Ohio Municipal Money Market (since 9/02), New York Municipal Money Market (since 9/03), New York AMT Tax-Free Money Market (since 9/03), and AMT Tax-Free Money (since 9/3). He previously managed Arizona Municipal Money Market Fund (10/01–8/03), Michigan Municipal Money Market (11/01–8/03), and Pennsylvania Municipal Money Market (11/01–8/03). He received a BA from College of Holy Cross in 1979, a JD from Syracuse University in 1982, and an LLM from Boston University School of Law in 1984.

Darren Maupin has managed Europe Capital Appreciation since January 2006. He received a BS from Boston College in 1998.

Christine McConnell has managed Floating Rate High Income since August 2000. She received a BS from Boston College in 1980 and an MBA from Cornell University in 1985.

John McDowell has managed Blue Chip Growth since March of 1996, runs trust accounts for Fidelity, and serves as a senior vice president. He has also managed Large Cap Stock (6/95–3/96) and Select Retailing (12/85–12/86). He joined Fidelity in 1985 as a securities analyst following the footwear manufacturing and retailing industries. Prior to joining Fidelity, McDowell worked for Corning Medical and Scientific Corporation from 1981 to 1985, finishing as a data processing consultant. McDowell earned his BA from Williams College in 1980 and his MBA from Harvard in 1985 and is a Chartered Financial Analyst (CFA).

James McElligott has run Select Natural Gas since November 2005. He received a BA from Harvard University in 2003.

Doug McGinley manages Municipal Money Market, California Municipal Money Market, and California AMT Tax-Free Money Market, all since July 2006. He previously managed Advisor California Municipal Income, Advisor Intermediate Municipal Income, California Municipal Income, California Short-IntermediateTax-Free Bond, Florida Municipal Income, Intermediate Municipal Income, Michigan Municipal Income, and Ohio Municipal Income. He received a BA from Northwestern University in 1988 and an MBA from Harvard University in 1994.

Anmol Mehra currently manages Select Automotive (since 3/04). He previously managed Select Paper and Forest Products (2/04–2/06). He received a BS from the University of Texas in 1995 and an MBA from the University of Texas in 2002.

James K. "Kim" Miller is a vice president and portfolio manager for the Fixed-Income Division. He manages Variable Insurance Products (VIP): Money Market Portfolio, Institutional Money Market: Money Market Portfolio, FIMM Prime Money Market Portfolio, and Money Market Central. He managed Michigan Municipal Money Market and Pennsylvania Municipal Money Market (5/01–10/01), Connecticut Municipal Money Market (5/01–8/02), and Spartan Connecticut Municipal Money Market (5/01–3/02). He managed Tax-Exempt Cash Portfolio, Tax-Exempt Fund-Daily Money, New York Municipal Money Market, Spartan New York Municipal Money Market, New Jersey Municipal Money Market, and Spartan New Jersey Municipal Money Market from May 2001 to September 2003, at which time he assumed responsibility for VIP Money Market Portfolio and FIMM: Money Market Portfolio. He also managed Tax-Free Money Market from June 2001 to August 2003. He assumed responsibility for FIMM Prime Money Market Portfolio in March 2004 and the Money Market Central Fund in April 2004. Prior to joining Fidelity Investments, Miller was a fixed-income securities trader at Stifel Nicolaus and Kemper Securities from 1985 to 1989. He received a BA from Brown University in 1985 and an MBA in finance and accounting from the University of Chicago Graduate School of Business in 1991.

Neal Miller has managed New Millennium since its December 1992 inception. He has also managed a number of Fidelity institutional trust accounts since 1988. Prior to joining Fidelity in 1988, Miller was employed by Chase Investors as a fund manager and as president of the Axe Houghton Stock Fund. He earned a BA from Carleton College in 1965 and an MBA from the University of Michigan in 1967.

Kenichi Mizushita has managed Japan Smaller Companies since December of 1996. Mizushita joined Fidelity as a research analyst in 1985, covering a variety of mostly cyclical industries. From 1979 to 1981 he worked as an officer in the Education Department of Tokyo. Mizushita received his Bachelor of Law from Gakushuin University in 1979 and his MBA from Central Missouri State in 1985.

Jeffrey Moore manages Investment Grade Bond, Advisor Investment Grade Bond, Spartan Investment Grade Bond, and the investment-grade bond portions of Asset Manager, Asset Manager: Income, Asset Manager: Growth, Asset Manager: Aggressive, and Advisor Asset Allocation. He also manages several fixed-income funds and the investment-grade bond portions of several asset allocation funds available exclusively to Canadian investors. Moore joined Fidelity in 1995 as a fixed-income analyst following several sectors including sovereign debt, energy, REITs, Yankee banks and Canada. He became a portfolio manager in June 2000 and began managing his current funds in April 2002. Prior to joining Fidelity, Moore was a credit analyst following Canadian provincial, municipal, and government debt for Dominion Bond Rating Service in Toronto, Ontario, Canada. From 1990 to 1994, he served as a financial analyst in the financial markets analysis and economic development groups for the Department of Finance of the Canadian government in Ottawa, Ontario, Canada. Born in 1965, Moore received a BA in economics from the University of Western Ontario in 1988 and a MA from the University of Waterloo in 1990. He is a Chartered Financial Analyst (CFA).

James Morrow has managed Select Technology since January 2005. He also manages Select Business Services and Outsourcing Portfolio (since 3/06), Select Electronics (since 2/04), and Advisor Electronics (since 2/04). He previously managed Select Business Services and Outsourcing (7/01–10/03), and Select Computers (8/05–4/06). He received a BS from the University of Buffalo in 1993 and an MBA from the University of Chicago in 1999.

Dale Nichols has managed Pacific Basin since October 2004. He received a B.B.Mgt. degree from Queensland University of Technology in 1990.

Mark Notkin has managed Capital & Income since July 2003. He also manages Strategic Income (since 4/99). Prior to this he managed VIP High Income Portfolio. He received a BS from the University of Massachusetts in 1986 and an MBA from Boston University in 1988.

Scott Offen has managed Value Discovery since inception in February 2002. He previously managed Select Energy (9/99–3/02) and Select Natural Resources (9/99–2/02). He has also managed Select Food & Agriculture (11/96–10/99), Select Paper & Forest Products (10/93–1/96), Select Brokerage (10/90–10/93), and Select Life Insurance (7/89–10/90). Offen joined Fidelity in 1985 as an analyst covering brokerage, investment management, and life insurance firms. He attended Hamilton College.

Ford O'Neil has managed U.S. Bond Index (since 10/01), Intermediate Bond (since 7/98), and Fidelity Total Bond (since 12/04). He also manages several bond portfolios for Canadian investors. O'Neil joined Fidelity in 1990 as an analyst covering electric, gas, and water utilities. Prior to Fidelity, he worked for Advest as an investment banking associate. O'Neil earned his BA from Harvard in 1985 and his MBA from the Wharton School in 1990.

Ben Paton has comanaged International Small Cap with Wilson Wong and Tokuya Sano since January 2004. He received an MA from Oxford University in 1982 and an MBA from London Business School in 1995.

Shep Perkins has managed Mid-Cap Stock since January 2005. Prior to this he managed Select Wireless since its inception in September of 2000 until April 2003. He previously managed Select Medical Delivery (8/99–2/00). Perkins joined Fidelity in 1997 as an equity research associate following health care services. Prior to Fidelity, he worked as an equity research associate at Donaldson, Lufkin & Jenrette. Perkins earned his BA from Amherst College in 1993.

Ramona Persaud has managed Select Banking since February 2006. Prior to that she managed Select Construction and Housing (4/04–1/06). She received a BS from Polytechnic University in 1997 and an MBA from the Wharton School in 2003.

Stephen Petersen took on the equity portion of Puritan fund at the end of January 2000, and he also manages Equity-Income (since August 1993), VIP Equity-Income (since January 1997), and several Fidelity trust accounts (since 1987). He has also run Balanced fund (3/96–6/97). Peterson joined Fidelity in 1980 as an analyst covering the airline and insurance industries. He earned a BA in 1979 and an MS in 1980 from the University of Wisconsin, and he is a Chartered Financial Analyst.

Keith Quinton has managed Tax Managed Stock since February 2004. He received a BA from Dartmouth College in 1980 and an MBA from the Amos Tuck School in 1982.

Lawrence Rakers has managed Balance Fund since February 2002. Prior to this he managed Select Computers (1/00–6/01) and Select Technology (2/00–6/01). He has also managed Convertible Securities (6/01–2/02), Select Energy (1/97–9/99), Select Natural Resources (3/97–9/99), Select Paper & Forest Products (2/96–10/97), Select Precious Metals (7/96–2/97), and Select Gold (7/95–2/97). Rakers joined Fidelity in 1993 as a research analyst covering the restaurant, precious metals, and coal industries. He earned his MS (1987) and BS (1985) from the University of Illinois and his MBA from Northeastern in 1993.

Gopal Reddy has managed Select Leisure since November 2005. He received a BA from Stanford University in 2001.

John Roth manages Select Consumer Industries (since 6/04) and Select Multimedia (since 5/04). Prior to this he managed Select Utilities Growth (11/99–2/02) and Select Chemicals (3/025/04). He joined Fidelity in 1998 as a summer intern and began full-time work in 1999. Roth has covered electric and gas utilities as well as energy service companies. Prior to Fidelity, Roth worked for Tucker Anthony as an equity trader from 1992 to 1997. He earned his BA from Colby in 1992 and his MBA from Sloan/MIT in 1999.

Matthew Sabel has managed Select Medical Delivery since January 2005. He received a BA from Tufts University in 1997.

Tokuya Sano has comanaged International Small Cap with Ben Paton and Wilson Wong since September 2002. He received a BS from Portland State University in 1993.

Andrew Sassine has managed International Small Cap Opportunities since August 2005. He received a BA from the University of Iowa in 1987 and an MBA from the Wharton School in 1993.

Christopher Sharpe comanages Delaware College Investment Plan, Fidelity AZ College Savings Plan, Strategic Real Return, U.Fund College Investment Plan, Unique College Investment Plan, and is lead comanager of Four-In-One Index, Strategic Dividend & Income, and Strategic Income. He received a BS from Brown University in 1990.

Jonathan Shelon manages Freedom Funds and comanages Delaware College Investment Plan, Fidelity Arizona College Savings Plan, U.Fund College Investment Plan, and Unique College Investment Plan. He received a BBA from Temple University in 1994.

Fergus Shiel has managed Capital Appreciation since October 2005. He has also managed Fidelity Fifty (6/02–4/03), Independence (6/96–4/03), Dividend Growth (4/94–5/95), Trend (5/95–5/96), Select Telecommunications (6/92–4/94), Select Multimedia (5/90–9/91 and 3/93–6/93), and Select Consumer Industries (9/91–2/93). Prior to joining Fidelity in 1989, Shiel was employed by Meritor Savings Bank as a manager of investment accounting. He earned a BA from the University of Virginia in 1980 and an MBA from Columbia in 1989.

Jody Simes has managed Select Industrial Materials since August 2003. She received a BA from the University of Massachusetts in 1992 and an MS from Boston College in 1997.

Douglas Simmons currently manages Select Environmental (since 2/04) and Utilities (since 9/05). He received a BBA from the University of Texas in 1997 and an MBA from Harvard Business School in 2003.

Steven J. Snider has managed Disciplined Equity since May 2000. He previously managed the equity portions of VIP Asset Manager and VIP Asset Manager: Growth and several Fidelity funds. Snider joined Fidelity in 1992 as an analyst in the quantitative research group. Prior to Fidelity, he served in the U.S. Navy. Snider received his BS from MIT in 1982 and his MBA from Duke in 1992, and he holds his CFA.

Mark Snyderman has managed Real Estate Income since its inception in February 2003. He received an AB from Dartmouth College in 1979 and an MBA from Stanford University in 1983.

Mark Sommer has managed Intermediate Municipal Income and Advisor Intermediate Municipal Income since July 2006. He also manages Short-Intermediate Municipal Income, Advisor Short-Intermediate Municipal Income, New York Municipal Income, Advisor New York Municipal Income, New Jersey Municipal Income, Connecticut Municipal Income, Pennsylvania Municipal Income, and Maryland Municipal Income. He received a BA from Colgate University in 1982 and an MS from Brown University in 1985.

Thomas Soviero has managed Convertible Securities since June 2005. He also manages Leveraged Company Stock (since July 2003). He received a BS from Boston College in 1985.

Victor Thay has managed Export & Multinational since October 2005. He previously managed Growth & Income II (6/05–10/05), Convertible Securities (2/02–6/05), Select Home Finance (3/99–1/01), Select Multimedia (1/01–2/02), and Select Natural Gas (12/97–8/99). Thay joined Fidelity in 1995 as a research associate following Canadian equities, and in 1996 began covering exploration and production firms. He received his BA and BS from UC Berkeley in 1995.

Christine Thompson has managed the Spartan state muni bond funds for Arizona, Florida, Massachusetts, and Minnesota, all since July of 1998. She also manages Municipal Income and Tax-Free Bond. She has also managed Spartan Intermediate Municipal Income, Spartan Short Intermediate Municipal Income, Spartan state muni bond funds for California and Pennsylvania, International Bond (2/96–2/98), Intermediate Bond (10/95–7/98), and the three Target Timeline bond funds (2/96–7/98). Thompson joined Fidelity in 1985 as a senior bond analyst. She earned her BA from Tufts in 1980 and her MBA from the Wharton School in 1985.

Richard Thompson has managed Small Cap Independence since October 2005. Prior to this he managed Small Cap Stock (4/05–10/05). He received a BS from Bentley College in 1991.

Joel Tillinghast has managed Low-Priced Stock since its December 1989 inception. He joined Fidelity in 1986 as an analyst covering natural gas, personal care products, appliances, and tobacco. Tillinghast was previously employed at BankAmerica as a vice president and research director, at Drexel Burnham as a research economist, and at Value Line as an analyst. He earned a BA from Wesleyan in 1980 and an MBA from Kellogg/Northwestern in 1983.

Trygve Toraasen has managed the Europe fund since January 2006 and the Nordic fund since June of 1998. He joined Fidelity in 1994 as an analyst for United Kingdom and European Equities at Fidelity Investments Services, Ltd. Before working for Fidelity, Toraasen was a partner and analyst for Fortuna Corporate Finance in Oslo, Norway. He earned his BS from California State in 1985 and his MBA from the University of Southern California in 1994.

Robert von Rekowsky has managed Emerging Markets since January 2004. He received a BA from the University of New York at Albany in 1988, an MA from Northeastern University in 1992, and an MS from Brandeis University in 2005.

Jason Weiner has managed both Fidelity Fifty and Independence since April 2003. Prior to this he managed OTC Portfolio (2/00–4/03), Discovery (3/98–2/00), Export & Multinational (1/97–9/98), Select Air Transportation (12/94–5/96), and Select Computers (3/96–1/97). Since joining Fidelity in 1991 as a research associate, Weiner has covered biotechnology, retail products, and technology industries. He earned a BA from Swarthmore in 1991.

Michael Widrig manages Arizona Municipal Money Market, Institutional Tax-Exempt Portfolio, Michigan Municipal Money Market, New Jersey AMT Tax-Free Money Market, New Jersey Municipal Money Market, Pennsylvania Municipal Money Market, and Tax-Free Money Market. He received a BS from Kansas State University in 1985 and an MBA from Columbia University in 1989.

Wilson Wong has been comanager of International Small Cap since July 2005. Prior to this he managed Select Technology (9/03–11/04). He received a BBA from the Chinese University of Hong Kong in 1995.

Steven Wymer has managed Growth Company since January of 1997. He has also managed Dividend Growth (5/95–1/97), Select Chemicals (1/93–1/95), and Select Automotive (10/90–12/92). Wymer joined Fidelity in 1989 as an equity analyst following the chemical, automotive parts, and leisure durables industries. He earned his BS from the University of Illinois in 1985 and his MBA from the University of Chicago in 1989.

Derek Young has managed Global Balanced since January 2006. He is also comanager of Strategic Real Return and lead comanager of Four-In-One Index, Strategic Dividend & Income, and Strategic Income. He received a BS from Troy State University in 1986 and an MBA from Vanderbilt University in 1991.

Brian Younger has managed Select Telecommunications since March 2002 and Select Utilities Growth and Select Wireless since May 2003. Prior to this he managed Select Biotechnology (9/00–2/02). He earned his BA from Harvard in 1998.

Martin Zinny currently manages Select Retailing (since January 2005). Prior to this he managed Utilities (3/02–10/03). He received a BS from Boston College in 1993 and an MBA from the University of Chicago in 2001.

Lowell and Lynch

Peter Lynch is arguably the best-known fund manager in the world, despite the fact that he hasn't managed a fund for more than a decade. Still, in the coming-of-age of mutual funds, few stars ascended as high as Lynch's, and deservedly so. He was a stock picker's stock picker. An analyst's analyst. A proven performer where it counted most: running Fidelity Magellan as the world's largest open-end mutual fund with consistent outperformance success. What Lynch *wasn't* was equally important: He wasn't a braggart or show-off; he wasn't one to covet ideas and ignore others' insights; he wasn't fixated on his own success. Instead, by staying focused on his charge he quietly and deliberately helped to create more millionaires than a Fortune 500 company could claim during his manager tenure. Even more remarkable, to this day Lynch remains a key ingredient in the continued success of Fidelity's new fund managers, serving a crucial and informed role as something more than a mere mentor.

I last spoke to Peter directly nearly four years ago, which makes the inclusion of that conversation somewhat suspect in a book that's being penned in 2006. That is, it would be if Peter Lynch were the kind of cat that changed his stripes to suit his suitors. But unlike the salesman who yells "turn on the green light Harry, the man wants a green suit," Lynch's investment style, experience, and insights are timeless ones. As a consequence, I know that new and veteran Fidelity investors alike can and will benefit from our conversation.

Here it is.

LOWELL: Thank you for taking time to speak with me, Peter. With so many issues facing mutual find investors today, from known scandals to bear market memories, I think now is the perfect time to speak with you about the benefits of investing in actively managed mutual funds. To that end, I'd like to begin with your definition of an investor—as opposed to a market timer or speculator.

LYNCH: Right. As you know, we've often talked about the issue that behind every stock is a company. If you have a portfolio of 200 stocks, you own a piece of 200 companies. And some companies lose it. Some companies basically lose their way, like Eastman Kodak. I bought Apple Computer when it came public. I bought Federal Express when it came public. I remember when Staples came public, or when Amgen came public. These are very significant—but maybe the next one's going to be Krispy Kreme for all I know. But, take Kmart. Basically, a great firm once that lost their way and went bankrupt. If you put $20,000 into Kmart 20 years ago, you'd have $0 today. But guess what? If you put $10,000 into Wal-Mart 20 years ago and $10,000 into Kmart, you'd have $0 on your Kmart, but you'd have made a lot of money on your Wal-Mart, so you'd be happy on the two investments. And you could have done the same thing with Xerox that has had bad earnings the last 40 years and it's been a bad stock, and McDonald's has had good earnings and it's been a good stock. And Gillette's had good earnings. It's been a good stock. And Johnson & Johnson's had good earnings and it's a good stock. So the good companies more than offset the ones that go out of business, like Burlington Industries or Bethlehem Steel.

LOWELL: Twenty years is a reasonable investment horizon—but for many people, 20 months seems like the limit on their patience.

LYNCH: I don't know what the next 12 months are going to do, but it'd be pretty hard to think that stocks are *not* going to be higher in 10 years. Certainly 20 years from now companies' profits will be higher and that's why their stocks go higher. And that's the essence of investing. You have to understand that there's a reason that if you'd owned McDonald's bonds over the last 40 years or 30 years at maturity, they say thank you very much and here's your money back, and they pay you the interest rate. But if you're a shareholder, you share in the success of the company.

LOWELL: Sharing in the success of a known company is one thing—but sharing in the success of an unknown company is another.

LYNCH: People laughed when Starbucks came public, and it's up 30 to 40-fold. So I think you can make more on a stock than you can lose. I can lose 100 percent in a stock—and I've done it a few times. But I've been right, like I did in Stop & Shop, or Taco Bell, or Chrysler, or Fannie Mae. You can make 10 to 20 times your money. That's why you own stocks; the upside is very big and, over time, corporate profits have grown, per share, 7 or 8 percent a year. You've got a 1 or 2 percent dividend return, just historically. So you made 10 percent on stocks. And the average person today can buy a 10-year bond, they're going to make 3 percent. If they put the money in a money market fund, they're going to make 1 percent.

So I've always said that you can flip a coin in terms of what the market's going to do over the next 12 months, but it's very predictable over 10 years, over 20 years. When you think of all the bad things that happened in the last 100 years, the worst 10-year market in the stock market was 1928 to 1938, when we had a depression. You had no FDIC, so a high percentage of people lost money in their bank accounts. You had no social security system, no unemployment compensation, no SEC. It was just a major depression. And from '28 to '38, you lost about a little less than 1 percent a year in the stock market, but it's the worst 10 years in the last 100 years. So I'm more of a historian than I am a predictor, because predicting the future is like predicting the weather in New England, not predicting it in Arizona.

LOWELL: Is predicting the future as foolhardy as gambling on the present?

LYNCH: The average person buys stocks based on hot tips—that basically turns stocks into poker chips—based on what they've heard from people on a bus, or they hear a story, or they just say this sounds good. This is gambling. This is not investing. A lot of times they're buying stocks, three a week, and the next week they buy three more, and so they're just spending a huge amount in commissions. It depends how much churning they're doing in their own accounts. At Fidelity, you get professional management, you get diversification, and you get very low costs.

LOWELL: Many investors didn't hold onto the gains that the greatest bull market of all time delivered. Why not?

LYNCH: Why did people do so badly in the greatest bull market of all time? Their methods must have been flawed. And some people were buying stocks on margin. They wound up losing everything.

It's a funny business. You don't have to be right in this business more than 5, 6, 7 times out of 10; if the times you're right, you get double and triple, and the times you're wrong, you lose 50 percent, you win—big.

You've got to get those big hits, and that takes—if you're just in a stock to make 30 percent, that doesn't pay for your mistakes that are 30 percent losers for starters, as we can see with AT&T and we can see with Westinghouse and we see with Xerox. Who'd believe you could lose 90 percent of Xerox and 90 percent of Westinghouse? The losses in some of these so-called conservative companies have been pretty staggering.

LOWELL: Some investors think that investing in individual stocks is the only way to invest. These same people often look down their stock-picking noses at mutual fund investors—as if investing in an equity mutual fund isn't investing in stocks. My belief is that for a handful of these people, owning both stocks and mutual funds makes sense, but that for the majority of investors, the inability to stay fully informed about all the potential opportunities in the thousands of individual stocks is simply beyond their means. Your thoughts?

LYNCH: You're right. Some people can do both: They can own mutual funds and occasionally, if they do good research, they know the company, know the balance sheet, and they know the business, they can invest in stocks. I've written several books (I've given all the profits to charity), not encouraging people to invest, but to help them understand that if you invest you ought to do certain things. I always thought of myself as a ski instructor. I don't encourage people to ski, but if you go to a mountain, you've got to learn how to fall down, you ought to learn how to turn sideways, you ought to learn how to stop, you ought to start on a small hill, not a double black. That's what I've tried to show people in my investing books, the things that worked for me and things that don't work, and not say people should ski, or not saying people should invest directly. But if they're going to do it, they'll do better if they do some homework—not just watching stock tickers and find out what stock had a leading volume last hour. That's total gambling. That's not investing.

LOWELL: There's another group of investors who seem to think that index investing is the only way to go. What do you see as the advantages of active management versus index investing?

LYNCH: I think the biggest benefits are in the fully, actively managed funds. There's plenty of benefits in the largest 200 or 300 stocks, but when you get out of the largest 200 and 300 stocks, there's much more room for inefficiencies, where some of these companies are not covered by anybody. If 100 people visit them, 99 people would say, wow, this sounds pretty good.

Obviously, I know that index funds are a way to invest, but then you have to decide what one to invest in, because you can get whipsawed by owning the wrong index. Clearly, if you're in an index fund, you're going to have to be careful. You can look at the incredible differential between the S&P 500 and the Russell 2000. In the late '90s you could have been in the Russell 2000 and say, why am I getting single digit returns when the big stocks are going up 25 percent a year? and then you would—just when the market was about to go south—you would have sold your small-cap or your value stocks and bought the Nasdaq or the S&P 500 Index Fund, and you would have lost 50 percent or 75 percent while the value stocks went up. That's an amazing differential. We're not talking about one going down 20 percent and one going up 10 percent. We're talking one going down 50 percent, one going down 75 percent, and one going up 20 percent.

So just saying you have an index fund isn't good enough. You have to say, well wait a second, what index fund do I have? Do you understand that the Wilshire is different than the S&P 500 and the Russell is different than that and that the overseas is different and small cap is different? Because they have these different patterns and if you don't understand where you are, and you have a narrow part of the overall global market, just when your area's about to heat up, you're probably depressed and say "get me out of that one." And then you're going to some other index and then you have the danger of being whipsawed.

LOWELL: Fidelity has an anomalous statistic, namely, in a world where half of any group has to be below average, two-thirds of its managers outperform the market. That's in direct contrast to the overall pool of fund managers, where more than two-thirds fail to beat their market benchmarks. I often speak of Fidelity as a high-minded university. When I worked at Fidelity, I was only a few years out of Harvard, but felt like I was instantly back in the midst of a place that valued talent, effort, and thought, and I think that accounts for more than some of the answer. But what's your answer?

LYNCH: I've got a unique perspective. For the last 13 years I've worked with most of our managers—we hire either six or nine MBAs a year, and I get them for two or three years. (If we hire six, I'll keep them for three years. If we hire nine, I'll keep them for two years.) I have one-on-one meetings with them. Some of those stay with us, some go back to business school, some become analysts. We interview 500 to 1,000 people, and these are not human resource–delineated. These are fund managers and analysts. I interview 500 people on campus. We narrow it down to 40. We bring them back to Fidelity and we make a select few job offers. These are incredibly talented people, screened by talented people. It's an incredible exercise.

In addition, we have summer students every year. In fact, I was a summer student here—back in 1966. Again, we probably interview about 500 people and have five or six summer students join us for the internship. These are typically people between their years of graduate school. And normally we hire about half of those people. If I look at our current managers and analysts, I can see that about half of our employees are people who were summer students here once. But they key is that we really hire great people, and they're all different individuals. Their backgrounds are really unique and they're very enthusiastic, very bright. And we don't hire a person that's a biochemist to be our biotech analyst. And we don't hire an insurance actuary to manage our insurance fund—we just hire raw talent and enthusiasm and say "go forth into insurance, banking, energy, electronics."

I think it's this great tradition [that] is matched by another: We don't have teams. We don't sub-advise the work that can be best done here. Instead, we have people that work in a group where they compare ideas. I think what's important about those groups is they don't beat each other up. There are some firms dominated by one individual, and if that person happens to hate a stock, they're not going to let you buy it, or you'll be so cowardly you'll buy a quarter of 1 percent. But in our meetings, if somebody doesn't like a stock, all they say is "here's why" . . . or "here's my idea and if people don't like it, tell me why you wouldn't buy it." So you don't dump on somebody else's idea. You just listen to it and say, "Well, that's interesting, but I'd still rather buy stock X to stock Z." You compare your ideas and people get the benefit of your research, and you get the benefit of their research. And it's important to note that all our managers started as analysts of ours—and that all our fund managers remain analysts. Every one of our fund managers is looking at two or three companies a day as an analyst, not simply looking at other analysts' reports on those companies. In this light, it can be said that the highest position at Fidelity is an analyst.

At some firms, people stop analyzing when they reach what they consider to be the top: a fund manager. They say, "Well, I can stop traveling now. I can just add some value to the ideas that are coming in through the research department." That's *not* what we do here. A lot of times managers don't agree with the capital analysts. They don't agree with the drug analysts. They don't agree with the auto analysts. And they're buying a stock when the analyst thinks of a sale, and a lot of times that's the right thing to do—but it's always a fully informed, well-thought-out move.

LOWELL: The difference between being a great analyst and a great money manager can be dramatic. Fidelity's Select funds provide a unique testing ground for this.

LYNCH: I don't know if I'd call it a testing ground, but I do think that the Select funds are a fantastic product because it puts our best analysts on a fund, in the role of putting their best theories into practice themselves. It's different to recommend a stock at 10 as an analyst to a roomful of managers than it is to be the manager buying that stock. A lot of times, as an analyst, you say to people "you really ought to get out of this at 14." But if you never change your recommendation and it goes up to 40, it looks like you got a four-bagger out there. Actually holding on to that stock is a different story. When you're a fund manager, you get that test. You're always tempted to sell if the damn thing is going up, because it's easier to get rid of than the ones that are going down. You've got to really concentrate on saying "this is a really good idea and of all my stocks, I had two up today and I'm trying to raise some money, but I'm not going to sell this one." It's awfully tempting to sell the ones that are up, but that may be the company that's going to go up significantly.

LOWELL: You don't have to be right all the time, just most of the time.

LYNCH: And we hire unbelievable people and we don't say, "Oh, my God, why is that guy going to California in the winter?" It looks like he's off on a boondoggle or he's going to Florida to fish. There are people that literally won't approve trips. They won't let their analysts travel. You laugh at this, but there are—I know other firms that literally say "you can do that by phone" or "wait until they come to Boston." Our people go where they want to go, and when they want to. They go to North Carolina, to Highpoint for the furniture shows. They go to Dalton, Georgia, for the carpet shows. They go to every single convention, every single deal. They're on the road seven, eight, nine days a month. And, of course, they're on the phone and seeing companies when they come to Boston.

LOWELL: Why do you think some of your most talented managers leave while others stay?

LYNCH: You've often mentioned Harry Lange and Charles Mangum as managers you're glad to see haven't left us. And we have had people that have basically retired that were great, like George Vanderheiden or

Beth Terrana. These are very good people. But guess what? We trot out new folks. We always have a bench of people that are in their third through fifth year that are extremely talented, and we keep adding to that bench. We've never stopped adding to it. We're going to add this year and—and occasionally, we'll pick somebody out from the outside, like Joel Tillinghast or Neal Miller. It's not our favorite method, but if we find a really staggeringly good person, like Joel or Neal, we'll go outside.

Look at our small-stock team. No one has got a team that just works in the small stocks like we do. We built that up and that helps all our funds. We're much more organized than we were 10 years ago, but our relationship with our people in Japan, our relationship with our people all over Asia, and the people in our London office, they just simply weren't that talented 10 years ago. Now in the last 10 years we've trained our own people. We've brought them up. We've just brought raw talent in [inaudible]—we used the same Fidelity method we used in Boston. They were hiring retreads from insurance companies and banks that weren't good people. Now we have very good people overseas and we're getting a lot of benefit from that. You can see the results in our European funds.

LOWELL: There's a positive impact to tell on this side of the pond, too, in terms of your Asian- and European-oriented funds.

LYNCH: That's another strength that our competitors don't have. And the final part, I think, that has paid off this year and probably if we'd paid more attention would have paid off more last year is the incredible team we have in high-yield. Now they're in the same building as our equity managers. If a company's bonds are a buy, guess what? Maybe their stock's a buy. And these bonds that have gone from 30 cents to a buck, the stock's gone from a buck to $12. Now, maybe it could be said that when it comes to high-yield bonds there's somebody in the same league with us, but there's certainly no one better than we are in dealing with the low-investment-grade bonds—whether it's research, analysis, or execution. And that is a skill set that actually helps all our funds. Also, it's not a very big market, so people won't devote a lot of people to the high-yield market because it's just not a very big market. We kept a big staff there just to help our funds. Public companies with below-investment-grade debt are a dynamic group. So is our group that tracks them, and they've really helped all our managers in 2002 and 2001 in the down leg, and they've really helped in the recovery of 2003.

LOWELL: That's why we owned Leveraged Company Stock.

LYNCH: Right. But the benefits of those ideas have helped 20 or 30 of our equity funds—not just buying high-yield bonds, because some of our funds can do that, but mostly just buying the equities of these companies.

LOWELL: What parting word could you give Fidelity Investor members who are looking out over the horizon?

LYNCH: First I would say that when it comes to investing there's always something to worry about. If you look back 10 years from now, 20 years from now, there'll be a terrible bunch of bad things that happened and that worried all of us. That's the nature of our world and our markets—there has always been something to worry about 100 years ago or 400 years ago and 1,900 years ago, but you just didn't have CNN—you didn't know what was going on in these other times. Today, information is inescapable, and information overload is itself a worry. How do you use it to your advantage?

The good news is that so many aspects of our lives are getting better and better. We have invented artificial hips, artificial knees, pacemakers, stents. People that used to not be able to leave their house can take an antianxiety pill. There's been some staggering advances in the world in addition to Krispy Kreme and Starbucks, which maybe people may not regard as a great advance, but they are. Years from now, people will simply assume that living in a wireless world is a given. Today, that's still a goal—but we're advancing on it.

What I'm saying is that it's human nature to worry about the bad news and to forget all the great things that have happened. I remember when personal computers came along. We tried to figure out what the heck people were going to do with a personal computer. People said, well, women can put their recipes on it. Now I wonder if a woman has ever put their recipes on a personal computer. But when we were trying to figure out what the function of these things was, the answer simply wasn't clear. Today, they're an enormous industry, and ubiquitous in our daily lives. But I think the good things that come along, like PCs, are eventually taken for granted, and it's always just bad things that take center stage. As a result, I think people get so overwhelmed with what I call *background noise*. Lately, that noise has all been about the recession. We've had nine recessions since World War II. This last one was number 10. We've got a perfect record. of recoveries from all of them. Recovery is part of the nature of our system. It beats the hell out of the one they used to have in East Germany or the one they've got in North Korea.

LOWELL: That's for sure.

LYNCH: So I think that's the thing, that you get so tied up in what's happening now and what's happening next week, which is not what investing is all about. Investing is not a sprint, it's a marathon. You're in it for 10, 20, 30 years and say, "Am I coming with a third in equities, one-half, 75 percent? What's my tolerance for pain?" You've got to say what's right for you and then stay with it. Just don't be persuaded by background noise to abandon your plan of action. Stocks are volatile things. Theoretically, the market's supposed to be up 10 or 12 percent per year. That's supposed to be your average annualized return. But you never get a year that delivers a perfect 10 percent. (Maybe this year, it's going to be proven wrong and it will turn out to be 10 percent.) But the historical reality is that 70 percent of the time the market's either up over 20 percent or down in any given year—this is precisely what people don't want. They want predictability, and we just don't get it in the short term. In the long run, as you well know, Jim, if you're in the right managers and funds, the rewards are plain to see.

LOWELL: Thanks, Peter.

Glossary of Investment Terms

Advance/decline ratio. The number of stocks whose prices have advanced versus those that have declined over a given day. Typically calculated at the close of market, this ratio is used to represent the general direction of the market.

Assets ($ millions). The size of the fund's total portfolio, in millions of dollars. In general, the larger a fixed-income fund portfolio, the lower the operating expenses, which can mean higher returns. With stock funds, however, larger portfolios can become unwieldy, especially for smaller-cap stock funds. For example, a manager of a small-stock portfolio that becomes too large may be unable to invest his or her cash without either purchasing too many shares of individual companies or building such a diverse portfolio that no one stock has much of an impact upon the fund's performance.

Annual report. Yearly report of a company's overall financial condition (from operations to balance sheet), which, by law, must be sent to all shareholders.

Asked price. A security's (or commodity's) price as offered for sale on an exchange or over-the-counter (OTC) market. (See **Bid price**.)

Asset. Value attributed to stocks, bonds, real estate, mutual funds, or, in terms of a company, the value of owned equipment or plants.

Asset allocation. A strategy for diversifying money in major investment categories as well as particular types of investments within each category.

Automatic investment. A method for investing in mutual funds that enables you to select a specific amount to be withdrawn from your bank savings or checking account on a regular, scheduled basis and invested in a mutual fund. It's a great low-cost way to start investing in mutual funds, since many funds are willing to waive their minimum in order to get what they hope will be your long-term participation in their fund.

Automatic reinvestment. Typically, the automatic reinvestment of dividends in new shares of a company's stock or a mutual fund. Some companies and almost all mutual funds allow automatic reinvestment. A smart move, even though you will have to pay taxes on the dividend amount (whether you reinvest or receive it in cash).

Average maturity. The average maturity is the weighted average of the maturities of all of a fund's bond holdings. (The maturity of a bond is the date the debt is due and payable.) Typically, the longer a fund's average maturity, the greater its interest-rate risk. Not as meaningful as a bond fund's duration.

Average annual return. A measure of historical return. The amount per year you would have had to earn to achieve the same total return over the time period in question.

Balanced fund. A fund that invests substantial portions in both stocks and bonds.

Balance sheet. A company's accounting of its current assets, liabilities, and owner's equity at a specified point in time. Found in the company's annual report.

Bear market. A sustained period of falling stock or bond prices. In the stock market, fear of economic downturn, and proof of it, tends to bring the bear out of hibernation. In the bond market, rising interest rates bring on the feared animal.

Beta. The extent to which a fund or stock's value tends to go up or down as the market goes up or down. A growth fund with a beta of 1.5 would most likely go up 15 percent when the market as a whole is up 10 percent (or down 15 percent when the market is down 10 percent).

Bid price. The highest price a prospective investor (or market maker) is prepared to pay for a security, usually just under the asked price, the lowest price a seller is willing to accept.

Blue chip. Large, well-known, established companies whose stock is considered to be a solid investment and safer than other companies' stocks, since a blue chip is unlikely to go bankrupt.

Bond. An IOU issued by a corporate or government entity in return for a pledge of repayment of the original face value invested, plus interest payments to be paid on specified dates.

Bond fund. A mutual fund that invests primarily in bonds.

Capital gain. Profit made on the sale of securities or property. Federal capital gains taxes are currently capped at 28 percent, even for investors whose income is taxed in a higher bracket.

Capital gains distribution. A mutual fund's distribution to shareholders of gains realized on the sale of securities within the fund's portfolio. Typically, the distributions are made once per year, and they can affect the optimal timing of your own purchase or sale of the fund.

Capital loss. When the amount realized on the sale of an asset is less than the amount originally paid for it, the investor has suffered a capital loss.

Capital preservation. Investors who have already grown their seed money into a harvestable crop want to protect what they have. Capital preservation refers to the objective of ensuring that the amount of capital doesn't become reduced over time, which in turn means that risks are avoided in favor of a defensive portfolio. Nevertheless, some growth of capital must ensue, if only to be able to safeguard the capital from inflation's toll, and some income is also usually sought to allow periodic withdrawals without depleting principal.

Cash. The most liquid asset, typically thought of in the form of negotiable currency, but inclusive of cash equivalents: interest-bearing short-term instruments such as a money market fund or Treasury bill.

Cash cow. A business that generates a continuous cash flow that, in terms of companies that issue publicly traded stocks, typically results in reliable dividends.

Cash dividend. Taxable cash payments made to shareholders from a corporation's earnings. Some companies issue a stock dividend in lieu of a cash payout.

Cash flow. A company's net income after expenses but before accounting for abstract costs such as depreciation. Cash flow is one indicator used by stock analysts to evaluate a company's ability to pay off debt and keep paying dividends.

Certificate of deposit. Better known as a CD, it is a specified-term, fixed-interest-earning debt instrument issued by a bank or savings and loan.

A good temporary parking place for cash you may need at a specified date in the near future (CD maturities can range from three months to five years). Penalties apply for early withdrawal. Most are FDIC insured; forget those that aren't.

Certified Financial Planner (CFP). This certificate, issed by the Institute of Certified Financial Planners, signifies that the holder has passed a series of tests showing the ability to advise clients on a host of financial concerns, including banking, estate planning, insurance, investing, and taxes. Be advised that tests are no substitute for experience, intelligence, and integrity.

Certified Public Accountant (CPA). A rigorous examination process, coupled with relevant experience and state licensing, combine in this certification process to yield one of the more meaningful professional designations for those whose career is focused on accounting, auditing, and tax preparation. This designation is an excellent indicator of a level of proficiency in the aforementioned fields, but is less indicative of the person's ability to advise you on non-tax-related investment matters.

Chartered Financial Analyst (CFA). Like the CPA designation, this one designates that a person has passed a rigorous (three-year) examination process coupled with relevant experience in the fields of economics, ethics, financial accounting, portfolio management, and hard-core security analysis. CFAs stand out among those who would proclaim themselves qualified to analyze an investment's fundamental worth and appropriateness to particular portfolios.

Chartered Financial Consultant (ChFC). An excellent addition to the CFP designation, this charter is offered to CFPs who have also passed a four-year program at Bryn Mawr College that covers economics, insurance, investing, and taxes.

Chartered Mutual Fund Counselor. A new designation, offered by the National Endowment for Financial Education, showing a financial adviser's enhanced ability to advise clients on their mutual fund questions and concerns.

Closed-end investment company. Contrasted with an open-end fund, which issues new shares per new purchase, a closed-end fund sells a fixed number of shares in its portfolio of securities. Closed-end fund shares trade on the major U.S. exchanges and over-the-counter market. Their market value is determined by supply and demand, which leads to shares being sold at either a premium or a discount to the actual net asset value of the fund's portfolio.

Commission. Percentage (based on selling price, amount managed, or service rendered) charged by a brokerage firm—be it real estate or investment.

Commodities. Goods, from foodstuffs to metals, that are traded on several exchanges by traders speculating on supply and demand's effect on the goods' prices.

Common stock. Share of ownership in a company. Stock prices can rise or fall with the company's fortunes, or even with stock market supply and demand fluctuations (which may or may not be entirely rational).

Compound interest. Interest earned on previously paid interest as well as on original principal amount. Example: $500 principal at 10 percent annual interest would become $550 in one year, but going forward, that $550 at 10 percent would become $605, after realizing $55 in interest during the second year. ($50 on the original principal, plus $5 on the first year's interest.)

Contrarian. An investor who examines the investments and trends that consensus wisdom is buying into, and then invests in their opposite. To a contrarian, the crowd is always wrong. But, you might ask, what happens if there's a crowd of contrarians?

Corporate bond. Debt instrument (IOU) issued by a private or public corporation as opposed to a government entity. Corporate bonds typically share the following characteristics: Their income is taxable; they have a par value of $1,000; they have a specified maturity; and they're traded on one of the major exchanges.

Correlation. The extent to which a fund and the stock market (usually as measured by the S&P 500 Index) tend to move together. An S&P 500 Index fund would have a correlation of 99 percent or 100 percent. A fund invested in smaller stocks not found in the S&P 500, or one that makes big bets on narrow sectors, or one that invests heavily overseas, would tend to have a much lower correlation (most likely less than 50 percent).

Coupon. The original interest rate paid on a bond's face (or par) value. A $1,000 par bond paying $50 per year has a 5 percent coupon.

Credit rating (bond). A letter grading of potential risk. Standard & Poor's (S&P) and Moody's are the top rating agencies, and both rate companies based on their ability to repay bondholders' interest and principle. Standard & Poor's ratings of AAA (Moody's highest rating is Aaa) to BBB (Baa) signify a range of "investment-grade" bonds, while ratings of BB (Ba) or lower denote "below-investment-grade" bonds, more commonly referred to as *junk bonds*. A rating of D signifies the bond is in default.

Credit rating (consumer). A report of a consumer's history of timely (and untimely) bill paying, used to determine potential credit risk for mortgages, new credit cards and other loans.

Current yield. Current yield is determined by dividing the bond's annual interest by its current market price. It differs from the coupon rate in that it accounts for the price paid for the bond (as opposed to its par value). For example, while the coupon rate of a $1,000 par bond paying $50 per year is 5 percent, the current yield of a bond bought at $950 with a $50 income would be 5.26 percent.

Cyclical stock. A stock whose performance is closely tied to the health of the economy. In tough times, these stocks falter. In good times, they typically rise rapidly. Housing, cars, and "deep cyclicals" like steel manufacturers are directly affected by the consumer's (and industry's) willingness and ability to purchase goods.

Debt-to-equity. A ratio that is calculated by dividing a company's total liabilities by total shareholder's stock in the company and that is used to help measure a company's ability to pay its creditors if the company itself fails.

Default. Failure of a company or other debtor to make principal and/or interest payments on schedule. A bad thing.

Defensive stocks. These stocks are the antonym of cyclical stocks, since the company's products tend to be staples (like food) that consumers can't or won't do without (unlike a new car). As a result, their performance is less affected by economic downturns.

Derivative. A bet on the direction of interest rates or the price of some other security or commodity. Some funds and investors use derivatives aggressively to enhance the yield or potential return of their portfolio, while others use them in an attempt to reduce the risk of their portfolio. Derivatives aren't all bad—but, like a dark freckle, excessive proliferation of them is a potential warning sign.

Discount. Just as you'd find on products at Wal-Mart, discounts reflect a price reduction in the product or security you're buying at market. For example, relating to bonds, a discount is the difference between the bond's par value and its current market price, where that price is lower than the par value. (In contrast, buying a bond at a premium would mean the current market price is higher than the par value.) For a closed-end fund, a discount is the amount by which the purchase price is less than net asset value.

Discount broker. A broker that typically charges less (in comparison to full-service brokers) for services rendered—from trades transacted to reports and recommendations issued. There's a wide variance in such costs and services among discounters and deep discounters.

Discount rate. The interest rate the Federal Reserve Board charges member banks on loans. This rate in turn affects the interest rates that consumers will pay on loans, since banks use the discount rate as the benchmark from which they mark up the rate on their loans to customers.

Distribution. A payment made to a shareholder. Except for income from municipal funds, distributions are taxable events. Distributions amount to a return on your capital, because (except for monthly bond fund dividends) share prices are reduced by the same amount as the dividend. This share price reduction occurs on the ex-dividend date.

Diversification. A strategy for reducing investment risk by investing in different categories and types of investments as well as (within the stock market) different industries and company market capitalizations.

Dividend. A distribution of earnings to shareholders, by either an individual company or a mutual fund.

Dividend reinvestment plan. Like automatic reinvestment, the reinvestment of dividends in new shares of the stock or fund. A smart move, even though you will have to pay taxes on the dividend amount (even if you don't receive it in cash).

Dollar cost averaging. Investment method in which a specific, equal amount of money is regularly invested on a scheduled basis. This method can reward the investor who employs it with more shares bought at lower prices than at higher prices.

Dow Jones Industrial Average (DJIA, or "the Dow"). A stock market index that has withstood the test of time by adequately reflecting the movement of the market as a whole. It's calculated by adding up the prices of 30 large-cap stocks, which results in a potential flaw (according to some critics), namely, its narrow definition and exclusion of newer industries and companies. Nevertheless, this index is the most widely used measure of the market—and it has certainly earned its place as a standard worth watching.

Duration. A measure of a bond fund's interest-rate sensitivity, based on the maturities of the bonds in the portfolio. A fund with an effective duration of 4 should lose 4 percent if interest rates rise 1 percent, or gain 4 percent if interest rates fall 1 percent.

Earnings per share (EPS). Portion of a company's profit allocated to each

318 WHAT EVERY FIDELITY INVESTOR NEEDS TO KNOW

outstanding share of common stock (total profits divided by number of shares of common stock).

Economic indicators. Statistics used to represent the current state of the economy and also to predict (with a meteorologist's accuracy) the direction of the economy.

Efficient market theory. A theory that suggests that market price reflects market value, meaning that dart throwers and analysts have an equal chance of selecting the best stocks. Contentious, but hardly groundless.

Equity. A fancy name for common stock. If you're in the habit of saying "tres good," by all means call stocks "equities."

Ex-dividend date. The date on which stocks (or mutual funds) effectively pay out their dividends. Shareholders who own the fund on this date receive the dividend, the share price tends to fall by the amount of the dividend on this date, and automatic reinvestments are made on this date. (However, actual dividend checks may be delayed by several days.)

Expense ratio. The amount investors in a fund pay for expenses incurred in the operation and management of the fund during the year. This expense may be 1 percent or more. A higher expense ratio reduces the fund's total return; therefore, two funds of equal strength but with unequal expense ratios present a clear choice—opt for the one with the lower expense ratio.

Face value. Worth of the bond or other security as stated on it.

Family of funds. Group of funds "owned" (i.e., managed and operated) by the same investment management company. (Technically, each fund is owned by its shareholders, who could vote to move the fund to another fund family.)

Fixed-income fund. A mutual fund that invests in fixed-income securities such as corporate bonds or Ginnie Maes.

401(k) plan. Employer-sponsored tax-advantaged retirement plan that enables contributors to put pretax dollars in the investment vehicles offered by the plan. The employer often matches the contributions of participating employees.

403(b) plan. Equivalent to 401(k) plans, but for nonprofit employers.

Fundamental analysis. Analysis of a company and its securities based on hard data from its balance sheet and income statements, sales, earnings, and management, as well as extrinsic economic factors that affect the company's ability to operate profitably. Such analysis can be used as a predictor of future potential. Contrast with **Technical analysis.**

Fund of funds. A mutual fund whose portfolio consists of other mutual funds.

Futures contract. Written agreement to buy or sell a commodity or security for a specified price at a specified future date.

Growth fund. A mutual fund that invests in growth stocks. In doing so, this type of fund seeks to deliver capital appreciation, rather than income, to its shareholders. As a result, a stock's earnings growth is favored over its actual or potential dividends.

Growth and income fund (G&I fund). A mutual fund that typically combines the objective of capital appreciation with the generation of some income. Note: Some G&I funds are very close to growth funds, offering virtually no income; others look almost like bond funds, with little room for capital appreciation. Match your objective with a G&I fund's actual portfolio.

Growth stock. A stock in a company characterized by above-average growth in earnings or sales. Growth stocks tend to have a high price relative to earnings, and they provide little if any dividend. Growth stocks also tend to have a high beta (or risk), but can offer long-term investors the potential for solid capital appreciation. Contrast with **Cyclical stock** and **Value stock.**

Hedge. Not a rhododendron. A hedge, or hedging, is a strategy that is used to neutralize the risk inherent in an investment. The phrase, "hedging one's bets," accurately reflects the objective: to break even whether the hedged assets move up or down. Hedging, which is often accomplished with the use of derivatives, sometimes fails to protect against risks as planned.

Index. A standard or benchmark against which the performance of a market, industry, company, or security (stock, bond, real estate, mutual fund, and more) is measured.

Index fund. A fund whose objective is to match a specific market index (most commonly the S&P 500 stock index). Since most funds fail to beat their relevant index benchmark, an index fund is likely to perform slightly better than most funds in the long term.

Inefficient market theory. This theory holds that an informed investor stands a better-than-even chance of outperforming a chimp and a dart board. Contrasted with the efficient market theory, this one encourages research, analysis, and the ability to beat a fellow investor to the punch—finding hidden profits or pitfalls in a given company.

Inflation. The rise in the prices of goods and services as reflected in the consumer price index (CPI), which tracks consumer goods, and the producer price index (PPI), which focuses on industrial goods and materials. Inflation decreases the purchasing power of your dollar in the long run. The cause is usually attributed to an increase in the money supply.

Investment company. An arrangement whereby investors pool their assets into a corporation or trust, which then employs professional management to invest the assets according to a stated objective. Mutual funds are one form of investment company. See **Unit trust, Mutual fund,** and **Closed-end investment company.**

Investment objective. A fund's aim, as stated in its prospectus. Investors should choose a fund whose objectives match their own—although they need to go beyond the stated objective and examine the fund's history of actually hitting what it says it's aiming at.

IRA. An acronym for *individual retirement account,* which can provide you with a tax-deductible retirement investment plan—or at least a tax-deferred one. Penalties apply for early withdrawal.

Load. A mutual fund's sales charge. See Chapter 2 for a list of the ways a mutual fund can take a bite out of your investment.

Mutual fund. A professionally managed portfolio of securities (one or a combination of stocks, bonds, cash, real estate investment trusts) that enables investors to pool their money and reap the potential rewards (or suffer the possible consequences). An excellent investment vehicle for getting you to your investment destination—the problem is, there are so many cars on the lot, and only a few of them have a full tank of gas.

Net asset value (NAV). The market price of a fund (its NAV) is derived at the close of market every day by determining the value of the fund's total assets (the value of each security as well as cash and cash equivalents) less its liabilities, divided by the total number of its outstanding shares.

No-load fund. A mutual fund whose shares can be bought and sold at NAV without any sales charge—but be forewarned that there may be redemption fees (fees charged for selling the fund, generally within a specified time of purchase).

Offering price. The net asset value per share, plus the sales charge. Also called the *asked price*. For no-load funds, the NAV and offering price are the same.

Open-end fund. See **Mutual fund**.

OTC (over-the-counter). The Nasdaq is the leading over-the-counter market in the United States. OTC stocks aren't listed on any exchange. Instead, they are bought and sold through a computerized network of traders.

Par. The face value of a bond (i.e., the principle amount that should be paid when the bond matures).

Portfolio. Term used to describe an investor's or fund manager's investment holdings.

Premium. The opposite of discount.

Prospectus. The fund's equivalent to a company's annual report. The Securities and Exchange Commission (SEC) requires every fund to provide each shareholder a prospectus, wherein the fund describes its investment objectives, investments, past performance, fees, and services. Get it. Read it. Know it—before you invest in it.

Sector. Sectors are the constituent parts of an overall industry. For example, pharmaceutical companies and semiconductor manufacturers as distinct from health and technology.

Sector fund. Fund that invests in companies in one defined sector or in a group of related sectors. Fidelity's Select funds are perhaps the best-known funds in this rather speculative genre.

Technical analysis. Using charts of a security's past price performance, technical analysts look for trends (and other, more abstract, symbols) to tip them to an investment's future prospects. Contrast with **Fundamental analysis**.

Tenure. This term refers to a fund manager's time at the helm. Since managers are responsible for the performance of the portfolios they run, tenure is an excellent way to determine the manager's experience, the relevance of any performance history, and the potential for problems should he or she choose to leave the fund. Note that just because a manager may not have a lengthy tenure at the fund you're thinking of buying (the average tenure is under four years), doesn't mean he or she didn't have solid experience elsewhere. Researching a manager's past history of performance at their present and preceding funds is a critical step in a comprehensive fund selection process.

Total return. Total return is the annual appreciation of an investment (including its capital appreciation, dividends, and/or interest) and thus a clear marker showing how much your investment has grown since you bought it.

Turnover rate. Calculated by taking the value of all the fund's trades (buys and sells) and dividing it by twice the net assets of the portfolio, this figure indicates how aggressive a manager is being in regard to trading in and out of (or within) the market. A turnover rate in excess of 100 percent generally means a pretty aggressive manager. If the manager is good, that's not a problem, but excessive turnover can drive up fund expenses and hurt returns.

Value stock. A stock that is considered cheap relative to earnings or assets. Value stocks tend to be stodgier players in slower-growing, defensive, or cyclical areas. Contrast with **Growth stock**. (Note that almost all fund managers at least pay lip service to the concept of value; even some aggressive growth players claim to be seeking value-growth issues!)

Year-end NAV. The fund's price, or net asset value per share. When you buy shares in the fund you pay this price plus any fees.

Yield. The rate of interest payments on a bond. The current yield on a bond is the amount of yearly interest divided by the current value of the bond. A more useful measure of yield is the yield to maturity, which takes into account the fact that bonds selling at a discount or premium to their par value will get closer to par value as they near maturity. The SEC now requires that funds report yield to maturity.

Yield spread. The difference between the yield on one kind of income investment and the yield on a standard investment, usually U.S. Treasury bonds. The yield spread between a bond and the benchmark U.S. Treasury would tend to indicate the degree of credit risk expected for the bond. Not surprisingly, yield spreads are much higher for junk bonds than for high-quality corporate bonds.

Glossary of Fidelity Investors' Terms for Quick Reference

The profiles in this book offer a wealth of information about Fidelity and its funds. They are arranged in a simple format that typically includes the following terms. There are many investment terms that you ought to know. This glossary is divided into most commonly used terms and more generally relevant ones.

Asset allocation. The broadest groupings of the fund's assets. Includes one or more of the following categories: *equity* (mostly common stock, but can also include some preferred stock positions); *convertible securities* (bonds and preferred stock that can, at the holder's option, be converted into a fixed number of common stock shares); *bonds* (fixed-income securities with a maturity longer than cash); *cash & other* (not literally cash stuffed in a safe, but holdings in money market accounts and other stable income securities with a very short term maturity, usually defined as under one year).

Composition. A fund's breakdown by major type of bond issuer. This may include, on the one hand, cash & other, and on the other hand some equities (stock) in a more aggressive bond fund.

Country diversification. For funds with considerable foreign positions, the top country breakdown is an important consideration. The U.S. position generally includes U.S.-held cash, so even truly foreign funds typically have a U.S. position.

Credit quality. Bond fund holdings are listed by their Standard & Poor's or equivalent credit quality, where AAA is the highest rating (given to a few of the stablest corporations and to U.S. government issues), followed by AA, A, and BBB (which is the lowest investment-grade rating). Below BBB are the junk-bond ratings: BB, B, and CCC. Other positions are listed as "NR" for Not Rated or "NA" for Not Applicable; in a junk bond most of these can be expected to be of very low quality or to be stock positions. In a government bond fund, NA positions tend to be very safe cash holdings.

Major market sectors. For stock funds, top industries are one way of forecasting how volatile a fund is likely to be, both as such and relative to a specific market benchmark. These are broad industry groupings, standardized across the Fidelity funds.

Objective. This tells you, very broadly, what type of investments your fund is expected to hold and to what extent it is seeking longer-term, more volatile (riskier) growth versus current income.

Ticker. Found at the top right of the page. The ticker or Quotron symbol is a five-letter code universally used for computerized retrieval of fund (and stock) prices and information.

Top 10 holdings. The largest 10 positions in the fund. It does not include cash positions, but does include any bonds and/or futures. Under this list is shown the *percent of the portfolio* that the 10 holdings make up, which is a measure of how concentrated the fund is in the manager's favorite positions. A high concentration (say, where the top 10 positions make up over 30 percent of the fund) generally means a more aggressive, riskier fund, but for government bond funds, diversification is not important for keeping risk low.

Total holdings. The total number of positions in an equity fund. Does not include positions in cash and equivalent securities.

Fund Risk

Beta. This is a measure of a fund's movement relative to the overall stock market. The stock market, as defined by the S&P 500, has a beta of 1.00. Beta is always the same as or less than relative volatility, as beta measures only stock market risk, whereas relative volatility measures all risk. For example, Select Precious Metals has a very high relative volatility (2.89) but a fairly low beta (0.85), because its movements tend to be independent of the broader stock market. The Equity-Income fund has a relative volatility of 0.97 and a beta of 0.90; the two numbers are close because the fund is well diversified and tends to move up and down (although not quite as much in either direction) with the market.

Date of inception. The month the fund began operations. Useful when comparing funds that may or may not have been in existence during severe bull or bear markets. For instance, many funds experienced their maximum cumulative loss during the fall of 1987. However, newer funds have no track record for that particular period, so their MCLs may not appear as deep as those of older funds.

Distributions. The months when the fund may make a distribution of income and/or capital gains, if it has accrued and/or realized any. In taxable accounts, you might want to delay new purchases until after a distribution, but distributions have no effect on IRAs and other tax-deferred accounts.

Expense ratio (percent). The portion of the fund annually consumed by Fidelity. It includes management, accounting, distribution, and other miscellaneous costs as a percentage of the fund's assets. The lower the expenses, the more frugal the fund. This number does not include the costs of trading commissions. Note that *total return* numbers already incorporate the effects of fund expenses.

Fees. Many Fidelity funds have initial sales charges and/or redemption fees, which are levied as a percent of assets. Spartan funds may also levy smaller fixed fees, such as $2 per check and $5 for other redemptions (generally waived on accounts over $50,000).

IRA minimum. How much you generally need, in an IRA or other retirement account, to make your initial purchase of the fund. Most funds have a $500 IRA minimum, although the Spartan funds' minimums are the same $10,000 to $25,000 as for non-IRA investments. Company-sponsored payroll-deduction plans like 401(k)s are usually not subject to even these lower minimums. Note that tax-free municipal income funds cannot be bought in a retirement plan (you wouldn't want to, anyway).

Minimum initial investment. How much you generally need, in a retail account, to make your initial purchase of the fund. (Current shareholders can usually make smaller additions to existing accounts, and many funds allow smaller investments if they are used to start a regular automatic account-building plan.) Most Fidelity funds aimed at individual investors have minimums of $2,500, although the Spartan funds' minimums are $10,000 to $25,000.

Portfolio manager (tenure). A fund's primary portfolio manager, as well as his or her tenure at the fund is a crucial factor to any fund selection.

Investors should note the current manager's tenure when looking at historical performance figures, since a fund's past performance—good or bad—is less relevant for periods under a different manager.

R^2 **(R-squared).** This tells us what portion of a fund's movements can be explained by the U.S. stock market's movements. Equity-Income, which is fairly broadly diversified in large-cap U.S. stocks, has an R^2 of 86 percent, while the narrowly invested and volatile (and heavily foreign) Select Precious Metals has an R^2 of 9 percent.

Relative volatility. This measure is derived by taking the standard deviation of fund returns over the past 36 months and dividing it by the standard deviation of returns for the S&P 500 Index for the same period. A fund whose relative volatility is greater than 1.00 is more volatile than the market. Conversely, a volatility rating of less than 1.00 indicates a fund is less volatile than the broad stock or bond market.

Style. Categorized as "value," "growth," or "blend." *Value* stocks are cheap relative to their underlying companies' current earnings or book value. *Growth* stocks are expensive (usually because analysts hope for above-average earnings growth in the underlying company). *Blend* stocks are in between.

Turnover (percent). This is a measure of trading activity in the fund's underlying portfolio. The higher the turnover, the more that is likely to be spent in brokerage commissions. High turnover also generally increases the fund's need to distribute capital gains, which can mean higher tax bills for taxable investors. A turnover rate of 100 (percent) indicates that in one year the fund manager has bought and sold securities with a value equal to the fund's portfolio value. In general, a lower turnover rate is desirable.

Yield. For stock funds, this is the current 12-month yield. It reflects the dividends paid over the past 12 months divided by the fund's share price. For bond and money market funds, this is the current 30-day or 7-day yield, respectively. Among stock funds, a higher yield usually means more conservative, dividend-paying holdings. (Paradoxically, among bond funds a higher yield usually means riskier, lower-credit-quality holdings, but we address credit risk separately.)

About the Author

James H. Lowell III is the editor in chief of the multiple-award-winning independent newsletter, *Fidelity Investor* (and fidelityinvestor.com), the weekly electronic *Fidelity Sector Investor*, and the customized, independent *401K Focus* service, as well as the founding editor of *The ETF Trader* on *Marketwatch from Dow Jones*. Lowell is the president of the Fund Family Shareholder Association.

Lowell is also the editor in chief of *The Forbes ETF Advisor by Jim Lowell*, an independent investment advisory service focused exclusively on exchange traded funds.

In addition, Lowell is the founder and chairman of The Rankings Service (www.trsreports.com). The Rankings Service (is an independent, objective, third-party research service for institutional clients, providing proprietary review, analysis, and monitoring of individual investment manager performance.

Lowell is also a prolific author. He has written several books on investing, most recently *Smart Money Moves* (Penguin) and *Investing from Scratch* (Penguin, 1997, revised edition in 2005). He is a past editor in chief of America Online's *FundWorks* and of *Funds Net Insight*, a national mutual fund newsletter.

He has written and lectured extensively on investing and personal finance for national audiences, magazines, TV, radio, and online media, including Bloomberg (radio and TV), CNN, and CNBC. His market views and opinions appear frequently in such publications as *Barron's*, *BusinessWeek*, the *New York Times*, the *Wall Street Journal*, *Fortune*, *Investment News*, *Money*, and *Smart Money*, to name but a few. He has given numerous speeches, most recently (December 2005) to the annual CFA Boston Chapter event and the AAII.

Lowell is a partner in, and chief investment strategist for, Adviser Investment Management, a private money management fee-only firm advising on over $900 million, based in Newton, Massachusetts. (Adviser Investment Management receives no fees or compensation from any fund family, nor does it sell or promote investment or insurance products. It is a fee-only firm.) Before joining Adviser Investment Management, Lowell was chief portfolio strategist for the Boston-based investment division of Adams, Harkness & Hill.

He is also the president of FundWorks, Inc., a financial publishing firm, and was the featured contributing editor for *Investment Advisor* magazine (ia-mag.com), where he focused on equities, closed- and open-end funds, and exchange traded funds. Lowell's columns frequently qualified for Certified Financial Planner (CFP) continuing education credits. He is also the author of the College of Financial Planning's Exchange Traded Funds curricula.

Lowell was formerly employed by Fidelity, where he was the senior financial reporter for *Investment Vision* and participated in the formative stages of *Worth* magazine.

Lowell has both his Series 7 and 65 securities licenses. He was educated at Vassar College (B.A.), and holds master's degrees from both Harvard University and Trinity College (Dublin, Ireland). In addition, Lowell is a published poet, a former teaching fellow at Harvard University, and former lecturer in the Philosophy/Religion Department at Northeastern University College in Boston. He is an accomplished sport fisherman. Lowell lives west of Boston, Massachusetts—a stone's throw from the hub of the mutual fund industry.

Index